KATE DALLY

PAUL MILGATE

PHILIP WEBSTER

TIM KELLY

CAMBRIDGE LEGAL STUDIES

Preliminary

CAMBRIDGE
UNIVERSITY PRESS

CAMBRIDGE UNIVERSITY PRESS
Cambridge, New York, Melbourne, Madrid, Cape Town, Singapore, São Paulo

Cambridge University Press
477 Williamstown Road, Port Melbourne, VIC 3207, Australia

www.cambridge.edu.au
Information on this title: www.cambridge.org/052168661X

First published 2006

Designed by Mason Design
Typeset by Palmer Higgs
Cartoons by Paul Konye
Edited by Anna Fern
Printed in China by APOL

National Library of Australia Cataloguing in Publication data
Dally, Kate
Cambridge Legal Studies Preliminary
ISBN-13 978-0-52168-661-7 paperback
ISBN-10 0-52168-661-X paperback
1. Law – Australia - Textbooks 2. Law – Examinations – Study guides.
3. Higher School Certificate Examination (N.S.W.) – Study guides. I. Dally, Kate.
349.94

ISBN-13 978-0-52168-661-7 paperback
ISBN-10 0-52168-661-X paperback

Contents

Introduction		v
Cases, statutes, media reports (CSM)		vi
Media notes pro-forma		viii
Glossary of key words		ix
About the authors		x
Acknowledgments		xi

Part I The legal system — 1
1 Basic legal notions — 2
2 Sources of law — 11
3 The constitutional system in Australia — 29
4 The operation of the legal system — 47

Part II The individual and the state — 67
5 Power and authority — 68
6 Legal controls on state power — 79
7 Duties — 90
8 Rights — 100

Part III The law in focus— focus groups — 109

SECTION A ABORIGINAL AND TORRES STRAIT ISLANDER PEOPLES — 110
9 The status of Aboriginal and Torres Strait Islander peoples under the law — 111
10 Mechanisms for achieving justice for Aboriginal and Torres Strait Islander peoples — 120
11 Responsiveness of the legal system to Aboriginal and Torres Strait Islander peoples — 130

SECTION B MIGRANTS — 138
12 The status of migrants under the law — 139
13 Mechanisms for achieving justice for migrants — 156
14 Responsiveness of the legal system to migrants — 173

SECTION C WOMEN — 185
15 The status of women under the law — 186
16 Mechanisms for achieving justice for women — 204
17 Responsiveness of the legal system to women — 223

SECTION D MEMBERS OF OTHER GROUPS NOT COVERED BY HUMAN RIGHTS LEGISLATION—CHILDREN AND YOUNG PEOPLE — 242
18 The status of children and young people under the law — 243
19 Mechanisms for achieving justice for children and young people — 263
20 Responsiveness of the law to children and young people — 275

GLOSSARY — 292

ANSWERS TO MULTIPLE-CHOICE QUESTIONS — 297

INDEX — 298

Introduction

To the student

Congratulations on choosing legal studies as a part of your pattern of study in your senior years. Legal studies was first introduced into the NSW Curriculum in 1989 and since then thousands of students have finished their secondary schooling better informed and able to think critically about the processes and institutions that shape their lives.

The rights people enjoy within democratic societies have at times been eroded by governments when electorates become apathetic about their freedoms and liberties. Legal studies will allow you to explore the power vested in our democratic institutions and wielded by our elected leaders. It explores issues fundamental to our way of life and will challenge the way you see the world.

Legal studies will give you more confidence to enter the wider world with your eyes wide open, hopefully with a healthy cynicism and a willingness to participate in the social and political world that we live in.

As you negotiate the course work, you will derive your information from many sources. These will be statutes of parliament, cases handed down in the courts and reports found in the media. Page vi has some useful advice on using these sources.

Good Luck.

Guide to icons

 Additional related material available on the *Cambridge Legal Studies Teacher* CD-ROM.

Additional resources available at
www.cambridge.edu.au/education/nswlegal

Cases, statutes, media reports (CSM)

In legal studies it is important that written answers are backed up by cases, statute law and media reports. This means learning the key pieces of statutory legislation (treaties for international law), knowing the basic facts about a few high-profile cases, and being able to cite recent events that relate to the topic (media reports). Always remember 'CSM' when writing essays and ask yourself 'Have I included some cases, statutes and media reports?'

When citing statutes or treaties in exams, always include the date. For example:

- *Family Law Act 1975* (Cwlth)
- Kyoto Protocol 1997.

Cases should be cited like this:

- *Mabo v. Queensland* (1992)

A media report is anything that has happened in the news. Most commonly this means newspapers, but media reports can also include magazine articles (eg. *Time*) and documentaries. The law is a dynamic thing and sparks much public comment. Luckily for students of legal studies, the media is always carrying an item, or making a comment that is relevant to the law. It is important that you recognise this and stay aware of current events in the legal arena. This will not only help you gain a greater understanding of the concepts and content that you are covering in the course, but it will also give you relevant, up-to-date examples to use in your written responses. However, be aware that outrage sells, and sometimes the headline and the article have very little in common. Thus, as you regularly peruse the media horizon for reports, evaluate the information that is being provided and be alert for bias and sales factor.

Try keeping a media file of relevant articles throughout the year. Set up a folder (either hard copy or electronically) with four subdivisions—'Law and society', 'Crime' and one for each of the focus studies. Articles relevant to any of the topics, even if they have not yet been studied in class, can be placed into plastic sleeves under the relevant heading. Make some brief notes and include these in your folder with the article. You may wish to make a pro-forma for the notes, or alternatively use the one supplied on page viii. Ensure that you write down the source and date of each item.

You can regularly check newspaper websites, as they allow you to access their most recent articles (e.g. the *Sydney Morning Herald* allows you access to articles that have appeared in the previous eight days). In accessing newspaper articles electronically, it is important to do so as soon as possible as it is difficult to get old articles without being asked to pay for them. Articles can be copied in a word program for easier manipulation, then placed in the relevant folder. An even better method of storage it to use a commercially available database such as Procite or Endnote or to make a database yourself. However, do not forget to evaluate each item and its source for reliability, validity, bias and usefulness.

When writing a research essay, correctly cite your media reports in a consistent way in footnotes or endnotes. For example:

• *Sun-Herald*, 'Churchill speaks against terror law', 27 Nov. 2005.

However, when writing in an exam, it is not necessary to remember exact citations— simply placing the event or issue that has been reported in the media in a timeframe is sufficient. For example, 'the recent debate on terror laws', 'in recent months', 'earlier this year' or 'in 2003'.

The Internet is a valuable source of information for legal studies students. However, there is a lot of misinformation posted on the Internet. Some websites will not be updated for months at a time, so the information will be old and irrelevant; some sites are just venues for individulas or groups to spout their views, or for businesses to sell items; and some have incorrect facts and figures. Therefore, any website accessed must be looked at for reliability, validity, bias and usefulness.

The most useful sites are those provided by government departments, as these websites are dynamic and the information provided is reliable. The websites of large-scale newspapers, magazines and television networks are useful in the same way, although it must be remembered that most of these are commercial organisations. Therefore when you surf the Internet looking for information, it is important that you check to see who is the provider of the website and the last time that the site was updated.

As you work through this course, you will probably find that multiple-choice questions will be part of some of your assessment tasks. It is important that you develop skills in this style of question not only for success in these tasks, but also for the Higher School Certificate examination, where you will find fifteen multiple-choice questions.

Here are some tips to help you answer multiple-choice questions.

• READ the whole question and make sure that you understand what the question is asking you to find.
• READ all of the choices.
• Eliminate all of the choices you know are WRONG.
• Look at your remaining answers and make a choice.

Media notes pro-forma

MEDIA REPORT

Newspaper: _____

Date: _____

Article title: _____

☐ Law and Society   ☐ Crime

☐ Focus Study _____   ☐ Focus Study _____

Description of article:

_____

_____

_____

_____

_____

_____

_____

_____

_____

Legal issues:

_____

_____

Glossary of key words

Syllabus outcomes, objectives, performance bands and examination questions have key words that state what students are expected to be able to do. A glossary of key words has been developed to help provide a common language and consistent meaning in the Higher School Certificate documents. Using this glossary will help teachers and students understand what is expected in responses to examinations and assessment tasks.

Key words	Meaning
account	account for, state reasons for, report on, give an account of; narrate a series of events or transactions
analyse	identify components and the relationship between them; draw out and relate implications
apply	use, utilise, employ in a particular situation
appreciate	make a judgment about the value of
assess	make a judgment of value, quality, outcomes, results or size
calculate	ascertain/determine from given facts, figures or information
clarify	make clear or plan
classify	arrange or include in classes/categories
compare	show how things are similar or different
construct	make, build, put together items or arguments
contrast	show how things are different or opposite
critically (analyse/ evaluate)	add a degree or level of accuracy, depth, knowledge and understanding, logic, questioning, reflection and quality to (analysis/evaluation)
deduce	draw conclusions
define	state meaning and identify essential qualities
demonstrate	show by example
describe	provide characteristics and features
distinguish	recognise or note/indicate as being distinct or different from; to note differences between

Key words	Meaning
evaluate	make a judgment based on criteria; determine the value of
examine	inquire into
explain	relate cause and effect make the relationship between things evident provide why and/or how
extract	choose relevant and/or appropriate details
extrapolate	infer from what is known
identify	recognise and name
interpret	draw meaning from
investigate	plan, inquire into and draw conclusions about
justify	support an argument or conclusion
outline	sketch in general terms, indicate the main features of
predict	suggest what may happen based on available information
propose	put forward (for example a point of view, idea, argument, suggestion for consideration or action)
recall	present remembered ideas, facts or experiences
recommend	provide reasons in favour
recount	retell a series of events
summarise	express concisely the relevant details
synthesise	put together various elements to make a whole

About the authors

Kate Dally BA Dip Ed is head teacher of social sciences at Birrong Girls High School. She has extensive experience in the social sciences, teaching the subject for the last 15 years at numerous schools, and being head teacher for 6 of those 15 years. Her experience also covers HSC marking in both business and legal studies, and she has also written for Success One HSC business studies for the last couple of years.

Paul Milgate Dip Teach BEd is head of legal studies, business studies/commerce and economics at Xavier Catholic College on the north coast of NSW. He has extensive experience in Legal Studies, having taught it since its inception. He was a foundation member of the North Coast Legal Studies Teachers Association which runs student seminar days and provides funding for teacher in-service in collaboration with Southern Cross University Faculty of Law and Justice. He is happily ensconced in his north coast lifestyle.

Phil Webster BA DipEd MEd MACE is head of HSIE at Casimir College in Marrickville, after teaching for many years at Knox Grammar School. Quite new to legal studies, his background is in geography and society and culture. His area of expertise is in individual rights and the plight of minority groups in Australia. He currently lives in Collaroy on the northern beaches with his wife and child.

Tim Kelly BA DipEd DipLaw obtained his BA DipEd from the University of New South Wales in 1984 and completed his Diploma in Law from the Legal Practitioners Admissions Board in 1996. He began teaching legal studies in 1993 at St Mary's Maitland and since 1998 has been at St Mary's Casino, where he is the HSIE coordinator.

Acknowledgments

Thanks to my family, and the principals and head teachers who never said 'you can't …'. Special thanks to Harry—the dog who missed out on many afternoon walks for this book but quietly kept me company anyway.

KATE

Thanks to my wife Barbara, my daughter Ebony and my son Zach. A great team.

PAUL

I would like to thank Abby and Frankie for being so supportive of me during the writing period. Also Tristan Tipps, senior policy officer at NSW Department of Aboriginal Affairs for her assistance with Chapter 9.

PHIL

To Amanda, Jack and Hannah. Thanks.

TIM

PART I

The legal system

THE LEGAL SYSTEM

Basic legal notions

- anarchy, custom, rules, law, fairness, equality and justice, values and ethics
- relationship between rules, laws and custom

The constitutional system in Australia

- constitutional division of power between the Commonwealth, states and territories
- the role of the High Court in constitutional interpretation, the system of judicial review and separation of powers
- the gradual transfer of legislative power from the imperial government to the colonies, states and the Commonwealth

Sources of law

Aboriginal and Torres Strait Islander customary law prior to 1788
- the spiritual nature of customary law
- diversity of laws
- ritual and oral traditions
- conciliation and mediation
- enforcement and sanction
- the significance of land and bodies of water

Sources of contemporary Australian law
- common law and uses of the term 'common law'
- the system of precedent
- statute law and delegated legislation
- the Constitution
- criminal law and civil law

Sources and framework of international law
- origins and sources: treaties, customs, legal decisions, legal writings
- principal international organisations: United Nations, International Court of Justice

Operation of the legal system

- structure of state and federal courts
- the adversary system and the legal profession
- court procedures in civil and criminal proceedings
- observation of civil and criminal cases in the local court
- enforcement agencies: police, government departments, other authorities
- legal aid

CHAPTER 1

Basic legal notions

law a set of rules which are enforceable and officially recognised and binding on all members of the community

The **law** is a dynamic thing, although it often seems to be playing catch-up as it tries to keep pace with our ever-changing society. The law is also complex, evolving from hundreds of years of tradition, culture and values.

The law can be defined as a set of enforceable rules of conduct which set down guidelines for relationships among people and organisations in the society in which they live. It provides methods for ensuring the impartial treatment of people, and outlines punishments for those who do not follow the agreed rules of conduct.

To understand how these rules (known in modern society as 'the law') came about, we also need to understand why we live in a society. A society is a group of human beings who are linked by mutual interests, relationships, shared institutions and a common culture. In earliest history, people usually banded together for basic survival and would make up rules that protected their lives and their property.

This tradition has carried on through history. As groups of people form societies and cultural groups within these societies, they have established and enforced rules about the conduct of relationships.

ANARCHY

anarchy the absence of order

When they believe that the law has let them down in some way, some people will proclaim 'We live in a state of **anarchy**!' What exactly do they mean by this?

The word 'anarchy' comes from the Greek word *anarchia*, which means 'without a ruler'. Thus, anarchy is the description given to the state of a society which has an absence of laws or authority figures. While many people believe that an absence of rules leads to a disorganised, chaotic society, an anarchist believes that anarchy does not imply chaos, but rather a ruler-free society with voluntary social harmony.

Anarchist Social Club Rules

1. There are no rules.

2. Failure to follow the rules will see cancellation of membership.

The club requires neat dress at all times.

Figure 1.1 Anarchy: voluntary social harmony... ?

THE NEED FOR RULES

So what are the chances of modern-day Australians living in a lawless, rulerless state? 'Very limited' would seem to be the answer, as most people want and accept rules as part of their everyday life. This is because of the belief that all persons, including ourselves, should be treated equally and with fairness. Thus, rules are needed to ensure that this happens. The rules that evolved for different societies are based upon their **customs** and the values and ethics that are part of these traditions.

Custom

Custom can be described as a common practice among people. This practice can depend upon country, culture, religion and history.

In law, custom (or **customary law**) consists of established patterns of behaviour which are accepted within a particular social setting. Modern law developed out of the customs, rules and expressions of law that were developed in particular communities and slowly collected and written down. Over time, these became the law of the land with enforeceable punishments for going against these laws.

Rules

If you were to look in a dictionary or on the Internet, you would find many meanings for the word 'rules'. Generally for our purposes, rules refer to prescribed directions for conduct in certain situations. For example, there are rules for playing games, behaviour in the classroom, how we eat food and so on. If we break these rules, there is some form of punishment attached, enforceable by those involved in the making of the rules or the playing of the game. Rules can also be altered by these people to deal with changes in situations. This usually happens after consultation with the community involved.

When we look at rules in the legal sense, they are the basis of our laws. However their punishments are more strictly enforced and more severe, and changing the law or its punishment is not a quick and easy process.

Law

The law, as we know it, is made up of the formal rules of society. These 'legal rules' have been agreed upon by the group and govern their behaviour and activities.

Laws are different from rules. For example, at the shopping centre, a sign on the escalator requests that you stand to the left and do not take strollers on it. These are just rules of using the escalator and that is why you will still see people standing on the right and taking their prams on the escalator. These rules exist for the safety and comfort of shoppers. However, there are also signs telling you that you can't smoke in shopping centres. This is a law and if someone did 'light up', they would be asked to leave the shopping centre by security or the police and might incur a fine.

Laws allow and prohibit a whole variety of activities, from where rubbish should be placed to how we should treat fellow human beings. Failure to follow these regulations incurs penalties ranging from a fine to imprisonment.

customs collective habits or traditions that have been developed by a society over a long period of time

customary law principles and procedures that have developed through general usage according to the customs of a people or nation, or groups of nations

Laws have certain characteristics that make them different from rules:

1 Laws are binding on the whole community. This means that they apply to all members of society.
2 Laws can be enforced. This means that penalties apply if a law is broken.
3 Laws are officially recognised. This means that governments and courts recognise laws and enforce them.
4 Laws are accessible (or discoverable). This means that people can find out which law applies to a particular situation.
5 Laws relate to public interest. This means that laws only exist for things that interest the whole of society, which is why there are no laws, for example, about doing the vacuuming in your house.
6 Laws reflect rights and duties. This means that everyone in society has responsibilities to do the correct thing by others, such as not drive dangerously, and that they have the right to be treated in the same way by others.

Today, in Australia, the laws of society are decided on by elected government officials at the local, state or federal government levels. (You will learn more about this process in following chapters.)

In most countries only professionals trained in the law can understand and explain legal principles, draft relevant documents, and guide parties through legal disputes. It is expected by society that the law will look after all members of the group, and as such any laws made will be fair, just and equitable. It is also expected that they will reflect traditional and current ethics and values.

Figure 1.2 There's no law about vacuuming, but there might be a rule...

Fairness

Fairness and **justice** are usually associated with each other. The difference is that the term 'fairness' applies to everyday life, whereas 'justice' has more legal connotations. Fairness is concerned with everyday activities and is based on personal opinion. For example, what one person may see as unfair will not worry another person. (Missing out on an item on ebay by one dollar may seem unfair to you, but be of no concern to your friend.) However, when rules are made, it is expected that they will be fair to those covered by them. In the same way, when a rule is translated into law, it is expected that it will be fair to all in society.

Equality

A basic definition of **equality** is the equal treatment of everyone. Although we would like to think that equality applies to everyone, our society tolerates many types of equality, and thus many forms of inequality. For example, a 10-year-old child will be treated differently to a 17-year-old teenager or a 40-year-old adult, so it is very difficult for true equality to exist in society.

justice the principle of upholding generally accepted rights and enforcing responsibilities, ensuring that equal outcomes are achieved for those involved

equality the equal treatment of everybody

The law does try to make this happen, but it takes into account that some people are more vulnerable than others, and so includes protection of them. Examples of this are not allowing teenagers to buy alcohol, and not holding children under a certain age legally accountable for their actions.

Justice

The concept of 'justice' involves the fair, moral and impartial treatment of all persons, especially in law. It is the continued effort to do the right thing by everyone. When it comes to making laws in a society, being just involves consulting the majority. If a person lives under a certain set law, making the person follow the law and applying punishment if they do not is considered to be justice. Thus, justice is different to fairness, as it is more specific and can be applied to actual situations covered by the law. Using the ebay example again, losing by one dollar is not unjust, as everybody had the same chance to win the item following the rules of the auction.

Values and ethics

We all have values by which we try to live. These are referred to as our 'ethics'. Having ethics means that we do things that we consider to be good and right.

Lawmakers try to incorporate these values and ethics into laws. However, it is very difficult to make rules, and thus laws, about everyone's values, especially as there are often groups in society that have different standards of what is morally right or wrong. For this reason laws will only cover those ethical values which are most common to all. An example of this is that everyone considers murder to be ethically wrong and thus this is incorporated into our laws with appropriate penalties.

Relationship between rules, laws and customs

Over time, as people have joined together in communities, a relationship has developed between rules, laws and customs.

- Whenever people have lived together in groups, they have developed rules to govern their behaviour and thus maintain the smooth running of activities.
- These rules were based on the traditions, customs and values of the group.
- These rules have penalties attached if members of the group fail to follow them.
- Groups usually put someone, or a small group, in charge to enforce these rules and the associated penalties. In modern times, this became the government.
- Over time, these rules became formalised laws, known in society as 'the law'.

Thus, a rule, when it is seen to be fair and just and based on the customs of the majority of the people in the community, will become a law accepted by the people.

Figure 1.3 Elected officials make laws on behalf of society.

Why do people obey the law?

People like to have rules, and thus laws, because they create order in society. They help each person to have a sense of security, as the law tells them what is expected of them, and what they can expect from others. As the law is based on custom, it also reinforces the values of the members of society. It says that what individuals feel is important has the same importance to the larger group.

Laws also have the function of providing protection for all members of the society, not only from their own actions, but from those of others. Laws tell society what actions are not allowed. They also provide freedom to do things by telling society what actions are allowed. In addition, they resolve disputes as they have penalties for behaviour which goes against the law and empower the police force and the courts to enforce and administer the law.

People will not follow rules if they do not agree with them or see that they have no connection to them. This is especially so if the penalty attached to the rule is seen as inadequate. (For example, think again about the penalties attached to standing on the wrong side of the escalator.) However, as laws do have a range of penalties attached to them that will make a person think twice about breaking the law, people are more inclined to follow the law.

Figure 1.4 People sometimes disobey laws if they do not perceive the penalty to be harsh.

REVIEW 1.1

1 Why do we need laws? For what reasons do members of society obey the law?
2 How would you explain the meaning of the following basic legal notions to someone else? You could use words, pictures or cartoons. Use a double-page spread in your workbook to do this. Write an explanation about your chosen format.
   a anarchy
   b custom
   c rules
   d law
   e fairness
   f equality
   g justice
   h values
   i ethics.

MEDIA CLIP

SYSTEM DISABLED
BY MATTHEW MOORE

Sydney Morning Herald, 28–29 January 2006

Losing a leg, needing a wheelchair, or being unable to walk 100 metres are the main disabilities the Roads and Traffic Authority says warrant a disabled parking permit.

- More than 256,000 permits issued, 13 per cent of all vehicles.
- Free parking all day on meters.
- All-day parking in zones of more than 30 minutes
- Two hours in 30-minute zones
- Costs $30.00 for three years

But thousands of Sydneysiders with no hint of a limp have found ways to get the tags that allow free parking on meters where others pay $4.40 an hour or more. The authority has issued more than 256,000 disabled permits, enough for 13 per cent of NSW vehicles.

On Wednesday morning in Kent Street scores of physically able drivers parked all day using the permits in scenes played out wherever parking spots are at a premium.

Just before 8am a black Alfa Romeo grabbed one of the few vacant spaces near the corner of Market Street. Before the driver got out he checked he had placed on the dash on of the white Mobility Parking Scheme cards that were on most other cars in the street.

Dressed in a snappy suit, the man, who appeared to be in his early 30s, left on the leather seat a well-thumbed copy of *Rich Kids*, Paul Barry's account of Jamie Packer and Jodee Rich's One.Tel venture. Then he opened the door and strode quickly across the road.

Asked whether he had a disability, he replied: "I do have a disability."

"Can you tell me what it is?"

"Not at all, sir." He gave the same answer when asked for his name.

Similar replies came from almost every motorist who parked in the block between Market and King streets between 6.30am and 9.30am. Nearly all drivers claimed a legitimate reason for using their cards, but nearly all refused to give their names or have their stories checked.

Russel Gordon was an exception. Asked why he had a permit, the fit young man in the silver Pulsar said: "Oh, I must have forgotten it was there. My parents are away so I'm using my mum's car, and sometimes I just forget."

Although he gave his name, he was reluctant to give his address.

"Just from the eastern suburbs," was all he would say before walking 100 metres back to his car and parking it elsewhere.

Most drivers showed no hint of remorse. First to arrive that morning was a slim young woman in high heels, still using P-plates on the Fairmont Ghia, who parks in the same place each day.

"It's my granny's sticker, it's in her name," she said, identifying herself only as an accountant who works at King Street Wharf.

"She lives around the corner in a flat. I pick her up at eight every morning to take her to the doctor's in Elizabeth Street and bring her back at 11...They have to inject her every day for vertigo."

She had only just got the permit, she said, and would not keep it long, although the sticker carried an expiry date of May 2007.

She must have lost track of time and her grandmother, as her car had not moved at 9.30am.

Other regulars arrived soon after. A young man pulled up in a Ford Explorer, put his permit on the dash as he does each morning and ran across the road into a cafe where he slipped behind the counter and began his shift. Half an hour later another young man parked his Honda, got the sticker and ducked into the Subway fast food joint through a door marked "Employees only".

A couple in a Honda Accord insisted they were not abusing the scheme, which says the tag can be displayed only when the car is being used to transport the person to whom it is issued.

The man said they were picking up his mother-in-law, but would not give his name. Ten minutes later his wife returned. She said she was Giovana Gualloupo and offered to take me to meet her mother. "She's got rheumatoid arthritis; she's at the blood bank giving blood. She does that about every two months."

But when I tried to get into the car, Ms Gualloupo changed her mind. "Will I get paid?" she asked. When told the *Herald* did not pay for stories, she said she could not take me. Nor would she reveal her mother's name or contact details.

While it is impossible to be certain who is using a permit legitimately, the authority restructured the scheme two years ago because so many people were misusing it.

New permits with photographs were issued, but for privacy reasons the photos are not visible when the tag is displayed. All you need to get a permit is find a relative or friend with an injury or disability. You get a doctor's certificate, take it and the relative to the authority, and get the tag. They last up to three years and cost just $10 a year.

The vice-president of the Physical Disability Council of NSW, John Moxon, said it was outrageous that so many abused the scheme. He said the State Government was not interested in policing it, as it does not operate the meters, so does not lose revenue.

A spokesman for the authority said the new scheme had cut abuse, with the number of new permits and renewals dropping by 25 per cent. But only 23 permits had been cancelled in the last two years, while nearly 1000 new permits were issued every week.

"The MPS changes have met the objectives of improving the integrity of the scheme," he said.

REVIEW 1.2

1 What is the article about?
2 Explain how and why the permit system has been changed.
3 Does society need a stronger type of legislation? Write two paragraphs, one arguing in favour of the legislation, one arguing against it.

RESEARCH 1.1

Prepare a report on anarchy. In your report include the following:
- a definition
- a history
- information on two anarchist organisations and their beliefs
- modern-day anarchists and their activities.

   To help you with your research, you could do an Internet search on the following:
- Some modern anarchist groups:
   - black bloc
   - WOMBLES
   - Wild Greens
- These groups often protest at:
   - G8 meetings
   - European Union meetings
   - World Trade Organisation meetings
- They are also anti globalisation.

   The Internet encyclopedia Wikipedia (http://en.wikipedia.org/) will help in providing information.

Figure 1.5 Modern anarchist groups protest about the dominant power of governments and large corporations.

MULTIPLE-CHOICE QUESTIONS

1 Which of these statements about the difference between a rule and a law is true?
   a rules are not binding on the whole of the community
   b rules do not involve rights and responsibilities
   c rules are not enforceable
   d rules have nothing to do with ethics

2 What is anarchy?
   a a state of chaos
   b having no rules
   c wearing black clothes to break the rules
   d rebellion against the government

3 What are ethics?
   a allowing people to be different.
   b a mix of equality and fairness
   c the principles that help us make decisions about right and wrong behaviour
   d different people's perceptions about the law

4 A police officer charges a man for crossing the road against the lights, but does not book a pretty woman doing the same thing. Why is this unjust?
   a the police officer should concentrate on serious crimes
   b studies show that women are better at crossing roads
   c the police officer has not treated all pedestrians equally
   d you should be allowed to cross the road wherever you want

5 What is the purpose of the law?
   a to divide power in society
   b to allow stability for the ruling government
   c to maintain order in society
   d to make people do things that no-one wants to do

CHAPTER SUMMARY TASKS

1 Describe the difference between anarchy and the law.
2 Explain how anarchy and a structured system of law are not compatible.
3 Account for the relationship between rules, laws and custom.
4 Compare and contrast rules and laws.
5 What is the relationship between fairness, equality and justice?
6 Is law necessary? Justify your answer.
7 Why do people have different perceptions about the law?

CHAPTER SUMMARY

- The law of a country has developed from the rules of the dominant community.
- These rules are based on the customs, values and ethics of that community.
- Rules and laws have different characteristics.
- The term given to a society where citizens are not required to obey laws is 'anarchy'.
- The law is based on the notions of fairness, equality and justice.
- The law covers all members of society and has penalties attached for infringements of the law.
- People follow the law because it provides them with protection against wrongful behaviour.

CHAPTER 2

Sources of law

ABORIGINAL AND TORRES STRAIT ISLANDER CUSTOMARY LAW PRIOR TO 1788

The Indigenous cultures of Australia are the oldest living cultures in the world. Over time, other peoples who have come to Australia to stay and peoples who visited Australia for trade or other reasons, but did not stay, have influenced Indigenous Australia. Indigenous peoples also traded among themselves and exchanged ideas, songs and dances. Songs and dances were displayed and exchanged usually at large ceremonial gatherings where many people collected together. These gatherings often occurred at a time and place when there were plenty of particular foods.

Like all cultures, Indigenous Australian cultures have changed and developed over time. Colonisation of Australia brought rapid changes to Indigenous society and dramatically affected the land and the way people lived.

Prior to European settlement, only Indigenous people populated Australia. When the First Fleet sailed into Sydney Harbour, in 1788, Aboriginal people inhabited the whole of Australia and Torres Strait Islanders lived on the islands between Australia and Papua New Guinea. Australia had many different Aboriginal and Torres Strait Islander communities, speaking different languages and with various cultural beliefs, practices and traditions.

It was very much a hunter-gatherer lifestyle, where men hunted the large animals such as kangaroos, emus and turtles, and the women and children hunted smaller animals and collected fruits, berries and other plants. On the coast, people relied on catching fish and collecting many types of shellfish. Most Indigenous people would stay in an area only for a certain time because of seasonal variations and to maintain the fragile environment.

There is no single system of Aboriginal and Torres Strait Islander law. The separate Indigenous nations developed their own law that was unique to their particular society, but did share common aspects with other groups. All of these laws are spiritually based and closely linked to the land. Aboriginal and Torres Strait Islander law is based on tradition, ritual and acceptable conduct. For this reason it is known as 'customary law'.

A main difference between Aboriginal and Torres Strait Islander customary law and the British legal tradition is the area of land ownership. The right to possess property is a key principle of English and European law. However, to Aboriginal and Torres Strait Islander peoples, land is sacred and cannot be owned. Instead people are custodians of the

terra nullius land belonging to no-one —the idea and legal concept that when the first Europeans came to Australia the land was owned by no-one and thus was open to settlement. It has been judged legally invalid.

Dreamtime also known as 'the Dreaming', the source of Indigenous Australian customary law

kinship family relationships, including all extended family relationships; an important part of Indigenous cultures and values, dictating how all people in the group behave toward each other

elders older and wiser men and women who are the keepers of traditional knowledge within Indigenous communities; they are responsible for such things as initiations and the handing down of punishments when community laws are broken

mediation a process whereby a third party intervenes in a dispute between two parties with the intention of resolving the conflict. The third party does not, however, adjudicate or impose penalties.

land, looking after it for future generations. This collective guardianship is a key feature of customary law. However, this lack of tangible ownership is the reason why the British people felt that they could impose settlement and the associated laws in Australia. The British considered Australia to be an unoccupied land, as they could not see any signs of ownership, such as fences and signs. The term that they used for this is '**terra nullius**', a Latin expression meaning 'empty land'.

It is important to remember that although laws set down by federal and state common and statute law govern Australia, many Indigenous people still follow the ideals of their own customary law. This will be explored further in the course.

The spiritual nature of Indigenous customary law

The Dreaming is the basis of much Aboriginal and Torres Strait Islander law. The Dreaming, also known as the **Dreamtime**, is the history of Aboriginal and Torres Strait Islander peoples. It explains how the land, animals, plants and sky were created and has a very strong religious element.

Diversity of Indigenous societies

Aboriginal and Torres Strait Islander law is tribal and as such different tribes have variations of customary law. Australia is a large land mass and, as a result, different languages and modes of conduct developed. However, the similarities in customary law outweigh the differences.

Ritual and oral traditions within Indigenous societies

Aboriginal and Torres Strait Islander law is part of everyday life. The law is an integral part of the values, customs and ethics of Aboriginal and Torres Strait Islander peoples and so has developed over many thousands of years. Most laws relate to marriage, child rearing, religion and **kinship**. Customary laws have been passed from generation to generation by word of mouth. Stories, songs and dances are used to help people remember the laws of their group. Different people in the tribe know different laws. For example, women have knowledge of some laws that they pass on to young females at a certain age. This lack of written law was another reason that the British considered Australia to be an 'empty land'.

Conciliation and mediation within Indigenous societies

When customary laws were broken or disputes arose, **elders** and influential members of the tribe were involved in their resolution through **mediation** and conciliation. With mediation, the elders of the group would get together to make a decision about how to deal with the dispute. Conciliation involves the elders of the tribe meeting with the people in conflict and using discussion and dialogue in an attempt to settle the dispute.

Enforcement and sanction within Indigenous societies

When a dispute is settled and a decision made about a punishment, the relatives of the wronged party or ceremonial leaders will usually enforce the punishment. These punishments range from ridicule, to exile, spearing or death.

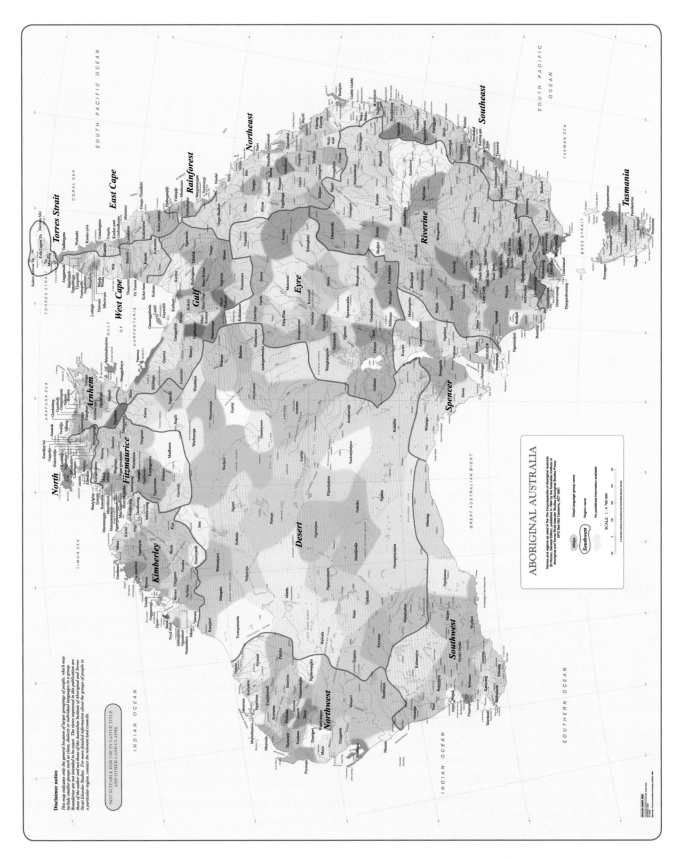

Figure 2.1 This map shows Indigenous Australian language regions.

The significance of land and bodies of water to Indigenous societies

Figure 2.2 In Indigenous societies, land belongs to a group and not to individuals.

The idea of individual land ownership is alien to Aboriginal and Torres Strait Islander thought. Being a member of a tribe means that a person is able to live on and use the resources of certain lands. Thus, the land belongs to the group and loss of this land means losing the tribe's culture and history. In the same way, Aboriginal and Torres Strait Islander people have links with the sea, lakes, rivers and all bodies of water. These are not owned by individuals, but are cared for by the group under customary law.

The relevance of customary law today

In the past twenty years there has been greater legal recognition of Aboriginal and Torres Strait Islanders' rights as the traditional landholders of Australia. Many aspects of customary law can be seen embodied in Australian law today. The philosophy of sustainable development has always been very important to Aboriginal and Torres Strait Islanders and is very much the basis for current environmental laws. Conciliation and mediation play an integral role in contemporary criminal, consumer and employment law in resolving disputes.

REVIEW 2.1

1 Describe the importance of tradition in Aboriginal and Torres Strait Islander customary law.
2 Explain the different relationships that Europeans and Aboriginal and Torres Strait Islanders have with the land.
3 Why is it not possible to refer to a uniform Aboriginal and Torres Strait Islander customary law?
4 What do the laws of Indigenous Australian peoples have in common?
5 Identify how customary law is relevant to the Australian contemporary legal system.

RESEARCH 2.1

Visit the website http://www.dreamtime.net.au/, go to 'Stories of the Dreaming' and complete the following activities:
1 Explain the importance of the Dreaming to Aboriginal and Torres Strait Islander peoples.
2 Identify how Dreaming stories are passed on through generations.
3 Who has custody of these stories?
4 Discuss why many of these stories are called 'sacred' and 'secret'?
5 Look at the list of stories and their summaries and distinguish the common themes of many of these stories.
6 Choose a story and briefly tell what it is about.

SOURCES OF CONTEMPORARY AUSTRALIAN LAW

Australian legal processes and practices are based on the English model. This is because when the British came to Australia in 1788, they brought with them the law that applied in Britain, **common law**. Australian contemporary law evolves from common law and **statute law**.

Common law refers to laws created in court by decisions made by judges. Statute law refers to laws made by parliament. These concepts are discussed below.

common law the law made by courts, historically, law common to England

statute law law made by parliament

Common law and the different uses of the term 'common law'

The concept of common law has many different uses, as you would find if you were to put the term into a search engine on the Internet. The law in Australia today includes elements of the following definitions:
- court-made law (as opposed to laws made by parliament)
- law developed by courts of common law as distinct from the courts of equity and merchant courts
- the system of court-based law used in countries such as Australia and Great Britain.

Courts of equity

These courts were developed in England in the thirteenth and fourteenth centuries by the Court of Chancery to deal with injustices that had crept into the common law.

Each case would be looked at by Chancery and, using a set of rules, it would decide what was fair or just in the particular circumstances. These standards are called the rules of **equity** and are still used today.

equity judging each case on its merits to correct any injustices

Mercantile law

Mercantile law was developed by merchants to enable them to settle disputes between themselves. It applied to all merchant countries, but, by the eighteenth century, these rules had merged with common law.

mercantile law laws that relate to trade

Court-made law

The common law originally developed in England after the Norman invasion in the eleventh century. Before the institutional stability imposed on England by William the Conqueror in 1066, the people of England were governed by unwritten local customs that varied from community to community and were enforced in often arbitrary fashion.

Courts generally consisted of informal public assemblies that weighed conflicting claims in a case. If unable to reach a decision, the court might require an accused to test guilt or innocence by carrying a red-hot iron or snatching a stone from a cauldron of boiling water or some other test of innocence in a system known as 'trial by ordeal'. If the defendant's wound healed within a prescribed period, he was set free as innocent; if not, execution usually followed.

MEDIA CLIP

TRIAL BY ORDEAL—SOME EXAMPLES

- The accused walked barefoot over red-hot iron. If the accused survived that, and the resultant wound healed after three days they were considered innocent.
- The accused had to carry a bar of red-hot iron in his hands while they walked nine marked paces. In the unlikely event of no burns appearing on their hand, they were judged innocent.
- Another trial by ordeal was the plunging of the arm into boiling water. If no blisters appeared innocence was assumed.
- The accused was thrown into a river; if they sank they were considered innocent.
- Another method was the eating of food containing a feather. If the accused choked they were assumed guilty.

Figure 2.3 'Don't worry: if you drown, we'll know you're innocent!'

In order to consolidate his hold on the country, William the Conqueror sent judges (or justices) around the country with three main tasks to carry out:
1 administer a common set of laws throughout the country
2 report on any threats to the throne
3 assess the wealth of the country so that taxation could be levied.

When the next ruler, Henry II, came to the throne in 1154, there was a well established practice of sending royal justices throughout the countryside to listen to disputes, work out solutions and apply punishments, and ensure that common rulings were made overall. These judges also had authority to make decisions when they heard new cases. In this way, a set of uniform laws developed throughout England. Thus common law as we know it today has evolved from judicial decisions that were based in tradition, custom and precedent.

The system of precedent

While common law is made in the courts and has rules about the presentation of evidence and the running of the case, one of the main features of common law is that it is adjusted by judges on a case by case basis. However, to do this, judges must review decisions made in previous cases. This is called 'following precedent'.

The **doctrine of precedent** works to limit the ability of a judge to be creative when it comes to making a decision and imposing **sanctions**. It gives the judicial system guidelines in making a decision. Precedent in law is based on custom and case law.

Custom

Custom can be deeply embedded in society and so gain the force of the law. Thus, custom sets a precedent in expected behaviour and has traditionally been recognised by courts and judges.

Case law

Case law is decisions made in previous court cases which make new interpretations of the law and, therefore, can be cited as precedents. When using case law, a judge will weigh up the similarities of a court case to previous cases. The judge will adjust the standards set by the other court cases to the circumstances of the current case.

When a judge gives a decision in a case, it usually is made up of two parts. They are:
1 **ratio decidendi**, or the legal reason why a judge came to a particular decision. Precedent usually plays some part in this decision.
2 **obiter dicta**, or other remarks made by the judge regarding the conduct of the trial, for example, about the credibility of a witness. These remarks do not form part of the decision and thus do not set a precedent.

The general rules for the process of precedent are as follows:
- Lower courts are bound to follow decisions in superior courts. This is known as 'binding precedent'.
- Superior courts do not have to follow decisions made in lower courts. They may, however, use them to help make a decision. This is called 'persuasive precedent'.
- Decisions made in other court heirarchies such as the United States or Great Britain may influence decisions made in an Australian judgement. This is 'persuasive precedent'.

doctrine of precedent the process whereby decisions made in earlier court cases help decide the outcome of the present case being considered

sanctions official permission or approval for a course of action

ratio decidendi the legal reason why a judge came to a particular decision

obiter dicta comments from a judge in a case not directly relevant to the case before them and therefore not legally binding

Sometimes judges try to avoid using precedent. For example, a judge may decide that the facts of a current case are significantly different to a precious case and so ratio decidendi does not have to be followed. Precedents can serve to establish trends and take into account changes in society. For instance, if minority groups have been receiving greater and greater equality under the law, then the next legal decision on that subject may serve to bring still greater equality.

Figure 2.4 The judge acts as an 'umpire' in a court case.

defamation an act of communication that causes someone to be shamed, ridiculed, held in contempt, and to lose their standing in the community or their place of work

CASE SPACE

The law of defamation and the Internet
Gutnick v. Dow Jones & Co Inc [2001] VSC 305

Precedent was established in this case where the plaintiff argued that he had been defamed over the Internet. The respondent Dow Jones publishes an online news magazine. It accused the plaintiff, a prominent Melbourne businessman, of improper dealings. Even though the news item originated in NewYork, USA, the plaintiff successfully argued that he had been defamed in his own city because more than 300 people had accessed the report in Melbourne. He was awarded damages in the court case.

A new legal precedent was set in this case as it was one of the first legal cases to look at the Internet as a source of defamation. The case sparked international interest because of this precedent. The fact that the World Wide Web is so accessible by everybody in today's world means that a legal minefield has been laid for anybody to take civil action over information placed on an Internet site. In awarding damages to the plaintiff, the court set a new standard for legal action and a basis for an injured party to take this legal action.

Statute law and delegated legislation

Statute law is the law made by parliament. It is also known as 'legislation' or 'acts of parliament'. In Australia, any parliament has the power to make statute law. This means that state, territory and federal governments all have the right to make laws. The Australian Constitution sets out the different levels of authority that the state and federal parliaments have to make law.

The Constitution

A **constitution** is a set of rules that set out how a country is governed and how laws are made. The Australian Constitution was passed by the British government in 1900 in a statute named the Commonwealth of Australia Constitution Act 1900 (UK). In Australia, each of the six states has its own constitution. The citizens of New South Wales are not only governed by the Australian Constitution but also the Constitution of New South Wales, created by the *Constitution Act of New South Wales 1902* (NSW). The Australian Constitution is the supreme law in Australia. It provides for the following:

- the establishment of federal parliament
- the division of powers between the federal and state governments by outlining what the states are allowed to do and what the federal government is allowed to do
- the **separation of powers** between legislature, **judiciary** and the **executive**
- establishment of a **High Court**
- the rights enjoyed by all Australians.

    The Constitution will be looked at in more detail in the next chapter.

Parliamentary structure

A parliament is a body of elected representatives. It debates proposed legislation, passes, rejects or amends legislation. Apart from Queensland and the territories, all state parliaments and the federal parliament are **bicameral**. This means that they have two houses, an upper house and a lower house. Queensland's parliament is unicameral as it only has a lower house.

    In federal parliament, the two houses are the Senate (the upper house) and the House of Representatives (the lower house). The Governor-General oversees them.

    There are key players in parliament. These include the government that is formed by the political party that has the majority of seats in the lower house. Sometimes parties will unite to form a government (such as the Liberal/National Coalition). The prime minister is the leader of the government. The political party or parties who have the remaining seats in the lower house form the Opposition. Ministers are those members of the government who have a special responsibility for particular departments. Some or all of the ministers form the Cabinet. Cabinet makes decisions on policy and laws to be drafted for consideration by parliament.

    The Executive Council is made up of Governor or Governor-General and selected ministers. It is the body that enables legislation to be put into operation. The British monarchy still plays a role in parliament in Australia. The Queen must assent to laws. She is represented in Australia by the Governor-General at federal level and governors at the state level.

Figure 2.5 Parliament House, Canberra.

constitution a set of rules; the fundamental law of the state

separation of powers the idea of preventing one person or group gaining total power by dividing power between the executive, legislature and judiciary

judiciary the court system

executive an arm of the federal government that is controlled by administrative law

High Court the highest court in Australia, it hears appeals and decides questions of interpretation of the Australian Constitution

bicameral containing two chambers or houses of parliament

Passing legislation

One of the most important functions of parliament is the passing of law. The making of a law can be time consuming and difficult. The process is open to public scrutiny and, as a result, well-organised pressure groups and members of electorates can influence parliamentarians' opinions. As members of parliament are subject to elections every few years, they are well aware of the consequences of passing unpopular legislation. This means that proposed legislation will undergo much discussion in parliament and could be redrafted many times. Before a law is made, it requires the approval of both houses of parliament and the Governor-General.

The process of passing a bill through parliament

STAGE 1

Cabinet discusses a proposed new law or change to an existing law. This proposal usually comes because of pressure from some parts of the public who see a need for change. A decision is made by Cabinet on whether or not to proceed.

If a decision is made to go ahead with the change, parliamentary clerks are asked to draft a bill. Then a minister in the government introduces a bill to the House of Representatives to either create a new law or change an existing law. Before it leaves the lower house, the bill must pass through at least three readings. The first reading is just the introduction of the bill. In the second reading any contentious points are debated and the minister responsible for the bill will highlight its purpose and benefits.

The bill is scrutinised, analysed and evaluated by parliamentary committees. Changes to the bill may be made. It will then go back to the lower house for a third reading. A vote is taken and, if the majority agree to the bill, it is passed to the Senate.

delegated legislation laws made by authorities other than parliament, who are delegated the power to do this by parliament

STAGE 2

The bill goes through all of the same processes in the upper house (Senate). Sometimes the bill will be sent back to the lower house for further amendment. The Senate must then vote on the bill and, if the majority says yes, it will progress to the next stage.

STAGE 3

The Governor-General meets with a select number of government ministers in a meeting of the Executive Council. If approval is given and the bill signed, it then becomes a law or act of parliament.

Delegated legislation

Delegated legislation is legislation made by non-parliamentary bodies. It involves 'less important' laws that parliament does not have time to draft, consider and pass, and so delegates the responsibility to 'subordinate' bodies.

Types of delegated legislation are:

1 Regulations—laws made by the Governor-General, state Governors or members of the Executive Council
2 Ordinances—laws made for Australian territories such as Norfolk Island and the Australian Antarctic Territory
3 Rules—legislation made for government departments, usually by the department involved
4 By-laws—laws made by local councils which are restricted to the area governed by that council

TABLE 2.1

The advantages and disadvantages of delegated legislation

Advantages	Disadvantages
• The people making the legislation are usually experts in that field. • Delegation of minor legislation frees up parliamentary time for very serious issues. • It is easier to amend delegated legislation and thus it is more flexible.	• Members of parliament do not have the time or expertise to fully check the delegated legislation. • With many different bodies involved in making delegated legislation there can be inconsistencies. • Little publicity surrounds the delegated legislation and thus the public usually cannot voice their views.

REVIEW 2.2

1 Explain how common law originated.
2 Describe how people were tried before William the Conquer came to England. What were the problems with this system?
3 Give meanings for mercantile law and equity law.
4 Account for the reason why Australian law is based on common law principles.
5 Identify the differences between court-made law and statute law.
6 How is the principle of precedent used in court decisions?
7 Evaluate the importance of the *Gutnick v. Dow Jones & Co Inc* case.
8 Describe the importance of a constitution. What does the Australian Constitution cover?
9 Construct a way to explain to the public how an act of parliament is made. You may wish to use a series of cartoons or a storyboard.
10 Define delegated legislation. Demonstrate your knowledge with appropriate examples.

Criminal and civil law

The law can be divided into **public law** and **private law**.

Criminal law is a form of public law. It covers acts or omissions against the whole community and its main focus is to maintain public safety and order for the whole of society. In criminal law, an offence is seen as being against the whole community even if only one individual is affected. This is because the offence is seen to damage the order of society.

Another name for private law is **civil law**. It means law relating to disputes between individuals or institutions and thus the aim of civil law is to regulate the relationship between individual citizens.

public law constitutional, administrative, industrial, and criminal law

private law also known as civil law, contract law, torts, family law and property law

civil law the area of the law that deals with disputes between private individuals

jury a group of people who listen to all of the evidence in a court case and decide on the verdict

There are many differences between criminal and civil law court cases.

In a criminal case, the state brings the case to court. 'The state' is a term used for the government and the people that it governs. In less serious criminal court cases, the state is represented by the police. The police pursue the criminal act and its perpetrator, they collect the evidence and ensure that the prosecution has all it needs to carry the case in court. Sometimes the state is also known as the Crown.

In a civil offence, an individual or an organisation brings the case to court. Criminal and civil law can overlap. An individual who has had a crime committed against them may also wish to take the perpetrator of the crime to civil court to gain compensation for injuries committed against them. However both court cases are based on an adversarial system of trial. This means a judge, and sometimes a **jury**, hears both sides of the case as put forward by representatives of the parties involved. The judge deliberates over the evidence and makes a decision in favour of one of the parties.

The differences between criminal and civil law will be covered further throughout this course.

Civil law systems in other countries

The term 'civil law' causes some confusion. In the Australian legal system it refers to private law, disputes between individuals. However it also describes the legal systems of those countries that have developed from the Roman law system instead of the English common law system.

Today, countries such as France, Germany and Italy are civil law countries. Civil law countries usually have an inquisitional system of trial as opposed to the common law adversarial system. In an inquisitorial system of trial, the judge collects the evidence for both sides in a dispute.

REVIEW 2.3

1 Distinguish between public and private law.
2 Outline the differences and similarities in civil and criminal court cases.
3 Why does the term 'civil law' cause confusion?
4 Discuss the differences between the adversarial and inquisitorial court systems.

Figure 2.6 If only civil law was more civil!

SOURCES AND FRAMEWORK OF INTERNATIONAL LAW

States and sovereignty

Each country has laws for its own people, known as **domestic law**. A country can do this because in the eyes of the rest of the world it is an autonomous (independent) state which has sovereignty to make laws.

domestic law the law of a nation

A state, in the legal sense, is an independent entity that is recognised by other states on an international basis. In order to be a state, a place must have a defined territory, a permanent population, an effective government and the capacity to enter into international negotiations. Sovereignty means that the state has the authority to make rules for its population and the power to enforce these rules. Although we call New South Wales a state, in international eyes, Australia is the recognisable nation state.

International law governs the relationship between nations. International law enables nations to participate in trade and commerce, and relieves areas of conflict between countries. International law also covers fundamental human rights, making it illegal to do such things as torture political prisoners or to commit genocide.

International law has a major problem in its enforcement: it relies on countries consenting to cooperate in the enforcement of these laws. As the world is made up of diverse cultures and values, not all countries will agree with all international laws and may ignore a law if they feel that it is irrelevant to them.

Origins and sources of international law

Sources of international law are treaties, customs, legal writings and legal decisions.

Treaties

Treaties are the most commonly used source of international law. They are written agreements between different nations that state their obligations to each other. Treaties usually take two forms:
- bilateral—between two nations
- multilateral—between many nations.

The more nations that sign a **treaty**, the more powerful that treaty will be.

Treaties are used to make specific laws and to control conduct and cooperation between and within nations. A treaty may also establish an international organisation.

treaty an international instrument that governs relations between two or more nations

There is no set way of making a treaty, but most treaties are made through direct negotiations between nations. If all parties involved agree, the treaty will be signed. The treaty only becomes binding when ratified by the signatory nations. In Australia, the Executive Council must ratify (or approve of) the conditions of the treaty. The conditions of the treaty are then enacted into domestic law.

HOW DOES A TREATY BECOME DOMESTIC LAW?

The signing of a treaty does not automatically make the conditions contained in the treaty part of the law of the country. The Australian government may sign a treaty, but, if it wants the substance of the treaty to be made into domestic law and followed by the Australian people with suitable penalties for non observance, it must ensure that it is able to do this under its constitutional powers. The proposed legislation must go through the processes discussed previously.

Most treaties that are signed by Australia do not need corresponding legislation as they are to do with trade and defence matters. However, treaties in regard to human rights have had elements of them embodied into federal and state laws. For example, parts of the United Nations Declaration of Human Rights can be seen in the state and federal antidiscrimination legislation.

Conventions and declarations

conventions procedures that people are expected to follow; a general agreement between nations

Conventions and declarations are forms of treaties. Their aim is usually to regulate a particular aspect of international law.

Customs

Customary international law is based on long-established traditions followed by many nations to the point that they are accepted as being fair and right by the international community. Examples of international customary law are the condemnation of slavery and genocide. The law of the seas and airspace are other examples.

Legal decisions

United Nations a world organisation that is dedicated to world peace and equality for all

While each country has its own laws, laws are also needed to regulate behaviour between nations. The main source of international law is the **United Nations**. It writes legislation and treaties that member countries vote upon. For example, an area of international law is basic human rights. Under international law, set down by the United Nations and agreed upon by the majority of members, it is illegal to torture political prisoners. The International Court of Justice deals with most disputes involving international law.

If enough countries pass an international convention, legal decisions of international organisations such as the United Nations and the International Court of Justice often become part of international customary law, even if the decision is not enacted into the domestic law. An example of this is the banning by the United Nations of driftnet fishing, a fishing technique now used by very few countries. The elimination of driftnet fishing has been carried out more with public awareness and education than with the use of domestic law.

However, the main problem with legal decisions is the difficulty in enforcing them. As international law relies on the consensus and cooperation of all parties, little can be done against countries that fail to follow international law or have a looser interpretation of the law.

Legal writings

Legal writings are the writings of well-respected international lawyers, judges and participants in world affairs (such as journalists and politicians). These writings and their ideas can be incorporated into customary law and treaties.

Principal international organisations: the United Nations and the International Court of Justice

The United Nations

The United Nations (UN) is the chief organisation involved in international law. It was established in 1945 by the Charter of the United Nations as an outcome of World War II. Since this time it has grown in significance. In 1945, fifty-one countries were members of the United Nations and this has since grown to 191 by 2003.

The UN was established to look after world affairs. Its main objective is to maintain global peace and security. The UN has no powers to make countries enact its suggestions into domestic law. It relies on consensus and cooperation of all member countries to follow, implement and reinforce its initiatives.

Key UN bodies

THE GENERAL ASSEMBLY

The **General Assembly** is made up of representatives from all member nations. It passes resolutions on the operation of the UN and on conflicts between nations. It creates organisations and considers aspects of customary international law.

The General Assembly meets every year and can meet more often if required. It works on agreement between its members. As the United Nations has no real power to enforce decisions upon countries of the world, it relies on the consensus and cooperation of its member nations.

General Assembly the main body of the United Nations, made up of all of the member nations

THE SECURITY COUNCIL

The **Security Council** is the most powerful part of the UN. It is the executive of the United Nations and has the final say about the security and peacekeeping activities of the General Assembly. The Security Council has the right to stop or ignore General Assembly decisions. This is called the 'power of veto'.

Security Council a council of the United Nations responsible for preserving world peace

The Security Council consists of five permanent members: Great Britain, the United States of America, Russia, China and France. There are also ten non-permanent members who serve for two years each. Australia has been a member of the Security Council four times since 1945.

The Security Council has control over UN peacekeeping corps, comprised of troops and equipment supplied by member nations. The Council has the authority to send these forces into areas of conflict.

Figure 2.7 The UN Security Council controls the UN peacekeeping corps.

International Court of Justice

The International Court of Justice (ICJ) is the principal judicial organ of the United Nations. It was established in 1946 and its main functions are to settle disputes submitted to it by states and to give advisory opinions on legal questions submitted to it by the General Assembly or Security Council or other bodies as permitted by the General Assembly. The ICJ can only hear disputes if the nations involved accept the **jurisdiction** of the court.

There are two distinct types of cases upon which the court may rule. The first is on contentious issues between states in which the court produces binding rulings between states that agree, or have previously agreed, to submit to the ruling of the court. The second is advisory opinions, which provide reasoned but non-binding rulings on properly submitted questions of international law, usually at the request of the United Nations General Assembly. Although advisory opinions do not have to concern particular controversies between states, they often do.

Other international organisations

Other international organisations that have an impact on international law can take the form of government or non-government bodies.

International governmental organisations (IGOs) are usually susidiaries of the UN. These bodies are established to meet and decide upon certain international issues such as refugees, tariffs and wealth. The International Labour Organisation is an example of an IGO. Its aim is to ensure the safe and fair treatment of workers.

Regional organisations also play an important role in international decision-making. The European Union is an example of a regional organisation. It consists of European nations and has powers to regulate the economies of member nations for the common good. These regulations cover such things as human rights, the environment and trade.

Non-government organisations (NGOs) such as the Red Cross and Greenpeace unofficially contribute to world peace, human rights and other issues. They do this by lobbying organisations and informing the global public about the infringements of human rights and environmental concerns.

jurisdiction the power of a court; the types of matters that it is allowed to hear and decide upon

---

REVIEW 2.4

1 Explain two different ways that the term 'state' can be used. In what ways is Australia a 'state'?
2 Identify what is meant by international law. Outline the different ways that international law is made.
3 Why was the United Nations established?
4 Account for the limitations of international law.
5 Describe the functions of the General Assembly.
6 Explain the importance of the UN Security Council.
7 Outline the role of the International Court of Justice. Discuss its limitations.
8 Identify the organisations that influence international law.

RESEARCH 2.2

Go to the United Nations website http://www.un.org/english/. Choose one of the issues that the United Nations covers (for example, human rights).

Write a news report about some of the recent initiatives taken by the UN in this area. Outline any problems that you see the UN facing as it makes these efforts.

RESEARCH 2.3

Investigate adversarial and inquisitorial legal systems.

Write a report that looks at the origins and workings of adversarial and inquisitorial legal systems. Include a comparison of the systems looking at the advantages and disadvantages of each system. You might like to look at Indonesia and the recent trials that have taken place with regard to terrorist activity and drug smuggling.

Come to a conclusion about which system you think is best for Australia.

Figure 2.8 The United Nations in action.

MULTIPLE-CHOICE QUESTIONS

1 What is common law?
   a parliament-made law
   b judge-made law
   c the legal principles developed in England and followed in Australia
   d law that resolves disputes between two individuals
2 When is a binding precedent set?
   a when it is established by a higher court
   b when a judge has determined that the facts of a case are similar to another case
   c when a judge accepts the advice from a judge in a higher court
   d when parliament passes a law about a case
3 What is the main purpose of equity?
   a to achieve justice
   b to achieve fairness
   c to achieve equality
   d to achieve damages
4 Which of these statements about the Security Council is true?
   a it is open for all countries to join
   b it has the authority to send armed forces into countries
   c it takes advice from the General Assembly
   d it has limited powers
5 Which of these features does the adversary system involve?
   a the use of a jury in all court cases
   b the payment of damages to the victim
   c judges collecting evidence
   d each side presenting their case and testing the opposition's evidence

CHAPTER SUMMARY TASKS

1 Explain the difference between common and statute law. Analyse their relationship.
2 Describe the distinguishing features of Indigenous Australian law.

3 Discuss the relationship between the government and parliament when it comes to making new laws or amending current laws.
4 Evaluate the influence of international law on domestic law.
5 Compare and contrast the features of criminal and civil law.
6 Critically analyse the ways that areas of Indigenous Australian law has been, and can be, incorporated into the contemporary Australian legal system.

CHAPTER SUMMARY

- The law in Australia, prior to European settlement, was customary law based on Aboriginal and Torres Strait Islander traditions, rituals and acceptable conduct.
- Customary law still has relevance in Australia today and elements of it have been incorporated into alternative dispute resolution procedures.
- Contemporary Australian law is based on common law developed from English traditions and rituals.
- The Australian Constitution sets out Australian law. Parliament has powers to make changes to these laws as long as due processes are followed. The government in power at the time will influence changes to the law.
- The doctrine of precedent is an element of common law which allows judges to follow rulings made in previous court cases and adapt them to suit the needs of a current court case.
- The law is divided into public and private law. There are similarities and differences in the ways that infringements of public and private law are dealt with by the courts.
- Australia is recognised internationally as an independent state and thus has the sovereignty to make its own laws.
- Australia also takes part in international law-making through its membership of the United Nations and by being a signatory of international treaties.

The constitutional system in Australia

A constitution is simply a set of rules that may apply to a social club, a large-scale organisation or even a nation. On 1 January 1901, Australia gained a Commonwealth Constitution which outlined the legal framework and rules that apply to the governance of Australia.

THE FEDERATION PROCESS

Prior to the Australian Constitution coming into force, Australia consisted of six colonies which were independent of each other with the right to govern within their own borders. These six colonies were not answerable to any authority in Australia, but rather to the British government. By the 1880s various groups and individuals began to promote the concept that Australia would be better off if the six colonies amalgamated into one nation under one centralised government. An emotional and sometimes bitter debate raged for two decades until **Federation** was achieved.

It is important to investigate the arguments for and against Federation because these different perspectives formed the basis of the final constitution document. As with any democratic process, politicians have to persuade the public to vote for their proposals, and sometimes they have to make trade-offs to ensure they gain voter confidence. This was essential to get the necessary votes in the Federation **referendums**.

Federation a national government formed through the aggregation of several states

referendum the referral of a particular issue to the electorate in a vote

Arguments for and against Federation

The fundamental reasons put forward arguing for Federation were:

- economics—the removal of trade barriers between the colonies would result in a more efficient economy with a broader range of markets available to manufacturers and farmers. (This was addressed in section 51 (ii) of the Constitution.)
- transport—the farcical situation of the colonies having different **rail gauges** meant that goods had to be off-loaded at colony borders to be reloaded again before reaching their final destination in another colony (New South Wales, Victoria and Queensland initially all had different rail gauges and this problem was addressed under section 51 (xxxii), (xxxiii) and (xxxiv) of the Constitution).

rail gauges the distance between the inner sides of the two rails of a train line

- defence—Australia's vast distance from Britain meant that the colonies felt vulnerable to a range of foreign powers who sought to expand their interests in the South Pacific region. With the existing military technology of the period, any attack on a colony could not be resisted by British forces for many months after the attack. There were specific concerns about France, Russia and Germany, especially after Germany took control of parts of New Guinea in 1883. The colonies had their own military outfits, but a unified defence force would obviously be far more effective. (This was addressed in section 114 of the Constitution.)

- Racial 'purity' and immigration—one common unifying factor amongst all the colonies was the desire to keep Australia white. If Federation was achieved, then a nation-wide immigration law could be introduced which could ensure a '**White Australia**'. In the first year of the new federal parliament, the *Immigration Restriction Act (1901)* and the *Pacific Island Labourers Act (1901)* ensured it was nearly impossible for non-Europeans to migrate to Australia. (Addressed in section 51 (xxvii) of the Constitution.)

- nationalism—in the late nineteenth century, a strong desire to foster a unique Australian identity had begun to emerge and, while the strong links to the **mother country** were not challenged, this movement did promote Federation. This emerging nationalism was evident in sport, literature, media, the arts and language.

Obviously the proponents of Federation were ultimately successful, but the groups arguing against Federation were able to influence those drafting the Australian Constitution, and their concerns were reflected in specific parts of the Constitution.

Those opposing Federation put forward the following arguments:

- trade—the colonies had different views on the use of **tariffs**. Victoria in particular wanted to protect their industries, whereas New South Wales wanted free trade between the states. (See section 51 (i), (ii) and (iii) of the Constitution.)

- fear—the smaller states harboured views that if Federation was achieved then their interests would constantly be overlooked by the larger, more populous states. A constitution which required matters to be decided by a simple majority was not deemed to be in the smaller states' interests. Consequently, the so-called 'states' house' (the Senate) ensures there is a check on the power of the House of Representatives, since each state has an equal number of representatives in the Senate. Currently each state has twelve senators, regardless of the size of their population, and there have been numerous examples of individuals from a smaller state holding the balance of power in the Senate and thus having the power to pass or reject proposed laws which have come from the House of Representatives. When an individual holds the balance of power in the Senate it means they have the deciding vote on whether a bill becomes an act. In the late 1990s an **independent** Senator from Tasmania (Brian Harradine) held the balance of power in the Senate. (See section 7 of the Constitution.) This was further reinforced with the requirements to successfully pass a referendum as outlined in section 128 of the final document, which clearly protects the smaller states from domination by the larger states.

- irrelevance—there was widespread apathy about the Federation proposals, as many people believed it would have no impact on their

White Australia the official government policy of excluding non-Europeans and non-English-speaking people from coming to Australia; it was fuelled by fears of the country being overrun by Asians

mother country Britain (in 1900, 96 per cent of Australians were of British origin)

tariffs a tax that must be paid on imports and exports

independent free from another person's authority; not aligned with a political party

Figure 3.1 This medallion was produced in 1906 to promote White Australia.

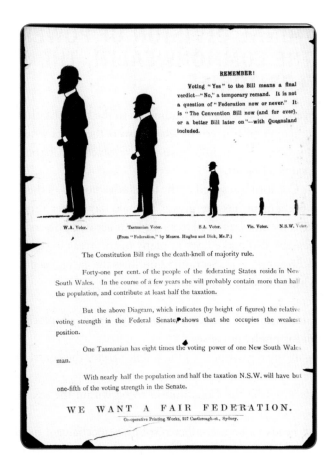

Figure 3.2 A poster from the turn of the century promoting a fair Federation.

day-to-day lives. Some thought it was only of concern to the wealthy and the upper classes. The severe economic depression of the 1890s also compounded this problem, as the bulk of the population focused on mere survival rather than the theoretical debate of what should be contained in a constitution a decade away.

The colonies decide

After a series of referendums in 1898, 1899 and 1900, the colonies eventually found a compromise position on a proposed constitution, but, before it could take effect, approval from the British Parliament was required. The Commonwealth of Australia Constitution Act 1900 (UK) was passed and Australia came into existence as a nation on 1 January 1901. The key features of this British act were:

- Australia was a federated nation consisting of six states (Western Australia joined shortly after the other states) and two territories.
- There was a bicameral Federal Parliament (House of Representatives and Senate).
- A High Court of Australia was established to oversee any other courts and provide 'final and conclusive' judgements upon any appeals it hears (see section 73 of the Australian Constitution).
- It outlined both the division of power and the separation of powers as they would apply in Australia.
- It enabled the Constitution to be altered by a referendum (section 128 of the Australian Constitution).

CONSTITUTIONAL DIVISION OF POWER BETWEEN THE COMMONWEALTH, THE STATES AND THE TERRITORIES

After all the controversy and discussions leading up to the formalisation of the Australian Constitution, the fundamental concern of what powers the states would retain and what powers the federal government would have was resolved in Chapter I, Part V of the Constitution, in sections 51 to 60.

legislative powers having the power or capacity to make laws

concurrent existing at the same time; where both state and federal parliaments can make laws on particular matters

exclusive in this context restricted only to the federal parliament

Section 51 of the Constitution specifies the **legislative powers** of the federal parliament, that is, the federal parliament has the power to make laws over those matters listed in Section 51 (these are sometimes referred to as the 'enumerated powers'). It is important to realise that the states can also make laws in many of the areas in section 51, as these are also considered **concurrent** powers. Section 52 outlines the **exclusive** powers of the federal government over which the states have no power.

Section 52 covers:

i the seat of government of the Commonwealth, and all places acquired by the Commonwealth for public purposes

ii matters relating to any department of the public service the control of which is by the Commonwealth

iii other matters declared by the Constitution to be within the exclusive power of the parliament.

Obviously there needs to be a conflict resolution mechanism in place to overcome conflicting laws if a state and the Commonwealth made contradictory laws. This is found in section 109 and will be discussed later in this chapter.

residual those matters remaining which the states can legislate on which are not referred to in the Constitution

Those powers which belong solely to States are known as the **residual** powers. Each state has its own constitution, which enables states to make laws in various areas, but excludes any area directly denied in the Australian Constitution. Chapter V 'The States' outlines some of these prohibitions, for example, section 114 forbids them from raising any military force, and section 115 forbids the States coining money. Some of the key residual powers are de facto relationships, same sex relationships, crime, hospitals and public transport.

Figure 3.3 Public transport is a residual power.

LEGAL INFO

Commonwealth Government legislative powers

The following extract from the Australian Constitution lists some of the legislative powers of the federal parliament.

Section 51.

The Parliament shall, subject to this Constitution, have power to make laws for the peace, order, and good government of the Commonwealth with respect to:-

    (i) Trade and commerce with other countries, and among the States:

    (ii) Taxation; but so as not to discriminate between States or parts of States:

    (v) Postal, telegraphic, telephonic, and other like services:

    (vi) The naval and military defence of the Commonwealth and of the several States, and the control of the forces to execute and maintain the laws of the Commonwealth.

    (xii) Currency, coinage, and legal tender:

    (xv) Weights and measures:

    (xix) Naturalization and aliens:

    (xxi) Marriage:

    (xxii) Divorce and matrimonial causes; and in relation thereto, parental rights, and the custody and guardianship of infants:

    (xxiii) Invalid and old-age pensions:

    (xxiiiA) The provision of maternity allowances, widows' pensions, child endowment, unemployment, pharmaceutical, sickness and hospital benefits, medical and dental services (but not so as to authorize any form of civil conscription), benefits to students and family allowances:

    (xxvi) The people of any race, ~~other than the Aboriginal race in any State~~, for whom it is deemed necessary to make special laws:

    (xxvii) Immigration and emigration:

    (xxviii) The influx of criminals:

    (xxix) External Affairs:

    (xxxi) The acquisition of property on just terms from any State or person for any purpose in respect of which the Parliament has power to make laws:

    (xxxii) The control of railways with respect to transport for the naval and military purposes of the Commonwealth:

    (xxxiii) The acquisition, with the consent of a State, of any railways of the State on terms arranged between the Commonwealth and the State:

    (xxxiv) Railway construction and extension in any State with the consent of that State:

    (xxxv) Conciliation and arbitration for the prevention and settlement of industrial disputes extending beyond the limits of any one State:

    (xxxvii) Matters referred to the Parliament of the Commonwealth by the Parliament or Parliaments of any State or States, but so that the law shall extend only to States by whose Parliaments the matter is referred, or which afterwards adopt the law:

ultra vires acting
beyond their power
or in excess of their
authority

CASE SPACE

The Franklin Dam case

If either the Commonwealth or a state government passes a law that contravenes the Australian Constitution, then that law would be deemed unconstitutional and thus be declared invalid. Technically the government would be said to be acting 'ultra vires'. But what happens if the state and Commonwealth laws were both valid, as can often be the case with a concurrent power? This situation arose in *Tasmania v. Commonwealth* [1983] 158 CLR1, known more commonly as the Franklin Dam or Tas Dam case.

Tasmania wanted to build a hydroelectric dam on the Franklin and Gordon river system. A group of environmentalists began a protest campaign against this proposal and the Wilderness Society and the Australian Conservation Foundation got actively involved. Nationwide protests were organised under the 'No Dams' slogan, and a range of high-profile personalities took up the cause.

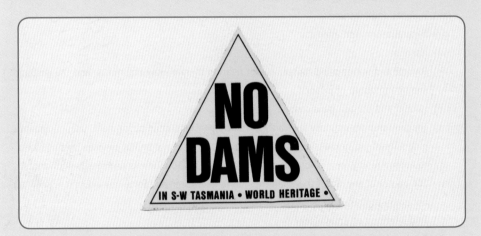

Figure 3.4 There were numerous street marches protesting against the construction of the Franklin Dam.

Tasmania refused to budge. The Tasmanian government argued that the building of the dam was a residual power and the protesters, while entitled to their view, were not going to change their decision. In the lead-up to the 1983 federal election, the Labor leader promised to stop the dam if elected. Labor won the election, but Tasmania continued to build the dam.

The federal government recognised the Wild Rivers area as a region of special significance and it was listed under the World Heritage Convention. The federal government passed the *World Heritage (Property Conservation) Act 1983*, which specified that such areas of special significance should be protected. The Franklin was included as one such area. Now there was a state law allowing the construction of the dam and a federal law which demanded it be stopped. The case went to the High Court.

There are seven judges on the full bench of the High Court and, in a 4/3 decision, the court ruled that the federal government was validly using the external affairs power of the Constitution (section 51 (xxix)) and, by applying Section 109, the federal law would override the state law so the dam was stopped. Section 109 states that 'When a law of a State is inconsistent with a law of the Commonwealth, the latter shall prevail, and the former shall, to the extent of the inconsistency, be invalid'. It was under this authority that the Franklin River was ultimately preserved for future generations.

external affairs
interpreted by the
High Court to mean
that when the
Commonwealth signs
an international
treaty or convention
it has the authority
to enact laws to
give effect to this
international law
within Australia

Amending the Australian Constitution

The law and the legal system must be dynamic to be effective. Mechanisms must be in place to change ineffective, obsolete or unfair laws. Statutes (acts of parliament) can be changed through the parliamentary process. Common law can be changed through the courts when a judge sets a new precedent. The Australian Constitution, while technically being a statute, has a unique reform process embedded into it. It can be found in Chapter VII 'Alteration of the Constitution', section 128, and the process is known as a 'referendum'.

As mentioned earlier, this referendum process was included as an added protection for the smaller states, and it makes it very difficult for proposed changes to the Australian constitution to be made. In fact, of the forty-four proposed amendments to the constitution, only eight have been successful. If you have access to a recent copy of the Australian Constitution, these successful amendments are often shown in bold type or by having deleted parts ruled through (see section 51 (xxvi)). The margin notes also indicate alterations made to the Constitution after a successful referendum.

The specifics of successfully altering the Australian Constitution, as per section 128, are:

1 The proposed change must pass both houses (Senate and House of Representatives) with an absolute majority.
2 The proposed change must be put to the electors 'not less than two months nor more than six months' after going through both houses.
3 There must be an absolute majority of voters Australia-wide who approve the change, that is, 50 per cent of voters plus one.
4 There must be a majority of states that approve the change, that is, four of the six states must vote for the change.
5 The alteration must go to the Governor-General for royal assent.

In 1967, one of the more popular referendums altered section 51 (xxvi) and deleted section 127, which enabled the Commonwealth Government to pass laws in relation to Aboriginal and Torres Strait Islanders. This ensured consistency of laws, as some states had discriminatory laws and were reluctant to change them. Other successful referenda included amending section 72 so that judges in the High Court and the other federal courts had to retire at age 70. This was the last successful referendum; the next nine proposals were all defeated. The last referendum was held on 11 November 1999 and involved changing Australia to a republic with a president appointed with the **bipartisan** support of the parliament. It was soundly defeated, but the push to make Australia a fully independent nation remains.

RIGHT WRONGS WRITE YES for ABORIGINES!
On May 27

Authorised by J. McGuinness, 9 Gough Street, Cairns. Issued by Federal Council for the Advancement of Aborigines and Torres Strait Islanders.

Figure 3.5 In 1967, Australia voted 'yes' to allow the government to make laws about Indigenous people.

bipartisan involving the support of two political parties

REVIEW 3.1

1 Define the term 'constitution'.
2 Outline the main reasons for and against Federation in Australia.
3 Explain why section 7 and section 128 of the Australian Constitution were included to protect the smaller states.
4 Use examples to outline the constitutional division of power. In your answer distinguish between:
   a legislative powers
   b enumerated powers
   c concurrent powers
   d exclusive powers
   e residual powers
5 Study the extract of section 51 and answer the following questions:
   a Under what section of the Constitution can the federal government legislate with respect to imports and exports? Explain your answer.
   b With specific reference to section 51(xxi) and (xxii) outline the grounds on which de facto relationships and same sex relationships are considered residual powers. Explain why these relationships were not covered in the Constitution by our 'founding fathers'.
   c Outline the process by which the federal government could construct a rail line from Brisbane to Melbourne.
   d What part of this extract has been altered by a referendum? Explain the impact of this amendment.
   e Explain section 51 (xxxvii) in your own words.
6 Write a summary of *Tasmania v. Commonwealth* [1983] 158 CLR1 under the following headings:
   a facts
   b issue
   c judgement.
7 With specific reference to section 128, outline why it is so difficult to alter the Australian Constitution, even if more than 50 per cent of voters want the proposed change.

THE ROLE OF THE HIGH COURT IN CONSTITUTIONAL INTERPRETATION

Chapter III of the Australian Constitution is titled 'The Judicature' and it is within this chapter that the judicial system of the Commonwealth is created. Section 71 creates the High Court of Australia and specifies that it must contain one Chief Justice and at least two other judges.

The first sitting of the High Court was on 6 October 1903, with three judges. In 1906 the number of judges was increased to five and in 1912 the number of judges was further increased to its current level of seven.

Section 71 also allows the Commonwealth Parliament to create other courts and, over time, parliament has created the Federal Court, the Family Court and the Federal Magistrates Court, which all come under federal jurisdiction.

Section 72 outlines how High Court judges are appointed and, as a result of a successful referendum in 1977, how they must retire when they reach the age of 70. Most High Court judges come from the bench of the state Supreme Courts or the Federal Court. They are chosen by the 'Governor-General in Council', which essentially means they are chosen by the government of the day. While most sittings are in Canberra, cases can be heard in the other capital cities and even by video link if it is warranted.

High Court jurisdiction

The High Court has both **original** and **appellate jurisdiction**. The original jurisdiction of the High Court is outlined in section 75 and 76.

Section 75
In all matters—
 (i) Arising under any treaty:
(ii) Affecting consuls or other representatives of other countries:
(iii) In which the Commonwealth, or a person suing or being sued on behalf of the Commonwealth, is a party:
(iv) Between States, or between residents of different States, or between a State and a resident of another State:
 (v) In which a writ of **mandamus** or **prohibition** or an **injunction** is sought against an officer of the Commonwealth:
    the High Court shall have original jurisdiction.

Section 76
The Parliament may make laws conferring original jurisdiction on the High Court in any matter—
 (i) Arising under this Constitution, or involving its interpretation:
(ii) Arising under any laws made by the Parliament:
(iii) Of Admiralty and maritime jurisdiction:
(iv) Relating to the same subject matter claimed under the laws of different States.

Cases which come under original jurisdiction begin in the High Court itself. Matters relating to the interpretation of the Constitution fall under section 76 (i) and this role of the High Court has at times had an enormous impact on determining the division of power between the states and the Commonwealth.

As community conditions, standards and attitudes evolve, they should be reflected in the views expressed by the judiciary. The law and the legal system need to be dynamic to be effective and relevant to the society to which it is being applied.

When a case concerning the interpretation of the Constitution comes before the High Court, all seven judges hear and decide the matter. Seven judges are used because this ensures a final decision, even though decisions need not be unanimous. The High Court is the highest court in the Australian judicial system and, since 1986, there are no other avenues of appeal available. The *Australia Acts 1986* (Cwlth) severed the judicial link with

original jurisdiction the ability or power of a court to hear a case in the first instance

appellate jurisdiction the ability or power of a court to hear appeals of the decisions of lower level courts and to reject, affirm, or modify those decisions

mandamus a court order compelling a government official or organisation to perform a particular task

prohibition a court order that forbids a lower level court from hearing or taking further action in a case or matter

injunction a court order stopping an individual or organisation from performing a particular action

Figure 3.6 The High Court of Australia is situated in Canberra.

England and stopped any appeals from the Australian judicial system going to the Privy Council in England for final determination.

The impact of the High Court on the states and Commonwealth

Invariably the High Court's interpretation of the Constitution involves stipulating what areas the Commonwealth can legislate on and what areas belong to the states. In association with such decisions, the High Court makes statements on how each level of government can use their powers and outlines any limits on such powers.

For example, in the Tas Dam case, the High Court said in obiter dictum that the Commonwealth can only use the external affairs power when entering legitimate international treaties or conventions. In other words, it said that the Commonwealth Government could not enter a treaty with another country simply to gain legitimacy to override a state law it disagreed with.

Initially High Court decisions favoured the states, but over time a broader approach to interpreting the Constitution has seen a shift in the legislative balance between the states and the Commonwealth. The following cases are examples of the High Court exercising its original jurisdiction to interpret the Constitution:

1 The uniform tax case (1942)

Section 51 (ii) clearly gives the Commonwealth the legislative power to collect taxes. This was considered a concurrent power, so both the Commonwealth and the states were collecting income taxes until 1942. As a wartime emergency measure, federal laws were introduced which effectively made the Commonwealth the only level of government able to collect income taxes. In return, the Commonwealth agreed to return to the states a grant of money about equal to what they could no longer collect as income tax.

These grants are under section 96, which states that 'the Parliament may grant financial assistance to any state on such terms and conditions as the Parliament thinks fit'. The states believed the new law would not only deny them financial independence, but would allow the Commonwealth to dictate how they spent these grants.

The states did not like this proposal, as it would make them reliant on the Commonwealth for the bulk of their revenue. The states went to the High Court, claiming the new law was aimed primarily at denying them collecting income tax and thus reducing their **fiscal** independence. The High Court ruled that it was irrelevant that this would limit the power of the states; the proposed law was constitutional and therefore valid.

fiscal relating to government financial matters

Figure 3.7 Fraser Island, situated off the south-east coast of Queensland, is now World Heritage listed.

2 *Murphyores v. The Commonwealth* (1976) 136 CLR1

This case is sometimes referred to as the Fraser Island case. Murphyores extracted rutile and zircon from mineral sands on Fraser Island under a lease granted by the Queensland government. Such a lease was certainly constitutionally valid, and the environmental consequences were also a state concern.

The Commonwealth Government disagreed with the project, but had no constitutional power to simply shut down the operations on Fraser Island. Instead it relied on one of its legislative powers, specifically section 51 (i) Trade and Commerce, to prohibit export of the rutile and zircon. Murphyores relied on exporting the mineral sands for its financial viability, but the Commonwealth exercised section 112 of the *Customs Act 1973* (Cwlth), under which it could prohibit the export of any goods from Australia.

Murphyores went to the High Court, arguing that the Commonwealth had acted outside its constitutional power, but the High Court strictly applied section 51 (i) and noted that, while the effect may well be to override a traditional state power, the Commonwealth was certainly within its rights to prohibit the exporting of the mineral sands.

3 *R v. Brislan; ex parte Williams* (1935) CLR 262

In this case, Dulcie Williams was charged with operating an appliance for the purpose of receiving messages by 'wireless telegraphy' without proper authorisation. The plaintiff objected, claiming that the Commonwealth had acted ultra vires when implementing the *Wireless Telegraphy Act 1919*, as the device did not fall within the description of a 'postal, telegraphic, telephonic and other like service' as per section 51 (v) of the Constitution.

The High Court ruled that 'upon its true interpretation' the Commonwealth is able to legislate in respect of any such broadcasting services and, consequently, the Commonwealth has been able to control any new technologically advanced broadcasting service, such as television and the Internet.

R *R* at the beginning of a case name refers to *Regina* (Latin for 'Queen'). Since Australia is a constitutional monarchy this refers to our head of state on whose behalf the prosecution case is run. If our head of state was a male the R would stand for *Rex*, which is Latin for 'King'.

ex parte refers to one side of the story; in a case this may mean the other side is absent or unrepresented

RESEARCH 3.1

Go to: www.austlii.edu.au and do a search for 'constitutional law'. Write a report on any TWO cases dealing with the Constitution, outlining:

a the facts of the case

b which section of the Constitution the case refers to

c the High Court's decision

d the significance of the decision.

Appeals to the High Court from lower courts

Section 73 outlines the appellate jurisdiction of the High Court. It stipulates that the High Court has jurisdiction to 'hear and determine all judgements' from any cases emanating from:

- the High Court exercising its original jurisdiction
- any Federal Court exercising federal jurisdiction
- the Supreme Court of any state.

Section 73 also states that 'the judgement of the High Court in all such cases shall be final and conclusive'. Currently, all appeal cases must be granted **special leave** before the case will be heard by the High Court. Chapter 4 of the High Court Rules 2004, which became effective on 1 January 2005, deals with the practice and procedure of the High Court in its appellate jurisdiction.

Generally, appeals relate to **questions of law**, or whether the matter is of such significance that it warrants the attention of the High Court, or when a final adjudication is needed to resolve a dispute between the opinions of various courts. The workload of the High Court has built up over the decades and there are numerous examples of the High Court deciding matters in their appellate jurisdiction. One of the more famous cases, *R v. Zecevic* (1987) came from the Victorian Supreme Court.

special leave where the High Court grants approval for the case to go before it on appellate jurisdiction

questions of law a disputed legal contention that is left for the judge to decide (e.g. whether certain evidence is admissible)

CASE SPACE

R v. Zecevic (1987) 162 CLR 645

Zecevic had an argument with his neighbour over a parking space. The 'difference of opinion' became heated and turned violent. Zecevic then kicked in the glass panel on his neighbour's front door. In return, the neighbour threatened Zecevic with a gun and stabbed him with a knife. Zecevic sought safety back in his home, but saw the neighbour approaching armed with the gun. Zecevic shot and killed the neighbour.

At his trial, the judge in the Victorian Supreme Court would not allow Zecevic to use the defence of self-defence. He was convicted of murder and appealed to the High Court on the grounds that he should have been able to use self-defence to gain an acquittal.

The High Court granted special leave to hear the case because they believed the matter warranted their attention as the laws regarding self-defence were quite complex. In the end Zecevic was acquitted, as the High Court redefined self-defence, stating that the accused must believe, on reasonable grounds, that it was necessary to do what they did. Furthermore, the High Court said that the actions of the accused must not only be reasonable in the circumstances, they must also be proportional to the danger at hand.

Figure 3.8 Action taken in self-defence must be proportional to the threat.

RESEARCH 3.2

Conduct an Internet search and write a one-page report on each of the following:

- a family law case that went to the High Court on appeal
- criminal law case that went to the High Court on appeal.

THE SYSTEM OF JUDICIAL REVIEW

The system of judicial review involves review by a court of law into the actions of a government official or department. Generally the system of judicial review involves investigating the legality of a decision or action. The High Court exercises judicial review whenever it makes a decision about whether a particular law is constitutionally valid or not.

The Federal Court undertakes most judicial reviews by applying the *Administrative Decisions (Judicial Review) Act 1977* (Cwlth). It is important to realise that this act applies strict rules and does not give the power to the Federal Court to review a decision on its **merits**. Appeals can go by leave to the High Court. A far more effective and efficient way to appeal the decision of a government official or body for individuals is through non-judicial review of administrative action in the Administrative Appeals Tribunal (see Chapter 6).

Generally judicial review involves the court with appropriate jurisdiction investigating whether a government official or department has acted ultra vires, or whether they have followed the rules of **natural justice** (procedural fairness). (These concepts are covered in the HSC course.)

merits judgment based on an analysis of the facts presented in the case

natural justice procedures set in place to ensure fairness in legal proceedings; in Australia it generally refers to a right to be heard, that is, present your version of the facts, and the right to freedom from bias by decision-makers, whether real or perceived

SEPARATION OF POWERS

The separation of powers doctrine was developed by the eighteenth-century French writer Montesquieu. He believed that the civil liberties of the public were at risk if the key organs of government were controlled by one person or group.

Montesquieu identified these key organs of government as:
* the legislature—the law-makers (in Australia this is the parliament— the House of Representatives and the Senate)
* the executive—the ministers and government departments which administer the laws made by parliament (in Australia the Governor-General, the Prime Minister and Cabinet are members of the executive)
* the judiciary—the courts which interpret and apply the law.

If one person controls all three organs or arms of government, then that nation is under a dictatorship because the ruler has unfettered absolute power. By having the three arms independent, there is a constant check and balance in place so that **civil liberties** can be preserved.

civil liberties basic individual rights, such as freedom of speech and religion, which are protected by law

Australia's founding fathers certainly wanted the doctrine of the separation of powers to apply upon Federation. The first three chapters of the Constitution are set out in accordance with the doctrine:
* Chapter I—The Parliament (sections 1 to 60)
* Chapter II—The Executive (sections 61 to 70)
* Chapter III —The Judicature (sections 71 to 80)

In theory Australia has strictly adopted the doctrine of the separation of powers, but the reality is different. By virtue of the fact that some members of the Executive are members of the legislature, that is, the ministers and the Prime Minister are members of both the executive and the legislature, the separation of powers does not exist in its pure form in Australia.

The key point is that there is a clear distinction between the judiciary and the other arms of government. For a true democracy, and in the interests of justice, it is imperative that there be no blurring between the judicial and non-judicial arms of government.

Protecting the independence of the judiciary is one of the cornerstones of our democracy. This becomes evident when a court makes a decision that is not in accordance with government policy.

REVIEW 3.2

1 Use examples to distinguish between original and appellate jurisdiction.
2 Outline the reasons why the High Court might grant special leave to hear an appeal.
3 Explain how the High Court interpreting the Constitution in a case can impact on the division of powers between the states and the Commonwealth. Refer to the uniform tax case (1942) in your answer.
4 Define the term 'judicial review'.
5 Outline the concept of the separation of powers and explain how it operates in Australia.
6 Discuss whether the separation of powers is important for Australian society.

RESEARCH 3.3

Investigate the concept of mandatory sentencing and discuss how this may come into conflict with the independence of the judiciary when determining punishments.

THE GRADUAL TRANSFER OF LEGISLATIVE POWER FROM THE IMPERIAL GOVERNMENT TO THE COLONIES, STATES AND THE COMMONWEALTH

colonialism the political, social, legal and cultural domination of a territory and its people by a foreign power for an extended time

The eighteenth century was a period of **colonialism**, and Britain was one of many European nations looking to extend their sphere of influence around the globe.

Britain had taken India by force, that is, they conquered India and included it as part of the British Empire. Under international customary law at the time, it was accepted practice that if a nation was conquered then local laws had to be taken into account when formulating the legal system that was to apply. When Captain Cook claimed Australia for Britain, he did so on the assumption that it was terra nullius. Cook noted in his journal at the time that the Aborigines had:

'... no fix'd habitation but move on from place to place like wild beasts in search of food ... we never saw one inch of cultivated land in the whole country.'

SUPPLEMENT TO THE ILLUSTRATED SYDNEY NEWS DECEMBER, 1865.

CAPTAIN COOK TAKING POSSESSION OF THE AUSTRALIAN CONTINENT, ON BEHALF OF THE BRITISH CROWN, A.D. 1770,
UNDER THE NAME OF NEW SOUTH WALES.
FROM THE GREAT HISTORICAL PAINTING BY GILFILLAN, IN THE POSSESSION OF THE ROYAL SOCIETY OF VICTORIA.

Figure 3.9 Captain Cook claims Australia for Britain.

Consequently, when Captain Arthur Phillip brought the First Fleet to Sydney in 1788, he established the penal colony based on the notion that Australia was terra nullius. In effect this meant that Australia was not conquered like India, but settled.

The ramifications for Indigenous Australians were enormous, since it meant that British law applied automatically without any need to take into account the laws and customs of the local people (after all, under terra nullius they technically did not exist). From this point on, Indigenous Australians were systematically dispossessed of their lands and the whole social fabric of their society was destroyed. Chapter 4 will look at the Mabo decision and its ruling that terra nullius was a **legal fiction**.

Over the subsequent two and a half centuries, there has been a gradual shift in the ability of, first the colonies, and, after Federation, the states and the Commonwealth, to make laws independently from Britain. By the beginning of the twenty-first century, the only remaining link is that our head of state is the Queen, who is represented in Australia by the Governor-General.

New South Wales was established as a penal colony in 1788, with the other colonies being established in subsequent decades. Since there were very few free citizens at this time, **military rule** was used to administer justice, and the Governor's authority was paramount. As the colony developed and more free settlers arrived, there grew more and more demands for a fairer and more democratic system of government.

legal fiction the presumption of a fact assumed by a court for convenience, consistency or to achieve justice

military rule the performance by the military of all the functions of government, notably the executive, legislative and judicial functions

representative government where law-making is under the control of voters, since parliamentarians are elected by eligible voters. Abraham Lincoln famously referred to representative government as 'government of the people, by the people, for the people'.

During the nineteenth century, a series of acts from the imperial government in England saw the gradual shift from a penal colony controlled strictly by the Governor to a legal system which allowed for **representative government.** The key developments were:

1823 The New South Wales Act (4 Geo IV c 96 Imperial) established a Legislative Council consisting of between five and seven members. The Crown determined who these members would be and they had no authority to initiate legislation. The Governor also retained the authority to make laws in an emergency without consulting the Legislative Council.

1828 Australian Courts Act (Imperial) removed the power of the Governor to make laws independently in 'emergency' situations and it stipulated in Section 24 that:

> '... all laws ... in force in England ... shall be applied in the courts of New South Wales and Van Diemans Land.'

1842 Australian Constitutions Act (Imperial) increased the Legislative Council to thirty-six, twelve of whom were nominated by the Crown and the remaining twenty-four elected by eligible voters. The Governor was no longer a member of the Legislative Council. In effect this meant that New South Wales had representative government, as the Legislative Council could make laws for the 'peace, welfare and good government of New South Wales in all cases whatsoever'.

1855 New South Wales Constitution Act (Imperial) confirmed an 1853 act made in New South Wales establishing a bicameral legislature and limiting the power of the Governor to reject laws passed by the New South Wales parliament.

1865 Colonial Laws Validity Act (Imperial) further increased the independence of the colonial parliaments in Australia by declaring that the colonies could pass any law they saw fit as long as it did not come into conflict with British law and they could not reject any law directed at them by the imperial parliament.

1901 Commonwealth of Australia Constitution Act 1900 (Imperial) established Australia has an independent nation (see earlier sections in this chapter).

1931 Statute of Westminster (Imperial) recognised the fact that Australia was operating well as an independent nation and thus gave the Commonwealth Government the power to apply British law in Australia when it chose to do so. In other words, Australia could pass any law, even if it conflicted with a British law. Technically Australia became a sovereign nation from this point on.

1986 The Australia Acts removed the last legal links between Britain and the states and the Commonwealth, as it ensured that the British parliament had no power whatsoever to make any laws that applied to Australia. This act also made the High Court of Australia the final court of appeal by stopping any appeals going to the Privy Council in England.

1999 Republic referendum asked the Australian people if they wanted to remove the Queen as our head of state. The Queen herself has publicly stated that the decision on whether Australia becomes a republic is entirely in the hands of the Australian people, and in the lead-up to the 1999 referendum she said:

> 'I have always made it clear that the future of the monarchy in Australia is an issue for the Australian people and them alone to decide, by democratic and constitutional means.'

TABLE 3.1

1999 republic referendum results

State/Territory	Yes	No
New South Wales	1 817 380 (46.43%)	2 096 562 (53.57%)
Victoria	1 489 536 (49.84%)	1 499 138 (50.16%)
Queensland	784 060 (37.44%)	1 309 992 (62.56%)
South Australia	425 869 (43.57%)	551 575 (56.43%)
Western Australia	458 306 (41.48%)	646 520 (58.52%)
Tasmania	126 271 (40.37%)	186 513 (59.63%)
Northern Territory	44 391 (48.77%)	46 637 (51.23%)
Australian Capital Territory	127 211 (63.27%)	73 850 (36.73%)
TOTAL AUSTRALIA	5 273 024 (45.13%)	6 410 787 (54.87%)

REVIEW 3.3

1 Outline the significance to Indigenous Australians of Captain Cook declaring Australia to be terra nullius.

2 Explain the difference between settled and conquered nations with regard to colonisation.

3 Explain the significance of:
   a Australian Constitutions Act 1842
   b Colonial Laws Validity Act 1865
   c Statute of Westminster 1931
   d Australia Acts 1986

4 Refer to Table 3.1 and outline the reasons why the referendum failed under section 128 of the Constitution.

Figure 3.10 The 1999 republic referendum aroused strong feelings on both sides of the fence.

MULTIPLE-CHOICE QUESTIONS

1 Which section of the Constitution outlines the legislative powers of the Commonwealth Government?
   a section 51
   b section 73
   c section 96
   d section 128

2 On what grounds would it be unconstitutional for a District Court judge to be elected to the House of Representatives?
   a it offends the division of powers
   b it offends the separation of powers
   c it would be ultra vires
   d it is not allowed under the referendum provisions of section 128

3 Which of the following was not promoted as a reason for Federation?
   a to ensure a 'White Australia'
   b to improve Australia's defence capabilities
   c to make the economy more efficient
   d to protect certain industries by imposing tariffs on some imports

4 Referring to the extract of section 51, which of the following statements is true?
   a Victoria would be able to produce its own notes and coins
   b Queensland is able to pass laws to allow migrants in to work in agriculture
   c New South Wales is able to legislate to legalise same sex marriages
   d South Australia can build a rail line along its southern coastline

5 How would the High Court decide a case where a concurrent power exercised by a state comes into conflict with the Commonwealth exercising its jurisdiction over that power?
   a it would rule in favour of the State as its law was passed first
   b it would apply Section 109 and rule in favour of the State
   c it would apply Section 109 and rule in favour of the Commonwealth
   d it would rule in favour of the Commonwealth because it must act in accordance with the Prime Minister's wishes

CHAPTER SUMMARY TASKS

1 Outline the competing points of view that influenced the final Australian Constitution produced in 1901.
2 Explain the difference between the 'division of power' and the 'separation of powers' under the Australian Constitution.
3 Use examples to describe the role of the High Court when it is exercising judicial review.
4 Construct a timeline indicating the transition of power from the imperial British government to the Australian governments.
5 Class debate: If the Constitution were to be rewritten today, what current state government powers should go directly to the federal government?

CHAPTER SUMMARY

- The Federation process was responsible for formulating the Constitution.
- The Constitutional division of powers outlines the responsibilities of the Commonwealth and the states by referring to legislative, concurrent, exclusive and residual powers.
- The High Court has the ultimate responsibility for interpreting the Constitution.
- The High Court is the final court of appeal in Australia (its appellate jurisdiction) but it also has original jurisdiction for some matters, notably constitutional law.
- The Constitution indicates how the separation of powers operates in Australia. It is important to note that only the judiciary is truly independent in Australia.
- The separation of powers ensures that individual rights and the democratic system are protected.
- There has been a gradual transfer of legislative power from the imperial British government to the colonies, states and the Commonwealth over the nineteenth and twentieth centuries. Currently, the only remaining link is that Australia is a constitutional monarchy, with the Queen as head of state.

CHAPTER 4

The operation of the legal system

So far in the course you have looked at how laws come into being. After laws are made, they need to be put into effect and administered. The main ways that this is done in Australia is through the court system.

STRUCTURE OF STATE AND FEDERAL COURTS

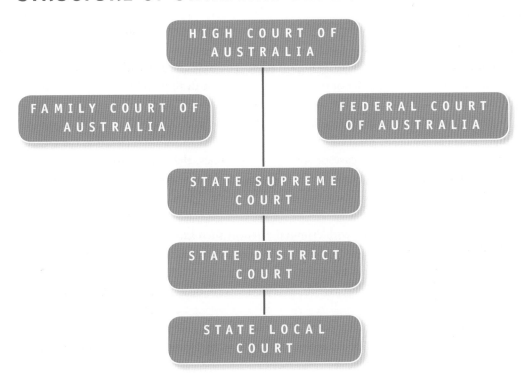

Figure 4.1 The court hierarchy in Australia

Australia has two levels of law—state and federal. As a result, there are separate state and federal jurisdictions, each with their own court structure.

State courts

The state court system in New South Wales operates under a hierarchy. The more serious or important the matter, the higher up in the court hierarchy it will be dealt. Each court has its own jurisdiction, or area over which it has authority. At the top of the court hierarchy is the Supreme Court, which deals with the most serious criminal and civil cases, while at the lower end of the hierarchy are the Local Courts.

Local Courts

Local Courts deal with minor criminal matters and minor civil disputes. In these courts a magistrate will hear the case, decide the verdict and set the punishment. Magistrates are usually qualified legal practitioners who have had many years of experience in matters of law.

Local Courts in New South Wales have jurisdiction to deal with the following areas:
- most criminal and summary prosecutions
- civil matters with a monetary value of up to $60 000
- **committal hearings**
- family law matters
- **child care proceedings**
- juvenile prosecutions and care matters (in a special Local Court called the Children's Court)
- **coronial inquiries** (in a special Local Court called the Coroner's Court).

The District Court

The District Court of New South Wales deals with more serious criminal matters. These include everything from charges of **larceny** to more serious charges like manslaughter, sexual assault and large-scale drug importation. The only charges with which the District Court cannot deal are murder or treason, which must be dealt with by the Supreme Court. More expensive civil matters are also heard in the District Court.

A judge and sometimes a jury will hear cases tried in a District Court. Most criminal matters are heard in the local court as only very serious crimes are referred to the District or Supreme Courts. In the case of some serious crimes, the magistrate will listen to an outline of the evidence to determine if the prosecution has a strong enough case to be able to try the defendant in the District Court or Supreme Court. This is called a 'committal hearing'.

The District Court deals with criminal offences such as:
- offences against the person, including manslaughter, malicious wounding to inflict grievous bodily harm and dangerous driving
- assaults, including common assault, assault occasioning actual bodily harm and assault of police officers
- sexual assaults, including indecent assault and carnal knowledge
- offences relating to property, including robbery, breaking and entering, larceny and embezzlement
- offences involving drugs, including the importation of heroin and other drugs into Australia, supply of prohibited drugs and possessing prohibited drugs
- offences involving fraud, including passing valueless cheques, obtaining money by deception and forgery.

committal hearing an inquiry held in the Local Court to see if there is enough evidence against the defendant to warrant a trial in a higher court (this is called establishing a prima facie case)

child care proceedings matters of child custody and access. When dealing with family law matters, the Local Court has federal jurisdiction and in these matters is essentially part of the Federal Court hierarchy.

coronial inquiry an investigation into a death that has occurred in unusual circumstances, held in the Coroner's Court and overseen by a magistrate called the Coroner. The Coroner will recommend whether further action should be taken over the death.

larceny wrongfully taking or withholding another's property with intent to permanently deprive the owner of the property

The District Court also handles civil cases where the amount being claimed is up to $750 000. If both parties agree, the court can deal with cases where larger amounts are involved. The court has an unlimited jurisdiction in claims for damages for personal injuries arising out of a motor vehicle accident. In addition, the court deals with cases under a number of acts of parliament such as the *Property Relationships Act*, *The Family Provisions Act* and the *Testator Family Maintenance and Guardianship of Infants Act*.

The Supreme Court

The Supreme Court is the highest court in the state hierarchy. It deals with the most serious criminal matters and civil cases involving large sums of money. It also deals with appeals from the two lower courts. The Supreme Court is a court of record. This means that decisions made in this court set a precedent and thus are an important means of establishing common law.

The Supreme Court has criminal jurisdiction over the most serious indictable offences such as murder and manslaughter, attempted murder, kidnapping, major conspiracy and drug-related charges, and Commonwealth prosecutions for more serious breaches of the **corporations law**. All cases are heard before a judge and jury.

In civil matters, there is no upper limit in the Supreme Court. It hears matters on claims for damages for personal injury, breach of contract, professional negligence, possession of land, and defamation. Only a judge deals with most civil matters, although a jury is used in some circumstances.

The Supreme Court also hears appeals. The Court of Appeal is the highest civil court in the state. Three judges hear most appeals, but some are heard by two, and, in special cases, they may be heard by more than three. If the judges cannot agree, the majority view prevails. To appeal to the High Court from the Court of Appeal, a special permission must be granted by the High Court.

corporations law legislation that regulates corporations and the securities and futures industry in Australia, it is administered by the Australian Securities and Investments Commission (ASIC)

The High Court

The High Court of Australia is a federal court located in Canberra which deals with appeals from the state or territory Supreme Courts. It also deals with cases concerning the interpretation of the Australian Constitution. It is the highest court in Australia and its decisions are final and applicable to the whole of the country.

Figure 4.2 The High Court of Australia is located in Canberra.

REVIEW 4.1

1 Account for the reasons that we need courts.
2 Explain the meaning of 'court hierarchy'.
3 Which court is the highest in Australia?
4 Outline the types of matters that are heard in the local court. Who hears these matters?
5 Indicate the types of cases that are dealt with in the District Court. Who decides these cases?
6 Describe the role of the Supreme Court.
7 Explain the importance of the High Court.

8 In which court would the following matters most likely be heard?
   a a murder trial
   b an appeal from the NSW Supreme Court
   c a hearing for a drink-driving offence
   d an investigation into a suspicious death
   e an armed robbery trial
   f the preliminary hearing for a kidnapping case
   g a civil dispute between business partners involving $100 million
   h a case dealing with an aspect of the Australian Constitution

THE ADVERSARY SYSTEM AND THE LEGAL PROFESSION

The adversary system

adversary system a legal system that relies on the skill of persons from different parties (as opposed to a neutral party, for example, a judge) in trying to come to the truth of a case

As you have read previously, the Australian legal system is heavily influenced by the English system of law. As a result, Australia has the **adversary system** as part of both criminal and civil court proceedings. This means that in a trial the two sides of the case try to prove their version of the facts and disprove the version of the other side. The defendant, in theory, does not have to prove anything as they are assumed innocent until proven guilty. However, most people accused of a crime will retain the services of a legal team to help them prove their innocence.

An impartial judge (and sometimes a jury) will listen to the evidence presented by both parties and make a decision as to which side has proved their case, and thus disproved the other side's case.

The inquisitorial system

An inquisitorial system is a legal system where the court is actively involved in determining the facts of the case. It is different from the adversarial system where the role of the court is to act as an impartial referee.

The inquisitorial system is usually found in Europe among civil law systems (those deriving from the Roman or Napoleonic codes). This system has a judge or a group of judges who work together and whose task is to investigate the case before them.

Indonesia has an inquistorial system of criminal trail. This means that the judges in a criminal trial in Indonesia will conduct an inquiry into the truth of what occurred, that is, the facts behind the legal issues in dispute. They are able to make rulings on the admission of evidence that probably could not have occurred in an Australian court. Judges are empowered to decide which witnesses will be called, and could even call for outside testimony that had not been requested by either side.

The legal profession

A court case will involve a number of personnel. Attending a court case may be members of the media reporting on the case, members of the public who might have an interest in the proceedings, the judge and the judge's associates, court reporters who take official records of the case, the defence and prosecution lawyers, the accused, a prison officer guarding the prisoner, witnesses to the crime and specialists who give evidence, and members of the jury. Some of these people play an official role in the court proceedings.

Judges and magistrates

Judges and magistrates preside over court cases. They are seen as the umpires of court cases, making sure that the rules are followed and that a fair trial is carried out. They are legally qualified professionals who have considerable experience in the law.

Judges sit in intermediate and superior courts. (In NSW they sit in District and Supreme courts.) They adjudicate in cases, which means that they make decisions about points of law and give instructions to the jury to make sure that they understand the proceedings and evidence offered. The judge is required to hand down sentences and rulings. In some civil cases, the judge will sit without a jury and therefore is responsible for the final decision.

A magistrate is in charge of a lower court. After hearing both sides of the case, the magistrate will decide whether a person is guilty or innocent. The magistrate will decide on the punishment in criminal cases, and the amount of money awarded in civil cases.

Magistrates will refer very serious criminal offences to the District Court. The magistrate will hear some indictable matters to determine if such a matter should go to trial. If there is enough evidence to establish a **prima facie** case, and thus justify the expense of a trial, it will be referred to a higher court.

prima facie the establishment of sufficient evidence against a defendant to warrant a trial in a higher court of law

Solicitors

When a person is seeking legal advice, they will usually go to a solicitor first. Solicitors give legal advice to people on a large range of legal issues. They have studied a recognised law course and carried out relevant work experience to achieve their qualification.

The main duties of solicitors involve family law, conveyancing for real estate transactions and the preparation of wills and contracts. Although a solicitor may appear in court, they will most often prepare a brief for a barrister when a case must go before a court. However, it is very rare to see a barrister in a local court where, due to the nature of the crime, solicitors will appear on behalf of their client.

Barristers

The barrister has two main roles. The first is to provide legal advice based on the facts presented to them by their client on the likely outcome of a court case. This allows the client to decide which course of action is best.

The second role is to present their client's case in court.

A solicitor will approach a barrister on behalf of their client. The barrister will then represent the client in either criminal or civil court.

Over years, the barrister has specialised in one particular area of court and this has allowed them to develop a large amount of expertise in the area.

REVIEW 4.2

1 Explain the differences between the adversary and inquisitorial systems.
2 Outline the role of a judge or magistrate in court proceedings.
3 What forms of legal representation are available to a person who is having legal problems?

Figure 4.3 Lawyers play a role in court cases.

COURT PROCEDURES IN CIVIL AND CRIMINAL CASES

What happens in a court hearing depends on the nature of the case being heard. These cases may be of a civil or criminal nature, involve a juvenile or be a coronial inquiry. In each of these situations, proceedings will be of a different nature.

Coronial inquiries

A coronial inquiry will occur when there is an unnatural death or an unexplained fire. The proceedings are more inquisitorial than normal court proceedings, as the coroner's office will gather all of the evidence. If there is evidence that a serious crime has been committed, the coroner will recommend that an indictment be issued and the accused will be tried in a court of law in the usual way.

Children's Court hearings

Children charged with a crime are treated differently by the court system. This is because it is believed that they are not always fully capable of making mature and sensible decisions, or may have been led into wrongdoing by older persons, and this resulted in them committing a criminal act. Most charges against people under 18 years of age are heard in a special Children's Court hearing. They are usually heard before a magistrate who specialises in children's cases and takes reasonable measures to ensure that the child understands the proceedings.

The case is heard in a closed court and the public is not allowed to attend. If the media is present, they are not permitted to publish the identity of the offender. If the child is under sixteen years of age, no conviction is recorded.

Civil court proceedings

Court procedures in civil and criminal cases have several differences. Civil proceedings are court actions and processes that are the result of disputes between individuals. They have a non-criminal basis and deal with such matters as breach of contract, property disputes and negligence. The person who initiates the civil action is called 'the plaintiff' and will start proceedings by issuing a statement of claim on the party they feel has wronged them. This party is called 'the defendant' and could be an individual or an organisation.

The statement of claim outlines the circumstances of the dispute and the parties involved in the dispute. The defendant responds with a statement of defence. At this stage the parties are able to obtain more information about each other's arguments through a process called 'discovery'. This allows information to be shared between the two parties to assist them in responding to the claims and allegations. At this point, many civil disputes are resolved. In most cases legal practitioners prepare the documents, as they have an understanding of the processes and can give appropriate and timely advice on legal matters.

If the dispute cannot be settled, the matter will be referred to trial. During the trial, each side has the right to produce evidence, call witnesses and carry out cross-examination. When both sides have presented all evidence, the judge or jury will make a ruling. If the plaintiff wins their case, the judge will make a decision about the amount of relief (or compensation) to be given to them by the defendant. This compensation usually takes the form of damages in a monetary form or injunctions, which are special court orders that prohibit certain activities or behaviours.

Standard and burden of proof in civil cases

The **standard of proof** means the level of proof that is needed to win a case. The **burden of proof** in a civil case refers to the obligation of the 'injured' party (the plaintiff) to prove their allegations during a trial.

standard of proof the level of proof needed by each party in a court case to prove their case

burden of proof the responsibility of a party to prove a case in court; to show that an allegation is true

The defendant is given the opportunity to submit evidence to rebut the plaintiff's case. To rebut generally means to contest a statement or evidence presented by another.

In a civil case, the standard of proof is determined on the balance of probability. This means that the plaintiff, who has the burden of proof, must prove that there was a probable cause for insult and thus they have been injured by the actions of the defendant.

Criminal law proceedings

Criminal law proceedings are the legal processes whereby the defendant is prosecuted to secure a conviction and punishment, such as a fine or imprisonment. The two main types of criminal hearings are summary hearings and trial by jury. The type of hearing depends upon the seriousness of the offence that the accused is alleged to have committed, that is, whether it is a summary or indictable offence.

Summary offences are relatively minor and include traffic offences and offensive behaviour. They are heard and decided by a magistrate or judge without a jury.

An indictable offence is a serious criminal offence and may be heard by a judge and a jury. Crimes in this category include murder, sexual assault and malicious wounding.

Sometimes, before a case is sent to a trial by jury, it undergoes a committal hearing. To have the matter put before a jury the prosecutor must convince the magistrate that there is a sufficiently strong case that the accused has committed an indictable offence.

In a criminal matter, the two parties involved are called 'the prosecution' and 'the defence'. The prosecution represents the interests of the community. During the trial they are referred to as 'the Crown'. In most criminal trials, the Department of Public Prosecutions conducts the prosecution's case. If a criminal matter is heard in a Local Court, the police prosecutor, a specially trained police officer, conducts the case.

The accused, known as 'the defendant', will usually employ a barrister to represent them. Some people may choose to represent themselves, depending on the seriousness of the charges. The case that the accused puts forward is called 'the defence'.

Criminal trials are heard before a jury of twelve people. These people are ordinary citizens selected at random. The jury considers whether there is enough evidence to convict the accused. The judge advises the jury and deals with questions of law. The jury will consider the evidence provided in a court case and decide on issues of fact on the basis of this evidence. The jury must come to a unanimous verdict, that is, they must all agree on the outcome.

The jury is selected from the jury list, which is compiled from the electoral role. When proposed jurors go to court, they are questioned by the lawyers for both the prosecution and defence to see if they have any biases or prejudices that might influence the outcome of the case. They are either accepted or challenged until the required number of jurors is selected.

Figure 4.4 Jurors sit in the courtroom's jury box.

Standard and burden of proof in criminal cases

In criminal cases, the defendant is presumed to be innocent until the contrary is proved. The burden of proof rests on the prosecution, which must prove beyond reasonable doubt that the accused has committed an offence before they can be convicted. The prosecution needs to convince the jury that the crime was committed by the defendant for the defendant to be found guilty. Thus it is the job of the defence to disprove the prosecution's case and provide evidence to show the innocence of their client.

In NSW, all members of a jury in a criminal trial must unanimously agree with the decision either to convict or acquit the accused. The defendant is acquitted if the jury returns the verdict of 'not guilty'. If the jury returns a verdict of 'guilty', the accused is convicted. Sentencing occurs either then, or at a later date determined by the court.

Observation of civil and criminal cases in the Local Court

The Local Court provides the first point of contact for most matters requiring judicial (legal) intervention. This means that most cases are dealt with by the Local Court unless they are very serious or expensive. The Local Court does not make use of juries and judges. Rather, a magistrate makes the decision. The length of matters is very brief in the Local Court. As a result, the Local Court is cost-effective and efficient in the way that matters are decided.

In the Local Court, the lawyers and magistrates do not wear traditional robes and solicitors carry out most legal work. The proceedings are less formal than the higher courts. Many defendants choose to represent themselves and so argue their case without the help of a lawyer.

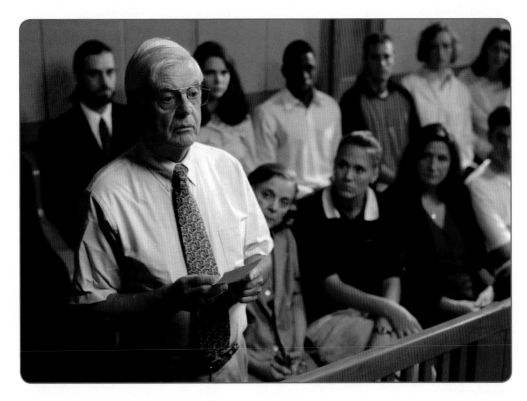

Figure 4.5 A court case involves many participants, each with roles in the procedures.

REVIEW 4.3

1 What is a coronial inquest?
2 Outline the ways in which children charged with a crime are protected. Account for this protection. Do you think this is reasonable?
3 Explain the difference between civil and criminal law. Give examples of each.
4 Draw a flow diagram showing the steps taken in civil legal action.
5 Describe the role played by a jury. How are they selected?
6 Draw up a table to show the different court proceedings for civil and criminal cases.
7 Explain the difference between indictable offences and summary offences.
8 Decide whether the following cases involve criminal law or civil law.
   a You are held up at knifepoint and your mobile phone is stolen.
   b A man trips over a box on the supermarket floor and breaks an ankle.
   c A woman is convicted of driving with a blood alcohol level of 0.08.
   d Your friend is caught with marijuana.
   e You find a cockroach in a salad you just bought from a café.
   f A neighbour's music at 3 a.m. every night wakes you up constantly.
9 With a classmate, make a poster (either drawing or cutting out pictures) showing as many civil wrongs and criminal actions as you can. Draw up a table to list these.

RESEARCH 4.1

Go to the following site: http://www.lawlink.nsw.gov.au/
   Who hosts this site? Why was it set up?
   Go to 'Courts and Tribunals'. Imagine that you are doing work experience at the local primary school and have to teach Year 6 about the Local Court. Develop an Internet activity based on the information on the website.

ENFORCEMENT AGENCIES: POLICE, GOVERNMENT DEPARTMENTS, OTHER AUTHORITIES

law enforcement making sure that the laws of the state are followed

Law enforcement agencies are those agencies that have the role of enforcing the law. These bodies are created by acts of parliament and include the police and government departments.

The police

Police do not make the laws, they only enforce them. They try to see that law and order in a community is maintained by preventing unlawful acts, investigating crimes and arresting offenders.

The police have rules that they must obey when they perform these duties. To ensure that evidence is collected correctly and thus is able to be used by the prosecution on a court case, the police are covered by a code of practice. This code covers:

- police powers to stop, search and detain people
- police powers to enter and search premises and seize property
- police powers to arrest, detain and question suspects
- the way in which suspects and others are to be treated by police.

Each state and territory in Australia has its own police force. The New South Wales Police Force is primarily concerned

Figure 4.6 Maintaining law and order at a large-scale sporting event.

with enforcing criminal law, particularly those crimes outlined in the *Crimes Act 1900* (NSW) and the *Motor Traffic Act 1909* (NSW).

The Australian Federal Police are responsible for enforcing federal law and criminal law where crimes cross state boundaries. The key role of the Australian Federal Police is to protect Australia's security and prevent and detect crimes against Commonwealth law within Australia and, in certain circumstances, by Australians overseas.

Government departments and other authorities

Some Commonwealth and state government departments have the authority to enforce specific laws. The taxation office, customs and transport authorities have been created by acts of parliament and thus have the power to enforce certain laws for the protection and good of society. For example, the Australian Tax Office (ATO) has powers under the *Income Tax Assessment Act 1936* (Cwlth) to investigate and prosecute matters in relation to tax.

LEGAL AID

The Australian legal system does not give a person an automatic right to a lawyer. However, it is recognised that a person without legal representation is unlikely to receive a fair trial. In order to give everyone the opportunity to have legal representation, Legal Aid was established.

In New South Wales, the Legal Aid Commission was established under the *Legal Aid Commission Act 1979* (NSW). This independent statutory body provides legal aid and other legal services to disadvantaged people.

A legal aid practitioner will respond to general queries about legal problems and eligibility for representation. Legal aid is available for family and criminal matters, but to be eligible for this service a person must be unable to afford legal representation in their own right and have a case that has a reasonable chance of a successful outcome.

ALTERNATIVES TO THE COURT SYSTEM

Going to court can be expensive both in money and time. There has been pressure to provide alternatives to court processes for solving legal disputes.

Administrative and other tribunals

One response has been the establishment of a range of quasi-judicial tribunals. Administrative and other tribunals are bodies that review decisions of government departments. They offer a time-efficient, low-cost means of resolving legal disputes and problems. They are different from courts as they have narrow areas of jurisdiction, are less formal, usually do not allow legal representation and are not bound by rules of evidence and so can take into account a variety of factors in finding a solution.

Some examples of tribunals in New South Wales are the NSW Consumer Trading Tenancy Tribunal, which deals with disputes between consumers and businesses, and the NSW Administrative Decisions Tribunal, which hears cases involving allegations of discrimination, professional misconduct and administrative decisions by NSW government bodies.

Alternative dispute resolution

Alternative dispute resolution (ADR) uses a variety of methods to resolve disputes between parties without involving court processes. ADR allows the participants to not only save time and money, but also to have more control over proceedings.

Alternative dispute resolution may be as simple as two parties talking through their dispute, or as complex as court-ordered mediation or arbitration. Mediation involves a neutral third party who attempts to help the parties come to an agreement. In arbitration, the neutral third party will make a decision that is binding on the parties involved in the dispute.

Self-help remedies

Taking legal action is expensive and time consuming, thus it always best for people to try to deal with an issue without resorting to court processes. Self-help dispute remedies can be as simple as the two parties in dispute discussing the issue, making a complaint to an organisation that has given bad service, or returning a faulty product to the manufacturer. However, if these fail to bring about resolution, there are other dispute resolution procedures. These are discussed below.

Ombudsmen

Many governments have established offices of ombudsmen. Their role is to act as a link between the people and the government and its agencies. An ombudsman has powers to investigate complaints and to write reports and make recommendations, but does not have power to institute civil or criminal proceedings.

If a complaint is made in writing, the ombudsman's office will investigate and assess whether the complaint is justified. If it sees that the complaint is justified, the ombudsman will make recommendations for rectifying the problem.

Some private sector industries have also adopted the model of an ombudsman to deal with complaints by consumers (e.g. the banking ombudsman, the telecommunications industry ombudsman and the energy and water ombudsman).

Political processes

Members of the public can also go to their local member of parliament if they feel they have been wronged by a government department or agency. Local members and councillors can help in resolving the dispute so that it does not need to go to court or a tribunal.

A person can write to or request an interview with their local or council representative to state their concerns. Local members and councillors rely on being re-elected to their position, so it is in their interest to help their constituents resolve disputes quickly.

Community justice centres

Community justice centres (CJCs) aim to resolve disputes through mediation. There are six centres throughout NSW, providing informal and impartial dispute resolution services to all sections of the community and government agencies. CJCs are funded by the NSW Government and provide their services free of charge.

Matters dealt with by CJCs include family disputes and youth conflict, workplace grievances, neighbourhood arguments and community disputes.

CJCs are designed to resolve disputes between members of the same community. As these people usually have an ongoing relationship, it is important that a dispute over something like a fence is resolved as quickly and economically as possible with no long-lasting acrimony. A dispute over an issue such as who is responsible for the repair of a fence can be resolved at a CJC by the parties talking through their dispute with a neutral mediator. It will be more satisfactorily resolved here than in a formal and confrontational courtroom.

REVIEW 4.5

1 Describe the role administrative and other tribunals play in settling legal disputes. Give an example.
2 Discuss the reasons why self-help is the best way of settling disputes. What forms can self-help take?
3 Define ADR. Outline some of the forms it may take. Which one do you think would have the most desirable results? Justify your answer.
4 If you are having problems with your neighbours, why should going to court be the last step taken?
5 What options are there for settling a dispute with your neighbour?
6 Outline the role of an ombudsman. How is an ombudsman limited in solving disputes?
7 In what ways can local politicians help with legal problems?

THE NAKED TRUTH AND THE MYTH OF NEIGHBOURLY LOVE
BY MATTHEW BENNS

Herald-Sun, 21 August 2005

Neighbours are more likely to argue with each other about garden fences than any other issue, new figures have revealed. In one instance, two neighbours ended up in court 78 times—their latest stoush involving claims of genital exposure.

Almost one-third of all neighbour disputes that go to mediation with the Community Justice Centre Program involve fences. "People fight about everything to do with a fence—colour, height, paling or Colorbond, trellis or not," Program director Deborah Sharp said. But she suspected that, behind the fights over the garden fence, lay deeper issues that only came to a head with a disagreement about the fence. "Fences can cause conflict but quite often they argue about the fence when it's really about lifestyle or cultural issues," Ms Sharp said.

If mediation fails, neighbours turn to the courts. At Warriewood, two neighbours have taken each other to court 78 times, with the latest conflict being over an illegally constructed fence one claims she put up to protect her from her neighbour's naked genitals.

After disputes about fences, the next big cause of offence between neighbours is invasion of privacy, which could be anything from noise to arguing over a shared driveway. Neighbours also rowed about each others' children, lifestyle and environmental factors such as smoke or noise, visitors, parking and plants, trees and shrubs in each others' gardens.

"The issue can seem quite small but because people get very distressed by it they lose perspective," Ms Sharp said. "We don't make a judgement on the issue. Quite a lot of disputes start with the way children play in a neighbourhood. There is a domino effect—people take their children's sides and whole streets get involved. Eventually somebody rings us and we go to everybody involved in pre-mediation to find out what the issues are." A time is then set for a meeting. If the parties do not agree to setting the time the mediators know there is little hope of ever reaching a settlement.

Sometimes the solution is as simple as organising a barbecue and ensuring that all the neighbours attend and get to know each other. Social analyst David Chalke of AustraliaSCAN said people felt their home, their neighbourhood and local area had become far more important in recent years.

"In the 1980s and 90s we were cocooning and fortressing and running away from the world," Mr Chalke said. "We have invested a lot of money renovating our homes and installing massive TVs [so] that home is incredibly important to us. Before, it was just a base we used to go out into the world. Now home is our world. Also, because of the turmoil we have been through in the past decade, we are far less tolerant of people whom we believe are breaking the rules. We saw it over the Tampa episode where people were saying it was OK for Australia to take refugees, but they had to follow the rules. We want the system to force people to stick to the rules. We see on TV every night people grizzling about councils and neighbours. We see people getting compensation for wrongs and they think, hey, I can do that too."

NSW has 3000 disputes a year that are mediated by the Government funded Community Justice Centre Program—1000 of those are in Sydney. The Law and Justice Foundation carried out a survey two years ago in Bega in southern NSW and found that 12.7 per cent of the population had taken some form of legal action after a dispute with neighbours.

OPERATION OF THE LEGAL SYSTEM IN RELATION TO NATIVE TITLE

The Indigenous cultures of Australia are the oldest living cultures in the world. As well as having rich and diverse cultures, Aboriginal and Torres Strait Islander people also had a well developed structure of laws that governed how they lived in their community and how they looked after the land. All of this changed with European settlement. It was to take 200 years before this lifestyle was formally recognised.

Figure 4.7 Indigenous Australians have a strong bond with the land.

The doctrine of terra nullius in Australia

The term 'terra nullius' means 'land belonging to no-one'. It refers not only to uninhabited territory, but also to territory that has no recognisable system of law, or social or political organisation. Terra nullius appeared as a legal concept in English law in the seventeenth century. It was based on the concept that, when a new land was discovered by the English, English law would dominate when no other system of law was apparent. This became known as the 'doctrine of reception'.

As discussed earlier, Indigenous Australians have a strong bond with the land, which they nurture, but feel that there is no need to put fences around it and signs proclaiming ownership. However these views are very different from the European idea of land ownership and thus enabled the English to proclaim Australia terra nullius in 1788 and enforce English law as the law of the land. The English saw Australia as being uncultivated land and, under the doctrine of reception, if an English colony was established in an uncultivated land, English law automatically applied to the colonists and any other people in that land.

Governor Arthur Phillip and subsequent governors of the colonies of Australia did try to negotiate treaties with local inhabitants, but language and cultural barriers meant that negotiations had limited success. Terra nullius then dominated the white settlement of Australia.

The concept of terra nullius has had a vast impact on the Indigenous population. Their treatment by the non-Indigenous colonists, loss of land, loss of culture and dispersal, has not only led to the decimation of the population, but considerable social problems. This will be discussed in more detail later in the course.

The growth of recognition of native title in some countries

Native title means the right of indigenous people to live on their land and use it for traditional purposes. Throughout the world there has been growing recognition of the rights of indigenous peoples to their own lands. Hunting, fishing and land ownership rights have been returned to many indigenous groups in different countries.

There has also been a move to give greater self-determination to indigenous groups. Self-determination means the rights of indigenous peoples to control their traditional lands and the use of these lands, the local economy and social policy. Maoris in New Zealand, Innuits in Greenland and Canada, and Aboriginal and Torres Strait Islanders are three indigenous groups who have been given greater recognition in terms of native title and self-determination in their own countries.

CASE SPACE

Recognition of Maori land rights

Unlike Australia, the recognition of Maori land rights in New Zealand was accepted early in European settlement. However, this is not to say that conflict did not occur over the ownership and use of the land, both with Europeans and with other Maori tribal groups. The result has been not so much land ownership as assimilation of cultures.

The Treaty of Waitangi, first signed on 6 February 1840, gave recognition to Maori sovereignty while making them British subjects. The Treaty allowed the following three important aspects:

- Maori would have greater control over their lands and resources .
- Maori land could only be sold to the Crown, who would then either keep it as Crown land or sell it to settlers.
- The Queen would promise to maintain law and peace in New Zealand

Not all Maori chiefs signed this treaty and there was quite a deal of confusion about the meaning of sovereignty and how far it actually went. Conflicts arose once again between Maoris and the European settlers and with other Maori tribal groups. By 1920, only 4.8 million acres of land in New Zealand was held by Maori people.

Unlike Australia, there were no laws or policies for removing Indigenous children from their families. However, a formal policy of assimilation was in place towards the end of the nineteenth century. The government argued that the most effective way of integrating Maori people into white culture was through education. Under the Native Schools Act, 1867, English became compulsory for all Maori students.

Maori people began moving to the cities and away from traditional lands in the middle of the twentieth century. By 1945, Maori ownership of land had decreased to just over 3 million acres. As their landownership gradually reduced, many Maori people relocated to the cities to live and work. In 1960, the government introduced an 'urban relocation program'. This encouraged Maori people to move into cities. Under this program, 400 families were relocated in 5 years.

Major High Court decisions on native title and subsequent legal developments

Native title was not recognised in Australia until 1992. This was when the High Court, in the *Mabo* decision, overturned the doctrine of terra nullius.

The Mabo case

The *Mabo* case is important because it led to the introduction of native title legislation. It is also significant because it gave recognition to the Indigenous inhabitants of Australia.

In this case, the High Court recognised the existence of native title for a group of Murray Islanders in the Torres Strait. Eddie Mabo and four other Murray Islanders launched legal proceedings against the Queensland Government in 1982. They stated that they could prove uninterrupted occupancy of traditional lands, and thus their right to the land was greater than the Queensland Government's right.

The case required the High Court to consider the legality of the declaration of terra nullius. The court ruled that the islanders were the traditional owners of the land and that they had the right to possess and occupy the islands and enjoy use of their traditional lands. The High Court also established guidelines for future claims of native title. These guidelines included the giving of compensation where the native title rights were taken back by the federal government.

As a result of the *Mabo* decision, the federal government enacted the *Native Title Act 1993* (Cwlth). The purpose of this act is to:

- provide for the recognition and protection of native title
- establish ways in which future dealings that affected native title may proceed and set standards for these dealings
- establish a mechanism for determining native title claims
- provide for the validation of past acts that may be invalidated because of the recognition of native title.

The act stopped short of defining native title and created the Native Title Tribunal to determine the validity of native title claims. If native title holders are unable to reclaim their lands and thus exercise their rights, the tribunal determines the compensation to be paid.

The *Mabo* decision and the Native Title Act resulted in other Aboriginal groups attempting to reclaim land. The Wik and the Thayorre people launched a case against the Queensland government in 1996, claiming native title rights on land that was being used as pastoral leases. The Federal Court ruled that the existence of pastoral leases extinguished the right to native title. This decision was appealed to the High Court where it was ruled that the Wik and Thayorre people should be entitled to their traditional lands. The court found that pastoral leases and native title could coexist, but that when conflict arose the pastoral leases would prevail.

Figure 4.8 Traditional life on the Torres Strait Island of Mer.

The Wik case

While the *Wik* decision did not grant automatic title over Crown land being leased, it caused concern among farmers and mining companies that they would have to enter into lengthy negotiations with Indigenous people over access to and use of land. In response to this growing concern in rural Australia, the federal government enacted the *Native Title Amendment Act 1998* (Cwlth). There was much debate in parliament over this act before it was passed.

The main provisions of the act are as follows:

- The act extinguished native title over any land that was considered privately owned prior to 1 January 1994.
- When native title exists alongside a pastoral lease, the pastoralist is allowed to use the land for primary production.
- Tough tests were imposed to determine right to native title. At least one member of the claimants must prove a continuous link with the traditional lands.

Figure 4.9 Gladys Tybingoomba, Wik woman, addresses the crowd at a reconciliation event.

The Native Title Tribunal

The Native Title Tribunal is an Australian Commonwealth Government agency set up under the Native Title Act. It is part of the Attorney-General's portfolio and mediates native title claims under the direction of the Federal Court of Australia.

The aim of the National Native Title Tribunal is to develop an understanding of native title and reach outcomes that recognise everyone's rights and interests in land and waters. The tribunal plays a variety of roles, for example, it acts as an arbitrator in some situations where the people involved cannot reach agreement about proposed developments. It also assists people who want to negotiate other sorts of agreements, such as Indigenous land use agreements. If requested, the tribunal will assist people in negotiations about proposed developments (future acts), such as mining.

State legislation

As discussed, the *Mabo* and *Wik* decisions led to Commonwealth legislation in the area of native title and self-determination for Aboriginal and Torres Strait Islanders. State legislation has also been enacted to give rights to and protect the interests of Indigenous Australians.

The *National Parks and Wildlife Act 1974* (NSW) provides for the protection of places and relics which are of significance to Aboriginal culture. Under this act, it is an offence to knowingly destroy, disturb or remove these places or relics.

The *Aboriginal Land Rights Act 1983* (NSW) recognises that:

- land was traditionally owned and occupied by Aboriginal people
- land has significance to Aboriginal people in a spiritual, social, cultural and economic way
- the importance of land to Aboriginal people must be acknowledged
- government decisions made in the past have impacted in a negative way on Aboriginal land ownership.

This act has been amended in 1990 and 2001. It provided for the ownership of reserve land to be transferred to the Aboriginal people, but this has in reality only seen a very small percentage of land transferred. Under the act a percentage of land tax revenue is paid into a fund to meet the costs of Aboriginal Land Council administrative costs and to finance land purchases and future development. This act also gives some rights to Aboriginal people to traditional hunting and fishing grounds.

Commonwealth legislation has been enacted to provide some Indigenous rights over bodies of water. The *Aboriginal and Torres Strait Islander Heritage Protection Act 1984* (Cwlth) is used to protect areas of water which have Indigenous cultural heritage, as well as areas of land.

Native title as a collective right

A collective right is one that is claimed and shared by a group of people. Native title is a collective right as it cannot be claimed by an individual—only by a group (for example the Wik people). All members of the group share the rights that are gained.

However, despite native title being a collective right, an individual can bring a claim before the courts, as seen in the *Mabo* case. As the individual is acting on behalf of the group, all members of the community that they represent will share the rights gained.

REVIEW 4.7

1 Explain the concept of 'terra nullius'. State the reasons why it was applied to Australia.
2 Define 'native title' and 'self-determination'. Which indigenous groups have gained greater recognition in these areas?
3 Draw a timeline showing the recognition of native title rights and self-determination for Aboriginal and Torres Strait Islanders in Australia and in New South Wales.
4 Assess the significance of the *Mabo* decision.
5 What was the impact of the *Wik* case?
6 Outline the main legislation that protects the land rights of Indigenous Australians.
7 In what way is native title a collective right?

MULTIPLE-CHOICE QUESTIONS

1 What did the High Court do in the *Mabo* case?
   a applied the doctrine of reception
   b overturned the doctrine of terra nullius
   c upheld the doctrine of terra nullius
   d returned all traditional lands

2 Which of these areas are NOT part of civil actions?
   a breach of duty
   b employment rights
   c murder
   d defamation

3 What does the adversary system involve?
   a judges cross-examining witnesses
   b the use of a jury at all times
   c the right to have a decision appealed
   d each side presenting their case and testing the opposition's evidence

4 Which of the following is a state legal response to land rights?
   a The Native Title Act
   b The Aboriginal Land Rights Act
   c The Native Title Tribunal
   d Reconciliation Day

5 What do courts and tribunals have in common?
   a they are both quick and inexpensive
   b they both require legal representation
   c they are used to settle legal disputes
   d judges and magistrates preside over them

CHAPTER SUMMARY TASKS

1 Outline the way that the law is enforced.
2 How are courts structured? Why?
3 Account for the ways that the adversary system affects the court process.
4 Distinguish between civil and criminal court procedures.
5 Explain why alternative dispute resolution mechanisms developed.

6 Discuss the role of legal aid.
7 How is the law on native title enforced?
8 Describe the structure of the Native Title Tribunal. Do you see any conflicts in this structure?
9 Discuss how the doctrine of terra nullius affected the status of Indigenous peoples.
10 How have recent legal developments affected the significance of the 1992 and 1996 High Court decisions in *Mabo* and *Wik*.

CHAPTER SUMMARY

- The legal system operates on a court hierarchy, which incorporates federal and state courts.
- The Australian court system is based on an adversarial form of trial.
- Court procedures may be either criminal or civil. Court procedures may also differ, depending on the nature of the case.
- The Local Court is at the bottom of the court hierarchy and hears the majority of cases in New South Wales.
- Various bodies are empowered to enforce the law. These include the police and government departments.
- Going to court is time consuming and expensive, so alternatives such as administrative and other tribunals have been established to review government decisions.
- Alternative dispute resolution mechanisms have been developed to resolve disputes in a time- and cost-efficient way.
- Under the doctrine of terra nullius, Aboriginal and Torres Strait Islanders lost most of their rights to own their traditional lands and follow customary law.
- The growing recognition of native title and the High Court decisions in the *Mabo* and *Wik* cases have given back some of these rights.

The individual and the state

THE INDIVIDUAL AND THE STATE

Power and authority

- concepts of power—social, cultural, economic, political, legal
- concepts of authority—customary, statutory, common law, delegated
- relationship of the individual to power and authority

Duties

Domestic
- the different meanings of duties: legal (statutory and common law), social and cultural, moral, religious and ethical
- the interrelationship of legal and other duties

International
- meanings of international duties and their evolving nature
- restrictions on the use of force as an instrument of national policy in international relations
- obligation on governments to practise tolerance and live together in peace as good neighbours and to work for the promotion of the economic and social advancement of all peoples

Legal controls on state power

- official duties and discretionary powers
- parliamentary control of executive: ministerial responsibility, parliamentary committees
- individuals' rights to access information: common law and statutory rights
- informal means of challenging state power through the media, members of parliament, trade unions, interest groups, including non-government organisations
- formal means of challenging power: internal and external review, including general merit review tribunals, privacy bodies, courts, Office of the Ombudsman, commissions of inquiry and the Independent Commission Against Corruption

Rights

Domestic
- legal basis of rights
- the distinction between moral, customary and legal rights
- different types of legal rights—common law and statutory rights
- self-determination

International
- international treaties and declarations of rights
- the limitations of international law in protecting rights
- self-determination

CHAPTER 5

Power and authority

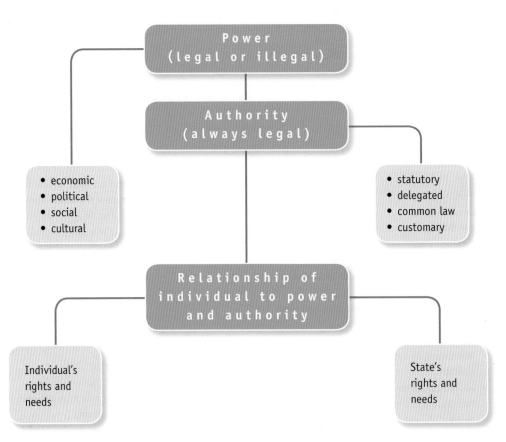

Figure 5.1 The rights of the individual must be balanced against the power and authority of the state.

Throughout this chapter, you will learn about the various meanings of power and authority. The power and authority that you have to act within society is controlled by various levels of government and there are many situations in which conflicts can arise between individuals and the state.

POWER

Power is the ability to force an individual or group to carry out any action against their will. Consider the power of your parents, guardians, teachers and even your friends in influencing you to act in a certain way. For example, when your teacher tells you to stop talking and continue with your work and you agree to stop, then your teacher has wielded power. The use of power is all around us in our immediate and broader world. When we hear the expression 'powerful person', it really means he/she is able to influence and control others.

Power is used and sometimes abused and therefore we can say that power is legal or illegal. A legal use of power is when it is associated with authority. All of the people who supervise us and with whom we associate have the authority to tell us what to do and expect us to follow their commands. In most cases we do.

However, power is often abused and is illegal. Consider a situation where a physically stronger student pushes their way to the front of a queue at a school canteen. Clearly they have forced others to move out of the way, disregarding the rule of lining up and waiting to be served.

Concepts of power

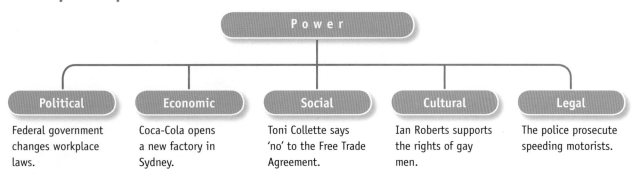

Figure 5.2 There are many different types of power.

Social
Social power is the ability to influence or control decision-makers through social status. Celebrities are often asked to conduct advertising campaigns for various products or political parties. When Kylie Minogue was diagnosed with breast cancer in 2005, the number of women visiting their doctors for breast cancer screens rose dramatically.

Cultural
Cultural power is similar to social power in that it is the ability to influence or control decision-makers through values and beliefs of certain bodies. Women's groups, gay rights groups and religious organisations can often speak out and create change over time. Ian Roberts, a high-profile NRL player of the 1990s, was the first homosexual football player to reveal his sexuality, openly discussing the difficulties of playing Rugby League and maintaining secrecy about his private life. However, it could be argued that he was able to use cultural power to create more tolerance towards homosexuals in Australian society.

Economic

Economic power is the ability to control or influence decision-makers through financial or monetary means. Your parents threatening to withhold money from you for not studying is an example in your immediate world. In a broader sense, a decision by a corporation such as Coca-Cola to build its new headquarters in Sydney or Melbourne would probably get the attention of the New South Wales and Victorian governments, both offering incentives of some kind to attract Coca-Cola to their state.

government policy decisions made by governments based on principles or ideals such as 'user pays', etc.

Political

Political power is the ability to influence and directly control **government policy** and the creation of statute law. The current federal government has recently changed workplace laws to better support its policies of greater employer control of workplace contracts. Political power is often created when political parties hold the majority of seats in parliament, thus allowing new legislation in support of particular policies to be passed.

Legal

Legal power is the ability to control or influence someone with the full backing of the law. When 40 km per hour speed limits were introduced outside schools, police had the legal power to fine motorists for speeding. In courts of law, judges hold legal power to make decisions on granting bail, sentencing and rules of evidence. When a judge sentences a guilty person to gaol, or orders them to pay a fine, legal power is being exerted.

Figure 5.3 The police have the legal power to enforce road laws.

REVIEW 5.1

1 Under each of the five categories of power above, list one more example of power from recent news stories.
2 Outline the difference between political and legal power.
3 Explain how power can be both legal and illegal.

AUTHORITY

Authority can be defined in exactly the same way as power, except that authority is always legal. A teacher who asks you to begin writing is acting with authority. A police officer who pulls you over for a random breath test is also acting with authority.

A bank robber may be able to force a teller to hand over all the money (illegal power), however he/she is certainly not acting with authority.

Concepts of authority

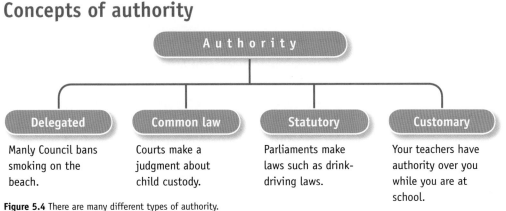

Authority			
Delegated	**Common law**	**Statutory**	**Customary**
Manly Council bans smoking on the beach.	Courts make a judgment about child custody.	Parliaments make laws such as drink-driving laws.	Your teachers have authority over you while you are at school.

Figure 5.4 There are many different types of authority.

Customary

Customary authority is the legal ability to control, influence or direct others because of traditions or history. Parents allowing or disallowing their children to attend certain functions or events is a clear example of customary authority. Families of all races and religions usually follow the custom of respecting and listening to elders. In times past, colonial people have enslaved Africans, men have dominated and controlled women, and royal families have ruled over their kingdoms. While much of this has changed in the **Western World**, many countries continue to enslave others, subordinate women and have a ruling elite.

Statutory

Statutory authority in this chapter refers to the ability to legally control persons or groups by acts of parliament. The Australian Taxation Office has the authority to investigate your tax affairs through the *Income Tax Assessment Act 1936* (Cwlth). The Roads and Traffic Authority can cancel a licence and issue a fine for speeding, using the *Road Transport (Safety & Traffic Management) Act 1999*.

Common law

Common law authority in this chapter refers to the power of judges to interpret statute law and make judgments about appropriate punishments. When an offender is accused of a crime (pleading not guilty) and brought before a judge, the court must decide whether a statute law has been broken. If the offender pleads guilty and the judge decides to impose a fine, then the order to pay the fine becomes known as 'common law'. If the offender does not pay the fine, they actually break common law for failing to abide by the court's decision. Therefore, the courts have common law authority to make judgments about breaches of statute law. Other meanings of common law can be found on page 15.

Delegated

Delegated authority means that authority is given to a subordinate (lower) body to act on the superior's behalf. For example, the New South Wales Government gives authority to local councils to collect your rubbish and recycling.

Western World
countries such as
Australia, United
States of America,
Great Britain and
New Zealand which
hold the principles
of Christianity,
democracy and
capitalism

THE RELATIONSHIP OF THE INDIVIDUAL TO POWER AND AUTHORITY

In most societies around the world, the needs of individuals will conflict with those of the state. Some of these may be minor conflicts, such as the desire to smoke on a beach or inside a restaurant; others conflicts, such as the refusal by persons to join military forces during times of war, may be more serious.

Over the past few years in New South Wales, smoking cigarettes in various places has become increasingly outlawed. Manly Council, which governs Manly Beach through delegated authority, introduced a no-cigarette policy for its beach in 2004. Council rangers are now able to fine smokers on the beach up to $50. The desires of individuals to smoke on the beach clearly conflict with non-smokers, and with the council's needs to keep the beach free of cigarette butts, which not only create an ugly sight for tourists, but can also interfere with marine life when they are washed into the ocean.

MEDIA CLIP

MANLY BANS BEACH SMOKING

18 May 2004

Manly Council has banned smoking on beaches, setting the example for other coastal councils. Mayor Peter Macdonald said council members were trailblazers who wished to see their no-smoking-at-beaches policy stretch as far away as Darwin and Hobart.

"I guess this is a bit of trailblazing but the important thing that's going to come out of it is it 'denormalises' smoking," Dr Macdonald.

"Tobacco companies have been putting out the message for years that smoking is normal. This is about saying smoking is not acceptable, it's not normal behaviour; there's a subtle educational effect."

The proposal passed council 8–3 tonight after "spirited debate".

The ban was designed to protect children from passive smoke as well as address the environmental impacts of cigarette butts on beaches and in waterways.

Such a ban makes Manly, on Sydney's northern beaches, the first area outside Los Angeles to ban smoking on beaches.

Pittwater mayor Lynne Czinner said it was sensible for neighbouring Pittwater and Warringah to follow Manly's lead.

But Ms Czinner joined Council of Civil Liberties president Cameron Murphy in questioning the policing of such a ban.

Dr Macdonald said council rangers would not become "smoke police".

"Once we get signage up and the public are aware of our no-smoking policy on the beach, these things tend to be regulated by the community themselves," he said.

Manly Council has also banned smoking within 10m of council-owned children's play areas, sporting fields and playing grounds.

Council-sponsored events will be smoke-free and signs will be erected highlighting environmental and public health issues associated with smoking.

REVIEW 5.3

Discuss the rights of a local council to ban:
1 smoking on a beach
2 the use of mobile phones
3 topless sunbathing.

You should try to write at least one point or argument for both sides of these scenarios.

Other relationships between individuals and the state

Throughout the 1960s and 1970s in Australia, the federal government used conscription to recruit soldiers to fight in the Vietnam War. Australia sent approximately 47 000 male troops to Vietnam from 1966–1972 by forcing soldiers to enlist to serve in Vietnam.

The government used statutory authority by passing a law that allowed them to select young men at random. This was done by picking various dates of birth from birth records. If an individual refused to respond to a letter from the government, they were pursued and often gaoled for breaking the law. In this case, an individual's religious or political beliefs that violence should not be used, or wars should never be fought, were ignored by the state. Such individuals were known as 'conscientious objectors', in that they objected to Australia's involvement in Vietnam, and to war itself.

There are many other situations where this particular conflict arises. Consider the situation in Israel, where all citizens, male and female, are required by law to join the military at age 18 and serve for a minimum of two years. There are also many countries where alcohol is banned for all citizens, as a government such as the Taliban in Afghanistan may wish to protect religious laws that forbid alcohol.

Figure 5.5 'Your country needs you!' 'Not me! I'm going surfing!'

Balancing the needs of individuals and the state

Since there are over six billion individuals living in our world in over 220 different nation-states, a huge variety of conflicts on various scales are obvious. However, the question of whether the needs of citizens can be balanced with the needs of the state is one that can be answered with both 'yes' and 'no'.

In all Western democratic countries, individuals can govern themselves in terms of what food they eat, what clothes they wear, what job they wish to do and how many children they have. However, there are examples where the state has tried to exert statutory authority within these situations.

In the United States of America state of Virginia, the government has attempted to outlaw the wearing by teenagers of pants that reveal underpants. Their view is that this practice is offensive to the remainder of the community. The fashion of wearing jeans off the hips has developed through the cultural and social power of hip-hop artists, who have displayed this fashion at concerts and on album covers.

On the other hand, recent terrorist attacks in Madrid, Bali and London have raised the level of security required on public transport and at major sporting and cultural events. The introduction of a national identification card would allow a government to monitor the movements of all its citizens in and out of the country and may reduce the number of potential terrorists from entering the country on false documents. It may also reduce the amount of fraud being carried out by having every citizen of Australia registered on a national database. However, there are many opponents of such a strategy. Such people are often known as **civil libertarians**, as they are protecting the civil liberties (freedoms) of civilians.

civil libertarians people who believe in personal freedoms such as the right to remain anonymous, the right not to be body searched at random etc; it is these issues that are becoming increasingly challenged as terrorist attacks occur around the globe

---

MEDIA CLIP

A BRIEF MATTER OF STYLE

VA. SENATE DROPS BAGGY PANTS BILL,
BUT HIP TEENS SAY LOOK IS PASSÉ ANYWAY
BY TARA BAHRAMPOUR

Washington Post, 11 February 2005

A proposal to impose a $50 fine on people who reveal their underwear in public died in the Virginia Senate yesterday, but according to young people who might have been affected, that "jont" was killed long ago.

Translation: The baggy pants trend already is fading on its own—and the state legislature was a little late catching on.

During a hastily convened meeting yesterday, the Senate Courts of Justice Committee voted unanimously against the bill, which the House of Delegates had approved Tuesday. Proposed by Del. Algie T. Howell Jr. (D-Norfolk), it was aimed at anyone who publicly and intentionally "displays his below-waist undergarments, intended to cover a person's intimate parts, in a lewd or indecent manner."

Howell's aides declined to specify what kind of underwear was being targeted, how many exposed inches might be deemed lewd or who would decide what constituted an offense. But the proposal was broadly understood to refer to a tendency, generally among young men, to wear baggy pants that hang several inches below the waistline, exposing the top—and sometimes a lot more—of boxer shorts.

But at the mall and skate park this week, only a few kids were still showing much underwear, even in the warm weather.

"That was back in the days," said Abbas Kandeh, 19, a senior at Annandale High School who was strolling through Landmark Mall in Alexandria with friends. Their waistlines were concealed by long T-shirts, and their jeans were baggy but did not hang as low as they might have four years ago when, they say, the trend peaked.

"Nobody does it these days," Kandeh said.

School officials also said they have noticed waistlines on the rise after hitting a low several years ago. "It kind of seems like a fad that has passed us," said Tammy Ignacio, an associate principal at T.C. Williams High School in Alexandria who is responsible for monitoring students' clothing.

That is not to say that anyone is about to return to 1980s-style peg-leg pants. Boys' jeans still tend toward the saggy, and the tops of undershorts still poke out, although these days they tend to be obscured by oversize T-shirts.

In fact, said Jaevon Thomas, 17, a sales clerk at Urban Styles, a hip-hop clothing shop at Landmark, boxers are now made to be seen. Pulling up his polo shirt, he displayed the top of a pair of red cotton boxers with "Tommy Hilfiger" printed on the front.

"Underwear are made to be accessories now," he said. "Underwear that matches your outfit, underwear that matches your clothes."

Figure 5.6 This look could have been illegal in the US state of Virginia.

Grown-ups in the Virginia Senate said they took up the legislation yesterday largely to quell the international attention it had received (Howell's office has gotten phone calls from the media as far away as Israel and Australia)—and express their concern that it posed constitutional problems. Before they killed the bill, several senators said they had received calls (including some from relatives) urging them to fight for the bill or admonishing them to focus on other matters.

"I would find this bill humorous or tolerable ... but for the indignity of the, no pun intended, international exposure," said Sen. Thomas K. Norment Jr. (R-James City). "That this is what is being associated with the commonwealth of Virginia is unacceptable."

T.C. Williams senior Jessica Miller, 18, agreed. The day after the House voted in favor of the bill, she organized a group of students who were planning to protest the bill in front of Alexandria City Hall this weekend wearing their underwear over their pants.

"Everyone thinks it's a joke," said Miller, whose faded jeans read "Make Love, Not War" in ballpoint pen. "They're using words like 'lewd'," she said. "War is lewd. Homelessness is indecent. Boxers showing—that's tacky. It's not worth spending taxpayers' money on."

For girls, she added, the bill would have posed a problem: Most jeans sold today are low-rise hip-huggers, a style that makes it hard to keep underwear from peeking over the top even if that is not the intent.

At American Eagle Outfitters, another clothing store at the mall, the best-selling girls' jeans are "Extreme Low Rise" and "Super Low Rise," low-cut hip-huggers often worn with thong underwear.

Victoria Martin, 19, a sales associate at the store, said she liked the idea of the bill. But when her manager pointed out that Martin's own red polka dot underwear was visible above her jean line, she smiled and acknowledged that staying legal might have been hard.

One person who was disappointed that the bill died is Marc Butlein, chief executive of Freshpair.com, the underwear company that started National Underwear Day (the second Wednesday in August) two years ago. On Wednesday, the company announced that it would send $100 of underwear to anyone who got an underwear ticket. "Underwear today is not what it was 50 years ago," Butlein said. "Underwear is something that, quite frankly, has come out of the closet."

For teenage skateboarders at the Schuyler Hamilton Jones Skate Park in Alexandria, staying legal was not a concern. While none was showing underwear as they swooped up ramps and crashed on asphalt, as soon as they were told that the House had voted for the law, they knew what to do. One of them tugged his jeans down to a gravity-defying level. Displaying his backside, clad in blue and white checked boxers, he scooted his board along the ground, gained speed and sailed away.

REVIEW 5.4

1 Read the article 'A brief matter of style'. Outline the reasons why the Virginian government was unsuccessful in outlawing the display of underpants.

2 Discuss whether a police officer in New South Wales could arrest you for indecency or offensive conduct under the *The Summary Offence Act 1998* (NSW). (This act outlaws offensive, indecent or antisocial behaviour.)

Figure 5.7 Sporting events frequently feature a police presence to keep crowds under control.

Discretionary powers

Almost all individuals around the world celebrate various social, cultural and sporting events. Celebrations such as birthdays, New Year, and sporting victories from World Cup Soccer, and our four football codes are a few examples. Many individuals would believe they have a right to celebrate such special events, but where are you allowed to hold a celebration, for how long and at what noise level?

It is widely believed that celebrations can be as noisy or loud as the participants wish before midnight, but what if you are living near a celebration and need to sleep?

Individuals have a right to complain about a celebration at any hour of the day if they believe that the noise level is too high. Police officers can be called to a party at any time and may decide to close down a celebration if they believe it to be invading the rights of other individuals. The decision by a police officer to allow a party to continue or close is known as **police discretion** and means that it is up to the officer on duty to consider the circumstances such as time of day, noise level and the nature of complaint by neighbours.

To use an example from overseas, China is reported to outlaw the religious practice known as Falun Gung as it believes this form of worship attempts to destabilise the government. Mr Chen, a Chinese diplomat in Australia, sought **political asylum** in June 2005. He claimed he was asked by the Chinese Government to spy on Chinese citizens in Australia who were involved with Falun Gung. He did not agree with the instructions he was given and feared for his safety if he was to return to China. Mr Chen asked the Australian Government for political asylum, which was eventually granted. It is clear from this the citizens of China do not have the same statutory rights as Australians have under Section 116 of our Constitution. There have been no recorded cases in Australia of citizens being threatened or fearing for their personal safety for refusing a government request.

In addition, since the 1980s the Chinese Government has attempted to restrict the number of children that parents can have. This concern arose out of the problem of rapid population growth. As a result of this policy, many parents are 'policed' once they have one child and encouraged not to have a second child. Some critics of the Chinese Government would label the policies discussed above as totalitarian. This is a situation in which individuals have no rights whatsoever, and the state has complete and total control of its citizens. It is a situation often involving military dictatorships and the absence of a separate judiciary.

Conversely, anarchy is a situation of lawlessness, with no state control whatsoever. It would be a situation of 'every person for themselves' and the elderly, weak and sick would not be protected by any form of police or army. Anarchy is said to exist in times of war and often involves horrific crimes against humanity as the offenders need not fear being caught for their actions.

police discretion the ability of police to make a decision about a situation as they see fit; for example, they do not have to follow a law in some situations

political asylum seeking refuge or shelter in a country by asking the state to protect you from another state; it usually means not being transported back to the country of origin

---

LEGAL INFO

The right to religious freedom is given to all citizens under the Australian Constitution.

Section 116   Right to religious freedom
The Federal Government is not able to make laws that restrict a citizen of Australia on the basis of their religious belief. For example, they would not be able to make a law that disallowed Buddhists from owning property.

REVIEW 5.5

Consider the following scenarios and discuss in small groups. Construct a table headed 'for' and 'against' and make notes on either side for each scenario.

1   An 18-year-old student wishes to drink alcohol on school grounds after a sporting victory. Should he/she be allowed to?

2   A female student wishes to wear her traditional religious clothing at a school that has a clear uniform policy. Should she be able to? Why or why not?

3   A 45-year-old man wishes to paint 'No War' on the Sydney Opera House to send his message to the federal government.

4   The Australian Government wishes to issue an Identification card and number to every citizen.

5   A police officer wishes to shut down your 18th birthday party at 9pm.

6   A school refuses to accept you as a student because you are Muslim.

MULTIPLE-CHOICE QUESTIONS

1 Complete the following definition of 'power': Power is the ability to control and influence others and is
   a always legal
   b never illegal
   c legal and illegal
   d illegal

2 Complete the following definition of 'authority': Authority is the ability to control and influence others and is
   a always legal
   b never legal
   c legal and illegal
   d government power

3 Which of the following fits the description of 'an independent government with control over a population'?
   a the state of NSW
   b state sovereignty
   c the United Nations
   d a local council

4 Which of the following is an example of political power?
   a the power of police to breath test a driver
   b sending troops to a war
   c a judge making a court ruling
   d a teacher keeping a student back at lunch break

5 What is legal power?
   a common and statutory authority to control and influence individuals
   b common but not statutory authority to control and influence individuals
   c statutory authority only to control and influence individuals
   d none of the above

CHAPTER SUMMARY TASKS

1 What do you understand by the term 'power'?
2 Explain the difference between power and authority.

3 What is the difference between political and economic power?
4 Why might the New South Wales Government want Coca-Cola to open a new factory in western Sydney and not in Victoria?
5 What type of power is involved in the scenario at question 4?
6 What is the difference between statutory and common law authority?
7 Identify how conflicts arise between individuals and the state.
8 List two statutory rights Australians have and where can you find a copy of these.
9 Describe the power police have to shut down a celebration and how this can be done.
10 Outline the difference between anarchy and totalitarianism.

CHAPTER SUMMARY

- Power can be wielded both legally and illegally, however authority is always legal. Consider the power of a police officer to conduct a random breath test as opposed to a criminal using a weapon to obtain money or property. Both wield power in legal and illegal ways.
- Authority can be classified into several categories. Authority allows individuals and states to always act within the law and with legal power.
- In democratic societies, the rights of the state are balanced with the rights of individuals to allow the protection of a state's resources and welfare without affecting the freedoms of individuals to express their opinions and choices.
- In a totalitarian state, the rights of the state are always placed above the rights of individuals.
- Anarchy is when individual rights are placed over all other rights, with no obedience to the state.

CHAPTER 6

Legal controls on state power

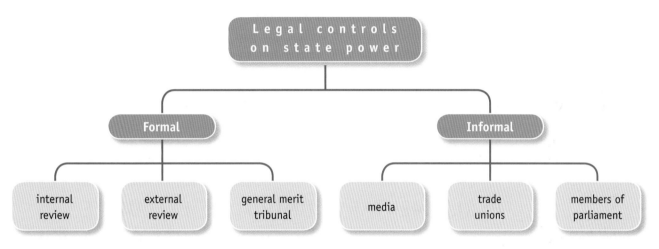

Figure 6.1 There are many ways of influencing state power, formally and informally.

In this chapter you will learn about how the state is controlled by laws and how individuals may challenge governments in Australia through a variety of means.

Legal controls on state power refers to the fact that Australian governments at all levels may not act in any way they wish and must abide by laws, rules and guidelines. When a government begins to act without following such laws, a dictatorship often follows and citizens' rights are often overlooked.

OFFICIAL DUTIES AND DISCRETIONARY POWERS

An official duty may be granted by statute law and means that individuals are compelled by law to behave in a certain way in various situations. For example, in NSW, motorists have an official duty to stay at the scene of an accident if they are involved. In other words, motorists *must* not leave the scene of an accident until instructed by police.

Powers may also be discretionary, in that individuals *may* behave in a certain way, depending on the situation. In a court of law, judges have discretionary power to determine punishment for guilty offenders which may differ from case to case. In the 1990s, under mandatory sentencing laws in the Northern Territory, judges were compelled by statute law to send offenders to gaol after committing three criminal offences. This led an offender to being sentenced to one year in gaol for stealing cordial and biscuits valued at $27.

Laws are enforced and upheld in three main ways:

1 By statute—that is, the passing of bills that outlaw, for example, drink-driving.
2 By decisions of the courts imposing sanctions for breaking laws. If, for example, a judge suspends a person's driver's license for 6 months, then that becomes a law that person must obey.
3 By the executive arm of the government as it has been elected to govern by the people. For example, the decision to send Australian troops to Iraq was made by the executive.

The executive arm of the federal government is controlled by administrative law. This law can be divided into two main areas: administrative duty and administrative discretion.

Administrative duty is when a minister is required by law to carry out an action. The word 'shall' is used in this instance and means 'must'. Administrative discretion, for example police discretion in applying the law in Chapter 5, means a minister or department 'may' carry out an action or make a decision

If a government wishes to change any part of our Constitution, it must call for a national referendum. The 1999 referendum to ask the Australian people whether they wished the nation to become a republic is an example. The Australian Constitution might have changed if enough people voted for a republic, but, in 2006, Australia was still a constitutional monarchy.

There are many controls placed on the Australian Government. The federal government, for example, is unable to extend the time it stays in power and must call an election every three years.

PARLIAMENTARY CONTROL OF EXECUTIVE

Political and legal power is separated into three distinct categories at both federal and state level. These three categories of areas of power are known as the executive, the legislature and the judiciary. In federal government, the executive comprises the Prime Minister and ministers of various departments.

Ministerial responsibility

Ministerial portfolios or responsibilities are granted by the Prime Minister, usually after a federal election. Ministers are responsible for various arms of government, as the Prime Minister cannot possibly control all aspects. The Prime Minister actually delegates responsibility to ministers for trade, finance, immigration, workplace relations and many other areas.

There have been many instances of controversy reported by the media where ministers have been called into question. In 2002, an Australian woman of Filipino descent was wrongly or mistakenly deported to the Philippines. This mistake was not discovered until 2005. Amanda Vanstone, the Immigration Minister, was not personally responsible for this incident because she was not the Minister for this portfolio at the time. However, her department, for which she had ministerial responsibility, was heavily criticised for the mistake. Some

Figure 6.2 Minister for Immigration Amanda Vanstone.

critics argued Minister Vanstone should resign because she had not competently carried out her duties as Minister. However, she did not resign. In a separate incident, the wrongful detention for 9 months of an Australian citizen, Cornelia Rau, caused some sections of the Australian public and media to call for the Minister to resign. It was argued that the Minister must take responsibility for the mistakes of her department. Such examples illustrate how ministers can come under close scrutiny in their daily responsibilities.

Parliamentary committees

Parliamentary committees can be set up where the parliament believes there may be a need for an issue to be investigated. Some examples include standing, select and joint committees, and the members of the committee are assigned a specific task to investigate and then report back to parliament.

These committees do not have to sit in Parliament House. Rather, they may travel the country to discuss issues with members of the public and seek expert advice or opinion from a range of citizens. One current example is the Standing Committee on Aboriginal and Torres Strait Islander Affairs.

Figure 6.3 Members of the Indigenous community together with members of the Standing Committee on Aboriginal and Torres Strait Islander Affairs.

RESEARCH 6.1

Go to the website http://www.aph.gov.au/house/committee/atsia/reports.htm and answer the following questions.

1 Outline the role of the Standing Committee on Aboriginal and Torres Strait Islander affairs.

2 Go to http://www.aph.gov.au/house/committee/atsia/indigenousemployment/index.htm and explain the reasons for Minister Vanstone's request for research into Indigenous employment.

3 Explain why parliament should have control over committees such as this.

INDIVIDUALS' RIGHTS TO ACCESS INFORMATION: COMMON LAW AND STATUTORY RIGHTS

What if you applied for a passport or a driver's licence and you were refused? What rights do you have to challenge the decision of a government department or delegated authority? Individuals in most circumstances have the right to challenge such decisions. This right is known as a **statutory right,** because legislation exists that allows individuals to access information about themselves.

statutory right
a right that has been enshrined in statute law

Consider the family who believe the Immigration Department is responsible for the death of their mother, Aziza Agha (see media clip below). They are challenging the decision of the Immigration Department to find out why the opinion of her local doctor was not sufficient to extend her visa.

The *Administrative Appeals Tribunals Act 1975* (Cwlth) and the *Administrative Decisions (Judicial Review) Act 1977* (Cwlth) require the federal government to release information about why a decision was made. Despite these laws, individuals still had to make the effort to bring such matters to tribunal and it was very expensive.

Under additional legislation, the *Freedom of Information Act 1982* (Cwlth) and the *Freedom of Information Act 1989* (NSW) allow individuals to pay a small fee and receive from a department information that related to a decision about themselves or deceased relatives.

MEDIA CLIP

FAMILY CONSIDERS LEGAL ACTION AGAINST IMMIGRATION DEPT

ABC News Online, 24 August 2005

Relatives of a Syrian woman are considering legal action against the Immigration Department after her death.

Aziza Agha, 79, died two days after she was forced to travel to central Melbourne for a consultation with a departmental doctor earlier this month.

Ms Agha flew to Australia from Lebanon in September last year, with a six-month visitor visa.

She applied to the Department of Immigration for a six-month extension on medical grounds, but the request was refused.

Ms Agha's GP Dr Chris Towie says he had warned Immigration officials she was too sick to travel and should remain in her home.

Dr Towie says he blames the Department of Immigration for her death.

Relative Massouna Najjarine says visa complications took a toll on Ms Agha's health.

"You could see that she was deteriorating. She became very weak and frail."

The Immigration Department's John Williams says the doctor should have given clear instructions.

"The advice to us was that she was fit to travel."

Dr Choong-Siew Yong, from the Australian Medical Association, says he is concerned the treating GP's advice was not considered sufficient.

"We'd support the Immigration Department taking GPs' advice seriously, particularly as the GP is the best placed person to know their patient's overall condition," he said.

"They're more likely to have seen their patient over several times, and got to know their medical history quite well. That's got to count for something when you're trying to make an assessment of someone's medical condition."

The case has been referred to the Victorian coroner.

REVIEW 6.1

1 Read media clip 6.1. Under what legislation could the family challenge the Department of Immigration?
2 Do you think there are adequate controls on state power in Australia? Give reasons for your response.

INFORMAL MEANS OF CHALLENGING STATE POWER

In addition to administrative appeal and review, citizens are also able to challenge government decisions through a number of other channels.

The media

By writing a letter, sending an email or calling television and radio stations, citizens are able to inform the media of a decision they think is unfair, unjust or harsh. There have been many instances in which major networks have taken on a story and caused the government to overturn a decision.

For example, it could be argued that children were released from migrant detention centres in August 2005 as a result of media pressure. If individuals and pressure groups constantly appear on television and radio, the government may choose to listen and reverse a policy decision. In this case, the Department of Immigration explained that it had 'softened' its stance on the detention of immigrants.

Another form of media, the Internet, provides a range of information, conferences and chat rooms where people can interact and discuss various cases or situations where public officers have allegedly acted unjustly. One such site entitled 'Whistleblowers Australia' states:

'The goal of Whistleblowers Australia (WBA) is to help promote a society in which it is possible to speak out without reprisal about corruption, dangers to the public and other vital social issues, and to help those who speak out in this way to help themselves.'

Members of parliament

Members of parliament (MPs) are those elected by voters at a state and federal level. These people are chosen to represent a particular area or electorate. For example, the Prime Minister John Howard holds the federal seat of Bennelong, in Sydney.

All citizens within an electorate are able to contact the office of their representative and speak to their MP about an issue that may trouble them. The MP may take this issue back to Parliament House in Canberra and discuss it with other MPs or the party that is in power.

For example, some electorates or regions are significantly more affected by certain issues than others. Consider the case of the Pacific Highway between Sydney and Brisbane being widened. Residents of towns along this highway could be directly affected, however this issue would clearly be irrelevant to residents of Western Australia. An MP in an affected area may be able to convince his or her party to reconsider an executive or Cabinet decision.

Trade unions

Groups of people in various industries unite to form trade unions to protect their rights and conditions of employment. You can often see various unions leading protests against a whole range of issues, such as workplace safety and changes to wages and conditions.

Figure 6.4 Heritage sites such as The Rocks have been saved by the protests of unions and other concerned citizens.

In the early 1970s, one union, the Builders' Labourers Federation, banned workers from worksites so that various sites of heritage value in Sydney were not demolished. These 'green bans' were highly successful, as a small park in Hunters Hill and terrace houses in Victoria Street, Potts Point, still exist today. The historic area of Sydney known as 'The Rocks' was also saved and protected by the actions of unions placing bans on work at the proposed demolition sites.

Interest groups, including non-government organisations

Groups of people can also form where they share a goal of challenging a state decision. Groups such as Greenpeace, the World Wildlife Fund and Oxfam are examples of non-government organisations (NGOs). Citizens can choose to donate money to these organisations or join the organisation and actively engage in protest or challenging state power.

For example, Greenpeace was actively involved in the protest and prevention of Japanese whaling in 2006. By manoeuvring their boats to positions that were directly in line with the whaling boat harpoons, Greenpeace members prevented the whale hunters from firing at whales.

Figure 6.5 The work of Greenpeace can challenge government decisions.

REVIEW 6.2

1 How would you go about challenging the state if they refused to award you the Higher School Certificate? What laws and means would you utilise to investigate why you did not receive your HSC?
2 Which of the informal means of challenging state power would be the most effective and why?
3 Evaluate the effectiveness of informal means of challenging state power.

FORMAL MEANS OF CHALLENGING POWER

As well as informal means of questioning state power, challenges can also be made on a formal or legal basis. These are listed below.

Internal reviews

In New South Wales, government departments can review their own decisions, procedures or behaviour. Such reviews are very cost effective, but can be ineffective if the people conducting the review have been involved with a decision that is not appropriate or incorrect.

External reviews

Reviews of government activities can also be undertaken externally. Individuals can utilise a range of external measures. As mentioned earlier in this chapter, the Department of Immigration and Multicultural Affairs was involved in two serious incidents that brought widespread public scrutiny and ridicule. A former Federal Police officer, Mick Palmer, was appointed by the federal government to conduct an external review into the causes of the mistaken deportation of Vivian Solon and the wrongful detention of Cornelia Rau.

General merit review tribunals

Decisions made by government departments may be reviewed by the Administrative Decisions Tribunal. The most frequent applications for review heard by the General Division of the Administrative Decisions Tribunal are freedom of information, privacy, and licensing matters relating to firearms, the security industry, passenger transport and the building industry. Most of the applications are made under the following legislation:
- *Fair Trading Act 1987*
- *Firearms Act 1996*
- *Fisheries Management Act 1994*
- *Freedom of Information Act 1989*
- *Home Building Act 1989*
- *Passenger Transport Act 1990*

Privacy bodies

All of us as individuals have a right to privacy and we often 'share' secrets with our friends and family. Most would agree that that it is not a pleasant feeling to know that somebody who is not close to you has access to information about you, whatever that may be. In a broader sense, laws have been created at both state and federal level to protect information about you being released to companies, government departments or other citizens.

The *Privacy Act 1988* (Cwlth) gives you the right to make a complaint if you think personal information, including health information about you, has been mishandled by a Commonwealth government agency or a private sector organisation.

For example, if you have a spent conviction (that is, you have served time in gaol), in most instances this is private information and should not be given to public or private bodies. Under the *Crimes Act 1914* (Cwlth), you are protected from discrimination on the basis of a spent conviction. In NSW, citizens are protected under the *Privacy and Personal Information Protection Act*. There are legal responsibilities that government departments must carry out in the collection and storage of personal information of individuals. If a person feels that their privacy has been breached (for example, a misuse of personal information), they may either request an internal review, or complain to Privacy NSW.

The courts

Law courts at both state and federal level have the power to review administrative decisions and actions in much the same way as the High Court is able to review the decisions of a constitutional nature made by lower courts. The term 'judicial review' is used to describe a process whereby one court can review the decisions made by a government department only on the basis of legality. What is legal can vary, depending on the circumstances of each case, but, as general rule, decisions are not lawful if they do not demonstrate the following:

Natural justice

You will study this concept in greater detail in the HSC course. In this context, natural justice refers to:

- a decision-making body ensuring that a person is given an opportunity to be heard. It is quite possible that a department may make a decision without hearing the person's circumstances.
- the decision being unbiased. This could mean that the department making the decision did not have a conflict of interest.

Limited rights of access

A person who wished a judicial review must have standing, that is, they must be directly involved in the case and not be an interested citizen wanting a review purely out of personal curiosity. In terms of resource efficiency, there would be huge costs associated with judicial reviews if they were to be ordered by any interested persons in society.

Court-based remedies

Once a judicial review has been undertaken, courts are able to offer the following remedies:

PROHIBITION

This means that a court is able to stop or prohibit a decision from going ahead, whereas **certiorari** allows a decision to be reversed after it has taken effect.

INJUNCTIONS

Injunctions can also be used and are often heard about in the media. One high-profile injunction that was widely publicised related to the release of the Mark Latham diaries in September 2005. 'Enough Rope' (ABC television) attempted to screen an interview with Mr Latham earlier than it had advertised. News Ltd, which also had an agreement with Mr Latham, requested an injunction, which was granted.

certiorari the issuing of a writ by a superior court requesting the record of a case heard in a lower court for the purpose of reviewing that case

The Office of the Ombudsman

In 1809, the Swedish Parliament created a new official known as the 'Justitie-Ombudsman'. This loosely translates as 'citizens' defender' or 'representative of the people'. The office of the ombudsman was created by statute in 1974 in New South Wales, and federally in 1977.

The office acts as a formal external control, with legal power to investigate complaints made by citizens. However, the current ombudsman in New South Wales, Mr Bruce Barbour, does not have the power to enforce any punishment or fine on a government department. He can, however, make recommendations to the department in question or to the New South Wales Parliament. Some of the main areas of complaint received by the office deal with:

- delivery of community services
- child abuse and neglect
- the operation of the police force.

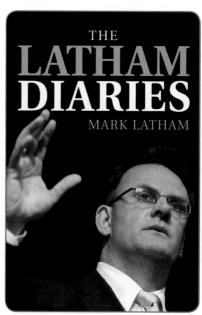

Figure 6.6 Injunctions to stop the publication of stories or interviews are often placed on the media.

Any citizen can make a complaint to the ombudsman, but it must be in writing. All complaints are taken seriously, but are only followed through if a prima facie case exists, that is, if the complaint would raise concern 'on first view'. Such concern could only exist if there were witnesses to an event or if a citizen had very strong and irrefutable evidence.

Commissions of inquiry

Commissions of inquiry are set up to investigate serious matters at both state and federal level. The most important type of inquiry is known as a royal commission. In the past, such inquiries have investigated issues such as Aboriginal deaths in custody 1987 (Cwlth) and the inquiry of the NSW police service which began in 1995 (NSW).

Such inquiries have been criticised for their expense, and questions could be raised about their resource efficiency, especially because, like many other forms of challenging state power, commissions of inquiry do not have the power to prosecute offenders. The government may decide to act on recommendations (a number of police officers were sent to gaol as a result of the NSW royal commission). However, there are still widespread problems with Aboriginal and Torres Strait Islanders' relations with police forces around Australia, and it could be argued that this commission failed in its goal to reduce deaths in custody.

Independent Commission Against Corruption

While the Ombudsman has the power to investigate complaints made by the public, the Independent Commission Against Corruption (ICAC) has greater power. The *ICAC Act 1988* (NSW) created the ICAC as an independent statutory body to investigate alleged corruption. ICAC attempts to protect the interests of the public, prevent breaches of public trust, and influence the behaviour of public officials so that the public is free from corruption.

Some examples of corrupt behaviour would include bribery, fraud or theft and it does not have to be carried out by a public official. ICAC has the power to investigate the activities of private citizens if such behaviour affects the proper administration of public offices.

ICAC has the authority to ask the police service to assist in its investigations, and is therefore able to search for and seize evidence where it sees fit. It does not have the power to prosecute offenders, but can state that corrupt behaviour has occurred, who committed it, and what further action should be taken.

At the time of writing, ICAC was investigating a claim that some local court officers were offering to help defendants with information about their cases in exchange for money. The operation known as 'Operation Hunter' illustrates how private citizens and public officials can engage in behaviour that would clearly corrupt the judicial process and therefore not deliver a just outcome.

If a citizen feels that they have been wrongfully accused of corruption, they may seek judicial review in the New South Wales Supreme Court.

REVIEW 6.3

1 Outline the importance of the role of the ombudsman.
2 Predict what may happen within some governments if the ombudsman was abolished.
3 What do you understand by the term 'natural justice'? Why should citizens be entitled to it?

MULTIPLE-CHOICE QUESTIONS

1 What are statutory rights?
   a rights granted by the courts
   b rights granted by the media
   c rights granted by parliament
   d rights granted by ministers
2 What does freedom of information allow individuals to access?
   a information about themselves.
   b information about themselves or a deceased relative
   c information about government departments
   d information about friends or relatives
3 Which of these statements about the executive arm of government is true?
   a it is controlled by administrative duty and discretion
   b it is controlled by administrative law
   c both A and B are true
   d it is chosen by democratic vote
4 Which of these statements about the *Administrative Appeals Tribunals Act 1975 (Cwlth)* is true?
   a it allows all decisions to be appealed
   b it requires the NSW Government to appeal federal decisions
   c both A and B are true
   d it requires the federal government to release information about why a decision was made
5 Which of these statements about the media is true?
   a it is an informal means of challenging state power
   b it is both a formal and informal means of challenging state power
   c it is able to broadcast all administrative decisions
   d none of the above

CHAPTER SUMMARY TASKS

1 Identify the difference between administrative duties and administrative discretion.
2 Describe what you understand by the term 'ministerial responsibility'.
3 List three ways in which law is upheld in Australia.
4 Explain the role that trade unions can play in challenging state power.
5 Outline one example of internal and external review of state power.
6 Explain the difference between internal and external review.
7 Analyse when you think an external review is more appropriate than internal review.
8 Evaluate the effectiveness of formal and informal means of challenging state power.
9 Discuss the problems individuals may have in accessing the legal system.

CHAPTER SUMMARY

• There is a range of legal controls on state power, and states are accountable to its citizens and other bodies such as the ombudsman.
• There are formal and informal means of challenging state power. These are available to citizens depending on the circumstances surrounding the case or scenario.
• Trade unions, the media and non-government organisations are examples of informal means of challenging state power.
• Internal reviews, privacy bodies, courts and legislation are examples of formal challenges to state power.
• Laws such as the *Administrative Appeals Tribunal Act* and the *Freedom of Information Act* require Australian governments to release information about citizens and relevant decisions. This means citizens have common-law and statutory rights.

CHAPTER 7

Duties

Individuals and states are obliged to carry out a range of duties to maintain order and control. As individuals we have duties at home, at school and in the local community. States have duties at local, national and international level and if these duties are ignored, serious consequences may eventuate.

From disposing of your garbage responsibly to international duties such as honouring the Geneva Convention, this chapter will guide you through a range of duties, illustrated with case studies and legislative obligations.

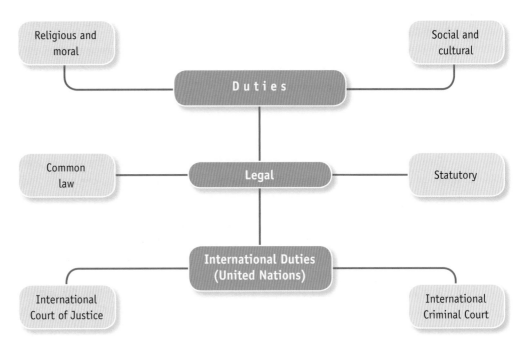

Figure 7.1 Types of duties.

THE DIFFERENT MEANINGS OF DUTIES

A **duty** is any action that a group or individual is obliged to undertake.

Having a driver's licence does not give you the right to drive over the speed limit or run red lights. The Roads and Traffic Authority would say that you have a right to apply for a licence and, if successful, you have the responsibility or duty to drive according to the laws that have been set down.

As members of society it could be said that we enter into a social contract or agreement. The agreement we have is that we carry out various duties expected of us, the most important of which is to obey the laws set down by the state. We are repaid by the state in the form of protection by police and defence forces.

One of the most important laws in this case is the law of paying taxes because, without tax revenue, the state would not be able to provide police, defence or judicial services. Consider also services offered by the government of Australia such as welfare for people who are out of work or people with disabilities.

duty work that someone is obliged to perform for moral or legal reasons

Legal duties

Legal duties are mandated by laws made by parliament (statute law duties) or by the courts (common law duties).

Most workers who earn an income are required by law to pay tax to their state. This is an example of a statute duty. Common law duties are those imposed by decisions of the courts.

Figure 7.2 A right to drive, but a duty to obey the road laws.

Common law duties

A famous case that set a precedent for common law duties is the *Donaghue v. Stevenson* case of 1932 in Scotland. This case concerned a woman, Mrs Donaghue, who bought a bottle of ginger beer and became sick soon after drinking it. It was found that there was a snail inside the bottle and she believed this caused her sickness. Since she bought the bottle from a shop that did not make the ginger beer, there was no case against that shop; rather the manufacturer of the ginger beer was thought to be at fault. Lord Atkin, a Scottish judge, ruled that the manufacturer, Stevenson, had a duty to protect their customers by making a drink which would not make you sick.

The concept of a duty of care emerged whereby people can take cases to court if:

• there is duty of care between two parties
• there is a breach of that duty
• there is damage to one of the parties.

In all schools in New South Wales today, such a duty of care exists between teachers and pupils and there have been legal cases in which students and parents have challenged the lack of care taken by schools or individual teachers.

The following is an extract from a guide for teachers in New South Wales.

'It is possible for you to become involved in court proceedings in a claim for damages if a parent/guardian claims that:
- a duty of care existed
- there was a breach by you of that duty
- injury to a pupil resulted from that breach.'

It is clear from the extract that these duties of teachers originated from Lord Atkins' judgment in 1932. One of the most common situations where teachers may breach duties of care is in their daily supervision or lack of supervision of students, particularly during break times.

Statutory duties

These are duties set out by parliament that govern relationships between people in certain instances. Doctors, lawyers, teachers and company directors all have statutory duties towards the people they deal with. For example, under the *Corporations Act 1996* (Cwlth) a company director has the following duties:
- to act honestly
- to not use information improperly.

insider trading using information that is not available to the public for personal financial gain

A director of a company that is listed on the stock exchange has a statutory duty under corporations law to disclose information that is relevant to stockholders. An accident in a mine, a factory fire or the resignation of key employees would be information that could affect overall company performance. In 2005, there were a number examples of company directors who were prosecuted under corporations law for using information improperly. The late Rene Rivkin was found guilty of **insider trading**, using information he was given about Qantas airlines.

Figure 7.3 QANTAS was going to buy Impulse airlines. Who knew about this before the public?

Social and cultural duties

Social and cultural duties are not enforceable by common or statute law, but are expected of all citizens. It is interesting to note how many of the duties listed below are beginning to change to statute duties such as:

- the duty to save water—in current circumstances you can be fined for washing your car with a hose in NSW
- the duty to stand up on a bus to give your seat to an elderly person
- the duty to keep the environment clean—there are fines for littering nowadays
- the duty to separate your waste into recyclable and garbage containers.

Moral duties

If you found a wallet at school or in your street, would you automatically hand it in to a teacher or the police?

Moral duties are not enforceable by law, but the majority of citizens would agree that there are various moral codes that we should uphold, like the example above. The duty not to commit **adultery** or to remain **monogamous** in a relationship is another moral duty.

Other examples of moral duties include:

- telling the truth at all times
- treating others as we would want to be treated.

Religious duties

Religious duties are based on religious beliefs and rules and are usually not enforceable by law. The exception is that in some countries, such as Saudi Arabia, religious law and statute law are the same. In some ways in Australia, religious law and statute do merge, as most religions denounce stealing, assault and, of course, murder.

adultery extramarital sex that interferes with marriage relations

monogamous having only one partner (refers to relationships)

Ethical duties

One of the most common ethical dilemmas for individuals is that of truth versus loyalty.

Consider a scenario where you know that a friend or relative has broken the law. Do you report them to the police, or do you decide to be loyal to your friend and say nothing? Which would you choose? Ethical duties, therefore, are those where our personal beliefs can influence our decision to carry out a duty. Similar to moral duties, they are not enforceable and are ultimately decided by individuals in different circumstances.

Figure 7.4 In some countries, religious law and statute law are the same.

perpetrator the person who committed or is responsible for something criminally or morally wrong

THE INTERRELATIONSHIP OF LEGAL AND OTHER DUTIES

As you have been reading through the chapter, you should have noticed that many of the duties discussed could be categorised in a number of different groups. Often legal duties are also found within other categories. For example, the decision to take another's life (excluding war) clearly is against legal, religious, moral and social duties. In some situations, moral and religious duties often evolve to legal duties.

Consider the fines imposed on water wasters, those who pollute the environment and the act of theft. All of these examples can be classified into various 'duty' categories.

There are also situations where a citizen's desire to uphold a particular duty can conflict with their legal obligation to uphold another. Whilst legal duties can be enforced if not upheld, other categories of duties may not carry the same punishment for breaches. It has been reported in some countries that women have been beaten or killed for committing adultery under the belief that it brings shame to the family. In this tragic situation, often the **perpetrator** is not prosecuted for murder. In Australia, strikes in the workplace have been made illegal if there is not sufficient reason to stop work. However, some workers may see it as their duty to stop work in support of a colleague.

REVIEW 7.1

1 List five to ten duties that you are required to perform at home or at school.
2 Classify each duty under the headings of 'legal', 'social', 'cultural', 'religious', 'moral' and 'ethical'.
3 Describe any interrelationships between these duties. Are there similarities and differences?
4 Explain what duties you may have to carry out if you discover a person who is unconscious. What legal issues may arise from this situation?

MEANINGS OF INTERNATIONAL DUTIES AND THEIR EVOLVING NATURE

Figure 7.5 The atomic bombing of Hiroshima in 1945: one of the events leading to the establishment of the UN.

Just as individuals have rights and responsibilities, so too do nation states. The United Nations (UN) was formed in 1948 after the horrific events of World War II, and many international duties are based around the resolutions, charters and conventions that have been written since the establishment of the UN. A significant number of international duties that Australia and other nations adhere to are based on customary law, treaties, conventions, agreements and decisions of international tribunals such as the International Criminal Court.

Customary international law refers to traditional relationships that nations have with each other. It entails respecting the legal customs and traditional practices between nations over a long period of time. It is not necessary for states to sign treaties with each other for customary international law to apply.

Codification of international customary law

An example of customary law would be the humane treatment of prisoners of war, whereby countries agreed to feed and provide shelter for prisoners if captured or if they surrender. This particular custom has since been codified into the Geneva Convention. The Geneva Convention consists of four treaties written in Geneva, Switzerland, and deals with the duties of nations to deal with the wounded, sick, captured and/or the civilian members of army or militia. You can read more about the Geneva Convention at: http://en.wikipedia.org/wiki/Geneva_Conventions

In 2005, Iraqi prisoners in Abu Ghraib prison were reportedly treated contrary to the Geneva Convention. Photographs were published revealing degrading and inhumane treatment of Iraqis at the hands of several United States soldiers. It could be argued clearly in this particular case that international duties and conventions were not upheld. A number of United States soldiers were reprimanded by military courts in the United States, raising the question about whether soldiers who take orders from their superiors are to be held responsible for their actions. This particular question has been highly controversial throughout history, particularly throughout World War II and with regard to the treatment of Jews in Nazi concentration camps. It was this type of behaviour that provided the catalyst for the formation of the United Nations in 1948 and a formalisation of international laws, customs, rights and duties.

International treaties

A treaty is a signed agreement between two (bilateral) or more (multilateral) nations about any particular issue or code of conduct. Australia has signed many treaties, both bilateral and multilateral, on issues such as defence, whaling, trade, Antarctica, the environment and the extradition of criminals. Therefore, Australia has legal duties to act according to these treaties.

One long-standing treaty of which Australia is a signatory is the multilateral treaty known as ANZUS, which involves Australia, New Zealand and the United States. Briefly, this treaty involves security and defence arrangements whereby each country agrees

Figure 7.6 The ANZUS Council meet for discussions with US Secretary of State, Dean Rusk, 1962.

to act together to achieve each other's aims. Australia, for example, has allowed the United States to set up the Pine Gap surveillance facility in the Northern Territory. This facility allows the United States to monitor the military movements by the Soviet Union during the Cold War of the 1950s to the 1980s. In the twenty-first century, the facility has been used to assist with NASA space-shuttle flights.

International tribunals such as the International Court of Justice (ICJ) and the International Criminal Court (ICC) can make decisions and judgments that would become law about a range of state or individual behaviour. Just as common law is made in courts, so too is international law, and there have been numerous highly publicised examples of individuals such as Slobodan Milosevic and Saddam Hussein who have been faced with international law violations. These involve the action known as 'genocide', the systematic murder of civilians during times of war and peace.

RESTRICTIONS ON THE USE OF FORCE AS AN INSTRUMENT OF NATIONAL POLICY IN INTERNATIONAL RELATIONS

judicial process allowing independent courts and judges to decide disputes

conciliation a process of solving disputes verbally, or through meetings and negotiations

One United Nations charter allows the use of force by a state in the following two circumstances:
- when the Security Council agrees that force is necessary under Chapter 7 of the UN Charter
- when self-defence is required because of an attack or an imminent attack.

In all other circumstances, the UN maintains that states should settle their differences or disputes by peaceful means. This could involve mediation, **judicial process**, **conciliation** or any other form of non-violent negotiation. States should also respect the sovereignty and territory of another. However, long-standing conflicts between, for example, Israel and Palestine or India and Pakistan demonstrate that settling disputes through peaceful means is more easily said than done.

Figure 7.7 Is a pre-emptive strike legal in international law?

The United Nations has, in the past, allowed one state to attack another (or defend itself) on the basis of self-defence. Such examples include Korea in 1950, Kuwait in 1991 and Kosovo in 1999. However, in these cases it was clear that an aggressor had already invaded another state. More recently, 'pre-emptive self-defence' is the term used by the Unites States Government and the 'coalition of the willing' (of which Australia was a part). The US argued that Iraq possessed weapons of mass destruction and an intention to harm the US, despite the lack of concrete evidence. Therefore, in March 2003, the United States invaded Baghdad, despite the UN refusing a pre-emptive attack.

Although the United Nations urges states to avoid armed conflict and passes resolutions to stop attacks, some states have chosen to ignore these resolutions, claiming that, in an age of international terrorism, pre-emptive strikes are justified.

> ## RESEARCH 7.2
>
> Evaluate the effectiveness of the United Nations in restricting the use of force by states to solve their differences. You could refer to Resolution 678 and 1441 to assist with your answer.

Obligation of governments to live together in peace

The following is an extract from the United Nations website, outlining the missions and goals of the UN:

'WE THE PEOPLES OF THE UNITED NATIONS DETERMINED

- to save succeeding generations from the scourge of war, which twice in our lifetime has brought untold sorrow to mankind, and
- to reaffirm faith in fundamental human rights, in the dignity and worth of the human person, in the equal rights of men and women and of nations large and small.'

In many respects, nations have international duties to fulfil as set out in the UN preamble. In order to achieve what has been set out above, states are obliged to carry out the following:

- to practise tolerance and live together in peace with one another as good neighbours
- to unite their strength to maintain international peace and security
- to ensure, by the acceptance of principles and the institution of methods, that armed force shall not be used, save in the common interest.

CASE SPACE

Australia's involvement in East Timor

East Timor (now known as Timor-L'Este), one of Australia's nearest neighbours, has experienced significant security problems since it claimed independence in 1975. Indonesia invaded East Timor 9 days after this declaration and, for the next 24 years, included East Timor as part of Indonesia. There was significant bloodshed and loss of life in which 100 000–250 000 deaths were reported.

In August 1999, the United Nations sponsored and supported a referendum which overwhelmingly favoured independence from Indonesia. Australian troops were also sent to help stem the violence and allow the voters to express their wishes without fear of retribution. However, many Indonesians were unhappy with this vote and the violence continues.

Many Australians protested that Australia should have sent troops sooner to end the violence and bloodshed. The other side of the argument held by successive Australian governments was that it was not to interfere with the internal problems of a neighbour.

Figure 7.8 Australian troops working with the people of East Timor.

Obligation of governments to work for the economic and social advancement of all peoples

The United Nations website states as one of its goals:

'To employ international machinery for the promotion of the economic and social advancement of all peoples'

Since the formation of the UN in 1948, a range of functions and various agencies have evolved, including the following:

- World Health Organisation (WHO)
- United Nations Children's Education Fund (UNICEF)
- International Labour Organisation (ILO)

Each of these bodies assumes responsibility for projects and goals of improving health, life chances for children, and the rights of workers throughout the world.

One of the first conventions published by the UN in 1948 was the International Charter of Human Rights. The list of thirty fundamental human rights can be viewed at http://www.un.org/Overview/rights.html.

As you view each of these rights, you may like to consider the question of what the world might be like if every one of these rights was respected, upheld and enforced by all states. The right to life and freedom, for example, would automatically eradicate the use of the death penalty, and see an end to child prostitution and slavery. In other words, global citizens would experience significant improvement in economic and social conditions. However, since the UN has no domestic legal power and very little means of enforcing the various charters, corrupt governments and individuals continue to abuse the weak, powerless and less fortunate. One of the greatest challenges for the UN and member states is to advance the social and economic wellbeing of all.

REVIEW 7.2

1 Discuss with your teacher and class the importance of the United Nations. If the UN is unable to enforce many of its goals and charters, is it worth maintaining?

2 Outline two international duties that the United Nations expects of states. Explain how they may or may not be enforced.

3 Assess the extent to which Australia observes all thirty articles of the 1948 International Charter on Human Rights.

MULTIPLE-CHOICE QUESTIONS

1 What is a duty?
   a a legal right
   b a statutory law
   c an obligation to carry out an action
   d none of the above

2 Which of the following statements is true of legal duties?
   a they are enforceable by statute and common law
   b they are enforced by courts only
   c they are enforced by parliament only
   d they are not enforceable

3 Which of the following statements is true of religious duties?
   a they are enforceable by statute and common law
   b they are enforced by courts only
   c they are enforced by parliament only
   d they are not enforceable

4 What was *Donaghue v. Stevenson*?
   a an example of criminal negligence
   b an example of customary law
   c an establishment of duty of care
   d none of the above

5 Which of these statements is true of the United Nations?
   a it establishes international duties to avoid war
   b it has a range of bodies and agencies
   c it attempts to advance the economic and social well being for all
   d all of the above

CHAPTER SUMMARY TASKS

1 Outline the difference between legal, common law and moral duties.

2 Explain the significance of the 1932 *Donaghue v. Stephenson* case for students and teachers in NSW schools today.

3 Describe some of the punishments individuals may face for not carrying out legal, social and moral duties.

4 Describe a situation in your family or school where a legal duty may conflict with a religious or moral duty.

5 Outline the importance of international customary law.

6 Explain the reasons why some countries may enter into bilateral or multilateral treaties.

7 Evaluate the effectiveness of the United Nations in maintaining peace throughout the globe.

8 Why would the UN allow or not allow the use of force between nations?

9 Outline the role Australia has played in recent years in promoting peace in our region.

10 Do you think Australia has an international duty to participate in the war in Iraq? Why or why not?

CHAPTER SUMMARY

- Individuals and states must carry out duties to maintain order and control at a local and an international level.
- Statute and common law duties are enforceable and often originate from religious, moral and ethical sources.
- States must enshrine international law into domestic legislation in order to uphold the missions and goals of the United Nations. Although the United Nations is able to prosecute some individuals through the International Criminal Court, some countries refuse to recognise this court.

CHAPTER 8

Rights

bill of rights a statement of basic human rights and privileges

In this chapter you will study the meaning of rights from a domestic to international level. Australian citizens have a number of rights protected by law in our Constitution but, unlike the United States and New Zealand, Australia does not have a **bill of rights**.

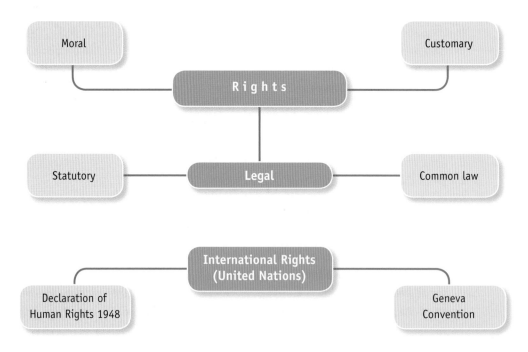

Figure 8.1 Types of rights.

The United Nations has constructed a range of charters, documents, conventions and treaties to protect the rights of all citizens, but with limited success. By the end of this chapter, you should have a better understanding of the powers of the United Nations and how it must rely on states to enshrine international law into domestic legislation in order to uphold human rights.

RIGHTS: DOMESTIC

Legal basis of rights

A right is something that a person is entitled to and cannot be denied. As discussed in chapter 7, a social contract exists in Australia whereby citizens enjoy certain rights, provided they carry out various duties in exchange. For a right to have a legal basis, it must be protected by law or it must be enforceable. In an Australian context, legal rights can be protected by statute or by common law.

In countries such as the United States, Britain and New Zealand, a document known as a bill of rights exists. Such a document sets out specifically what individuals are entitled to from their respective states. For example, in the United States the right to 'keep and bear arms' is quite well known by many people around the world, however, such a right can be misunderstood as, in fact, citizens of the United States may bear arms but may not 'conceal' a weapon such as a gun when in public. In any case, this particular right, referred to as the 'Second Amendment', is an example of a right set out on a separate document.

In Australia, such a document has never existed, as the founders of our Constitution believed that citizens' rights would be protected by decisions of the courts or by various statutes made as the need arose. As mentioned in chapter 5, the Australian Constitution does set out a number of rights, including the right to religious freedom and the right to trial by jury. However, the debate for and against Australia producing a bill of rights continues, particularly in an age of increased terrorist attacks around the world.

One of the most famous cases in Australia demonstrating rights being protected by common law is that of *Mabo v. Queensland* (see also chapter 4, page 57). Eddie Mabo fought through to the High Court of Australia and successfully argued that his people, the Meriam on Murray Island, should hold title or native title of the land. Prior to this case, the Meriam people had no legal rights to access the land. It was possible that the Queensland Government could have sold the land of the island to developers and there would have been no legal basis for the original inhabitants to fight such a sale.

As mentioned, New Zealand, Great Britain and the United States all have a bill of rights. Listed below are some examples of these rights

TABLE 8.1

Examples of rights enshrined in a bill of rights

New Zealand	United States	Great Britain
If arrested, citizens have a right to: • know the charge • consult a lawyer • be brought before a court as soon as possible.	Everyone has a right to bear arms (if a militia is necessary).	Everyone has the right to free speech.

The Australian federal government introduced the *Anti-Terrorism Act 2005* (Cwlth) to protect citizens from terrorism. Although not passed through parliament, one key criteria of the legislation denies citizens the rights of the New Zealand bill of rights, as set out in table 8.1. This particular right is given to ensure that, if arrested, citizens must be told what the charge is and be able to defend themselves in a court of law.

The distinction between moral, customary and legal rights

As discussed in chapter 7, moral duties are not enforceable by law, but most citizens would believe that a strong obligation exists to carry out various duties. Moral rights are similar in that there is no legal backing for an individual to be granted such a right.

The issue of euthanasia is controversial, as some people diagnosed with terminal illnesses may argue they have a right to die and not suffer pain and degradation. However, euthanasia is not a legal right and therefore, according to the law, citizens may not end their own life. In this instance the distinction between a moral and legal right is clear.

Another example involves your right in NSW to engage in sexual activity. Consensual heterosexual and homosexual sex is legal for persons over the age of 16. However, many social, religious and moral leaders in our community would argue that this age is inappropriate. Hence, whilst you have a legal right, a moral right may not exist.

Customary rights originate from customs and traditions however they have no legal basis. An example at home or school would be a group of friends that always sit in the same position at break times. Whilst this may be tradition for that group, they would certainly have no legal right to the spot if another group decided to sit there one day.

Figure 8.2 We have an expectation of customary rights in many everyday situations.

In a broader sense, the practice of 'squatting', or staying in houses or on land that you do not own, is an example of customary rights. Examples in the 1930s in Sydney at La Perouse and Palm Beach demonstrate customary rights to land but again, there was no legal basis.

Different types of legal rights—common law and statutory rights

Earlier in this chapter, examples demonstrated the difference between rights that are protected by common law and those protected by statute. In some respects, many of the human rights (to be discussed later in this chapter) set down by the United Nations are protected either by common law or statute. For example, in Australia, you cannot be sentenced to death for a crime, no matter how horrific such a crime may be. Therefore, it can be said that Article 3 of the UN Charter of Human Rights is upheld by statute, as a judge may not sentence a guilty offender to receive the death penalty.

Another type of legal right is the protection of your reputation from unfair attack. What can you do if a hurtful article is published about you in the school newsletter or local paper? If you know the article is false and can identify the writer, you may wish to simply contact the writer and ask for an apology.

On the other hand, suppose you are the author of the article. To what extent does free speech allow you to criticise your teacher, friend or boss, and possibly hurt their reputation? What legal rights do you have? And how well does the law work to protect reputations on the one hand and free speech on the other?

According to Associate Professor Brian Martin at the University of Wollongong (http://www.uow.edu.au/arts/sts/bmartin/dissent/documents/defamation.html) you have a right to free speech and you are legally protected from being sued if what you say is:

- true
- needs to be communicated out of duty
- is your personal opinion.

Needless to say, your right to free speech is not protected by either statute or common law as you can be taken to court for **slander** or **libel**. Even if you were taken to court and successfully defended your right to free speech on the basis of the three points listed, it may cost you a significant sum in legal fees to defend such an action.

slander the publication of non-permanent (verbal etc.) material that is defamatory

libel the publication of permanent (printed etc.) material that is defamatory

Figure 8.3 Defending free speech can be very expensive if you are taken to court for slander or libel.

MEDIA CLIP

AINSWORTH LOSES DEFAMATION CASE

BY GEESCHE JACOBSEN

Sydney Morning Herald, 3 November 2005

Poker machine baron Len Ainsworth has lost the latest of his long-running defamation actions against police.

Mr Ainsworth had sued the retired former licensing officer, Les Burden, over a letter that the officer had written in 1993 to then police minister Terry Griffiths about Mr Ainsworth's involvement in the gaming industry.

In the NSW Supreme Court yesterday a jury of four found the letter had said or implied Mr Ainsworth was not a "fit and proper person" to be involved in, or have a financial interest in, a licensed poker machine company or a licensed dealer of approved amusement devices (gaming machines with redeemable credit).

These meanings, contained in the letter which outlined some of the history of relations between police and Mr Ainsworth, had defamed the poker machine manufacturer, the jury found.

But the three women and one man found there was an excuse for the defamatory letter. They found Mr Burden had written it in such circumstances that Mr Ainsworth was unlikely to suffer harm.

The letter was not intended to be a complaint but "merely as an advice as to the past and for consideration of the action deemed necessary".

Mr Ainsworth had obtained the letter from police files when he had sought access to internal police documents under the Freedom of Information Act.

The letter had been sent, together with a police report, to the Nevada Gaming Commission. NSW police had advised their US counterparts that Mr Ainsworth was under investigation by them.

Mr Ainsworth had claimed the letter had adversely affected his attempts to become licensed in Nevada and cost him hundreds of millions of dollars in lost business.

Mr Ainsworth has been ordered to pay Mr Burden's legal costs.

REVIEW 8.2

Read the media clip and answer the following questions:
1 Describe the reasons for Mr Ainsworth suing Mr Burden and state the outcome of the case.
2 Explain the circumstances for the letter Mr Burden wrote.
3 Evaluate how the Freedom of Information Act might assist Mr Ainsworth gain a gaming licence in Nevada.

Self-determination

'The idea of self-determination is intimately linked with that of a people or political community having a right and ability to determine its own priorities and design its own instruments of governance.'

Source: ATSIC website

Should the rights of Indigenous people be different or separate from the rights of non-Indigenous people in Australia? Do groups of people of similar ethnicity who want independence from a colonial power have a right to such independence? From 1995 to 2004, the United Nations declared a decade for World Indigenous Rights. The UN hoped to promote the rights, languages and cultures of all indigenous people and to draft a Charter of Indigenous Human Rights.

In addition, Article 1 of the United Nations Covenant on Economic, Social and Cultural Rights (1966) states that:

> 'All peoples have the right of self-determination. By virtue of that right they freely determine their political status and freely pursue their economic, social and cultural development.'

Indigenous people are the original inhabitants of countries and, in the case of Australia, have lived here for over 50 000 years before European settlement. The 'doctrine of reception' was the accepted method of colonising Indigenous Australians into the British common law system. How appropriate is it to expect people of vastly different language, culture, beliefs and traditions into this way of life and law? One way in which self-determination is demonstrated in Australian Indigenous communities is through tribal law prevailing rather than the English common law.

LEGAL INFO

Circle sentencing

Circle sentencing involves taking a sentencing court to the local community, where the magistrate and the community sit in a circle, discuss the matter and arrive at an appropriate sentence. Community members include the offender and victim and their families and respected members of the local Indigenous community. Australian circle sentencing is based on Canadian experience. In New South Wales the scheme is invoked once the alleged offender has pleaded or been found guilty. Circle sentencing is an example of self-determination in relation to crimes within Indigenous communities.

Source: Australian Institute of Criminology
http://www.aic.gov.au/topics/indigenous/interventions/alternatives/circle.html

RESEARCH 8.2

Consider a scenario in Australia in which a mining company wishes to drill for uranium on land in the Northern Territory on a site considered sacred by Indigenous people. Whose rights should be more important?

You could research such a case study at: http://www.nlc.org.au/html/busi_mining_act.html

Self-determination for East Timor

An international example of self-determination includes the story of East Timor as discussed in chapter 7. The East Timorese people, indigenous to the island of Timor, voted overwhelmingly for independence from Indonesia in 1999. East Timor now enjoys such independence, but there was considerable violence and loss of life throughout the process. According to Article 1 of the United Nations Covenant on Economic, Social and Cultural Rights (1966), the East Timorese have the right to political and cultural freedom.

RIGHTS: INTERNATIONAL

International treaties and declarations of rights

Treaties and declarations to make clear the behaviours and rights of individuals and states have been made throughout history, and continue to be made. Such treaties and declarations can be made into law if states agree to make the same laws and enforce such laws. This will assist with the purpose of any law, which is to control behaviour and protect individuals from others.

The United Nations published the Declaration of Human Rights, which can be viewed at http://www.un.org/Overview/rights.html. The following list summarises what the UN is trying to achieve internationally.

LEGAL INFO

United Nations Declaration on Human Rights

Article 3 Everyone has the right to life, liberty and security of person.

Article 4 No-one shall be held in slavery or servitude; slavery and the slave trade shall be prohibited in all their forms.

Article 5 No-one shall be subjected to torture or to cruel, inhuman or degrading treatment or punishment.

Article 9 No-one shall be subjected to arbitrary arrest, detention or exile.

Article 10 Everyone is entitled in full equality to a fair and public hearing by an independent and impartial tribunal, in the determination of his rights and obligations and of any criminal charge against him.

i Everyone charged with a penal offence has the right to be presumed innocent until proved guilty according to law in a public trial at which he has had all the guarantees necessary for his defence.

ii No-one shall be held guilty of any penal offence on account of any act or omission, which did not constitute a penal offence, under national or international law, at the time when it was committed. Nor shall a heavier penalty be imposed than the one that was applicable at the time the penal offence was committed.

Limitations of international law in protecting rights

While the United Nations drafts laws, treaties, conventions and resolutions, states may choose to ignore these to suit their individual circumstances. This should not be considered unusual in the sense that many citizens choose to ignore the laws of their state. You may also choose to ignore a school rule from time to time, understanding there may be consequences for such actions.

To illustrate the concept of limitations, consider the case of East Timor. Indonesia, the former ruling power of East Timor, opposed the independence movement for many years. It argued that East Timor needed to stay as part of Indonesia as it contained considerable resource wealth and lay geographically within the Indonesian archipelago. By 1999, the

United Nations intervened and was assisted by Australian troops to hold elections and keep the peace between pro- and anti-independence supporters. Despite this, many independence demands continue today throughout the world such as the Basque movement in Spain and the Tamil Tigers in Sri Lanka. In both these cases, the United Nations has not intervened to assist the independence supporters.

In 2002, an Australian man, David Hicks, was captured in Afghanistan and transported to Guantanamo Bay, a US army base on the island of Cuba. It has been argued by many legal experts that Hicks has not been granted his rights as set out in articles 5, 9, 10 and 11 of the United Nations Declaration on Human Rights.

The UN, often with the cooperation of states, has been able to capture various individuals and states for a range of activities contrary to international law. (You will study human rights in more detail in HSC.) However, apart from the 1948 Declaration of Human Rights, there have been other important conventions, laws and treaties drafted and **ratified** by the UN. One of the main reasons why international law is limited in protecting rights is that not all states may agree with the laws. The case of David Hicks demonstrates that some states may deem it necessary to use torture or inhumane treatment to extract information that may lead to stopping more terrorist activities.

ratified approved and invested with legal authority

MEDIA CLIP

THE CASE OF DAVID HICKS

The Age, 14 June 2004

Hicks has been charged with conspiracy, attempted murder and aiding the enemy. But the charges are significant for what they do not spell out. Though they are extremely serious, there is no allegation that Hicks killed or specifically harmed anyone.

His captors assert instead that he trained in al-Qaeda camps, guarded a Taliban tank at Kandahar airport and travelled to Konduz in northern Afghanistan to join Taliban engaged in combat against US-led forces. They say he intended to kill coalition combatants in Afghanistan between September and December 2001. They assert he aided al-Qaeda and the Taliban in the context of armed conflict. In the absence of specifics it is impossible to make any further assessment.

The legal limbo in which Hicks and other detainees are held means they have been unable to invoke the writ of **habeas corpus** to test the legality of their imprisonment. They are held on Cuban soil, leading to the technical legal argument that this exempts them from the protection of the US constitution and the normal legal protections to which a prisoner is entitled. They have been held as enemy combatants, not prisoners of war, and so have been denied the protections of the Geneva Convention. Yet the charges against Hicks relate to belligerent conduct.

habeas corpus the idea that people should not be held indefinitely without being charged

REVIEW 8.4

1 Why did the UN construct the Declaration of Human Rights 1948?
2 Describe the UN's ability to enforce these rights.
3 'Everyone has the right to life, no matter what they have done.' Discuss this statement with reference to recent terrorist attacks in New York, Madrid and London.

MULTIPLE-CHOICE QUESTIONS

1 How are legal rights protected?
   a by statute law
   b by common law
   c by both statute and common law
   d by morals and customs

2 Which of these statements about moral and customary rights is true?
   a they have no legal basis
   b they can be enforced
   c they are the same as legal rights
   d none of the above

3 Which of these statements is true?
   a every state in the world has a bill of rights
   b a bill of rights can only be drafted by the United Nations
   c a bill of rights is a document setting out the rights of individual citizens
   d a bill of rights is part of Australia's Constitution

4 What sort of a right is euthanasia?
   a a common law right
   b a legal right
   c a moral right
   d none of the above

5 How is the right to freedom of speech protected?
   a by statute
   b by common law
   c both A and B
   d it is not protected by either statute or common law

CHAPTER SUMMARY TASKS

1 Outline the arguments for and against a bill of rights in Australia.

2 List two examples of how rights are protected by statute and common law in Australia.

3 Describe the difference between moral, customary and legal rights using examples.

4 Discuss the issue of the death penalty in Australia. Should Australia re-introduce death sentences for horrific crimes or acts of terror? Or, do all Australians have a right to life?

5 Discuss the right of Indigenous people in Australia to self-determination.

6 Explain the concept of circle sentencing. Why might it be effective?

7 Explain the reasons for constructing declarations of rights. List some examples of such declarations.

8 Evaluate the effectiveness of treaties, declarations or conventions in protecting rights.

9 Explain why the United States may detain terrorists at Guantanamo Bay, but not on United States soil.

10 'David Hicks was denied his rights under international law.' Discuss.

CHAPTER SUMMARY

- There is a significant difference in the level of rights that are available to you from a personal to an international level.

- Some rights, such as customary and moral rights, are not actually enforceable by law and therefore cannot be upheld in a court of law.

- As a student at school, you have a range of rights which are protected by law. The right to be free from physical punishment is one example and would be strictly enforced by the appropriate authorities.

- Internationally, numerous conventions, treaties and declarations have been published since 1948. Many of these remain unenforceable in law as some states do not recognise these documents or have not written these rights into domestic legislation.

- Since the United Nations has no sovereignty or territorial control, there are limitations on the protection of human rights.

- The case of David Hicks demonstrates how international rights can be manipulated to suit the ideals of a state, however, the International Criminal Court is currently hearing cases against war criminals and will have the power to incarcerate offenders, as the states involved have agreed to abide by its decision.

PART III

The law in focus—focus groups

Section A Aboriginal and Torres Strait Islander Peoples

- the status of Aboriginal and Torres Strait Islander peoples under the law
- mechanisms for achieving justice for Aboriginal and Torres Strait Islander peoples
- responsiveness of the legal system to Aboriginal and Torres Strait Islander peoples

Section B Migrants

- the status of migrants under the law
- mechanisms for achieving justice for migrants
- responsiveness of the legal system to migrants

Section C Women

- the status of women under the law
- mechanisms for achieving justice for women
- responsiveness of the legal system to women

Section D Members of other groups not covered by human rights legislation—children and young people

- the status of children and young people under the law
- mechanisms for achieving justice for children and young people
- responsiveness of the legal system to children and young people

Aboriginal and Torres Strait Islander peoples

ABORIGINAL AND TORRES STRAIT ISLANDER PEOPLES

The status of Aboriginal and Torres Strait Islander peoples under the law

- Pre-1967
- Post-1967
- Criminal law
- Civil law

History of government policy

Dispersal
Protection
Assimilation
Self-determination

Mechanisms for achieving justice for Aboriginal and Torres Strait Islander peoples

- Anti-discrimination legislation
- Racial vilification legislation
- Special commissions and government inquiries
- Self-determination and treaties
- Land councils and trusts
- Legal aid

Responsiveness of the legal system to Aboriginal and Torres Strait Islander peoples

How have governments responded and recognised Aboriginal and Torres Strait Islander people's rights?

1987 Deaths in custody
1995 Forcible removal of children
2005 Abolition of ATSIC
Practical reconciliation

CHAPTER 9

The status of Aboriginal and Torres Strait Islander peoples under the law

THEME EMPHASIS:
CULTURE, VALUES AND ETHICS; CONTINUITY AND CHANGE

In this chapter you will learn about the changing government policies in relation to Indigenous Australians since 1788 and how their legal status has developed, with particular reference to the 1967 referendum. There was a range of policies and laws designed to achieve goals of **dispersal**, protection, **assimilation** and possibly self-determination in the present day. The effects of such policies will be considered, as well as an analysis of contemporary policies and legislation. It may be useful to revise pp. 11–12 of chapter 2 before you begin this chapter.

HISTORY OF GOVERNMENT POLICY

Most Australian students who have attended school have studied Australian Indigenous populations from 1788 to the present day. 'Aboriginals', as they were called by past generations, are more appropriately referred to as 'Indigenous', as this term encompasses both Aboriginal and Torres Strait Islander peoples. Torres Strait Islanders are of Melanesian origin. One of the most famous Torres Strait Islanders is the late Eddie Mabo, who was born on Murray Island (Mer) and belongs to the Meriam people. We will refer to Eddie Mabo and his legal battles later in this chapter.

Aboriginal and Torres Strait Islander people have inhabited the Australian continent for the past 50 000 years, living a mostly **nomadic** lifestyle. Although they did not operate a legal system that utilised legal documents or written laws, there is no question Aboriginal and Torres Strait Islander people used oral law, customs and traditions to maintain order and control behaviour. Tribal elders had systems of negotiation, discussion and rulings when it came to unacceptable behaviour, and Aboriginal and Torres Strait Islander people did not in any way live an anarchic existence. There were punishments for crimes that involved physical force such as spearing and beating.

dispersal the distribution of people over a wide area

assimilation a policy based on the idea that the minority group should adopt the language and traditions of the majority group

nomadic people who tend to travel and change settlements frequently

By studying the map on page 13 in chapter 2, it is clear that Indigenous people lived in distinct tribal and language groups and it is not fair or accurate to categorise Indigenous people into one cultural group. In 1788, when the First Fleet arrived, the belief at the time was that Aboriginal and Torres Strait Islander people were 'savages', with no concept of land ownership. There were no fences, landlords, tenants or farms to speak of, and therefore the British Government declared the land terra nullius (land belonging to no-one, or uninhabited land).

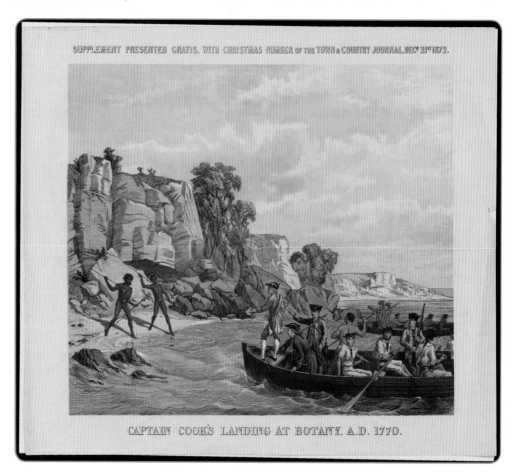

SUPPLEMENT PRESENTED GRATIS, WITH CHRISTMAS NUMBER of the TOWN & COUNTRY JOURNAL, DEC 21ˢᵗ 1872.

CAPTAIN COOK'S LANDING AT BOTANY, A.D. 1770.

Figure 9.1 The First Fleet arrives at 'New Land'.

It is very difficult to estimate the total population of Indigenous people in 1788, and figures range from 500 000 to 2 million inhabitants. In 2001, however, 2.2 per cent (410 000) of Australia's total population recognised themselves as of Aboriginal and Torres Strait Islander descent. A range of government policies and laws in relation to Indigenous peoples have been in place since 1788, as summarised in table 9.1.

In 1901, the following quote appeared in the *Bulletin* magazine:

'If this country is to be fit for our children and their children to live in, WE MUST KEEP THE BREED PURE. The **half-caste** usually inherits the vices of both races and the virtues of neither. Do you want Australia to be a community of mongrels?'

half-caste people whose parents are of different race and/or culture

Mr A. O. Neville, Chief Protector of Aborigines in Western Australia, made the following statement in 1937:

'We have power under the act to take any child from its mother at any stage of its life ... Are we going to have a population of one million blacks in the Commonwealth or are we going to merge them into our white community and eventually forget that there were ever any Aborigines in Australia?'

The term 'protection' clearly has two different meanings when used in the legislation listed. Governments felt that Indigenous people needed protection and as such were able to remove 'half-caste' children from their homes in order for them to grow up 'protected'. However, from an Aboriginal Torres Strait Islander point of view, such legislation and actions were far from 'protection'.

dispossession
expelling someone from the possession of land through lawful process

martial law law enforced by the military over civilian affairs that overrides civil law

TABLE 9.1

Government policies and their effects on Indigenous Australians

Policy/law	Effect/outcome
Dispossession/dispersal (1788–1800s) Since Indigenous people were not recognised as citizens, it was not a criminal offence to hunt, shoot and kill. The general belief was that Indigenous people would eventually 'die out'.	Massive reduction in Indigenous population. Traditional Indigenous areas converted to farming lands.
• *1816 Martial Law (NSW)* • *1824 Martial Law (Tasmania)*	• Aboriginal people could be shot on sight if armed with spears, or even if they were unarmed and within a certain distance of houses or settlements. • Settlers were authorised to shoot Aboriginal people.
Protection (1869–1909) • *Aborigines Protection Act 1869* (Vic) • *Aborigines Protection Act 1909* (NSW)	These acts allowed the appointment of a 'protector' of Aboriginal people. This included the power to remove children from homes to be placed in missions.
• *Vagrancy Act 1835* (NSW)	• Citizens could be sent to gaol with hard labour for 'lodging or wandering in company with any of the black natives of the colony'.
Assimilation and integration (1900–1970s) By this time, Indigenous populations were a long way from 'dying out', and the policy was to 'Europeanise' them. Leaving behind their language, culture, artefacts and traditions and becoming 'similar' and 'integrating' into mainstream society.	The European majority attempted to teach the Indigenous population to be white. This was met with both submission and resistance. The 1967 referendum recognised Aboriginal and Torres Strait Islander people as citizens with voting rights.

THE LEGAL STATUS OF ABORIGINAL AND TORRES STRAIT ISLANDER PEOPLES BEFORE 1967

The doctrine of terra nullius meant that in the eyes of the law Indigenous Australians did not exist as citizens for hundreds of years. The statements made by the *Bulletin* magazine and the Chief Protector of Aborigines highlight the legal status of Indigenous people since 1788. There were no criminal laws for European people to abide by in terms of harming or killing Indigenous people and, in the first 50 years or so, the government policy of dispossession and dispersal tended to condone violence. Indeed, martial law in both Tasmania and New South Wales allowed Aboriginal people to be shot and killed.

One of the most significant and tragic events of the 1800s occurred in New South Wales at Myall Creek, near Narrabri. In May 1838, forty Indigenous people set up camp on a cattle station and were brutally attacked and killed by stockmen who were angry about the theft of their cattle. Twenty-eight men, women and children were slaughtered, and the Governor of New South Wales ordered an investigation into the massacre. Such a legal process was probably the first of its kind and, initially, twelve men were found not guilty of the crime. However, a subsequent retrial sent seven men to their death by hanging. As a result of this event:

> 'The message that was received was that if you did kill Aboriginal people, don't tell the authorities and cover up any evidence. The result was that nearly all further massacres went unrecorded.'

> Source: *Blood on the Wattle: Massacres and Maltreatment of Australian Aborigines since 1788* by Bruce Elder

Indigenous Australians had no legal status until 1838. Up until the 1967 referendum, the Constitution referred to Aboriginal people in two sections—section 51 and section 127.

Section 51 gave the responsibility for Aboriginal affairs to state governments. Since there were no federal laws governing the welfare of Indigenous people, different states interpreted their rights and legal status in various ways. While most Aboriginal people were killed or removed from Tasmania by the 1840s, New South Wales at the same time sent seven men to death for the Myall Creek massacre.

Section 127 of our Constitution excluded Aboriginal people from the census and thereby from all citizenship rights. Citizenship rights involve being able to enjoy individual freedoms such as freedom of speech, the right to stand for election and the right to education.

Figure 9.2 An Aboriginal man exercises his new right to vote for the first time in 1962.

By the 1960s, as attitudes, beliefs and policies began to change, so too did the legal status of Aboriginal and Torres Strait Islander people. For example, the right to vote in federal elections was granted in 1962 and in all state elections by 1965. The 1967 referendum asked the non-Indigenous population to change section 51 and to totally remove section 127 of the Constitution. Over 90 per cent of the population voted 'yes' to these requests and, from this point on, Aboriginal affairs become a federal issue and Aboriginal and Torres Strait Islander people were counted in the census.

AFTER THE 1967 REFERENDUM

In 1968, Yolngu people from the Gove Peninsula, in eastern Arnhem Land, sent a bark petition to the Commonwealth Government protesting the removal of some 300 hectares of land for bauxite mining without their permission. The petition failed to move the federal government to recognise the rights of the Yolngu people and hence the *Gove land rights case (Milirrpum v. Nabalco Pty Ltd* (1971) 17 FLR 141) commenced in the Northern Territory Supreme Court in 1971.

In his ruling, Justice Blackburn stated that if the Yolngu people did have any type of **native title** rights, they would have been extinguished under common law. Thus, the doctrine of terra nullius prevailed and they could not prevent mining on the land.

In 1972, the Australian Labor Party, led by Gough Whitlam, was elected after 23 years in opposition. That year, the government established the Department of Aboriginal Affairs in response to the failure of the *Gove land rights case*. A royal commission into Aboriginal land rights under Justice Woodward was established, and its findings led to the drafting of the *Aboriginal Land Rights Act 1976* (NT). This was the first legislation in Australia to establish a land claim process by which traditional owners could claim various parcels of land that were listed as available for claim. The photo on the following page depicts the Prime Minister handing native title to the Gurindji people in 1975 in the Northern Territory.

native title the right of Indigenous people to their traditional lands

Between 1982 and 1992, Eddie Mabo and four other men challenged the Queensland Government in the Supreme Court (*Mabo v. Queensland* 166 CLR 186 8 December 1988), and the federal government in the High Court (*Mabo v. Queensland [No 2]* (1992) 175 CLR), over his people's rights to access Murray Island (Mer). Although Eddie Mabo and one of his fellow plaintiffs died during this time, in May 1992, the High Court ruled (by six judges to one) that Australia was not terra nullius and that the Meriam people clearly held native title to their land. The judgments of the High Court in the *Mabo* case inserted the legal doctrine of native title into Australian law.

In recognising the traditional rights of the Meriam people to their islands in the eastern Torres Strait, the court also held that native title existed for all Indigenous people in Australia prior to the British Colony of New South Wales in 1788. This decision altered the foundation of land law in Australia.

The federal government responded to this decision with the passing of the *Native Title Act 1993* (Cwlth). The *Mabo* case and the ensuing legislation, including the *Native Title Amendment Act 1998* (Cwlth) significantly changed the legal status of Indigenous people in relation to native title and allowed some people to access parcels of land throughout Australia to practise their traditional way of life. It did not allow Indigenous people to 'own' land, thereby restricting access to current owners. In December 1993, during the passage of the Native Title Bill through parliament, Prime Minister Paul Keating said:

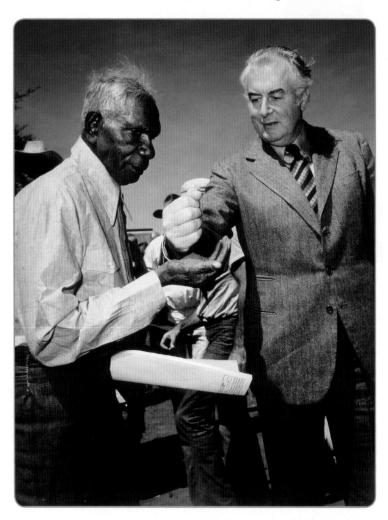

Figure 9. 3 Prime Minister Gough Whitlam symbolically poured a handful of sand into the hand of Gurindji elder Vincent Lingiari at the handback of the Gurindji people's traditional lands in 1975.

'... as a nation, we take a major step towards a new and better relationship between Aboriginal and non-Aboriginal Australians. We give the Indigenous people of Australia, at last, the standing they are owed as the original occupants of this continent, the standing they are owed as seminal contributors to our national life and culture: as workers, soldiers, explorers, artists, sportsmen and women—as a defining element in the character of this nation—and the standing they are owed as victims of grave injustices, as people who have survived the loss of their land and the shattering of their culture.'

Figure 9.4 Eddie Mabo took his challenge to the High Court and won.

REVIEW 9.2

1 Describe the changing legal status of ATSI people prior to 1967 and up to 1993. Why do you think laws have changed?
2 Explain the importance of the 1992 Mabo decision for the legal status of ATSI people.
3 Evaluate the statement made by Prime Minister Paul Keating in 1993 on the passing of the *Native Title Act*.

CRIMINAL LAW

In the cases of *R v. Ballard* (1829) and *R v. Murrell* (1836), in which Indigenous men (Ballard and Murrell) were charged with murdering other Indigenous men, the defence counsel argued:

> 'The natives were not protected by the laws of Great Britain, they were not admitted witnesses in Courts of Justice, they could not claim any civil rights, they could not obtain recovery of, or compensation for, those lands which had been torn from them, and which they had held probably for centuries. It therefore followed they were not bound by laws which did not at the same time afford them protection.'

In both cases the prisoners were dismissed. However, in the latter case, Justice Forbes reversed his decision and found the defendant guilty after consulting with three other judges.

Throughout all of the twentieth century and into the twenty-first, Aboriginal and Torres Strait Islander people continue to be significantly over-represented in rates of arrest, charge and gaol sentencing. It is estimated that Aboriginal and Torres Strait Islander people are between nine to fifteen times more likely to be arrested, charged and gaoled for offences commonly known as 'the trifecta'—public drunkenness, offensive language/behaviour, and resisting arrest. Indeed, in 2004, Aboriginal people (including people of Torres Strait Islander descent) in NSW appeared in criminal courts four times more frequently than non-Aboriginal people. In terms of incarceration, 16 per cent of Aboriginal people who appeared in court received gaol sentences, compared to just 6 per cent of non-Aboriginal people.

It has been estimated, however, that if all Indigenous people who were sentenced to gaol for less than 6 months were released, Indigenous gaol population numbers would fall by 56 per cent over 12 months (Jopson 2003). In addition the Royal Commission into Aboriginal Deaths in Custody 1987 found that:

> 'the more fundamental causes for the over-representation of Aboriginal people in custody are not to be found in the criminal justice system but in those factors which bring Aboriginal people into conflict with the criminal justice system in the first place. The view propounded by this report is that the most significant contributing factor is the disadvantaged and unequal position in which Aboriginal people find themselves in the society—socially, economically and culturally.'

In the last few years, a range of measures and policies to counter the statistics listed above have been put in place, including circle sentencing (see chapter 8). While circle sentencing continues in Dubbo and Nowra, there are examples of criminal cases whereby Aboriginal people are not excused from the current criminal justice system.

CIVIL LAW

Australia's adversarial legal system means that taking civil action against another person or company can be an extremely costly experience. The chances of winning a case with self-representation are extremely low and, as a consequence, very few Indigenous or non-Indigenous people can afford to act as plaintiffs in civil cases. However, in 1996, as a result of the *Mabo* decision, the Wik people of Cape York challenged in the High Court the legality of pastoral leases or land formerly under pastoral leases.

The major difference between the *Mabo* and *Wik* cases was that the Wik people were fighting against farmers who also felt they had legal rights and ownership. The High Court found in favour of the Wik people. In a judgment known as 'the *Wik* decision' the court found that native title was said to 'co-exist' with pastoral leases. This effectively meant that the Wik people could access their land for customary purposes and that this should not interfere with farmers or pastoralists. The court also handed down the decision that, should native title and pastoral leases come into conflict, then pastoralists' rights prevailed. The court explained that pastoralists had an exclusive right to pasture, but not exclusive rights to possession of the land.

Following this judgement, the federal government introduced the ten-point plan for native title, with the *Native Title Amendment Act 1998* (Cwlth). The implications of the act will be discussed in chapter 11.

MULTIPLE-CHOICE QUESTIONS

1 For how long have Aboriginal people occupied the Australian continent?
   a 5000 years
   b 50 000 years
   c 10 000 years
   d 1000 years
2 What does the doctrine of terra nullius mean?
   a land unoccupied
   b land occupied
   c legal systems in place
   d land owned by colonial powers
3 Citizenship rights require which three types of rights?
   a economic, social, educational
   b economic, political, employment
   c cultural, land and native title
   d civil, social and political
4 Why were the Yolngu people denied native title in 1971?
   a they did not have citizenship rights
   b they did not have political rights
   c terra nullius prevailed
   d they could not afford to purchase the land
5 What was the outcome of the *Gove land rights case*?
   a it was dismissed on the doctrine of terra nullius
   b Indigenous people were granted land rights for the first time
   c it allowed the constitution to be changed
   d it allowed co-existence on pastoral leases

CHAPTER SUMMARY TASKS

1 Describe the significance of the cases *R v. Ballard* and *R v. Murrell*.
2 Explain the possible causes of the over-representation of Indigenous people in the criminal justice system.
3 Justify the under-representation of Indigenous people in the civil law system.

4 Describe the circumstances and outcomes of the *Gove land rights case*.
5 Explain what you understand by the term 'co-existence' in relation to Indigenous people and pastoral leases.
6 Outline the federal government's responses to the *Mabo* decision.
7 Outline the federal government's responses to the *Wik* decision.
8 Describe the major difference between the *Wik* and *Mabo* cases.
9 Compare the *Gove* case to the *Mabo* and *Wik* decisions. Why do you think the judgments have changed over the last 20 years?
10 Analyse the changing land rights of Indigenous people since 1971.
11 'If Indigenous people stopped committing crimes, they wouldn't end up in gaol!' Discuss this quote with reference to your reading of this chapter.

CHAPTER SUMMARY

- Indigenous people occupied the Australian continent for over 50 000 years prior to 1788. They have experienced a range of government policies since 1788, from dispersal and dispossession to assimilation and reconciliation.
- There has been a range of legal challenges and changes since the 1960s, including constitutional change and land-rights challenges by the Yolngu people.
- The *Mabo* cases of the 1980s and 90s were the first successful legal challenges in Australia and led to the abolition of terra nullius. The *Native Title Act 1993* was passed as a result of this High Court decision.
- The *Wik* decision was also important for Indigenous people, as it led to the concept of co-existence between pastoralists and customary Indigenous practices.
- The *Native Title Amendment Act 1998*, passed in response to the *Mabo* and *Wik* cases, reduces the power and rights of Indigenous people.

CHAPTER 10

Mechanisms for achieving justice for Aboriginal and Torres Strait Islander peoples

THEME EMPHASIS:
LEGAL PROCESSES AND INSTITUTIONS; CONFLICT AND COOPERATION

In this chapter you will examine the mechanisms and methods available to Aboriginal and Torres Strait Islander people in contemporary times. Land rights, native title, Australian law and Indigenous customary law will be discussed within the context of legal, social and political changes since 2000.

AREAS OF DISADVANTAGE FOR INDIGENOUS AUSTRALIANS

As discussed in chapter 9, compared to non-Indigenous people, Indigenous Australians generally experience lower standards of health, education, employment and housing, and are over-represented in the criminal justice system. This is highlighted by the statistics in table 10.1.

This disadvantage was highlighted in the report of the Royal Commission into Aboriginal Deaths in Custody in 1991. In the report, Commissioner Elliot Johnston QC stated:

'the consequence of the history of Aboriginal people (since European settlement) is the partial destruction of Aboriginal culture and a large part of the Aboriginal population and also disadvantage and inequality of Aboriginal people in all the areas of social life where comparison is possible between Aboriginal and non-Aboriginal people.'

TABLE 10.1

Areas of disadvantage for Indigenous Australians

Health

Life expectancy (2001)

• Indigenous males: 56 years (compared to all Australian males: 77 years)

• Indigenous females: 63 years (compared to all Australian females: 82 years)

General health (2001)

Indigenous people were nearly twice as likely to report their health as 'fair or poor' (34%) compared to non-Indigenous people (18%). Based on self-reported height and weight, Indigenous people aged 15 years and over were more likely to be overweight or obese (61%) compared with non-Indigenous people (48%). Indigenous people were more likely to report asthma as a long-term health condition (17%) than the non-Indigenous population (12%). Indigenous people were more than three times more likely to report some form of diabetes than non-Indigenous Australians.

Education

School retention (2002)

38% of Indigenous students continued to Year 12 compared with 76% of non-Indigenous students.

Employment

Unemployment (2001)

The unemployment rate was 20% for Indigenous adults compared with 7.2% for non-Indigenous adults. This rate has improved since 1994 (when Indigenous unemployment was 27.8%), but has deteriorated since 2000, when Indigenous unemployment was 17.6%.

Criminal justice system

Juvenile detention (2001)

Indigenous youth aged 10 to 17 years were 19.9 times more likely than non-Indigenous juveniles to be detained in a juvenile justice centre.

Source: Australian Human Rights and Equal Opportunity Commission
http://www.hreoc.gov.au/racial_discrimination/face_facts/atsi.html#q4

REVIEW 10.1

1 With reference to table 10.1, outline the differences in life expectancy between Indigenous and non-Indigenous males and females.

2 Describe the differences in general health between Indigenous and non-Indigenous people.

3 Discuss the reasons for the overall disadvantage differences as outlined by Elliot Johnston QC.

RACIAL VILIFICATION

The *Racial Discrimination Act 1975* (Cwlth) was amended in 1995 to include the *Racial Hatred Act 1995* (Cwlth) and allows citizens to complain about offensive, abusive or racially motivated behaviour. This legislation aims to balance two rights discussed in chapter 8: the right to communicate freely and the right to live free from vilification. The act prevents public offence, insult, humiliation or intimidation of people of a particular race, colour or national identity.

racial vilification
a public act based on the race, colour, national or ethnic origin of a person or group of people which is likely to offend, insult, humiliate or intimidate. Types of behaviour can include racist graffiti, speeches, posters or abuse in public.

affirmative action
a policy designed
to address past
discrimination and thus
improve the economic
and educational
opportunities of
women and minority
groups

A recent case highlights the intent of this legislation: Mr Bowman shouted abuse from his front verandah to his Aboriginal neighbour, Mr McMahon, because he tried to retrieve his children's ball from Mr Bowman's front yard. The magistrate noted that passers-by could have heard them. The respondent (Mr Bowman) was ordered to pay $1500 in compensation as well as the complainant's (Mr McMahon's) legal costs. You can view this case (*McMahon v. Bowman*, Federal Magistrates Court, 13 October 2000, [2000] FMC 3) at http://www.austlii.edu.au/au/cases/cth/FMCA/2000/3.html.

There are exceptions to this legislation and these include:

- an artistic work or performance (for example, a play where racist attitudes are expressed by a character)
- an academic publication, discussion or debate (for example, discussing and debating public policy such as immigration, multiculturalism or **affirmative action** for migrants)
- a fair and accurate report on a matter of public interest (for example, a fair report in the media of an act of racial incitement or racially offensive conduct)
- a fair comment if the comment is an expression of a person's genuine belief.

In the case of *McMahon v. Bowman*, none of these exceptions applied and the respondent was ordered to pay a fine.

RESEARCH 10.1

Visit the site http://www.austlii.edu.au/au/cases/cth/FMCA/2000/3.html and view the cases on record.

1 Describe the events of each case and the judge's decision.
2 Evaluate the effectiveness of the law in dealing with racial vilification.

ANTI-DISCRIMINATION LEGISLATION

Figure 10.1 It is unlawful to treat someone unfairly because they are different.

Discrimination means treating someone unfairly because they belong to a particular group of people. Discrimination includes harassment.

Harassment is any form of behaviour that is not wanted and not asked for and that humiliates, offends or intimidates. The *Anti-Discrimination Act 1977* (NSW) outlaws this behaviour towards Indigenous people.

In May 2005, some amendments were made to this legislation which allowed lawyers to lodge complaints to the Anti-Discrimination Board (ADB) within 12 months of the offence, rather than the previous 6-month complaint period. In addition, the ADB will be able to hear part of a complaint rather than a complaint in total. This is designed to allow parts of a complaint to be dismissed if not covered by legislation, but remaining parts of the complaint will stand. Previously, whole cases have been dismissed because some of the behaviour of the respondent had not been covered by legislation.

equal opportunity
the right to
equivalent
opportunities
regardless of race,
colour, sex, national
origin, etc.

The Anti-Discrimination Board of NSW, which is part of the NSW Attorney General's Department, was set up under the *Anti-Discrimination Act 1977* (NSW) to administer that act. The ADB's role is to promote anti-discrimination and **equal opportunity** principles and policies throughout NSW.

The ADB provides an enquiry service for people who want to know about their rights or responsibilities under anti-discrimination law and accepts complaints of discrimination. More importantly, the ADB informs the people of New South Wales about their rights and responsibilities under anti-discrimination laws and explain how they can prevent and deal with discrimination. This is achieved through consultations, education programs, seminars, talks, participation in community functions, and the production and distribution of information, through printed publications and the ADB website (http://www.lawlink. nsw.gov.au/lawlink/adb/ll_adb.nsf/pages/adb_index).

LEGAL AID

'Legal aid' describes the provision of legal services to socially and economically disadvantaged people at no or very little cost to them. The government pays for legal aid so that people who cannot afford to pay a solicitor themselves are still able to access the legal services they require. Legal aid is provided by a number of different organisations, including the Legal Aid Commission of NSW, community legal centres generally and the Aboriginal Legal Service. All of these are funded by either or both of the Commonwealth and NSW Governments. Legal aid assists socially and economically disadvantaged people to understand and protect their rights. The legal system can only perform this protective role if people have equitable access to it. Socially and economically disadvantaged people, including many Aboriginal people (and people of Torres Strait Islander descent), may experience particular difficulties in accessing the justice system. Legal aid plays a special role in improving access to justice by providing a range of legal service to Aboriginal people.

The Aboriginal Legal Service (NSW/ ACT) Limited (ALS) provides legal aid services to Aboriginal people in NSW and the ACT in the areas of criminal and family law. It started operation on 1 July 2006 and has 24 offices across NSW and the ACT. The ALS replaced the six Aboriginal and Torres Strait Islander Legal Services (ATSILS) and their peak body the Coalition of Aboriginal Legal Services (COALS). The ALS won the government contract to provide legal services to Aboriginal people in NSW and the ACT on 28 April 2006, and receives government funding to do so.

Figure 10.2 28 April 2006: Vickki Armytage (L) and Matilda House (seated) sign a contract on behalf of the Aboriginal Legal Service to provide legal aid services to Aboriginal people in NSW and the ACT.

SPECIAL COMMISSIONS

ATSIC

ATSIC Aboriginal and Torres Strait Islander Commission, a legal branch designed to help Aboriginal and Torres Strait Islanders with the legal system, which was shut down in 2005

In 1989, the Commonwealth Government legislated the *Aboriginal and Torres Strait Islander Commission Act* to establish a body known as **ATSIC**. The purpose of ATSIC was to grant more political power to Indigenous people by allowing them greater participation in Indigenous affairs.

Government funding was provided to establish head and regional offices for the purpose of providing services such as health, substance abuse programs, housing and economic development programs. In March 2005, after a range of criticisms from the federal government and some personal issues with the chairman Geoff Clark, ATSIC was officially abolished.

GOVERNMENT INQUIRIES

Aboriginal deaths in custody

The Royal Commission into Aboriginal Deaths in Custody was established in 1987 in response to the unacceptable number of Indigenous deaths in police custody and gaol in Australia.

In summary, the commission found that there was no evidence of foul play by police officers in each of the deaths. However, suspicions were raised and this caused serious damage to relationships between Aboriginal and Torres Strait Islanders, the police and the wider community. The commission made 339 recommendations to assist in the reduction of custodial deaths. You can read the commission's findings at http://www.austlii.edu.au/au/special/rsjproject/rsjlibrary/rciadic/national/vol1/9.html.

LAND COUNCILS AND TRUSTS

The *Aboriginal Land Rights Act 1983* (NSW) was established to provide a mechanism for compensating Aboriginal people for their loss of land. The act states that land was traditionally owned and occupied by Aboriginal people and that it is accepted that as a result of past government decisions, the amount of land set aside for Aboriginal people has been progressively reduced without compensation.

The act aims to compensate Aboriginal people in New South Wales for their loss of connection to land. Therefore, a three-tiered network of Aboriginal land councils was established in New South Wales, consisting of the NSW Aboriginal Land Council, thirteen regional land councils and 120 local land councils.

Interestingly, this act came into effect at about the same time that Eddie Mabo was challenging the Queensland Government, and highlights the nature and operation of the Australian legal system with respect to Indigenous land rights and native title. At this point it is worth differentiating between these two terms.

Figure 10. 3 The push for land rights.

Land rights

Land rights granted to Indigenous people give legal rights to a parcel of land, but usually not exclusive rights to develop such land as the owners see fit. A legal document or 'title deed' is handed over to a community or organisation, and this land is usually passed down to future generations, as it would have been prior to 1788.

Native title

Native title is not a grant by a government to land. Rather, it is the legal recognition of Indigenous rights in Australian law and allows access and co-existence for customary lifestyles and traditions to be practised.

The NSW Aboriginal Land Council (NSWALC) works for the return of culturally significant and economically viable land. It pursues cultural, social and economic independence for Aboriginal people by being politically pro-active and voicing the position of Aboriginal people on issues that affect them. Some of the activities the NSWALC may engage in include administering funds from mining royalties, acquiring new lands from the Crown and allowing or rejecting mining activities on Aboriginal land.

POLITICAL POWER

As mentioned in chapter 5, political power refers to the ability to influence and directly control government policy. One of the most obvious ways to control and influence policy is to have Aboriginal and Torres Strait Islanders as members of parliament (MPs).

In 2005, Linda Burney was the member for Canterbury in NSW. In 2003, Burney was the first Aboriginal Australian to be voted into the 149-year-old NSW Parliament. She became the eleventh Aboriginal MP and only the fourth Indigenous woman elected to any Australian parliament.

Another way of wielding political power is through bodies such as the NSW Aboriginal Land Council and ATSIC. While ATSIC was an arm of the federal government, it was able to determine a range of strategies, policies and programs for Indigenous communities. However, since the abolition of ATSIC in 2005, a number of questions have arisen. According to Ms Jody Broun, director general of the NSW Department of Aboriginal Affairs:

> 'The Commonwealth Government is now using SRAs [shared relationship agreements] with Aboriginal communities to deliver funding for projects that do not involve core services. SRAs are voluntary written agreements around particular projects or activities which Aboriginal communities have identified as a priority. SRAs set out the outcomes to be achieved, and the agreed roles and responsibilities of the Governments and Aboriginal communities involved in the activity.
>
> While the primary objective of SRAs should be to bring benefits to Aboriginal communities, some Aboriginal leaders and State Government representatives have expressed concerns that SRAs may require Aboriginal people to do things to get services that non-Aboriginal people do not have to do. There is no clear evidence yet that this is the case. Aboriginal communities should be able to obtain benefits from SRAs, but this is dependent upon communities having good leadership and resources, and being able to negotiate on an equal footing with government officials.'

Figure 10.4 Who should determine Indigenous affairs?

Finally, the power of protest can sway political parties to change policy or legislation, depending on the issue and the timing of elections.

SELF-DETERMINATION, INCLUDING TREATIES

As mentioned in chapter 8, Article 1 of the United Nations Covenant on Economic, Social and Cultural Rights (1966) states that:

> 'All peoples have the right of self-determination. By virtue of that right they freely determine their political status and freely pursue their economic, social and cultural development.'

The following extract, written by Aboriginal and Torres Strait Islander commentator and journalist Tim Rowse, offers an opinion about Indigenous rights to self-determination in Australia.

> 'Citizens who are Indigenous are bearers of a right to self-determination which cannot be honoured by putting in their hands merely those instruments of self-determination that were afforded to all Australian citizens through the Australian Constitution. That is because Indigenous Australians were not parties to the federal compact of 1901. Giving Indigenous Australians the vote since federation cannot in itself redress their omission from the founding processes of nationhood. To admit them as parties to nation building it would be necessary to negotiate changes to the Constitution that acknowledge their collective interests in some way. This should have been the main business of the Centenary [of Federation] in 2001. Thus some advocates of a treaty now argue for constitutional recognition of an Indigenous order of government — the instrument of their self-determination as a distinguishable people within the Australian nation.

> 'John Howard's opposition to recognition of Indigenous Australians as Indigenous, with their own unique culture, religion, customary laws and communities, is well known. He frankly expressed his strong personal view in 1988, saying 'Aboriginal people should be brought into the mainstream of Australian society'. He reiterated such a view in May 2002 while commenting on the 'disgraceful' state of Indigenous communities, saying 'There are plenty of Aborigines, Indigenous Australians, who are fully integrated. But there are still quite a lot who aren't.'

Source: 'Treaty talk' by Tim Rowse, Australian Policy Online
http://www.apo.org.au/webboard/results.chtml?filename_num=12827

Many Indigenous people have debated and discussed a treaty between Indigenous and non-Indigenous Australians. Such a treaty could take many forms, such as a bill of rights, or an agreement on a range of issues. The Treaty of Waitangi in New Zealand between Maoris and the colonial powers settles the differences that existed over land occupation, and there is still a possibility in Australia of a treaty being signed.

In 2000, former chairman of ATSIC, Geoff Clark, made the following comments about a treaty:

'In fact what it can do is resolve all outstanding issues left in terms of **reconciliation**. Proper recognition of Indigenous people's rights, equality and fairness are all wrapped up in the treaty. At the end of the day a treaty is a settlement.'

REVIEW 10.2

Read the opinions of author Tim Rowse. Do you agree or disagree with these opinions in relation to self-determination? Discuss your views in class.

reconciliation
getting two parties to correspond, or make peace

REVIEW 10.3

1 Define the difference between land rights and native title.
2 Identify at least one problem with the abolition of ATSIC for Indigenous communities.
3 Discuss the advantages and disadvantages of a treaty between the federal government and Indigenous Australians.

Figure 10.5 Self-determination includes the rights of Indigenous people to practise their traditional way of life, language and culture.

MULTIPLE-CHOICE QUESTIONS

1 What is racial vilification?
   a any behaviour designed to humiliate on the basis of race
   b condoning violence between racial groups
   c proving that one race is superior to another
   d legal in the workplace

2 What body administers anti-discrimination legislation?
   a ATSIC
   b the NSW Anti-Discrimination Board
   c Coalition of Aboriginal Lands
   d Department of Aboriginal Affairs

3 Who can be provided with legal-aid services?
   a Indigenous people only
   b any financially disadvantaged person
   c divorce and family law litigants
   d people charged with criminal offences

4 How does native title differ from land rights?
   a native title delivers exclusive access to land
   b native title does not recognise the existence of non-Indigenous people
   c land rights usually involve a title deed to land
   d land rights enforce co-existence with pastoralists.

5 What is the Waitangi Treaty?
   a a treaty between pastoralists and Indigenous people of Queensland
   b a treaty made between governments and the Wik people
   c a treaty between Australia and New Zealand
   d a treaty between Maoris and non-Maoris in New Zealand

CHAPTER SUMMARY TASKS

1 Identify some statistics that highlight the disadvantage of Indigenous people.

2 Define the term 'vilification' and explain why you think it is outlawed in New South Wales.

3 Define 'harassment' and outline what citizens are able to do if they feel they are being harassed.

4 Outline the role of legal aid in improving access to the legal system.

5 Identify the difference between native title and land rights.

6 Explain two ways in which Indigenous people can gain political power.

7 Evaluate how the abolition of ATSIC impacted the ability of Indigenous Australians to achieve justice.

8 Analyse the impact of a treaty between Indigenous and non-Indigenous people. How would both parties benefit?

9 Define 'self-determination' and outline the reasons Indigenous people would seek it.

10 'Indigenous people should be able to determine their own social, political and economic future.' Discuss.

CHAPTER SUMMARY

- Indigenous people experience a range of disadvantages in areas such as health, education, employment and the criminal justice system.
- Legislation has existed for over 20 years that outlaws racial discrimination and vilification, yet conflict continues between the Indigenous and non-Indigenous population.
- The Anti-Discrimination Board of New South Wales and the New South Wales Legal Aid service provide support to Indigenous people who are socially and economically disadvantaged.
- The Royal Commission into Aboriginal Deaths in Custody made 339 recommendations to assist in the reduction of custodial deaths.
- ATSIC was established in 1989 and abolished in 2005. Practical reconciliation has emerged as the federal government policy, and involves shared relationship agreements.

- The *Aboriginal Land Rights Act 1983* (NSW) recognised that land was owned by Indigenous people prior to 1788. Currently the NSW Aboriginal Land Council aims to administer land now held on behalf of Indigenous people.
- Political power can be exerted in a number of ways, such as direct representation in parliaments, peaceful protests or through government agencies or departments such as ATSIC or the NSW Department of Aboriginal Affairs.
- Self-determination is a concept that is difficult to define, but involves recognition of Indigenous customary law and the rights of Indigenous people to practise their traditional way of life, language and culture.
- A treaty, such as the Treaty of Waitangi between Maoris and the New Zealand colonial powers, is a possibility in Australia.

CHAPTER 11

Responsiveness of the legal system to Aboriginal and Torres Strait Islander peoples

THEME EMPHASIS:
EFFECTIVENESS OF THE LEGAL SYSTEM; JUSTICE, LAW AND SOCIETY

The Australian legal system is based on an adversarial process, whereby opposing sides argue their cases with a judge acting as a 'referee'. The adversarial system is one of many justice systems used around the world, and it is certainly not the only system. As mentioned in chapter 9, Aboriginal and Torres Strait Islander people had a customary system of law and justice based on tribal elders settling disputes or handing out punishments (see *R v. Williams* on page 131).

MISUNDERSTANDINGS DUE TO IGNORANCE AND DIFFERENCES IN POINTS OF VIEW

The adversarial system is complex, expensive, time consuming and quite foreign to Indigenous people. Indeed, many would argue that it is difficult for any person without legal training to comprehend all of the rules and processes. It is therefore easy to see that misunderstandings due to ignorance are common.

Some people argue that Indigenous people are the proper owners of all land in Australia; others argue that Indigenous people should have no special rights.

Language and cultural differences

Indigenous people lived on the Australian continent for at least 50 000 years, and, prior to colonisation, there were approximately 500 different cultural and language groups. To categorise Indigenous people into a single ethnic group would be similar to categorising Caucasian, Asian or Arab people into one group. The European colonists did not grasp the concept that there were significant differences between these groups in terms of language, religion and culture.

There is evidence to suggest that not all Indigenous peoples were nomadic. Some groups lived a sedentary lifestyle, with permanent dwellings and clear physical boundaries. Indeed, as Eddie Mabo successfully demonstrated, the Meriam people (on the Torres Strait island of Mer) had a system of land ownership with identifiable boundaries, whereby land was passed down through generations.

As a general rule, Indigenous cultural beliefs emphasise the group rather than the individual. They have a strong connection to the land and the physical environment, believing that life comes from the land and returns to it upon death. This is in stark contrast to the non-Indigenous view of land as an asset that can be bought and sold for profit and changed or developed to suit the needs of people at the time.

For Indigenous people living in rural and remote parts of Australia today, English may not be their first language, and interpreters are often needed if an individual faces police and court proceedings. Placing an Indigenous person within four walls for an extended period of time may be viewed as more cruel and inhumane than for a non-Indigenous person because of the different cultural backgrounds discussed.

Customary law involves discussion, mediation and direct action, and a physical punishment may be administered. While this may also be viewed as cruel and harsh, it is dealt with quickly and does not involve incarceration. The 1976 case *R v. Williams* highlights the recognition of customary law by a South Australian judge.

CASE SPACE

R v. Williams (1976) 14 SASR 1

During the course of this criminal trial in South Australia, Justice Wells heard evidence that a woman taunted Mr Williams in relation to customary secrets. They had been drinking together and an argument broke out between them which led to the woman's death at the hands of the accused. Mr Williams was convicted of manslaughter.

The court decided that the provocation by the woman was sufficient to reduce the murder charge to the lesser crime. Justice Wells decided against sentencing Williams to imprisonment if he agreed to customary penalties dealt by Aboriginal elders. Justice Wells 'suspended' a two-year custodial sentence if the prisoner returned to his lands for customary punishment. The sentencing judge later gave his reasons:

'The fact was that he had very little English; it would have been impossible for him to have communicated with the staff of the prison or with any fellow prisoners, or to have related to them in any way ... To condemn a tribal Aborigine to such a fate was something which I wished, if possible, to avoid.'

Williams was later speared through the legs as required by the elders.

Source: http://beta.austlii.edu.au/au/special/alta/alta95/sarre.html

REVIEW 11.1

1 Outline Indigenous systems of justice and punishments.
2 Explain how non-Indigenous systems of law and punishment may be more harmful to Indigenous offenders.
3 Justify the decision of the court in the *R v. Williams* case. In your answer, consider whether being speared by elders is sufficient punishment for manslaughter.

Figure 11.1 English is not the first language of many Indigenous people.

THE EXTENT TO WHICH GOVERNMENTS HAVE RECOGNISED AND RESPONDED TO ISSUES AND RIGHTS

State and federal governments have recognised and responded to Indigenous issues in a range of ways. It is difficult to identify the most important issue, as opinions vary widely, but land ownership, recognition of customary law and an apology from a federal government for 'stealing' children from their homes will be dealt with in this section.

What if gold, oil or some other precious resource was discovered in your backyard or house? Would you automatically want to sell your house and allow this resource to be extracted for huge profit? Perhaps you and your family were so attached to your house that you would not dream of selling? This situation is similar to the issue of native title and land rights, as some citizens see the practising of Indigenous culture to be far less important than the economic gains of farming, forestry, fishing and mining. How do we decide whether access should be granted to Indigenous people?

What if a major deposit of a mineral is discovered on land owned by an Indigenous community and they do not wish mining to occur, despite large sums of compensation or royalties? As mentioned in chapter 9, the *Gove land rights case* commenced in the Northern Territory Supreme Court in 1971. The court found that if the Yolngu people did have any type of native title rights, the doctrine of terra nullius prevailed and they could not prevent mining on their land.

In response, the Whitlam government established the Department of Aboriginal Affairs in 1972. The *Aboriginal Land Rights Act 1976* (NT) established a land claim process for traditional owners. The *Mabo* cases demolished the notion of terra nullius and established the *Native Title Act 1993*, however, the *Wik* case and the government's ten-point plan (*Native Title Amendment Act 1998*) now means Indigenous people can be consulted on a land-use issue, but they have no legal power to veto a decision about land. In relation to the issues of customary law and self-determination, while some judges have recognised social, cultural and legal differences, the High Court dismissed the 1994 appeal by Denis Walker as explained below.

CASE SPACE

Walker v. New South Wales (1994) 69 ALJR 111

Denis Walker claimed that he could not be guilty of a crime of assault because he was not accountable under Commonwealth or state criminal law. Mr Walker claimed that Australian governments did not have the power to make laws for Aboriginal Australians without their consent. However, on 16 December 1994, the High Court decided to dismiss Walker's appeal against his conviction.

The High Court was not influenced by Walker's counsel's submissions. Chief Justice Mason stated that the concept of justice demanded that the same conduct receive the same legal response regardless of the race of the person charged with an offence.

Deaths in custody recommendations

The 1987 Royal Commission into Aboriginal Deaths in Custody was established in response to the unacceptable number of Indigenous deaths in police custody and gaol. The commission handed down 339 recommendations, some of which will be discussed here.

It is worth noting that the number of deaths in police custody has fallen because of a range of changes made to police cells, one of which reduces the possibility of suicide. However, the number of Indigenous people in gaol in 2005 and subsequent deaths in custody remains approximately seventeen times higher than the number for non-Indigenous inmates.

One of the main recommendations for reducing deaths was to reduce the number of Indigenous people going to gaol in the first instance. A diversionary program was suggested that involved punishment or rehabilitation rather than gaol.

Figure 11.2 Fewer Indigenous people in gaol should reduce the number of Indigenous deaths in custody.

In 1997, a 15-year-old boy died in juvenile custody in the Northern Territory. He had committed minor property offences, but was not placed on a diversionary program.

In 1992, the position of the Aboriginal and Torres Strait Islander Social Justice Commissioner was created by federal parliament in response to the findings of the Royal Commission and the National Inquiry into Racist Violence. It was also a response to the extreme social and economic disadvantage faced by Indigenous Australians. In his *Social Justice Report of 2000*, Aboriginal and Torres Strait Islander Social Justice Commissioner Dr William Jonas stated that the past 10 years had seen Indigenous issues become highly publicised and discussed, and the wider community had become more aware of a history of injustice.

Dr Jonas highlighted the reports of the Royal Commission into Aboriginal Deaths in Custody and the recognition of native title as exposing the foundational myths of our history. Australia was not terra nullius and Indigenous people did suffer at the hands of our custody system. Of particular importance was the documenting of the impact of the forcible removal of Aboriginal and Torres Strait Islander children from their families which occurred as government policy up until 1972. Many non-Indigenous Australians were unaware of such policy and the horrendous impacts on families and individuals who were removed.

Forcible removal of children from their families

As mentioned in chapter 9, the Chief Protector of Aborigines in Western Australia commented in 1937 that Australia had the power to take any child from its mother so that the nation could merge its 'black' population into the 'white'. The National Inquiry into the Separation of Aboriginal and Torres Strait Islander Children from Their Families

Figure 11.3 Stolen children—their lives 'protected' by white governments?

was established in May 1995 in response to efforts made by key Indigenous agencies and communities. They were concerned that the general public's ignorance of the history of forcible removal was hindering the recognition of the needs of its victims and their families and the provision of services.

The inquiry looked at four main issues or 'terms of reference'.

- The first was to examine the past and continuing effects of separation of individuals, families and communities.
- The second was to identify what should be done in response, to change laws, policies and practices, to re-unite families and otherwise deal with losses caused by separation.
- The third was to find justification for, and the nature of, any compensation for those affected by separation.
- The last looked at current laws, policies and practices affecting the placement and care of Indigenous children. This included looking into the welfare and juvenile justice systems, and advising on any changes in the light of the principles of self-determination.

The final report, entitled *Bringing them home*, made some recommendations that are listed as follows:

- Compensation for individuals and families affected including reunion and counselling services. This included an apology from all organisations involved in this policy.
- Enacting legislation ensuring Australia abides by the United Nations Convention on the Prevention and Punishment of the Crime of Genocide. Article II of that convention states that genocide includes the forced transferring of children of a group to another group. It could therefore be argued that for 24 years Australia was in breach of a United Nations convention.

Indigenous groups have sought an apology from the Prime Minister since 2000 as they believe this to be the origin of reconciliation. While the NSW and Queensland state parliaments have issued an official apology on behalf of their governments, the federal government has expressed 'deep and sincere regret for past injustices'.

Since the abolition of ATSIC in 2005, the federal government has embarked on a policy of 'practical reconciliation'. Such a policy implies that many of the problems faced by Indigenous people can be solved with simple, 'practical' solutions. Some of the gains the federal government has publicised are the increases in home ownership by Indigenous people and the rise in university qualifications. (There has, however, been a slowing down of Indigenous youth finishing secondary education.)

Finally and most importantly, the problems faced by Indigenous people in accessing the legal system to achieve justice are very complex, and an improvement in a range of statistics is not necessarily satisfactory. Aboriginal and Torres Strait Islander cultures have different social and spiritual needs that are not catered for within the policy of practical reconciliation.

REVIEW 11.2

1 Identify the basis of Denis Walker's appeal to the High Court in 1976.
2 Describe one or two of the 'foundational myths' referred to by Dr William Jonas.
3 Justify the request for the federal government to give an official apology to the stolen generation.

MULTIPLE-CHOICE QUESTIONS

1 On what type of process is the Australian legal system based?
   a inquisitorial
   b conciliation
   c mediation
   d adversarial

2 Approximately how many different Indigenous language and cultural groups were there in Australia before 1788?
   a 500
   b 50
   c 1
   d 50 000

3 Who was involved in the *Gove land rights case*?
   a the Wik people
   b the Mabo people
   c the Yolngu people
   d the Bundjalung people

4 In 1976, a South Australian judge allowed an Aboriginal man to be punished through customary law. What is the name of this case?
   a *R v. Burrell*
   b *R v. Williams*
   c *R v. Gipps*
   d *R v. Clark*

5 How many recommendations were handed down by the Royal Commission into Aboriginal Deaths in Custody?
   a 39
   b 339
   c none
   d 1987

CHAPTER SUMMARY TASKS

1 Identify one piece of legislation enacted in response or recognition of Indigenous rights since 1967.

2 Outline different outcomes of the *Williams* and *Walker* cases.

3 Describe the difficulties Indigenous people face with the adversarial system.

4 Discuss the fairness of diversionary programs for Indigenous people.

5 Explain the reasons for the establishment of the Royal Commission into Aboriginal Deaths in Custody and list some of the main findings.

6 Explain the reasons for the establishment of the National Inquiry into the Separation of Aboriginal and Torres Strait Islander Children from Their Families and list some of the main findings.

7 Define 'reconciliation' and 'practical reconciliation'.

8 Discuss the arguments for the current federal government to issue an apology of behalf of the nation to Indigenous people for past injustices.

9 'Indigenous people should be governed by customary laws in all criminal justice issues.' Discuss this statement with reference to self-determination.

10 Evaluate the effectiveness of government responses and recognition of Indigenous rights since 1967.

CHAPTER SUMMARY

- State and federal governments have responded and recognised Indigenous rights in a range of ways since 1967. Legislation has been passed that recognises both land rights and native title; however, current federal legislation 'waters down' the rights of Indigenous people under the ten-point plan.

- The different languages and cultures of Indigenous people may or may not be recognised by the law. Some court cases, such as *R v. Williams*, demonstrate a recognition of customary rights.

- The Royal Commission into Aboriginal Deaths in Custody handed down 339 recommendations in response to the unacceptable number of Indigenous deaths in police custody and gaol. There has not been a significant improvement in this area since the report was published.

- In 1995, the National Inquiry into the Separation of Aboriginal and Torres Strait Islander Children from Their Families was established in response to the policy of forcible removal of Indigenous children. The report 'Bringing them home' called for compensation, reunion and counselling services for the victims, as well as an apology from the federal government.

- Practical reconciliation is the current federal policy on Indigenous affairs. It has been widely criticised for lacking sufficient funding and a shallow understanding of the problems faced by Indigenous people in the past, present and future.

TOPIC REVIEW

EXTENDED RESPONSE

Evaluate the effectiveness of the legal system in achieving justice for Indigenous people since 1967.

Marking criteria for extended response

Criteria	Marks
• Makes judgments about the effectiveness of the legal system in achieving justice since 1967, based on valid criteria. • Makes comprehensive use of relevant cases, legislation and media reports. • Demonstrates excellent understanding of legal access and the operation of the legal system. • Presents a sustained, logical and well-structured answer to the question. • Communicates an argument/opinion using relevant legal vocabulary.	21–25
• Makes judgments about the effectiveness of the legal system in achieving justice based on valid criteria. • Uses relevant research from cases, legislation and media reports. • Presents a well-structured answer to the question. • Uses appropriate legal vocabulary competently.	16–20
• Demonstrates an understanding of justice for Indigenous people. • Refers to relevant cases and/or legislation. • Uses appropriate legal vocabulary.	11–15
• Mentions justice for Indigenous people. • Makes basic reference to cases and legislation. • Uses some legal vocabulary.	6–10
• Demonstrates a limited understanding of some aspects of the legal system. • Uses some elementary legal vocabulary.	1–5

Section B
Migrants

MIGRANTS

The status of migrants under the law

Different categories of migration

Family sponsored migrants
Independent migrants
Refugees
Humanitarian entrants
Unlawful non-citizens
(border entrants and
overstayers)

Application processes

People smuggling and trafficking

Disadvantages faced by people in these groups

Long waiting periods
Financial problems
Rejection of application
Emotional problems

Mechanisms for achieving justice for migrants

Development of multiculturalism

Treatment of migrants
in Australian society
(assimilation and
integration)

Legislation to prohibit discrimination (federal and state)

Access to housing, social services and the law

Court access

Going to court
Challenging immigration
decisions
Use of interpreters

Criminal law processes

Deportation
Extradition
Detention

Responsiveness of the legal system to migrants

Administrative review of immigration decisions

Responses

International treaties
Racial vilification legislation
Anti-discrimination legislation
Legal aid
Recognition of cultural diversity

Future responses

CHAPTER 12

The status of migrants under the law

THEME EMPHASIS:
CULTURE, VALUES AND ETHICS; CONTINUITY AND CHANGE

People from other countries cannot just decide to come and live permanently in Australia. Like other countries, Australia has restrictions on the types and numbers of people who can enter and settle permanently. In 2003–04, the number of new migrants who settled permanently in Australia was 148 884. These migrants consisted of:

- 111 590 people living overseas who were granted a visa allowing them to enter and stay permanently in Australia
- 37 294 people already living in Australia on temporary visas (such as student or business visas) who were granted a visa allowing them to stay permanently in Australia.

Australia has had a long history of migration since the arrival of the First Fleet in 1788. Gold rushes and world wars have seen Australia's migrant intake swell, and have changed the nature of Australian society. Despite this history of migration and **multiculturalism**, newcomers to Australia have not always been treated well and have suffered many disadvantages.

Not all people coming to Australia are given the same legal status. To maintain a harmonious, healthy and well-balanced society, the Australian Government puts prospective migrants through stringent application processes. These processes are covered by immigration law.

multiculturalism the recognition of cultural diversity and the right of all Australians to express and share their individual cultural heritage. It also refers to government policies and programs that are designed to support diversity.

Immigration law

The Australian Constitution gives the federal parliament the power to make laws about immigration. Section 109 of the Constitution states that in the event of conflict between laws, the federal law will override state law. Thus the states have allowed the federal government to make immigration laws for the whole of Australia.

Permission to settle in Australia in the form of a visa is given by the federal government. A visa is a formal endorsement placed by government authorities on a passport, indicating that the passport has been examined and found valid by the nation to be visited, and that the bearer may legally go to his or her destination. For those who wish to come for a temporary period of time, visas are issued for studying, short work placements and tourism.

Migration law is very complex. Current migration law is contained in the *Migration Act 1958* (Cwlth). This act has been amended many times and contains over 500 sections as well as 200 regulations. In Australia the Department of Immigration, Multicultural and Indigenous Affairs (**DIMIA**) assesses all applications of people who wish to migrate to Australia.

DIMIA Department of Immigration, Multicultural and Indigenous Affairs, the federal government body that controls migration in Australia

Figure 12.1 There is long tradition of people from other cultures migrating to live in Australia permanently.

RESEARCH 12.1

Go to the DIMIA website at http://www.immi.gov.au/ and answer the following questions:

1 Who provides this site?
2 What types of information does it offer?
3 Choose one of the areas on the home page and write a review on how easy to use the site is for a prospective applicant.

DISTINCTIONS BETWEEN VARIOUS CATEGORIES OF IMMIGRATION

For people wanting to come to Australia on a permanent basis, there are two programs designed to help them in this move—the migration program and the humanitarian program.

The migration program

The migration program is made up of:

- a skill migration stream—this has a number of categories for people who have particular work related skills, outstanding talents or business skills. There are certain occupations which, at different times, will be in high demand in Australia due to a domestic shortage. These are listed on the 'Migration Occupations in Demand List' found on the DIMIA website. In 2006 these occupations included accountants, anaesthetists, dental specialists, dermatologists, automotive electricians and stonemasons. (The full and current list can be viewed at
http://www.migrationexpert.com/content/skilled_visa_skilled_occupations.asp)
- a family migration stream—this is where people can be sponsored by a relative who is an Australian citizen or permanent resident
- special eligibility migrants—this allows former citizens or residents wanting to return to Australia, and certain New Zealanders, to migrate to Australia.
- The migration program for 2004–05 had 120 000 places available for migrants. This program put a strong focus on attracting skilled people and people who agreed to live in regional areas of Australia.

The migration process
GENERAL REQUIREMENTS
To be allowed to come to Australia, a person must meet certain requirements. Whether they are intending to stay for a short period of time or an extended stay, all visa applicants must meet the requirements of being of good character. A person who wishes to live in Australia on a permanent basis must also meet health requirements and in most cases pass the points test.

CHARACTER REQUIREMENTS
All applicants must be of good character. The character requirements are set out in the *Migration Act 1958* (Cwlth). A visa will be denied to any person who has been sentenced to at least a year in prison for a criminal act, who has been involved in criminal activities or associates with known criminals, who will likely commit a crime in Australia or will behave or encourage others to behave in a way that will bring contempt or hatred to members of Australian society.

LEGAL INFO

What happens if your character does not pass the test?

David Irving is a British historian who has regularly been denied a visa to enter Australia because of his views. Irving, whose theories denying that the Holocaust happened have caused outrage among Jewish communities and historians worldwide, has been refused entry to Australia in 1993, 1996 and 2003. Irving's application for a visa was rejected after he failed the character test.

In its decision, the Australian High Commission in London said it could not be assumed Irving would abide by Australian law. In its report it cited Mr Irving's defiance and contempt for the law of other countries that he had visited and that he had been deported and excluded from these countries. It could not be ruled out that he would not behave differently in Australia.

Irving was convicted in Germany in 1992 for defaming the memory of the dead and was expelled from the country the following year. He was also deported from Canada in 1992 for lying to an immigration adjudicator. He also owes the Australian Government $35 140 after previous failed appeals.

HEALTH REQUIREMENTS

All applicants must meet strict health standards designed to protect Australia from high health risks and costs, and overuse of health resources. These health standards are set out in the Migration Regulations 1994. To ensure that Australia's health requirements are met, applicants and dependent family members will be asked to have a medical examination, an X-ray (if aged 11 or older), and an HIV/AIDS test (if aged 15 or older).

POINTS TEST

People who wish to come to become permanent residents of Australia must complete a number of application forms and answer a range of questions. The answers are awarded points which, when added up, measure the desirability of the candidate in comparison with other applicants.

Different categories of migration are assessed on different features. Some of the things that are assessed in the points test include:

- the applicant's education level
- the skills possessed by the applicant
- the applicant's English proficiency
- the qualities of the sponsor (such as the sponsor's citizenship, employment and relationship to applicant).

Figure 12.2 All visitors to Australia must have a visa.

Family-sponsored immigration

The category of family-sponsored immigration covers people who are sponsored by relatives to come and live in Australia. The sponsor must be an Australian citizen or a permanent resident of Australia. Generally people who are sponsored by Australian citizens will be favoured over those who are sponsored by permanent residents.

In 2003–04, there were 42 229 family stream visas granted. Under the family migration program, certain people can apply to migrate to be with family members. These include spouses, fiancés, carers, dependent children and other relations under certain circumstances.

Spouses or de facto spouses of Australian permanent residents can apply for a provisional visa. They may be granted permanent residency two years after arrival in Australia if the relationship is ongoing. Fiancés are granted a nine-month conditional visa, in which time they are expected to marry. Permanent residency may be granted two years after the marriage.

Carers are allowed to come to Australia to care for a relative with special needs. Dependent children are allowed to come to Australia to be cared for by their parents. Orphaned and unmarried relatives under the age of 18 are allowed to migrate to be with family members if they have no one else to care for them.

Parents of Australian permanent residents may migrate to Australia if they pass the 'balance of family' test. Under this criterion, half of their children (including stepchildren) must live in Australia, or there must be more of their children living in Australia than anywhere else. Aged dependent relatives are allowed to migrate to Australia if they are over retirement age and have been dependent on their Australian relative for a period of time (usually three years). If a person has their parents, siblings and children living in Australia, they can migrate to Australia under the remaining relative category.

Applicants in all of the above categories must meet the general requirements. For most categories of family migration, the Australian relative sponsoring them must give an assurance of support. This means that the relative must sign a contract agreeing to provide financial support to the new resident for two years. However, this assurance does not apply to dependent children, fiancés or sponsors, as it is expected that the family member will support them anyway. With the exception of dependent children and spouses, any person applying for family migration must pay a bond and a Medicare levy before their application will be considered.

Australian residents who sponsor applicants under the family migration program can appeal to the Migration Review Tribunal if the application is rejected. A fee is charged for each type of visa. The amount differs depending on the visa. For example, a student visa in 2005 cost $420 and a prospective marriage visa cost $1035.

> ## RESEARCH 12.2
>
> Go to the Australian Human Rights and Equal Opportunity Commission (HREOC) website at http://www.humanrights.gov.au/ and then to http://www.humanrights.gov.au/voices/index.html. Read about the different experiences of migrants in Australia. Choose one of the stories and write a mock interview or a short play involving that person's experiences.

Independent or skilled migrants

Prospective migrants who can contribute to the economic wellbeing of Australia are accepted under the *Migration Act 1958* (Cwlth) as independent or skilled migrants. These people must pass a points test which allocates points according to the age, qualifications, work experience and language ability of the applicant.

An age limit of 45 years applies to independent migrants and they must have proficient English skills. Thus the points test favours young, English-speaking professionals and tradespeople. There are several independent immigration schemes, including business migration, employer nomination, investment-linked, and distinguishing talent schemes.

BUSINESS MIGRATION

Under this category, an applicant must plan to establish a business in Australia. The applicant must show that they will be directly involved in the management of the business and that the business will create employment or export opportunities. The applicant must have the assets to run the business financially and be able to prove a successful business career.

EMPLOYER NOMINATION SCHEME

Applicants must be sponsored by an Australian employer to fill a highly skilled permanent and full-time position. The applicant must have the skills needed, and sponsors must show that there is a shortage of workers with the requisite skills in Australia. Sponsors must also show that they are involved in the training of Australian residents to overcome this skills shortage.

INVESTMENT-LINKED MIGRATION

Applicants must invest in a designated Australian enterprise for at least three years. Similar criteria to those of the business migration scheme must be met.

DISTINGUISHING TALENT

Applicants must prove that they have an exceptional record in their profession.

Disadvantages encountered

Since 1996, the rules regarding family migration have been considerably tightened. This has made it harder for people to migrate to join their relatives already living in Australia and caused heartache for families in Australia and overseas. These difficulties have arisen for the following reasons:

1 The quota system—due to the limited number of places available each year, many people who wish to migrate to Australia to join their families are on a long waiting list.
2 General criteria—people who do not meet the general criteria usually cannot migrate to Australia.
3 Financial requirements—many relatives in Australia are stuggling to establish themselves financially and thus cannot take on the extra financial burden of their relatives wishing to come to Australia.
4 Long waiting periods—in some countries the processing of applications takes a long time.
5 Sponsors of employer-nominated or distinguished talent applicants can have their applications reviewed by the Migration Review Tribunal. Most other independent immigration applicants do not have the right to have their application reviewed if it is rejected.

Some groups are able to meet all of the above requirements more easily than others and thus the tightening of the rules can be seen to be discriminatory in many ways.

> **REVIEW 12.2**
>
> 1 Identify which applicants may have their migration sponsored by a relative who has permanent residency in Australia.
> 2 Why do you think DIMIA makes it easier for some family members to reunite than others? Do you agree with this policy? Justify your answer in half a page.
> 3 Describe the problems that prospective migrants encounter in trying to gain residency in Australia.

Refugee and humanitarian immigration

Due to harsh conditions in their own country, some people wish to come and live permanently in Australia. They apply to be allowed to migrate on humanitarian grounds. A person who is able to successfully prove refugee status or meet other humanitarian criteria is given a protection visa which allows them permanent residency in Australia.

Refugees are different from migrants, although the two groups are often confused. Migrants have choice over when to leave their country, where they go and when they return. Refugees flee their country for their own safety. They cannot return unless the situation that forced them to leave improves. The humanitarian program is designed for refugees and others deemed to be in special humanitarian need.

The offshore resettlement program is a major component of the humanitarian program. It assists people in humanitarian need overseas for whom resettlement in another country is the only option. Those people who are already in Australia on temporary visas or in an unauthorised manner and who claim Australia's protection are covered by the onshore protection component. There were 13 000 places in the 2004–05 humanitarian program.

> **REVIEW 12.3**
>
> 1 Outline the two streams of migration available for people wanting to come to Australia permanently. How many places were available in each in 2005?
> 2 Briefly describe the different parts of the migration stream.
> 3 For whom is the humanitarian program designed? What are the two components?

Figure 12.3 Many refugees have undergone hardship to find a new home.

Refugees

The Australian refugee program allows migration on the basis that the applicant is a refugee. To be considered a refugee, the applicant must meet the definition given by the United Nations, that is:

> 'refugees are people who are outside their country of origin and can prove that they have a well founded fear of persecution because of their religion nationality, membership of a particular social group or political opinion if they return to their country of origin.'

> Source: United Nations Convention and Protocol Relating to the Status of refugees 1951, 1968

It is very difficult to actually prove refugee status, and those people accepted in Australia as refugees are usually the ones who face a death sentence in their country of origin. The Department of Immigration, Multicultural and Indigenous Affairs (DIMIA) is responsible for deciding a person's refugee status. They consider each application separately. Children will not be granted refugee status just because a parent has been classified as a refugee, and a spouse cannot assume that they will be given **asylum** with their partner.

asylum a place of protection

The Australian community has been concerned that the refugee process is being abused by people who fraudulently claim refugee status. The federal government responded to this concern in late 2001 by making a number of amendments to the *Migration Act 1958* (Cwlth). These changes made it harder not only for fraudulent claims, but also genuine claims for refugee status.

The amendments cover the following areas:

- The behaviour of applicants once they arrive in Australia, such as hunger strikes and self-harm attempts, cannot be used as evidence of the applicant's desperation.
- If applicants have been involved in serious criminal conduct, their application will be rejected.
- Applicants must have identifying documents or their application will be rejected.

Under its refugee program, DIMIA aims to assist people in humanitarian need overseas to resettle in another country where this is the only available option, and to meet Australia's international obligations onshore under the Refugee Convention. The program is made up of two main parts—offshore resettlement and onshore protection. These are discussed below.

OFFSHORE RESETTLEMENT

The offshore resettlement program is for refugees and other 'humanitarian entrants' who apply for a visa from outside Australia. The main categories of visa given are:

- **refugee visas**

  These visas are for people outside their home country who satisfy the Refugee Convention definition of 'refugee' and who are in need of resettlement because they cannot return to their own country or stay where they are.

- **special humanitarian program visas**

  These are for people outside their home country who have experienced substantial discrimination amounting to a gross violation of human rights in their home country. Their application must be supported by a proposer, who is an Australian citizen, permanent resident, or eligible New Zealand citizen, or an organisation that is based in Australia.

- **temporary offshore humanitarian visas**

  Changes to the *Migration Act 1958* (Cwlth) introduced in September 2001 created two new categories of temporary offshore humanitarian visas. They were introduced to encourage **asylum seekers** to remain in their country of first asylum, that is, the first safe country where they sought protection outside their home country. These visas are only available to asylum seekers who have spent less than seven days in a country where they could have sought and obtained protection. The two types of visa under this category are:

  - **secondary movement relocation visa**

    This visa is available to asylum seekers who have moved from a safe first country of asylum, but have not yet entered Australia. This temporary visa is valid for five years and people who hold this visa may apply for a permanent protection visa after four and a half years if there is a continuing need for protection.

  - **secondary movement offshore entry visa**

    This visa is available to asylum seekers who enter Australia at a place outside Australia's migration zone (such as Christmas Island, Ashmore Reef or the Cocos Islands). This temporary visa is valid for three years and the people who hold this visa are not entitled to permanent residence. Holders of this visa are eligible for successive temporary protection visas if there is a continuing need for protection.

asylum seeker
someone who has fled their own country and applies to the government of another country for protection as a refugee

ONSHORE PROTECTION

A person can be recognised as a refugee once they are in Australia by applying for a protection visa (PV). The asylum seeker must show that they satisfy the definition of 'refugee' and that Australia has an obligation to protect them. Australia is only obliged to protect an asylum seeker if:

- the applicant has a well founded fear of persecution on grounds covered by the Refugee Convention
- the applicant cannot be given effective protection in another country
- the applicant is excluded from the operation of the Convention (e.g. because of security concerns).

The type of protection visa given is either permanent or temporary, depending on how the refugee entered Australia.

- **Permanent protection visas** (PPV) are for people who arrive in Australia with a valid temporary visa (such as a tourist or student visa) and then ask for refugee status. Applicants receive a **bridging visa** upon lodging a PPV application. In most cases, the bridging visa allows the applicant to remain lawfully in the community until the PPV application is finalised. Some bridging visas allow the applicant to work in Australia. Applicants are eligible for financial assistance for basic living costs and health care while their applications are being processed.

- **Temporary protection visas** (TPV) are for people who arrive in Australia without a valid visa and ask for refugee status. Applicants must meet health and character requirements. The TPV gives them temporary residence for three years. After three years, some can apply for a PPV while others can only reapply for another TPV. The TPV provides only limited access to government assistance for settlement compared with other protection visas. TPV holders are not automatically allowed to sponsor their families to join them in Australia. They also need special approval to re-enter Australia if they leave.

bridging visa a permit to stay in Australia for a temporary period of time so that arrangements can be made to either leave or apply for permanent residency

REVIEW 12.4

1 Give a definition of 'refugee'.
2 What criteria must a refugee meet?
3 Write a brief report on the offshore and onshore settlement programs. Include who is covered under each program and the different visas involved.
4 Explain the special assistance category.
5 What are the reasons for changing the migration categories?

SPECIAL ASSISTANCE CATEGORY

In 1992, a new category of immigration was created for those people who do not fit the traditional Australian refugee or humanitarian criteria. The special assistance category allows applications from persons who have suffered distress as a result of severe civil disorder or as a result of being a member of an oppressed minority.

Each year the Minister for Immigration decides which groups of people will be eligible for inclusion in the special assistance category. Eligible groups have included people from Sudan, the Former Republic of Yugoslavia, Burma and Sri Lanka.

PERSONS WITHOUT AUTHORITY TO REMAIN IN AUSTRALIA

Illegal immigrants

Illegal immigrants are people in Australia who do not have the proper authority to stay in the country, that is, they do not have the correct visa. Under the *Migration Act 1958* (Cwlth) they are called 'unlawful non-citizens'. If these illegal immigrants do not leave Australia voluntarily, they can be detained and removed from Australia. Under these circumstances they may be excluded from applying to re-enter Australia for a time.

There are two types of unlawful non-citizens in Australia. The first group are those who enter Australia on temporary visas but do not leave when the visa expires. This group, known as '**overstayers**', makes up the largest number of illegal migrants in Australia.

The second group are those who have arrived in Australia with no form of entry permit at all. Since the late 1980s, this group of illegal immigrants has been composed for the most part of people who have travelled by boat from overseas to the northern shores of Australia. They are known as **border applicants** or **boat people**, and they usually go about seeking asylum or refugee status so that they can gain legal residency in Australia.

overstayers people who come to Australia on temporary visas but who continue to stay when their visa expires

border applicants people who arrive in Australia without a valid visa

boat people people who arrive in Australia without a valid visa

All border applicants who are assessed as being refugees are granted a three-year temporary protection visa.

The legal treatment of unlawful non-citizens depends upon their category. Border applicants are illegal entrants who arrive in Australia without a visa. They are usually detained in a detention centre while their status as refugees is assessed. There has been much controversy in Australia about the detention of illegal immigrants.

In 2001, increased numbers of border entries and concern over their treatment saw amendments to the *Migration Act 1958* (Cwlth). The *Tampa* incident (see the legal info box below) expedited the need for change. The amendments to the act changed the status of some Australian islands such as Christmas Island and Ashmore Island to being 'excised offshore places'. This means that they are not included as part of Australia in terms of immigration law. If people land on an excised offshore place in order to enter Australia, they will be ineligible for a permanent Australian visa.

LEGAL INFO

The *Tampa* incident

In 2001 asylum seekers were rescued by a Norwegian tanker called the *Tampa*. The Norwegian vessel picked up 433 asylum seekers from a boat sinking in international waters between Australia and Indonesia.

The Australian Government ordered *Tampa* not to enter Australian waters, but the captain defied the order and moved towards Christmas Island. The Special Armed Services (SAS) was ordered to board the vessel, naval and air force patrols of international waters between Australia and Indonesia were stepped up, and the government rushed in legislation to give it more certain legal backing.

The government refused to accept the asylum seekers, saying that as they had left from Indonesia they either should go back to that country or be taken to Norway. The government declared that as Australia was a sovereign state and had a right to protect its borders it should be allowed to decide who could enter Australia.

The world watched as the stand-off lasted for ten days. Eventually Nauru and New Zealand took the group of people.

Australia introduced legislation to remove the outer islands as immigration zones. All asylum seekers must disembark on the mainland if they wish to have asylum. *The Migration Amendment (Exclusion from the Migration Zone) (Consequential Provisions) Act 2001* (Cwlth) introduced the new humanitarian visa system and increased the penalties for those caught people smuggling.

Figure 12.4 The *Tampa* picked up asylum seekers from a boat sinking in international waters between Australia and Indonesia.

Figure 12.5 Amendments to legislation have made it increasingly difficult for border applicants to land on Australian soil.

Offshore processing

People who arrive without authorisation at an excised offshore place are detained on Christmas Island or moved to offshore processing centres. These offshore processing facilities were established in Nauru and Papua New Guinea in September and October 2001 respectively. The facilities were set up in cooperation with the governments of Nauru and Papua New Guinea with the promise of assistance by the Australian Government.

Asylum seekers are not detained under Australian law, or the laws of Nauru or Papua New Guinea, but are instead granted special purpose visas by those countries while waiting for processing and resettlement or return. All asylum seekers in Nauru and Manus have had their refugee claims assessed by either the United Nations High Commission for Refugees (UNHCR) or the Australian Government. The result has seen resettlement in countries such as Australia, New Zealand, Sweden, Canada, Denmark and Norway.

Stopping people smugglers

People smuggling occurs when people pay smugglers to arrange for them to cross illegally into a another country. On the other hand, trafficking in persons often involves coercion and abduction in addition to false promises by the traffickers of jobs and a better life. The transaction often does not end at the point of destination, as traffickers may continue to exploit their victims through sexual exploitation, forced labour, and other forms of slavery.

People smuggling and trafficking in persons are serious global problems for the following reasons:

- They challenge national sovereignty in controlling borders and potentially threaten national security. An open back door to people smugglers is an open back door to criminal and terrorist activity as well as health issues.
- They undermine the integrity of the international refugee protection system, and they reduce public support for the legal migration programs that have so benefited and enriched Australia and many other countries.
- They can result in human rights abuses and humanitarian disasters, as smugglers and traffickers often send people across dangerous waters in unsafe and overloaded boats. Misleading information is given to women and children about their future employment and lives when they reach their destination.

Domestic laws and policies to deter people smuggling

Following concern about large numbers of illegal boat arrivals run by people-smuggling operations from Indonesia to Australia in 2000 and 2001 (6640 people arriving on 83 boats), the Australian Government instituted a broad range of domestic laws and policies to combat people smuggling and trafficking and provide appropriate assistance to the victims of this trade.

Australia has put in place policies, legislation and programs in order to achieve the following:

- to deter unauthorised boat arrivals
- to extradite and/or prosecute the smugglers and traffickers
- to provide appropriate assistance to the victims of trafficking
- to ensure asylum seekers have their claims assessed in accordance with the Refugees Convention
- to provide effective and safe return arrangements for those found not to be in need of protection.

The Australian Foreign Minister, Mr Downer, and his Indonesian counterpart, Dr Wirajuda, co-hosted a regional ministerial conference on 'People Smuggling, Trafficking in Persons and Related Transnational Crime' in Bali in February 2002 to build regional cooperative efforts to deal with people smuggling and trafficking. This has led to a better relationship between Australia and Indonesia in dealing with the issue and cooperation in reducing the human trade.

Disadvantages encountered by refugees and unlawful non-citizens

In their bid to gain permanent residency in Australia, refugees and unlawful non-citizens encounter many disadvantages. Some of the disadvantages are the same ones that all migrants face, but others are unique to their circumstances. They are as follows:

Rejection of applications

It is very difficult to prove refugee status, and many asylum seekers do not have the capacity to fight for their rights.

Poverty

Many illegal immigrants in Australia have limited access to job opportunities and as a result live in poverty. Even if they are given refugee status, they find it difficult to find a job due to language problems and their skills not being recognised.

Trauma

It must be remembered why refugees and asylum seekers have left their original country. The trauma suffered in these circumstances, the journey to Australia, and the waiting for their application to be assessed can only leave a lasting emotional and psychological legacy.

REVIEW 12.5

1 Recount the *Tampa* incident.
2 How did the *Tampa* incident change Australian migration law?
3 What has been the outcome for asylum seekers who are processed offshore?
4 Distinguish between people smuggling and people trafficking.
5 Explain why people smuggling and trafficking are serious problems.
6 Summarise what Australia has done to try to stop this problem domestically and regionally. Evaluate the success of these measures.
7 Discuss the special problems that refugees and migrants face in their bid to live permanently in Australia.

Isolation

Due to language and cultural differences, many new migrants are alienated from mainstream Australia. This isolation only perpetuates the language and cultural differences as the new migrant seeks out people from the same ethnic origins. As a result, communities develop with a large number of people who share ethnic origins. For example, the Sydney suburb of Cabramatta is known for its large Vietnamese population and Bankstown for its large Arabic population.

Stereotypes are created and this promotes misunderstandings about the values and behaviour of particular ethnic groups. This only increases the social isolation and creates barriers to overcoming language and cultural differences.

Exploitation

minority group any group of people that is disadvantaged, underprivileged, excluded, discriminated against or exploited

Poverty, isolation and language difficulties allow exploitation to take place. Some migrants will be taken advantage of through unsafe or unfair work practices. Migrants may not know their rights or do not want to create trouble. In the past, trade unions have neglected to protect **minority groups** and thus these work practices have continued. The use of outworkers in the clothing industry is an example of unfair work practices which use many migrant workers.

Financial hardship

Language difficulties, cultural differences, non-recognition of overseas qualifications and discrimination makes it very difficult for migrants to find employment. As a result they suffer financial hardship when trying to establish themselves in their new country.

Access to social security

Migrants are not allowed to access social security benefits in their first two years of residence in Australia, which adds to financial hardship. This is discussed in greater detail in chapter 13.

Figure 12.6 Alienated from mainstream Australia, new migrants often form ethnic communities. There is a large Vietnamese population in Cabramatta.

MEDIA CLIP

POMS, YANKS WORST ILLEGAL IMMIGRANTS

Afghan and Iranian boat people create headlines but it's the Poms and Yanks who make up the majority of Australia's illegal immigrants.

There were more than 10,000 illegal British and American immigrants in Australia on June 30, 2004, making up about a fifth of all people who overstayed their visas and remained in the country unlawfully. Another 3,900 Chinese illegal immigrants remained in Australia last year, along with 3,000 Indonesians and 2,800 South Koreans. Afghans don't rate a mention while there were less than 200 illegal Iranians in Australia in June.

The new figures on illegal immigration were revealed in a report on immigration trends released by Immigration Minister Amanda Vanstone. The report said that while visitors from the United Kingdom and the United States accounted for the highest number of visa overstayers, they were rated as low risk because the number was small as a percentage of the total number of Britons and Americans entering the country.

Around 15,000 illegal immigrants had been in the country for more than 10 years but many of the 51,000 unlawful visitors only stayed for a few days after their visa expired.

"Many people who are recorded as overstayers are simply extending a short stay in Australia by a few days or weeks and leave of their own accord within a short period," the report said.

Australia's population reached 20.1 million at the end of June last year. The population growth in the 12 months to June 2004 was made up of 121,000 so-called natural increases—births less deaths—and 117,600 in net overseas migration. Most migrants continue to come from the UK, followed by New Zealand.

The brain drain once again affected Australia, with the country losing almost 29,000 skilled workers—most of whom were young—through permanent emigration last year. However, more than 44,000 skilled workers settled in Australia.

In total, 59,078 people left Australia permanently in 2003–04, the highest ever number.

The report found a quarter of Australia's workforce was born overseas, with computer professionals, accountants and managers/administrators the top three occupations of migrants prior to coming to Australia.

Humanitarian visas were granted to 788 people already in Australia last year, down from 897 the previous year. The proportion of migrants settling in NSW was at its lowest level since 1983–84 as a result of a regional migration initiative. Senator Vanstone said students and skilled workers were driving the change in Australia's migration intake.

"In the case of students, in 2001 the government changed the rules to allow overseas students in Australia to be able to apply to stay permanently as skilled migrants at the end of their studies," she said.

The report predicted Australia's population would swell to around 26 million to 27 million by the middle of this century.

REVIEW 12.6

1 Explain why isolation causes problems for migrants in trying to establish themselves in Australia.

2 In what ways do migrants suffer financial hardship?

3 Explain why migrants are vulnerable to exploitation.

4 Read media clip 12.1 and answer the following questions:

  a Who do the headlines say make up the largest number of illegal immigrants?

  b In fact, who makes up the largest number of illegal immigrants?

  c Rank in order the ethnic groups that make up the majority of illegal immigrants in Australia?

  d What is the length of time that unlawful visitors stay?

  e How many skilled workers left Australia? Do you see this as a problem? Justify your answer.

  f How many skilled workers came to live in Australia? What types of skills did they bring?

RESEARCH 12.3

Write a report about migration in Australia. In your report look at:

- the history of migration
- the changing nature of migration
- where migrants live
- the impact of migration.

The following sites may help you:

- http://www.humanrights.gov.au/racial_ discrimination/face_facts/migrants.html
- http://immigration.museum.vic.gov.au/

MULTIPLE-CHOICE QUESTIONS

1   What is a visa?
   a   a stamp in a passport
   b   a formal endorsement placed by government authorities on a passport
   c   a credit card given to all migrants
   d   not necessary for short visits to Australia

2   Which of these statements about migration in Australia is true?
   a   migration is a relatively new event
   b   migration only occurred in the last century
   c   the Australian migrant population is made up of illegal immigrants
   d   migration has been an important part of Australia's history

3   What type of law covers migration?
   a   common law
   b   laws particular to each state
   c   federal law
   d   judge-made law

4   Which of the following statements about character requirements for a visa is true?
   a   an applicant cannot have a criminal record
   b   a reference from a previous employer must be included in the application
   c   character requirements must be met by every applicant
   d   character requirements need only be met by one member of the family

5   What is the points test?
   a   a test based on how much money you earned in the last five years
   b   a test that must be completed by all applicants
   c   a test made up of multiple-choice questions
   d   a way of assessing an applicant's desirability

CHAPTER SUMMARY TASKS

1   Make a timeline of important dates and events in this chapter. You will add to this timeline as you work through this topic.
2   Who is responsible for immigration law in Australia?
3   What is an assurance of support?
4   Outline the types of people eligible to come to Australia under skilled migration programs.
5   Explain who determines refugee status.
6   Discuss why there were amendments made to the *Migration Act 1958* (Cwlth) in 2001. What changes were made?
7   Analyse how you think the *Tampa* incident affected Australia's international reputation. Justify your opinion in one to two paragraphs.
8   Summarise offshore processing. Include a definition of offshore processing, where it takes place and who is processed there.
9   Define an unlawful non-citizen. By what other names are they known?
10   Outline the different types of unlawful non-citizens and how they are treated by the law.

CHAPTER SUMMARY

- There are different categories of immigration available to people who want to come to live permanently in Australia. These include family sponsored, independent, refugee and humanitarian categories.
- Prospective applicants must go through certain procedures in their bid to migrate to Australia.
- Australia has had an illegal migrant problem. In response to this issue, migration law has been amended.
- There are different visas available to legal and illegal migrants.
- New arrivals in Australia face disadvantages related to finances, employment opportunities and isolation.

CHAPTER 13

Mechanisms for achieving justice for migrants

THEME EMPHASIS:
LEGAL PROCESSES AND INSTITUTIONS/CONFLICT AND COOPERATION
Although when a person legally migrates to Australia it is expected that they will be afforded the basic rights of all other people who live in Australia, in reality this does not happen. Due to a number of reasons, migrants in Australia may face limited access to services such as housing and social services. Many find themselves subject to different levels of racial discrimination. As a result, legal processes and institutions have been developed to eliminate these inequalities. However, access to these legal processes is limited by such things as availability, funding and language problems. This has led to issues of cooperation and conflict. These issues will be discussed in the following pages.

DEVELOPMENT OF MULTICULTURALISM

Australia has been a culturally diverse nation for many years, however this does not mean that society and the legal system have fully embraced this diversity. In fact programs were initially put into place to ensure that any migrants who came to Australia were either very like the people already living here or would try their hardest to be like everyone else.

The system of multiculturalism as we know it today has developed over many years. With Federation in 1901 came the official policy of assimilation. The basis of this policy was that migrants were expected to adopt the 'Australian way of life' and reject their own cultural practices. This policy operated from 1901 to the mid-1960s.

From the mid-1960s to the mid-1970s, a system of integration operated. Integration allowed migrants to retain their own language and cultural practices while also embracing the 'Australian way of life'.

In the 1970s, the term 'multiculturalism' came into common use. Multiculturalism is based on the idea that minority groups should be given every opportunity to preserve their cultural traditions. Multiculturalism celebrates the cultural diversity of a society and the benefits that migration has brought to this society.

In 1972, the Minister for Immigration, Al Grassby, called for the abandonment of the policies of assimilation and integration. He called for a more tolerant approach to the cultures that existed in the community. The Australian Government investigated the needs of migrants and its findings were released in 1978 in the Galbally Report. The report declared that migrants were socially, economically and politically disadvantaged. The findings of the investigation were that the only way to overcome this discrimination was to adopt a policy of multiculturalism.

MEDIA CLIP

AL GRASSBY, FATHER OF MULTICULTURALISM, DIES
BY PAUL HEINRICHS

The Age, 24 April 2005

Father of multiculturalism, or just a colourful lair from Griffith? The Honorable Albert Jaime Grassby, who has died aged 78, was a bit of both, and then some.

His arrival in Canberra in 1969, and subsequent promotion to minister for immigration in the Whitlam government's first term from 1972–74, was a shock to the system. It was to Grassby's eternal credit that, through political vision, his wit and some outrageous stunts, he turned this into a plus, helping to bury the discredited White Australia policy of the Menzies era.

Grassby literally wore his politics on his sleeve—one that, often as not, was part of a purple or gold safari suit. Or, if the suit was conventional, there would be a wild tie. He called it his "Riverina rig", and it carved an eye-straining sartorial swathe through Canberra, about as subtle in the corridors of power as Sir Les Patterson at a cocktail party.

Grassby's policies began the transformation of an Anglo-centric, or at least Euro-centric Australia, to one that welcomed Asians and people from every part of the globe. When they got here, they were no longer pressed into jettisoning every bit of their culture to "assimilate" into the mainstream Anglo-Celtic community.

Grassby initiated reforms to help immigrants from non-English speaking backgrounds. Among them, he helped gain the right to remain in Australia for overseas students who had successfully completed their studies and were sought by an Australian employer.

He allowed the parents of Australian-born children to remain in Australia, and he granted assisted passage to Vietnamese orphans coming to Australia, then to orphans from any country.

He introduced non-discriminatory procedures for the selection of migrants and the issue of tourist visas, and began to extend the infrastructure of education and support for migrants within Australia.

Grassby lost his seat of Riverina in the 1974 election, a defeat he put down to racist elements campaigning against him. But there was no counteracting his influence. Whitlam made him the first Commissioner for Community Relations, and he had a big role in overseeing the introduction of the pioneering Racial Discrimination Act of 1975.

But times became tougher for Grassby, who had grown close to many of the Italian families of Griffith, not all of whom were law-abiding Calabrians.

Figure 13.1 Al Grassby's polices began Australia's multicultural development.

Grassby got to Griffith in a roundabout way. He was born in Brisbane in 1926 to an Irish mother who married a Spaniard from Chile. The family took off around the world in the 1930s, but Grassby's father was killed in a German air raid on London.

Grassby went to university in England, trained in journalism and served in the British Army Infantry and Intelligence Corps for the last two years of the war. He returned to Australia in 1948 as a "ten quid migrant", sponsored by an aunt, and soon moved to Griffith, becoming an information officer for the CSIRO.

Much of his work involved helping Italian farmers, and he went to Italy for a year to learn the language. His pro-Italian sympathies led him to become involved in the backwash over the Mafia-linked killing of Donald Mackay in 1977.

Concerned at a wave of anti-Italian sentiment, in 1980 Grassby allegedly asked a NSW politician, Michael Maher, to read in Parliament a document that imputed that Mackay's wife, Barbara, and her family solicitor were responsible for Mackay's disappearance.

Grassby was charged with criminal defamation of Mrs Mackay. He always maintained his innocence and fought a 12-year battle in the courts before he was eventually acquitted on appeal in August 1992. He was awarded $180,000 in costs.

Supporting multiculturalism

Multiculturalism has enriched Australian society. It has given the Australian people access to a diversity of such things as arts, literature, food and music that is widely appreciated. However, true multiculturalism needs to go further than this to produce a cohesive and equal society. In practice multiculturalism should do more than promote tolerance of people from different cultures; it should also allow people to live according to their own culture. Thus the idea of multiculturalism must be supported by providing services that will strengthen ethnic communities and encourage tolerance amongst the community.

Multiculturalism has been supported by the formation of many associations at state and national levels to promote the cultural heritage of different ethnic groups. The federal government has also established several bodies to raise awareness of multiculturalism and promote tolerance.

The Australian Institute of Multicultural Affairs (AIMA) was established in 1979 by the federal parliament. Its purpose was to raise awareness of cultural diversity and to promote social cohesion, understanding and tolerance. AIMA was replaced by the Office of Multicultural Affairs in 1986. It was part of the Department of the Prime Minister and this meant that multiculturalism was given a national prominence. This office has since closed.

In 1989, the National Agenda for a Multicultural Australia was produced by the federal government. It is supported by all political parties to this day. The agenda introduced many measures to help recognise the cultural diversity of Australia, including the expansion of SBS television services and the establishment of the National Office of Overseas Skills Recognition.

The National Multicultural Advisory Council (NMAC) was established in 1994 with the task of recommending policies for the implementation of multiculturalism in Australia. It ceased its operations in 1999. Before it stopped operating, the NMAC released a report called *Australian Multiculturalism for a New Century: Towards Inclusiveness*. The report concentrated on ensuring that Australia's cultural diversity was a productive and unifying force for the future. The federal government responded to this report with the release of its own multicultural statement in 1999, *A New Agenda for Multicultural Australia*.

The Council for Multicultural Australia was established in June 2000 to assist in the implementation of the New Agenda. The idea of multiculturalism has lost its impetus over the years with cuts to government spending in some areas such as English language classes. Legislation that does not have strong enough penalties and thus does not discourage racist views has meant that multicultural policy has been limited in its effectiveness.

REVIEW 13.1

1 Distinguish between 'assimilation' and 'integration'.
2 How did the government respond to the Galbally Report?
3 Explain how multiculturalism has been limited.
4 Read the article on Al Grassby and answer the following questions:
   a Who was Al Grassby?
   b What was the 'Riverina rig'?
   c Outline all of the ways that Grassby promoted the rights of migrants.
   d Discuss the role Grassby played in promoting multiculturalism.
   e What other political roles did Grassby hold?

LEGISLATIVE SANCTIONS AGAINST DISCRIMINATORY BEHAVIOUR

Both state and federal governments have passed legislation to eliminate discriminatory behaviour. Despite these laws, many migrants experience discrimination on a regular basis. The acts that apply to migrants are:

- *Racial Discrimination Act 1975* (Cwlth)
- *Human Rights and Equal Opportunity Commission Act 1986* (Cwlth)
- *Anti-Discrimination Act 1977* (NSW).

Commonwealth legislation

The *Racial Discrimination Act 1975* (Cwlth) prohibits any behaviour that discriminates against a person because of their race. This act was amended in 1995 under the *Racial Hatred Act 1995* (Cwlth) to outlaw racial vilification. Racial vilification involves behaviour that could encourage racial hatred, serious racial contempt or ridicule.

A person who has been the victim of racially discriminatory behaviour must prove that they have been treated differently or unequally because of their race, colour or ethnic origin.

The *Human Rights and Equal Opportunity Commission Act 1986* prohibits conduct that discriminates against a person because of their race. Migrants who believe that they have suffered racial discrimination should contact the Human Rights and Equal Opportunity Commission (HREOC).

If there is sufficient evidence that racial discrimination has occurred, the Race Discrimination Commissioner will carry out an investigation. The Commissioner does not have the power to force people to stop their discriminatory behaviour and can only make recommendations and mediate to resolve disputes. If a dispute cannot be resolved, it is referred to the Federal Court which will make a legally binding decision and award compensation.

Human Rights and Equal Opportunity Commission

The Human Rights and Equal Opportunity Commission is a national government body, established in 1986 by an act of the federal parliament, the *Human Rights and Equal Opportunity Commission Act*. The Federal Attorney-General is the minister responsible for the Commission.

Through its public awareness and other educational programs aimed at the community, government and business sectors, the Commission plays a central role in contributing to the maintenance and improvement of a tolerant, equitable and democratic society. These programs provide information and strategies to improve the enjoyment of human rights in Australia.

The key message the Commission sends is that the elimination of discrimination and harassment are prerequisites for the enjoyment of human rights by all Australians. A core responsibility of the Commission is education about human rights, along with the investigation and attempted resolution of complaints about breaches of human rights under anti-discrimination legislation.

The Commission also conducts public inquiries, including inquiries into the following areas:

- the separation of Aboriginal and Torres Strait Islander children from their families
- homeless children
- discrimination on the grounds of pregnancy
- the accessibility of electronic commerce and new service and information technologies for older Australians and people with a disability.

New South Wales legislation

The *Anti-Discrimination Act 1977* (NSW) prohibits direct and indirect acts of discrimination. To be unlawful, the discriminatory behaviour must fall into one of a particular group of activities—employment, provision of goods and services, education and entry to or membership of a registered club. In the area of employment the act provides that no person should be denied promotion because of his or her race.

If a migrant feels that they have suffered any discrimination as covered by the *Anti-Discrimination Act* they can contact the Anti-Discrimination Board. The Board will investigate the claim and organise mediation between the two parties in dispute. If the claim is particularly serious and proved to have occurred, compensation will be awarded.

Limitations of legal processes and institutions

Despite legislation and the best intentions of policy-makers, migrants in Australia still suffer discrimination in a whole range of areas.

Racial discrimination

Racial discrimination happens when someone is treated less fairly, because of their race, colour, descent, national origin or ethnic origin, than someone of a different 'race' in a similar situation. Racial discrimination can be in the form of direct or indirect behaviour.

Direct discrimination occurs when one person or group of people receives less favourable treatment than another person or group in the same position would have received on the grounds of their race, colour, descent or national or ethnic origin.

Indirect discrimination involves practices or policies that appear to be neutral or fair because they treat everyone in the same way, but adversely affect a higher proportion of people of one racial, national or ethnic group. For example, a factory that has all its procedures written in English, yet not all of its employees speak English. It is a lot easier to prove that direct discrimination has happened than indirect discrimination.

Figure 13.2 Indirect discrimination: employees of non-English speaking backgrounds cannot read signs in English!

Racial discrimination creates barriers to equity. When migrants are subjected to it they find it difficult to get employment, adequate housing and other services. Although it is impossible to stop people having racist thoughts, the government does try to prevent racist behaviour. Under the International Convention on the Elimination of All Forms of Racial Discrimination, the government is obliged to stop racist behaviour. State and federal governments have tried to meet this obligation by passing legislation that prohibits racially discriminatory behaviour.

Treatment of unlawful non-citizens

The treatment of different types of illegal immigrants by the Department of Immigration, Multicultural and Indigenous Affairs can be seen as discriminatory. Border applicants are detained while overstayers are usually free to move about in the community.

Racial hatred and the race debate

Despite anti-discrimination and anti-vilification laws, migrants are subject on a regular basis to racist views. This was highlighted in 1996 in the State of the Nation Report, where it was found that there has been widespread belief that migrants take the jobs of non-migrant Australians and cause unemployment. In addition, some politicians will fuel a media debate on the issue if they feel that it might win votes. Newspapers and current-affairs programs will also headline the debate if they feel that it will increase readers and viewers.

LEGAL INFO

State of the Nation Report 1996

This report outlined the key findings from community consultations held in 1996 with non-English-speaking-background communities. Feedback from these consultations revealed that, despite daily experiences of racism, many people do not lodge formal complaints under the *Racial Discrimination Act 1975* (Cwlth).

In the foreword to the report, Zita Antonios writes:

'Legislative redress is not the only means by which to counter racism in our country, but is an essential foundation. It plays a vital role in indicating that racial discrimination is unacceptable in our society. This report describes how the Act is being used by Australians of non-English speaking backgrounds and it identifies areas where change seems warranted to ensure that the Act becomes a more effective and accessible means of challenging racial discrimination in the future.'

Employment opportunities

Migrants can face discrimination when they are looking for employment. Once again it is very difficult to prove that a person did not gain a particular job because of their ethnic origin. In times of high unemployment there may be many applicants for a job. Migrants may also have difficulty in finding suitable employment because of non-recognition of overseas qualifications. Migrants may be discriminated against in other ways within the workplace which are very difficult, time consuming and costly to prove as being a direct result of ethnic origin.

Benefits to the economy of migration

The increased demand created by migrants in the economy in turn creates new jobs. The taxation revenue earned from migrants also contributes to programs that benefit our nation. Migrants have been successful business owners and thus are the generators of jobs, national and state income, export earnings and innovation.

REVIEW 13.2

1 Write a meaning for 'racial discrimination'.
2 Distinguish between direct and indirect discrimination. Give examples of both either in words or pictorially.
3 Outline the state and federal legislation that covers discrimination.
4 How does public opinion create problems for migrants?
5 Briefly describe the findings of the State of the Nation Report.
6 Evaluate the benefits that migrants provide for Australian society.

The effectiveness of legislative sanctions against discriminatory behaviour

The very existence of anti-discrimination laws goes towards recognising that discriminatory behaviour exists and should be eliminated. Thus the laws have been, and continue to be, effective in compensating those who have experienced discrimination, and punishing the perpetrators of discrimination. The introduction of anti-vilification legislation strengthened these laws. The legislation also sends a message that racist attitudes and behaviour are not acceptable in Australian society.

Limitations of the law

Despite these laws, several factors limit the effectiveness of anti-discrimination legislation. Slow processing of complaints reduces the impact of the legislation. It can take several years for a complaint to be finalised. As a result, some migrants feel that it is not worth taking their complaint to the Anti-Discrimination Board.

Many people are also dissatisfied with the outcome of their complaint and they believe that remedies available are not strong enough to stop further discrimination or send a strong message to the public. The NSW legislation provides heavy fines and imprisonment, but they are rarely used. HREOC has the power to make determinations, but is not empowered to make them binding on the parties involved.

Difficulty in proving that the discrimination took place and that the treatment was based on race also means that migrants are reluctant to access legislation. Problems continue today in the elimination of racial discrimination because of limited government authority, continued racist attitudes in the community as well as language barriers and ignorance of rights by migrants.

ACCESS TO HOUSING, SOCIAL SERVICES AND THE LAW

Migrants may experience discrimination in their search for somewhere to live and in their dealings with the suppliers of other goods and services.

Access to housing and other services

When renting accommodation, landlords have the right to choose tenants but are not allowed to discriminate because of race. However it is often difficult to prove that someone was refused tenancy because of race.

Migrants are usually low-income earners and as such have difficulty renting adequate accommodation, especially in expensive cities such as Sydney. Getting the bond and other money together is a hurdle. They have even greater difficulty in saving and borrowing the money necessary to purchase a home.

Poor English skills and lack of legal knowledge often means that migrants are unaware of their rights as renters and buyers. Waiting lists for public housing are very long, and this only adds to the problems faced by migrants trying to provide adequate housing for themselves and their families.

Mechanisms exist to help migrants overcome these problems. For example, migrant resource centres run by sponsored community groups supply information and assistance to new migrants. St Vincent de Paul, the Salvation Army and other charitable organisations provide emergency shelter, food and clothing.

Social security

Social security is available to migrants in Australia, however aspects of the law regarding social security payments have undermined the effectiveness of this measure. With the exception of refugees, migrants have to wait two years from the time of arrival before they can access welfare payments, including unemployment, sickness and student allowances. A 10-year wait applies to aged pensions and disability allowances.

Independent migrants are expected to support themselves, and family-sponsored migrants must be supported by their sponsor. Social security payments can only be claimed by a migrant during this waiting period if their circumstances have undergone unforeseen change out of their control, for example if they are injured in an accident. This waiting period has been criticised as being discriminatory, as it restricts access to those in need and only serves to further isolate migrants from society.

Issues of court access

While the courts should be a mechanism by which all Australian citizens and residents achieve justice, there are factors that contribute to them being less than accessible to migrants. When dealing with legal issues, migrants face the problems of language barriers, unfamiliarity with the Australian legal system, fear of police and authority figures, ignorance of the law and their rights, and financial issues.

Often the rights a migrant is entitled to in Australia are different to the rights that they had in their country of origin. This ignorance of the law often means that migrants will not try to enforce their rights. Language difficulties not only add to this lack of knowledge, but also a reluctance to pursue their legal rights.

On the other hand, this ignorance of the law can see the unintentional breaking of the law. Although ignorance of the law is no excuse for breaking the law, the punishment applied can be a harsh penalty for someone who was unaware of the law and whose language and cultural barriers prevented them from finding out about it.

Figure 13.3 Language and cultural barriers make it difficult for migrants to understand Australian law and legal processes.

Taking a case to court can be expensive and many migrants are socio-economically disadvantaged and cannot undertake a court case without financial assistance. Like other members of society, migrants have access to legal aid, but the waiting list is long and they may not necessarily get a lawyer who can bridge the cultural and language barriers. As a result, many migrants are reluctant to take their case to court.

Negative experiences that they may have encountered with the court system in their home country only add to this reluctance. Attending court can be an intimidating experience for anyone, especially someone who is yet to get a full understanding of the Australian legal system and is still coming to terms with the language. The use of interpreters helps alleviate the problem, but can draw out the whole frightening process, especially as legal terms are very hard to interpret into different languages.

Migrants will often be disadvantaged during police investigations. Language barriers may cause some migrants to incriminate themselves if they do not understand the questions being asked. Some ethnic groups say that the police discriminate against them, for example Arabic and Asian groups have complained that they are targeted by police.

Challenging immigration decisions

Everyone living in Australia is subject to Australian law. Migrants, however, are also subject to other criminal processes. These include deportation, extradition and detention

Bringing other cases before the courts

Migrants have the same rights as other people in Australia to take a case to court. However, as discussed above, limited knowledge of legal rights and court processes, fear of police and financial issues will often mean that a migrant will not pursue their rights in court. This has led to criminal actions and civil injustices against migrants (and other minority groups) being allowed to occur without penalty.

Use of interpreters

The Translating and Interpreting Service (TIS) is provided twenty-four hours a day by DIMIA. It provides a free telephone interpreting and document translation service. It also provides free face-to-face translation services for certain organisations such as medical practices and trade unions. For a fee, other people can also access a three-way interpreting service which involves English-speaking and non-English-speaking parties and the TIS interpreter. This can be done face-to-face or using telephones.

RESEARCH 13.1

Go to the HREOC site http://www.humanrights.gov.au/. Choose one of the areas that is relevant to migrants. Prepare a fact sheet or brochure for migrants letting them know how their rights are covered in this area. Remember, many migrants experience English language barriers, so your presentation of information should take this into account.

SPECIAL CRIMINAL LAW PROCESSES: DEPORTATION, EXTRADITION AND DETENTION

Deportation and removal

'Deportation' means the forcible removal of a person from a country. Removal is the most serious consequence of breaching the immigration laws in Australia. The term 'deportation' is only used today for people who are permanent residents and have committed a crime. Under the *Migration Act 1958* (Cwlth), a person who is not given legal permission to stay in Australia must be removed as soon as is practically possible. Thus those applying for refugee status must successfully prove their claim or they will be removed.

A person who is removed must meet the costs of the removal (or owe the Australian Government the cost of the removal). They are not allowed to re-enter Australia for up to three years. A person cannot be removed until all visa applications have been fully determined. This can be a lengthy process, and the successful applicant will often have resided in Australia for many years as they pursue all avenues. They may have formed relationships and had children during their time in Australia. As a result, the removal can have severe impacts, emotionally and financially.

Removal from Australia does not necessarily mean that they will be accepted into other countries. To stay in Australia, people should apply for a bridging visa, as they are available to unlawful non-citizens. This visa will allow the applicant to stay in Australia while their application is assessed.

Section 200 of the *Migration Act 1958* gives DIMIA the power to deport a migrant who commits a criminal act and as a result is sentenced to more than one year in jail. Those migrants who pose a threat to the security of Australia can also be deported.

DIMIA only deports people under extreme circumstances. A person who is being deported can appeal the decision to the Administrative Appeals Tribunal. A migrant who has become an Australian citizen cannot be deported.

Extradition

Extradition happens when a person who is currently residing in one country and accused of a crime in another country is handed over to that other country for trial or punishment. In Australia, the laws controlling extradition are contained in the *Extradition Act 1988* (Cwlth). The act covers everyone who lives in Australia.

A person will only be extradited if the crime that they are accused of committing carries a punishment of one year in Australia and the country where it was carried out. The Australian Government will detain the person to be extradited and hand them over to the officials of the other country. The accused will be taken to the other country and tried (and punished if found guilty).

The only person in Australia with the power to order an extradition is the Federal Attorney-General and they will not give the authority if they feel that the accused will be tortured or sentenced to death. Extradition is also unlikely if a person is seeking refugee status in Australia because of political reasons.

Detention

The *Migration Act 1958* (Cwlth) allows for the immediate detaining of any person who is in Australia without a valid passport. This covers unauthorised arrivals, people who stay beyond the expiry of their temporary visa and those who breach the conditions of their visa (for example by working when the terms of their visa prohibit it).

Since 1992, asylum seekers who arrive in Australia without a visa—both adults and children—have been subject to mandatory detention. For most, the detention ends only when they are recognised as refugees and granted a protection visa, or when they are removed from the country. The government brought in its detention policy in 1992 for the following reasons:

* It is easier to question a person about their application if they are kept in detention.
* It is easier to monitor the health of a detained applicant, especially if they have arrived from a country with known health problems.
* Applicants are less likely to become lost in the community if they are detained during the application process.
* It is easier to remove a failed applicant from a detention centre.

Australian detention centres

Since 2000, the main nationalities of people held in detention centres are Afghan, Iraqi, Iranian, Chinese, Indonesian, Sri Lankan, Palestinian, Korean, Vietnamese and Bangladeshi.

The main detention centres are:

* Immigration Detention Centres (IDCs), which are used to detain people in breach of their visa conditions, people refused entry at Australia's international airports, and overstayers. The IDCs currently operating in Australia are at Villawood (established in New South Wales in 1976), Maribyrnong (established in Victoria in 1966) and Perth (established in 1981).
* Immigration Detention Facilities (IDFs), which are used to detain a range of unlawful non-citizens. An example is Baxter Immigration Detention Facility (open since July 2002).
* Immigration Reception and Processing Centres (IRPCs), used for unauthorised boat arrivals. An example is Christmas Island Immigration Reception and Processing Centre (open since September 2001).
* Residential Housing Projects (RHPs), which allow women and children to live in family-style accommodation while remaining in immigration detention. An example is the Port Augusta Residential Housing Project.

RESEARCH 13.2

The main nationalities of people held in detention centres are Afghan, Iraqi, Iranian, Chinese, Indonesian, Sri Lankan, Palestinian, Korean, Vietnamese and Bangladeshi. Investigate one of these groups and find out what has happened in their country of origin to make them leave, how easy it has been to leave their country of origin, and the way that they came to Australia.

TABLE 13.1

Number of persons in immigration detention as at 10 August 2005*

Facility	Men	Women	Children	Total
Villawood IDC	324	43	0	367
Maribyrnong IDC	42	8	0	50
Perth IDC	14	0	0	14
Christmas Island IRPC	0	0	0	0
Baxter IDF	117	10	0	127
Port Augusta RHP		0	0	0
Total in IDFs (includes one in transit)				559
Other places of detention **	32	21	41	94

* Approximately 75 per cent of detainees arrived in Australia with a visa and have been detained as the result of compliance action by DIMIA. The majority of these detainees are not seeking asylum.

** Includes correctional facilities; watch houses; hotels; apartments; foster care; community; hospitals; illegal foreign fishers in harbours awaiting departure, removal or court appearance.

Source: HREOC (www.humanrights.gov.au)

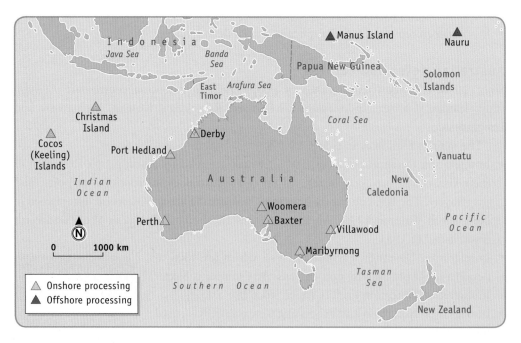

Figure 13.4 Location of Australia's immigration detention centres.

Criticism of detention

It is important to remember that the basis of keeping applicants in detention centres is as a form of immigration control and not as punishment. However, there has been much criticism both in Australia and internationally about the conditions in the detention centres and the right to keep people in them for extended periods of time.

One criticism revolves around the fact that border applicants are subjected to detention, but other unlawful non-citizens such as overstayers are generally allowed to stay in the community while their applications to remain in Australia are assessed. Thus discrimination takes place against certain groups of people.

Another criticism is that only in certain circumstances are bridging visas available to people in detention. They are only granted to those people who have applied for refugee status, and then only for children, people over 75 years of age, spouses of Australians and former victims of trauma and torture.

Criticisms have been made about the fact that border applicants who are detained only have the right to appeal to the Migration Review Tribunal if they claim refugee status.

People in detention are often unaware of their legal rights. Although all people in detention must be given the opportunity to gain legal assistance upon their request, they are not always informed of this right by immigration officers. On the other hand, overstayers who are detained must be informed of their rights.

Many see detention as an abuse of human rights under international law. The United Nations Human Rights Committee (HRC) has criticised such things as the lack of review rights for those in detention. In its decision in *A v. Australia (1997) HRC*, the HRC found that Australia had breached Article 9 (4) of the International Covenant on Civil and Political Rights 1996 (ICCPR). Article 9 (4) provides for the rights of people in detention to seek a legal determination on the legality of that detention without delay.

Australia's response to the HRC finding in this case was to dismiss the HRC's findings and no actions have been taken to rectify the matter in an effective way. This response has been criticised nationally and internationally.

Figure 13.5 Keeping children in detention centres is a contentious issue.

Australia has also been criticised for its detention of children of border applicants. From 1999, the number of children in detention rose significantly and there was widespread community concern about their treatment. While these children can be released, there is no such provision to release their parents or grandparents. So, with no one to look after them, the children remain in detention centres in their 'best interest'.

In response to criticism from such bodies as the United Nations Committee on the Rights of the Child, the Human Rights Commissioner announced the Human Rights and Equal Opportunity Commission's National Inquiry into Children in Immigration Detention in November 2001.

CASE SPACE

Children in detention centres

While there has been much controversy and criticism about the mandatory detention of all refugees/asylum seekers attempting to enter Australia, the loudest cries have been about the detention of children. It can be argued that the detention of children over an extended period is in contravention of the rights of children under the United Nations Convention on the Rights of the Child 1989, where the children in detention have the right to 'not be deprived of their liberty unlawfully or arbitrarily, with detention only in conformity with the law, as a measure of last resort and for the shortest appropriate time'.

Critics argued that, while detention for children accompanied by adult family members is traumatic, the detention of unaccompanied children is indefensible. They said that under the convention, the following rights of children in detention are not met:

1 **The right to protection from all forms of physical or mental violence**

   Woomera and Port Headland Centres were scenes of unrest and external and internal protest and as witnesses to this, the children in those centres were not protected from all forms of physical or mental violence.

2 **The right to rest and play**

   The location of camps in isolated areas precludes conditions and amenities that allow children to enjoy appropriate rest and play.

3 **The right to family life**

   The very nature of detention centres does not allow the practice of normal family life.

4 **The right to be treated with humanity and respect for their inherent dignity and in a manner which takes into account their age**

   This is particularly so in the case of unaccompanied children who are at the risk of being exploited in detention centres as they have no parent to protect them.

5 **The right to privacy**

   The very nature of mass detention does not allow the standards of privacy expected and enjoyed in everyday life.

The National Inquiry into Children in Immigration Detention was established to examine whether the laws requiring the detention of children and the treatment of children in immigration detention met Australia's obligations under international law, especially the Convention on the Rights of the Child.

The Commissioner of the Human Rights and Equal Opportunity Commission said he would examine possible breaches of the children's human rights and the long-term effects of their detention. "I am particularly concerned about the children who arrive in Australia without parents, often after a period of trauma, and who then face the prospect of being in a detention centre alone," he said.

The inquiry was conducted throughout 2002. It received over 340 submissions and visited all immigration detention centres in Australia.

Public hearings were conducted in Victoria, Western Australia, South Australia, New South Wales and Queensland. Experts with experience in dealing with children in detention gave oral testimony. In addition, the inquiry conducted confidential focus groups with former detainee children and young people.

In its *National Inquiry into Children in Immigration Detention Report—A Last Resort?*, released in May 2004, the Commission found Australia's immigration detention policy has failed to protect the mental health of children, failed to provide adequate health care and education, and failed to protect unaccompanied children and those with disabilities.

The key recommendations of the report centred around the following principles:

- Children can only be detained as a measure of last resort and for the shortest appropriate period of time.
- The best interests of the child must be a primary consideration in all actions concerning children.
- Unaccompanied children must receive special assistance so that they are in a position to enjoy the same rights as all other children.
- Children have the right to family unity.
- Children must be treated with humanity and respect for their inherent dignity.
- Children must enjoy—to the maximum extent possible—the right to development and recovery from past torture and trauma.
- Asylum-seeking children must receive appropriate assistance to enjoy their rights, including the right to be protected under the Convention relating to the Status of Refugees.

The federal government was slow to respond to the recommendations of the report, much to the criticism of HREOC. In fact it was not until the end of July 2005 that all children had been released from detention centres. This only came about because the Prime Minister was put under pressure from members of the Coalition to release all children who were still detained.

The children will be housed in serviced apartments under a community detention plan. They are being looked after by the Australian Red Cross and other non-government organisations funded by DIMIA, but they would still have to report to the department.

Community support groups, although pleased about the release of children, are concerned that they may also not have the necessary financial and social supports in place to help them make the transition.

REVIEW 13.4

1 Identify the circumstances under which a person can be deported from Australia.
2 Write a meaning for 'extradition'. Under what circumstances does extradition take place?
3 Which cultural groups make up most of the population in detention centres?
4 Where are the detention centres located?
5 Outline the arguments given against the detaining of children in detention centres. Can you recommend any arguments for keeping children in detention centres?
6 How did HREOC respond to the outcry over children in detention centres?
7 What were the findings of its report?
8 How has the Australian Government responded to the HREOC report?

MULTIPLE-CHOICE QUESTIONS

1 Which of these statements about multiculturalism is true?
   a under multiculturalism, migrants are expected to integrate into society
   b under multiculturalism, migrants are expected to assimilate into society
   c multiculturalism came about with federation
   d multiculturalism has come to prominence in the last 30 years

2 Which of these statements about racial discrimination is true?
   a racism has been eliminated by law
   b racism is acceptable as long as nobody is physically hurt
   c racism has been eliminated by multiculturalism
   d racism is difficult to prove

3 Which of these statements about racial discrimination law is true?
   a racial discrimination law falls under federal jurisdiction
   b racial discrimination law only covers discrimination in the work place
   c racial discrimination law prohibits discriminatory behaviour based on race
   d racial discrimination law is based on civil action

4 Which of these statements about HREOC is true?
   a HREOC is an international body
   b HREOC is funded by the federal government
   c HREOC is part of the United Nations
   d none of the above

5 Which of these statements about the *Anti-Discrimination Act 1977* is true?
   a it is federal law
   b it prohibits discrimination in the areas of employment, provision of goods and services, education and entry to or membership of a registered club
   c it prohibits discrimination in employment, provision of goods and services and education only
   d it was abolished in 2005

CHAPTER SUMMARY TASKS

1 Add all of the important dates and events from this chapter to your timeline.
2 Who can be detained under Australian law?
3 What does the Australian Government see as the main reasons for detention?
4 How has the treatment of migrants changed over the past 100 years?
5 Why is going to court to solve a problem not always an option for migrants?
6 How do language barriers cause problems?
7 What does the term 'multiculturalism' mean? When did this term start to be used?
8 What were the findings of the Galbally Report?
9 What is meant by 'racial vilification'?
10 What is HREOC? Describe the role that it plays in protecting migrants' rights.
11 In what ways do migrants face discrimination in the following areas?
   a employment opportunities
   b finding housing
   c being granted refugee status

CHAPTER SUMMARY

- Migrants have been treated in different ways in Australia in the last century. Although they were allowed to retain some of their traditional ways, it was expected that they would integrate into society and adopt Australian ways.
- Multiculturalism developed in the 1970s in response to identification of certain advantages brought to Australia by migrants.
- State and federal legislation has been introduced in attempts to eliminate racial discrimination.
- Migrants face problems in accessing housing, social services and the law.
- Other issues that migrants face involve going to court, challenging legal decisions and accessing interpreters.
- There are procedures that must be followed before a person can be deported or extradited.
- Amendments to migration law allows for the mandatory detention of illegal migrants.

CHAPTER 14

Responsiveness of the legal system to migrants

THEME EMPHASIS:
EFFECTIVENESS OF THE LEGAL SYSTEM; JUSTICE, LAW AND SOCIETY

Migrants may need to access the legal system to redress some of the disadvantages that they face and to appeal decisions about their applications or status. As in all cases, the legal system is limited in how well it can come to a solution that is acceptable to all parties. For various reasons, migrants are limited in their ability to obtain an acceptable solution. Thus the responsiveness and effectiveness of the legal system in the areas of migrant issues can be questioned.

ADMINISTRATIVE REVIEW OF IMMIGRATION DECISIONS

Prior to 1989, it was very difficult for prospective migrants to appeal decisions made about their applications. Challenging a government decision in court was a lengthy and expensive processs. However, in 1985 a review of the *Migration Act 1958* (Cwlth) was carried out by the Human Rights Commission (now HREOC) under Commissioner Fitzgerald. This review, called 'Human Rights and the Migration Act 1958', criticised the fact that there was very limited access to independent review of migration decisions.

In 1989, the Fitzgerald Report was released. Under its recommendations a system of merits review by independent tribunals was established. Merits review is a process where an authorised body has the power to look at facts of a case, consider the whether the final decision was correct and change the decision.

The new review system consisted of:
- The Migration Internal Review Office (MIRO), whose role was to provide independent internal review.
- The Immigration Review Tribunal (IRT), which reviewed decisions by MIRO and had the power to review on merits.

- The IRT could appeal to the Administrative Appeals Tribunal (AAT) and the Federal Courts only on matters of law, for example if correct procedure had not been followed in the previous reviews.

Under this system, when a refusal occurred, the applicant had a chance of seeking review under a two-tiered system. The first tier involved a review from an officer of the Migration Internal Review Office. The officer would undertake a total examination of the application and make a new decision. The applicant could also introduce new evidence at this point.

If the applicant was again unsuccessful under this review, they could then appeal to the Immigration Review Tribunal. This independent body had the power to review the decision made by the reviewing officer and within the department. It could make a new decision, but if it disagreed with the decision made by the Minister for Immigration, it could only make a recommendation.

The federal government had promised to review the new system after two years. In 1992, a review committee published its findings in a report called *Non-Adversarial Review of Migrant Decisions—The Way Forward*. While affirming that the two-tiered merit review system was working, it recommended that refugee decisions should also be handed over to an independent body. Thus the Refugee Review Tribunal (RRT) was created in 1993.

The RRT was established to review decisions regarding refugee applications. Just like the IRT, it can only appeal to AAT and the Federal Courts on matters of law. In 1999, the IRT and MIRO were almagamated and became the Migration Review Tribunal (MRT). This move was to try and make the review processes more efficient and economical.

RESEARCH 14.1

Go to the website of your local council. Write down all the ways that it supports migrants in your community. Put together a brochure for migrants new to your area outlining for them the services provided.

Review process

If prospective family-sponsored and independent migrants feel that their applications have been decided incorrectly, they can lodge a claim for further review in the Migration Review Tribunal (MRT). They must pay a fee to do this. A court-like hearing will be conducted by the MRT. Written submissions and any evidence presented by the applicant and DIMIA will be considered. The MRT is also able to conduct its own investgation, calling witnesses and subpoenaing documents.

The applicant and DIMIA may gain legal advice, but are not allowed to be legally represented during the hearing. DIMIA has the resources to gain legal advice from some of the most prestigious law firms in Australia, so most applicants are placed at a disadvantage during the court case. The MRT's decision is considered binding.

Refugees and humanitarian program applicants who have not been recognised as refugees may challenge this decision before the Refugee Review Tribunal (RRT). Their appeal must be lodged within twenty-eight days of the original decision. The RRT operates in the same way as the MRT. It cannot consider applications that have been refused because of the failure of the applicant to meet character or health requirements (the Administrative Appeals Tribunal hears these appeals).

If an applicant fails in their appeal to the MRT or RRT, they may choose to challenge the decision in the Federal Court. As with all court cases, this is time consuming and expensive and not recommended without legal representation. Thus it is not an avenue open to most unsuccessful applicants.

The Federal Court cannot make a decision based on a merit review. It can only consider whether the correct decision-making process was followed. In October 2001, amendments to the *Migration Act 1958* (Cwlth) took away the power of the Federal Court to overturn an MRT decision unless the decision-maker was found to have not acted in good faith (for example, shown bias) or did not have the legal authority to make the decision. Under the amendment, class actions are also not allowed.

The Administrative Appeals Tribunal (AAT) was established to hear appeals against Commonwealth Government ministers, officers and authorities. In this capacity, the AAT hears appeals on decisions made by DIMIA. The AAT has the power to conduct merits reviews and allows the parties involved to have legal representation. However, the only migration decisions that can be heard by the AAT are those related to cancelling a business skills visa, deportation of a person for committing a criminal act, and the refusal of an application on character or health grounds or that a person is not a refugee.

CASE SPACE

Muin and Lie v. Refugee Review Tribunal (2002)

In the class action *Muin and Lie v. Refugee Review Tribunal* an appeal was brought to the Federal Court of Australia. Mr Muin and Ms Lie were Indonesian nationals of Chinese descent who came to Australia in the mid 1990s. Both applied for asylum, claiming that they faced persecution in Indonesia because of their race.

They argued that the tribunal did not consider all of the evidence that supported their application. In addition, evidence against their case was admitted without their knowledge, thus they were not able to defend themselves.

The court ruled in favour of the appellants, saying that the Refugee Review Tribunal lacked procedural fairness. In their decision, the judges found that Muin and Lie had been denied procedural fairness in the way the tribunal dealt their with cases.

This case shows how the Federal Court can only review a case on matters of law and not on the merits of the application.

REVIEW 14.1

1 Explain the two-tier system of review.
2 Discuss the limitations of the review process.
3 Describe the role played by the Federal Court of Australia in the review process.
4 Summarise the case *Muin and Lie v. Refugee Review Tribunal*.

MEDIA CLIP

AFGHANS AFTER ALL—THE FAMILY
DEPORTED FOR BEING PAKISTANI FRAUDS
BY PAUL MCGEOUGH CHIEF HERALD CORRESPONDENT IN KABUL

Sydney Morning Herald, 28 September 2005

Afghan authorities have concluded that Roqia Bakhtiari, whose family's pleas for refuge sparked one of Australia's most bitterly fought migrant law challenges, is an Afghan citizen, not a Pakistani fraud as alleged by the Federal Government.

Figure 14.1 Long road to nowhere ... Ali Bakhtiari in 2002.

Although the Government insisted on deporting the family to Pakistan on December 30 last year, the *Herald* has confirmed that the Bakhtiaris then fled almost immediately to the greater harshness and impoverishment of postwar Afghanistan.

Their attempt to stay in Australia was a race against time that the family narrowly lost. The *Herald* has learnt that as they were returned to detention in Australia in preparation for deportation late last year Afghan investigators finally made contact with people who could vouch for Mrs Bakhtiari. They were on the verge of confirming the status of Mrs Bakhtiari, whose application for asylum included all six children, but the investigators told government officials they needed more time to formalise their findings. A source in Kabul had no doubt that this was "officially communicated" to the Department of Immigration in Australia.

In interviews in the Afghan capital this month the chief investigator and his deputy revealed that they were agreed on the citizenship of seven of the eight Bakhtiaris, and they had an open mind on that of the eighth, the enigmatic head of the family, Ali Bakhtiari, 48. General Mohammed Anaam Hoshmand, the head of the little-known Identity Checking Unit (IDCU), which is based in Kabul and is funded by the Australian Government, said through an interpreter:

"We never said 'no' about Mrs Bakhtiari. In a report on December 19 we said it [her citizenship] wasn't conclusive. However, [the report] did say there were people in Ghazni province who said she was from the Jaghuri district—we had to have more time. Our final report said that the district chief and four relatives had guaranteed Mrs Bakhtiari was from the village of Balaw Daoud—it was dated January 10. Mrs Bakhtiari is Afghan. But by the time we knew for sure, [the family] had been deported from Australia, so we just closed the file."

The *Herald*'s research uncovered a crucial document in the IDCU files that supports the claims of Mrs Bakhtiari, whose application for an Australian visa included all her children. In the document, a local mullah and the district governor counter-sign a declaration by four men from Balaw Daoud, in the Jaghuri district of Uruzgan province, that Mrs Bakhtiari is their cousin.

But the deputy secretary of the Immigration Department, Bob Correll, told the *Herald* that the department had not seen any of the IDCU's Bakhtiari reports. He said: "The reports produced by the IDCU are internal Afghan Government documents and are not provided to the Australian Government."

He said the reports had had no impact on the Australian decision to deport the family to Pakistan. In a written response to questions, Mr Correll said the Afghan evidence and the issue of the family's Afghan nationality were irrelevant as they were also citizens of Pakistan.

"The Bakhtiaris are citizens of Pakistan," he wrote. "Their return to Pakistan was fully consistent with Australia's international obligations. [Their] removal was authorised because they had run out of options. [The department] had an obligation to remove them. The IDCU investigation was just one of several lines of inquiry started well before the family were available for removal ... Any claims that the Bakhtiari family have a formal right of residence in Afghanistan do not affect the refugee assessments made in their cases—they had no legal right to remain in Australia [after] at least 20 different court appeals. We do note, however, that throughout their time in Australia, they claimed to need protection from persecution in Afghanistan—the country in which it appears they have now chosen to live, in preference to Pakistan, where they are recognised as citizens."

REVIEW 14.2

Read the above media clip and answer the following questions:
1 Why was the family deported?
2 What new evidence has emerged?
3 How was this evidence collected? How reliable do you find this evidence?
4 Give examples of communication breakdown between the Afghani and Australian authorities.
5 Outline the Australian authorities' response to the statements made in the article.

FORMS OF RESPONSES

There are a number of forms of responses to discrimination, disadvantages and other problems experienced by migrants in their bid to live in Australia, or once they have permanent residency. These responses range from international treaties to state and federal legislation.

International treaties

International law protects the basic human rights of all people and, as such, offers protection to migrants. This is important as ethnic minorities, who often make up migrant groups, lack the political power to assert their rights and so are more prone to disadvantage. They are able to turn to powerful international bodies such as the United Nations if they feel that their human rights have been violated.

These human rights are protected under a number of treaties that have been signed by Australia, including:

• the Universal Declaration of Human Rights (1984), a treaty outlining the fundamental rights that can be claimed by all people of the world
• the International Convenant on Civil and political Rights (1966), which protects the right to vote, freedom of expression and the right to a fair trial

Figure 14.2 The UN Human Rights Committee is mandated to protect all rights in international human rights laws and treaties.

• the International Convenant on Economic, Social and Cultural Rights (1976), a treaty that protects the basic needs that must be met (shelter, education and employment) for a person to live a dignified existance
• the Convention on the Elimination of all forms of Racial Discrimination, which gives special protection to ethnic minorities, including migrants.

The United Nations Human Rights Committee (HRC) or other United Nations committees can hear complaints if there has been an abuse of human rights. However, these committees are only available when all other avenues have been exhausted, and their decisions are not enforceable.

Group action

Often migrants can only force action through forming themselves into groups who will organise marches in protest of unfair actions. They can also ask for help from non-government bodies such as Amnesty International, who will in turn lobby governments and the United Nations on their behalf. This is very difficult because some cultures only have very small numbers in Australia, separated by large distances and so cannot create a very loud protest. Also, agencies such as Amnesty International have many demands for their time and financial support.

Racial vilification legislation

The federal and state governments have enacted laws to protect people from racial discrimination. This legislation has been widened to prohibit racially offensive behaviour and racial vilification. New South Wales legislation also includes penalties for racial harassment. Legislation does have its limitations as discussed earlier in this topic. Discriminatory behaviour can be hard to prove and is costly to pursue. In addition, penalties are not always seen as adequate.

Figure 14.3 A police strike force was established to patrol the streets in Sydney after the racially-motivated riots in December 2005 in Cronulla.

Anti-discrimination legislation

As discussed earlier, anti-discrimination legislation has been enacted by both federal and state governments. Protection of migrant rights is covered by these laws as they prohibit behaviour which discriminates against someone because of their race.

However, as already seen these laws are rendered ineffective because of the following factors:

- Migrants do not always understand their legal rights.
- Many migrants do not have the money or time to pursue discriminatory behaviour through the courts.
- It is very difficult to prove that discrimination has taken place.
- Penalties for wrong behaviour are seen as inadequate.

Thus the legal system's response to the protection of migrant rights can be regarded as lacking in many ways. This can be seen in the reduced access of migrants to social services, adequate housing and employment.

Legal aid

Pursuing legal rights is expensive for everyone, including migrants. There is very little legal or financial assistance available to migrants, prospective migrants and asylum seekers to pursue their applications or legal rights. The New South Wales Refugee Advice and Casework Service had to close in 1996 due to lack of funding.

The Immigration Advice and Application Assistance Scheme provides advice to asylum seekers during their application process, but cannot assist during appeals.

Migrants who use the courts to settle non-migration disputes are able to apply for legal aid if they meet the criteria. Free legal advice can be obtained over the telephone using the Legal Aid Hotline. Legal Aid can also represent a person if they claim they have encountered racial discrimination.

Recognition of cultural diversity

In a culturally diverse society, there will always be difficulties in reconciling the values of different cultures with the legal rights of the whole of society. An example of this is that in some countries a man can have more than one wife, whereas in Australia the law only allows one wife. Thus a man migrating from a polygamous country to Australia will find that only one of his wives will be recognised as his legal spouse.

The problem of different values in different cultures and the legal implications of this has been recognised by the Australian Law Reform Commission. In its 1992 report 'Multiculturalism and the Law', it was stressed that judges, lawyers and politicians need to have greater education on cultural awareness. The report urged that legal decision-makers need to be more aware of the impact of their decisions on particular cultures and for there to be greater awareness of the circumstances of some infringements of the law.

Although the law does exist to stop some undesirable cultural practices, sometimes it does not stop the practice, but just makes the carrying out of the activity more covert. For example, although the legal age of marriage in Australia is 18 years of age, in other countries the age is lower. Thus, a parent wanting to have their daughter married can send their daughter to one of these countries if she meets their entry requirements or has dual citizenship.

In an article on 2 August 2005 entitled 'Brides of Islam', the *Australian* newspaper reported that the Australian Embassy in Beirut had been approached by twelve women over the past two years, asking for help in returning to Australia to escape arranged marriages. The *Australian* reported that seven of the girls were minors, one of them aged 14.

A similar problem exists with female circumcision, a practice that is banned in Australia. Under law it is considered an assault, and any doctor who performs this operation will be prosecuted. However, health workers are concerned that the number of women affected by the practice in Australia has increased in the past five years with the migration of women from practising countries such as South Yemen, Oman, United Arab Emirates, Malaysia, Indonesia and more than twenty African countries. Thus the law has not abolished female circumcision, but sent it underground to be performed in unhygienic conditions by people with dubious medical qualifications.

RESEARCH 14.2

Go to the website of the Anti-Discrimination Board of NSW http://www.lawlink.nsw.gov.au/adb and look at conciliation cases.

1 Briefly outline two of the racial discrimination cases handled by the board.
2 How where they resolved?
3 Do you think this was a satisfactory resolution?
4 How else could the cases have been handled?

Other means of response

Federal, state and local governments have undertaken different ways to help migrants minimise the difficulties that they face in adapting to a new society. These include the following actions:

- printing important information in many different languages
- providing this information in different languages on electronic databases
- providing interpreters where possible
- providing special English classes for children and adults (although with funding cutbacks many of these are provided by volunteers)
- providing for recognition of overseas qualifications
- developing multicultural policies and principles to assist in multiculturalism
- providing settlement programs to assist newly arrived migrants.

Non-government bodies such as church and community groups and migrant organisations also offer support and provide networks to assist new migrants.

Future directions

Although federal and state governments have done much to recognise the needs of migrants and to minimise the difficulties that they face in establishing themselves as permanent residents in Australia, inequalities still exist. There is still the need for greater reforms in addressing the problems experienced by migrants in Australian society.

Possible reforms include the following areas:

- increased funding for English language programs
- promoting public education about multiculturalism to reduce racially discriminatory behaviour and vilification
- increasing the availability of and access to legal aid for migrants
- providing greater access to social security for migrants
- providing greater access to legal assistance for people in detention and increased access to review of immigration decisions
- streamlining application processes for migration so that they are the same around the world
- reforming the rules regarding mandatory detention.

REVIEW 14.3

1 In what ways can international treaties provide protection and remedy for migrants?
2 Evaluate whether legislation has provided protection for the rights of migrants.
3 Discuss how accessible legal aid is for migrants.

RESEARCH 14.3

Choose one of the areas of reform in 'future directions' above, and research how this reform will improve the rights of migrants. Write a speech or a letter to a newspaper strongly arguing for this reform.

MULTIPLE-CHOICE QUESTIONS

1   What is the name given to public behaviour which encourages others to feel hate for people of a particular race?
    a   racial harassment
    b   sedition
    c   racial vilification
    d   racial discrimination

2   Which of these statements about the Migration Internal Review Office is true?
    a   it was established as a result of the review called the *Human Rights and the Migration Act 1958*
    b   it was established as a result of the Fitzgerald Report
    c   it was established to carry out medical checks of migrants
    d   it was established by the federal government in 1986

3   What does the two-tier administrative merit review system involve?
    a   an unsuccessful candidate being allowed to appeal to the Immigration Review Tribunal if they are rejected by MIRO
    b   an unsuccessful candidate being allowed to appeal to the High Court if they are rejected by MIRO
    c   an unsuccessful candidate being allowed to appeal to the High Court if they are rejected by the Immigration Review Tribunal
    d   the Refugee Review Tribunal being responsible for all appeals

4   Which of these statements about the Refugee Review Tribunal is true?
    a   it was established after a review of the two tier merit system
    b   it was established to review decisions regarding refugee applications
    c   it began in 1993
    d   all of the above

5   Which of these statements about the Migration Review Tribunal is true?
    a   it is free
    b   it is available to prospective legal and illegal migrants
    c   it is a state body
    d   it is available to prospective family-sponsored and independent migrants

CHAPTER SUMMARY TASKS

1   Summarise the ways that the appeals process has changed over the last three decades.
2   What is 'merits review'?
3   Discuss how the legal system tries to recognise cultural diversity. Analyse if it has been successful in creating equal rights for everyone in society.
4   What is the AAT?
5   Explain what problems are created by having legislation which stops certain cultural behaviour.
6   Draw up a table that includes all of the actions that can be taken to help migrants listed under the heading 'Other means of response' on page 181 of this chapter. Next to each action, provide evidence to support its existence (you will have to look for information from the whole topic). For example:

Action	Evidence
Providing interpreters	Translating and Interpreting Service

7   Make a judgment about how effective legislative sanctions have been against discriminatory behaviour. Justify your opinion.
8   Propose other action, legal and non-legal, which could be taken to eliminate racial discrimination and racial vilification.

CHAPTER SUMMARY

- Prospective migrants can have decisions on their applications reviewed under certain conditions.
- The review process has developed over time and has adapted to change, but there are still limitations.
- Responses to migrant issues include state and federal legislation and international treaties.
- Migrants face several problems in accessing their legal rights, including the use of legal aid.
- The legal system tries to address the issue of cultural diversity but, because the law has be equal for everyone, recognition of unique cultural practices is limited.
- Further action could be undertaken to address problems faced by migrants, including allowing access to social security when needed.

TOPIC REVIEW

EXTENDED RESPONSE

Outline the legal issues facing refugees and illegal immigrants and evaluate the effectiveness of the legal system in responding to the needs of refugees and illegal immigrants.

Marking criteria for extended response

Criteria	Marks
• Clearly outlines a range of legal issues facing refugees and illegal immigrants and makes a balanced judgment on the extent to which the different remedies available to refugees and illegal immigrants achieve justice • Integrates relevant legislation, cases, documents and media reports to discuss issues faced by refugees and illegal immigrants and evaluates remedies available to them to achieve justice • Presents a sustained, logical and well-structured answer using relevant legal terminology	21–25
• Clearly outlines some legal issues facing refugees and illegal immigrants and makes some judgment on the extent to which the remedies available to refugees and illegal immigrants achieve justice • Uses a mix of relevant legislation, cases, documents and media reports to discuss issues faced by refugees and illegal immigrants and evaluates remedies available to them to achieve justice • Presents a logical and well-structured answer using relevant legal terminology	16–20
• Outlines some legal issues facing refugees and illegal immigrants and makes a limited judgment on the extent to which the remedies available to refugees and illegal immigrants achieve justice • States some relevant legislation, cases, documents and/or media reports to describe issues faced by refugees and illegal immigrants and attempts to evaluate remedies available to them • Presents a structured answer using relevant legal terminology	11–15
• Outlines some legal issues facing refugees and illegal immigrants and identifies some remedies available to refugees and illegal immigrants to achieve justice • Makes limited references to legislation, cases, documents and/or media reports to outline issues faced by refugees and illegal immigrants and identifies remedies available to them • Presents a general answer which includes legal information and terms	6–10
• Identifies a legal issue and/or identifies a remedy available to refugees and illegal immigrants to achieve justice • May make limited reference to legislation, cases, documents and/or media reports to identify an issue and/or remedy • Limited use of legal information/terms	1–5

WOMEN

The status of women under the law

Historical attitudes to the status of women

- marriage
- right to own property
- suffrage
- contracts/torts
- jury service
- education
- ability to join professions

Status of women under the law today

- pay equity
- occupational segregation
- sexual harassment
- equality of opportunity in the workplace
- domestic violence
- women's health
- post-school and workplace education and training

Mechanisms for achieving justice for women

United Nations

Convention on the Elimination of Discrimination against Women

Anti-discrimination bodies

State level: Administrative Decisions Tribunal
Federal level: Human Rights and Equal Opportunity Commission (HREOC)
State and federal anti-discrimination legislation

Affirmative action

Equality Opportunity for Women Agency (EOWA)

Education and training

Non-legal mechanisms

Unions, lobby groups, health and advocacy centres

Health

Responsiveness of the legal system to women

| International law | Pay equity | Anti-discrimination | Affirmative action |

CHAPTER 15

The status of women under the law

THEME EMPHASIS:
CULTURE, VALUES AND ETHICS; CONTINUITY AND CHANGE

For centuries, women have agitated for change to have their voices heard. Throughout history men have held most of the political power and owned the majority of wealth in most societies. Intended or not, the policies and laws that are a construct of the legal system have favoured men in all facets of society. Gender should not matter in determining the worth of an individual, but for years women have been discriminated against in many areas and denied equality of opportunity, especially in the workplace.

At a federal and state level there is a substantial body of policy and legislation that outlines the rights of women, and mechanisms in place to achieve equality for all women in Australian society. For the purposes of this unit of study, the changing status of women in the past and the status of women in Australia today will be examined. The rights of women (primarily in the workplace) will also be examined through anti-discrimination and affirmative-action legislation, and the extent to which the law has responded to the disadvantage and discrimination that women experience.

Other issues relevant to women in Australia today, such as domestic violence and rights and responsibilities in relationships, will be dealt with in the HSC course in family law.

THE CHANGING STATUS OF WOMEN

'"If the poor had more justice they would need less charity:"—If women had more justice they would have no need of appeals to sympathy.'

Jeremy Bentham (1748–1832), English philosopher and political radical

Historical roles and attitudes

For many years, the attitude that women were inferior to men has been reflected in the laws and policies of western societies. These attitudes confined women to short, formal working lives until they married and took up the role they were destined to fulfil—that of homemaker. As a result, women were discriminated against in many areas of life.

The relationship of women and men in early British and Australian society was that of servant and master. Men almost exclusively held all positions of power and owned practically all property. It followed that the position of women in society was one of subservience and powerlessness.

Such a position saw women performing domestic duties such as rearing children, preparing food, sewing and various other tasks about the home.

Figure 15.1 Historically, women were destined to fulfill a homemaker role.

This position was strongly influenced by biology. As most women were always bearing children (no reliable and safe contraception was available), they were left at home, dependent on their male partners.

The attitude of women being secondary to men was personified in various aspects of society and sometimes attempts were made to give reasons for this. Much was written and said by men, especially in Victorian England, about women, proclaiming an intimate knowledge of them, from reasons as to why they belong in the home bearing children to their sexual desires.

In a lecture to the Anthropological Society in London, in 1869, James MacGrigor Allen said:

> 'Women are unwell on average, two days in the month, or say one month in the year. At such times women are unfit for any great mental or physical labour ... In intellectual labour, man, has surpassed and does now and always will surpass women for the obvious reason that nature does not periodically interrupt his thoughts.'

On the subject of sexual desire, or lack thereof, Dr William Acton (1813–75) was quoted as saying that women are not troubled by sexual desires at all. He went to add:

> 'The best mothers, wives, and managers of households, know little or nothing of sexual indulgences ... As a general rule, a modest woman seldom desires any sexual gratification for herself. She submits to her husband, but only to please him; and, but for the desire for matrimony would far rather be relieved from his attentions'

Historical overview

There have been signature times throughout the last 120 years where women's restricted roles in society were more prominently challenged and questioned. The first two World Wars saw women, through necessity, take on non-traditional roles due to the shortage of men on the home front.

This was especially so in World War II. Women ran farms, worked in factories and generally helped maintain productivity at home. Although this work was at times hard and challenging, it was also liberating for many women, because for the first time they understood their full potential outside the traditional roles assigned to them in society.

Women also began to question why these areas of employment were denied them and, more importantly, why they did not receive equal pay. As a result the Australian Women's Charter was established in 1943. It contained twenty-three resolutions which affirmed such demands as the establishment of a national network of childcare centres, and equal pay.

For many women, though, the end of the war meant room had to be made for the returning soldiers, and they resumed their domestic roles as wives, mothers and homemakers.

The 1960s and 70s was the next significant period of time where women questioned their secondary status to men and why they did not enjoy the same rights as men. The feminist movement of this time challenged, for example, discrimination in the workplace and restrictions placed on women in pubs and clubs. Important pieces of legislation such as the *Family Law Act 1975* (Cwlth), the *Anti-Discrimination Act 1977* (NSW) and the *Sex Discrimination Act 1984* (Cwlth) were products of this era.

In 1975 the United Nations proclaimed that year to be International Women's Year to promote issues relating to women around the world.

Today in Australia there is significant legislation and policy that protects the rights of women and promotes equality of opportunity for women. Having said this, the status of women in society today is still affected by particular issues and concerns, which will be examined in this unit.

REVIEW 15.1

1 Describe the historical attitudes that men had towards women and explain why these attitudes permeated society at that time.
2 Prepare a detailed timeline to outline the historical development in the roles of women in society.

Marriage

When a woman married she effectively lost the legal identity she enjoyed as a single person. The law did not recognise the existence of the woman within the marriage, as her legal identity became that of her husband's. They were regarded as **unito caro** which meant 'one in flesh'.

William Blackstone wrote in 'Commentaries on the Laws of England, 1765', that in respect to marriage the husband and wife are one person in law. He said;

> 'By marriage, the husband and wife are one person in law: that is, the very being or legal existence of the woman is suspended during the marriage, or at least is incorporated and consolidated into that of the husband, under whose wing, protection, and cover, she performs every thing and is therefore called in our law-French a feme-covert.'

(Source http://www.pinn.net/~sunshine/whm2001/butler2.html)

unito caro 'one in flesh', meaning that when a woman married, in the eyes of the law she assumed the legal identity of her husband

The effect of this type of legal reasoning and attitude was far- reaching. Almost all women before the 20th century were married and as a result nearly all women were assigned an inferior status in society. Evidence of this can also be found in the areas discussed following.

Today the rights and responsibilities of men and women in relationships can be found in the *Family Law Act 1975* (Cwlth) and the *Property (Relationships) Legislation Amendment Act 1999* (NSW). The later piece of legislation covers people in NSW in relationships where they are not married. This includes de facto and same sex couples. These aspects of marriage and other relationships will be covered in the HSC course in Family Law.

The right to own property

Once a woman married she effectively lost control over any property she might have owned at the time of the marriage. A woman lost all control over any personal property she acquired before and during the marriage and any **real property** she owned came under the husband's control but remained hers for the purpose of inheritance. As the husband was the bread winner and the wife was dependent on him, (an inferior position), women were generally subject to the good favour of their husbands.

real property
property consisting of land and the buildings upon it

This situation stayed the same until the Married Women's and Property Act was passed in 1870 and 1872, and later a similar act in NSW, the *Married Persons (Property and Torts) Act 1901*. These acts gave women greater control over their personal property. At the time of its passing the 1901 act was seen as being forward thinking, progressive and for the first time established an independent legal status for married women.

The act effectively allowed women to retain ownership of any property they brought into the marriage and to make dispositions of property via a gift. The act also protected any property left to a woman in a will and protected a woman from a husband who was unscrupulous or a spendthrift. In other words a husband could not eat away at their wife's property inherited from her family or other sources.

Today men and women can hold, manage and dispose of property in their own right and as they see fit to do. The *Family Law Act 1975* (Cwlth) and the *Property (Relationships) Legislation Amendment Act 1999* (NSW), recognises the financial and non-financial contributions made by either party to a marriage, de facto or same-sex relationship before, during and after the relationship. As such these pieces of legislation recognise the role played by the homemaker in contributing to the assets of the family.

The *Family Law Legislation Amendment (Superannuation) Act 2001* (Cwlth) now allows superannuation to be divided up in the event of marriage breakdown. This was an important development, as superannuation is a sizeable asset, especially in the future when it matures. Prior to the passing of this act, there were strict rules about when and how you could collect your superannuation, for example when a person resigned from their job. As a result, a lot of women who had been contributing in the home but had no formal superannuation in their name, had no access to their share of the family's superannuation, usually in the husband's name. The legislation allows the superannuation to be split into two funds, one in each spouse's name. These aspects of property in relationships will be covered in the HSC course in family law.

The ability to sue and enter contracts

femme sole a single woman

A **femme sole**, or single woman, had the same rights for civil wrongdoing (torts), and the ability to sue or be sued and to enter into contracts. This was not the case for married women. A married woman could not be sued unless her husband was a co-defendant, and she could not sue unless her husband was a co-plaintiff. A husband and wife were also not permitted to sue each other.

Similarly, by herself, a married woman was not allowed to enter into a contract—her husband's signed authority was required. The legal position of women at this time reaffirmed the legal reasoning that husband and wife were one in law.

This situation changed with the *Married Persons (Property and Torts) Act 1901* (NSW). Either partner had the ability to sue or be sued, to sue the other and to obtain remedies to protect and seize their own separate property. Women also had the ability to enter into contracts on their own. Today the common law and legislation recognises the rights of all men and women who are not minors to sue and be sued and to enter contracts.

The right to vote

suffrage the right to vote guaranteed by the law

suffragette a woman supporter of women's right to vote

For women everywhere, the right to vote (**suffrage**) had always symbolised the fundamental right of all people in a democratic society. Many women, though, were denied this right until the early twentieth century. The right to vote was also an important symbol of women's struggle for equality. In Britain it was Emmeline Pankhurst who was the driving force behind the **suffragette** movement. Their marches on parliament grew in size from approximately 300 in 1906 up to 4000 in 1907. They chained themselves to pylons and gates and disrupted many political meetings.

Emmeline Pankhurst was driven by the injustice of a lack of universal suffrage. She was determined to right this wrong, as was evident when she said:

> 'You have to make more noise than anybody else, you have to make yourself more obtrusive than anybody else, you have to fill all the papers more than anybody else, in fact you have to be there all the time and see that they do not snow you under, if you are really going to get your reform realised.'

Rose Scott was a prominent figure in the suffragette movement in Australia. In a similar vein to the movement in England, she along with other women marched and held rallies to raise consciousness around the issue of the right to vote.

Politicians in Australia were certainly more receptive to the issue of universal suffrage. This may have been in part due to the fact Australia was a young country and that the contributions that women had made in a pioneering sense were well appreciated. Hence the vote for women in England lagged behind that of Australia even though it was the suffragette movement in England that inspired the movement in Australia. Regardless, Australia certainly was one of the world leaders in giving women the vote.

Figure 15.2 Many woman were denied the right to vote until the early twentieth century!

TABLE 15.1		
Years in which voting rights for Australian women were won		
	Voting rights	**Right to stand for Parliament**
South Australia	1894	1894
Western Australia	1899	1920
Australia (Commonwealth)	1902	1902
New South Wales	1902	1918
Tasmania	1903	1921
Queensland	1905	1915
Victoria	1908	1923

As can be seen in table 15.1, women in South Australia gained the vote in 1894, and all women were allowed to vote in Commonwealth elections in 1902. The rest of the states soon followed. Aboriginal women did not gain the right to vote until 1962. Until that time they had been excluded by the *Commonwealth Franchise Act 1902*.

Jury service

Even though women had gained the right vote, the right to serve on juries came much later. In New South Wales, like many other parts of Australia, a person had to satisfy certain property qualifications to serve on a jury. This was discriminatory because at the time most household property was in the husband's name. In 1947 this requirement was dropped, but there was still no automatic right to serve, as women had to apply to do so. In 1968, all women were obliged to be included on the jury roll, but could quite easily discontinue their responsibility to serve by notifying the officer responsible for the rolls.

In the parliamentary debates leading to the introduction of the *Jury Act 1977* (NSW), the Attorney-General the F. J. Walker stated:

> '... that because of an outmoded selection system and the proliferation of persons who may claim **exemption** from jury service, the stage has been reached where the jury rolls now in use are not truly representative of the ordinary citizen.'

As the main aim of the *Jury Act* was to ensure 'that jury service, so far as is practicable, will be shared equally by all adult members of the community', the liability to serve on juries was extended to all those enrolled to vote. This of course included all women.

exemption being immune from certain duties and obligations

Education, training and workforce participation

A person's status in society is greatly influenced by opportunities to acquire skilled employment. For women who wanted to enter professions, there were many barriers to overcome. The formal education that most young girls received was usually short in duration and mainly skewed towards being a homemaker.

There seemed no urgency for young women to complete their secondary education, let alone go to university. Those women who were able to attend university to study courses such as law and medicine did so in the knowledge that even if they passed their exams, they were not given degrees and effectively were barred from practising in their chosen field. This did not deter some women whose thirst for knowledge and a chance to use their talents spurred them on anyway.

The passing of the *Women's Legal Status Act 1918* (NSW), opened the way for a universal recognition of this right. Many women who had successfully completed their degrees were able to enter professions and some were elected to parliament in the 1920s.

Today the participation rate of young women aged 15–19 in education in NSW increased from 46.7 per cent in 1989 to 52 per cent in 2003. The retention rate in Year 11 and 12 has also increased steadily over the last 20 years, from 37 per cent to 81 percent in 2003. Women also comprised over 50 per cent of people studying in higher education and represented 49 per cent of students in vocational education.

Women, however, were under-represented in trade apprenticeships in NSW. Of all women undertaking apprenticeships in 2001, only 14 per cent were completing training in a 'trade' occupation. This seems consistent with the level of occupational segregation seen in NSW and throughout Australia today. Occupational segregation will be examined

TABLE 15.2

Students in vocational education and training, 2001

Training related to a person's career or occupation is mostly provided by TAFE institutions. Figures only include publicly-funded courses.

Discipline	Number of female students (000s)	Number of male students (000s)	Percentage of female students
Humanities	179.1	152.4	53.9
Social studies	46.0	17.3	72.6
Education	45.8	42.2	51.9
Sciences	66.3	88.8	42.7
Mathematics, computing	300.4	268.3	52.6
Visual/performing arts	46.7	30.2	60.5
Engineering/processing	43.0	274.4	13.5
Health sciences	293.1	311.2	48.4
Administration, business, economics, law	353.5	280.1	55.6
Built environment	15.2	99.3	13.2
Agriculture, renewable resources	30.4	82.0	27.0
Hospitality, tourism and personal services	158.9	127.9	55.3
Social, educational and employment skills	369.7	327.3	52.9
Total	**856.0**	**893.5**	**48.7**

Source: http://ofw.facs.gov.au/publications/wia/chapter6.html

in chapter 17. Post-school qualifications for women have also risen from a figure of 38 per cent in 1990 to 46 per cent in 2002.

Women also showed gains nationally in education with the retention rate for girls continuing to number higher than boys. In 1990 the retention rate for girls and boys was 70 per cent and 58 per cent respectively. This figure increased so that by 2003 the retention rates for girls and boys was 81 per cent and 70 per cent respectively.

In respect to labour-force participation, women have also made significant gains. Women aged over 15 made up 44.4 per cent of the NSW labour force in 2004, and the median age of women in the labour force was 37 years. Of all the women in NSW working, 43 per cent were employed part-time and they comprised 71 per cent of all part-time workers. In 2002, nationally, 66 per cent of all women aged 15–64 were in the workforce, with 39 per cent of these working part-time, while only 11 per cent of men worked part-time.

Across Australia, women still comprise the majority of part-time and casual workers, which raises issues about flexible work practices and the ability to access working conditions such as maternity leave and holiday pay. These and other issues such as pay equity and women in leadership roles will be discussed in chapter 17.

> ## REVIEW 15.2
>
> 1 Examine table 15.2 and outline the areas in vocational education and training in which women are well represented and under-represented.
> 2 Describe some possible reasons for women's under-representation in some areas of vocational education and training.

Social security

In the early twentieth century, the federal government did not see it as their responsibility to provide welfare payments to people who were unemployed or experienced other kinds of disadvantage that affected their ability to earn an income. The Great Depression in the early 1930s changed this mind-set because the government realised that at times people may be unemployed due to circumstances beyond their control. Today, women are eligible for unemployment benefits. Women are also eligible to receive family allowance payments to assist with the costs of raising children and, if they come from low-income families, they may also receive rental assistance to help with private rental accommodation.

All people who have carers' responsibilities for family members can receive a payment because their responsibilities impact on their ability to earn an income. The majority of carers are women. Women also comprise the majority of recipients who receive parenting payments. This is paid to parents regardless of their marital status, to assist the main carer. Other payments can be received for child-care assistance, child-care rebates and child-care support through the Child Support Agency.

Most people, women included, who are dependent on welfare as their main source of income live below the **poverty line**. Studies have also shown that over the long term, women fare far worse financially than men after divorce. This added to the fact that around 90 per cent of lone-parent families are headed by women, begins to paint a picture that many women on welfare face barriers to entering the workforce and are economically disadvantaged. Butterworth states that 'lone mothers are more likely to be income support recipients than partnered mothers, and they are also less likely to be working'. (Source: Butterworth, Peter, 'Multiple and severe disadvantage among lone mothers receiving income support' in *Family Matters*, No 64, Autumn 2003).

poverty line (also known as the Henderson poverty line) the level of personal income that defines the state of poverty

One aspect of the Howard government's suggested welfare reforms was to get single mothers looking for work, or back into the workforce once their children reach school age. This would be part of the conditions for receiving or continuing to receive welfare payments. It is suggested that many women forced to accept part-time or casual jobs will effectively be trapped in low-paid jobs without the chance to retrain or upskill.

REVIEW 15.3

Draw up a table like the one below and complete a detailed summary of the status of women for the areas listed.

Area of concern	Historical status	Current status
Marriage		
Right to own property		
Ability to sue and enter contracts		
The right to vote		
Jury service		
Education, training and workforce participation		
Social security		

Women from non-English-speaking backgrounds

Migrant women throughout Australia experience the same barriers as other women, but when you add to this a language barrier the problems compound, especially in the workplace.

Migrant women have been employed in factories in substandard conditions throughout Australia. Because these women have little English, they have not always been aware of their rights. Some of these workplaces are characterised by 'unsafe conditions, onerous shift work, little attempt to have multi-lingual health and safety signs, inadequate toilet and rest room facilities and little or no chance of promotion up the ladder'. (Source: http://www.eeo.nsw.gov.au/family/flexible/nesb.htm.)

Only recently have unions and governments taken up the cause of these workers. Over the last 10 years, occupational health and safety laws have made some progress in this area. A large section of migrant women also carry out home-based employment. While this work offers flexible hours and there is no need for child care, evidence suggests that many women work long hours in poor conditions and are paid a pittance on a piece-work basis. The federal government report *Half Way to Equal* states:

'a very distressing situation which has no place in a society which embraces the concept of social justice, the existence of widespread and grossly unfair exploitation of migrant women of non-English speaking background who are amongst the most vulnerable persons in the workforce.'

It has also been noted that immigrant women have an unemployment rate higher than Australian-born people. Immigrant women from non-English-speaking backgrounds have an even higher rate of unemployment again than immigrants from English-speaking backgrounds.

Women of non-English-speaking background also experience difficulties in relation to caring for children while at work.

'Most had no one to call on to help in emergencies, could not attend special occasions at their child's school and at times they had to leave sick children at home on their own when they were sick. They also have difficulty coping with hours of work (early starting times and shift work hours) that do not mesh with childcare or school hours.'

(Source http://www.eeo.nsw.gov.au/family/flexible/nesb.htm)

Compounding some of the issues outlined previously, women from non-English-speaking backgrounds are less able to afford to work part-time. They are usually concentrated in blue-collar jobs which are not known for flexible working hours, and generally have less confidence in negotiating job-sharing or part-time options with their employers.

Even those migrant women with a high level of educational qualifications usually cannot work in Australia without undertaking expensive bridging courses and this at times can be on top of a recognised language course. As a result of managing family commitments, many of these women suffer downward occupational mobility because their qualifications are not recognised.

> ## REVIEW 15.4
>
> 1 Explain some of the main issues in the workplace facing women from non-English-speaking backgrounds.
> 2 Outline why women from non-English-speaking backgrounds are more likely to be exploited in the workplace.

Indigenous women

Under the doctrine of terra nullius, all Indigenous Australians were dispossessed of their land. As a result, traditional Indigenous lifestyle was eroded quite quickly. Indigenous people living in the Botany region had lost their hunting skills within approximately 50 years of settlement.

The impact of terra nullius on Indigenous women was devastating. Disease and massacre decimated the population and this impacted greatly on the lives of Indigenous women. It is generally accepted that there were many examples of young girls and women being victims of sexual assaults from the non-Indigenous community. Many were members of the stolen generation, and the consequences of being taken from their families caused great suffering spiritually and emotionally. Like many Indigenous communities around the world, the effects of colonisation are a stark reality in contemporary Australia.

TABLE 15.3

Life expectancy for Indigenous people compared to the total Australian population

Population	Male life expectancy	Female life expectancy
Indigenous, 1996–2001 Australia	59.4	64.8
NSW/Vic	60	65.1
Qld	58.9	62.6
WA/SA	58.5	67.2
NT	57.6	65.2
Total population (Indigenous and non-Indigenous) 1998–2000	76.6	82

Source: http://www.healthinfonet.edu.edu.au

Figure 15.3 Life expectancy for Indigenous women is 65 years; for non-Indigenous women it is 83 years.

Today Indigenous women comprise approximately 50 per cent of the total Indigenous population. Compared to non-Indigenous women, Aboriginal women fall behind in most indicators. The life expectancy of Indigenous women is 65 years compared to 83 years for non-Indigenous women.

Indigenous women are twice as likely to suffer from cervical cancer and eight times more likely to die from it than non-Indigenous women.

Diabetes resulting from dietary and lifestyle issues is major problem facing Indigenous women. They are thirty-three times more likely to die from diabetes in the 35–64 age groups than non-Indigenous women.

Their labour force participation rate was 43 per cent compared to 52 per cent of non-Indigenous women in 2001. Retention rates to Year 11 and 12 was 24 per cent for Indigenous women aged 15 and over in NSW. Nationally only 16.3 per cent of Indigenous women had a post-school qualification compared to 34.2 per cent for non-Indigenous women. In respect to higher education only 3.5 per cent of Indigenous women held a degree, whereas 14 per cent of non-Indigenous women did so. So far, any government attempts to overcome these types of entrenched disadvantage have failed.

REVIEW 15.5

1 Describe how 'terra nullius' impacted upon Indigenous women in the years following European settlement.

2 Outline the main issues facing Indigenous women today.

3 Assess why some of the attempts to resolve these issues have failed.

4 Examine table 15.3 and answer the following questions:

   a Compare the life expectancy of Indigenous women with the rest of Australian women.

b Construct a line graph to represent the comparative life expectancy rates of Indigenous and non-Indigenous women in all Australian states and territories.

c Identify what part of Australia has the lowest life expectancy rates for Indigenous women and suggest possible reasons for this.

THE STATUS OF WOMEN UNDER THE LAW

International law—UN Convention on the Elimination of all Forms of Discrimination against Women

The main piece of international law that addresses discrimination against women around the world is the United Nations Convention on the Elimination of all Forms of Discrimination against Women (CEDAW). It came into force in 1981.

The preamble acknowledges that the Charter of the United Nations and the Universal Declaration of Human Rights affirms that all human beings are born free and are equal in dignity and rights. It also acknowledges that under human rights treaties, **nation states** have responsibilities to 'ensure the equal rights of men and women to enjoy all economic, social, cultural, civil and political rights'.

It also affirms that, despite these various instruments, there was still extensive discrimination against women around the world. The treaty states that this discrimination:

> 'is an obstacle to the participation of women, on equal terms with men, in the political, social, economic and cultural life of their countries, hampers the growth of the prosperity of society and the family and makes more difficult the full development of the potentialities of women in the service of their countries and of humanity.'

The Convention contains thirty articles. Articles 1–16 set out the main rights of women. Articles 17–30 outline the provisions with respect to the Committee on the Elimination of Discrimination against Women. This is the body set up to monitor the implementation of the treaty and other procedures for the operation of the treaty.

nation state
a politically independent country

LEGAL INFO

United Nations Convention on the Elimination of all Forms of Discrimination against Women

The main provisions in articles 1–16 of the Convention are:

Article 1   Defines discrimination against women as any distinction, exclusion or restriction made on the basis of sex that impairs or nullifies women's enjoyment of human rights and fundamental freedoms.

Article 2   States that are a party to the treaty will condemn discrimination against women and will pursue means to eliminate it.

Article 3   States should take all measures including legislation to ensure the full development and advancement of women guaranteeing them the same fundamental human rights and freedom as men.

Article 4   Parties are to adopt special measures to ensure the equality of de facto couples between men and women and to protect maternity. These positive measures are not to be considered discriminatory.

Article 5   Social and cultural patterns of men and women are to be modified with the aim of eliminating prejudices and customary practices that are based on the inferiority/superiority or stereotyped roles of men and women. The importance of maternity to children and as a responsibility of both men and women.

Article 6   To eliminate all forms of traffic in women and exploitation of prostitution of women.

Article 7   To eliminate discrimination against women in the political and public life in regards to voting, participation in government and non-government organisations.

Article 8   Women shall be given the opportunity to represent their government at an international level and to participate in the work of international organisations.

Article 9   Women shall have equal rights with men to acquire, change or retain their nationality.

Article 10   Women shall have equal rights with men in education and training.

Article 11   To eliminate discrimination against women in the workplace. This includes equality of opportunity, equal pay and conditions. This also includes the elimination of discrimination on the basis of pregnancy and maternity.

Article 12   To eliminate discrimination in the area of health care and ensure adequate services during pregnancy, confinement and the post-natal period.

Article 13   To eliminate discrimination against women in economic and social areas such as family benefits, finance and participation in areas of social life such as sports and cultural activities.

Article 14   To eliminate discrimination against women who face particular problems in rural areas.

Article 15   Equality with men before the law. This includes all aspects of civil law, in particular rights in respect to contracts.

Article 16   To eliminate discrimination against women in marriage and family relations. This can include equal rights with men in respect to entering a marriage and dissolution of a marriage. It also includes the same rights and responsibilities as parents.

As a signatory country, Australia has an obligation to ensure that laws and policies of all governments protect the rights of all women and promote equality of opportunity. The extent to which this occurs will be examined in chapter 17.

Domestic law—anti-discrimination legislation

One of the main methods for women to protect their rights when they have been discriminated against is through anti-discrimination legislation. Legislation exists at a federal and state level.

Being discriminated on the basis of sex occurs when you have been treated unfairly on the basis of your sex, marital status or because you are pregnant or likely to become pregnant. There are two types of sex discrimination, **direct discrimination** and **indirect discrimination**. Direct discrimination is a more blatant form of discrimination and more easily identified. An example of direct discrimination is where male employees were offered first choice for extra overtime ahead of female employees.

Indirect discrimination is usually harder to detect. This usually occurs when there is a procedure, rule or practice that on the face of it is the same for everyone and not discriminatory but when it is carried out it actually discriminates against a particular group of people. An example of indirect discrimination provided by the Human Rights and Equal Opportunity Commission is where a manager offers a wage increase to all employees who have worked continuously for the company over a number of years. On the face of it this may not seem discriminatory, however, given the fact that many more women interrupt their working lives to have children, this policy is discriminatory.

REVIEW 15.6

1 Select five articles of CEDAW. Outline some examples of domestic state or federal legislation that has provisions consistent with CEDAW.
2 Visit the CEDAW website at http://www.ohchr.org/english/law/cedaw.htm) and identify some countries that are not signatories to the treaty. Put forward a hypothesis on why this might be the case.

direct discrimination when one person or group of people receives less favourable treatment than another person or group in the same position would have received, on the grounds of their race, colour, descent, or national or ethnic origin

indirect discrimination practices or policies that appear to be neutral or fair because they treat everyone in the same way, but which adversely affect a higher proportion of people from one particular group. Indirect discrimination can occur even when there is no intention to discriminate.

CASE SPACE

Australian Iron and Steel v. Banovic (1989)

This landmark case of indirect discrimination revolved around the retrenchment policy of Australian Iron and Steel of last on, first off. On the face of it, this seems a reasonable policy to have. The High Court found this policy imposed a condition 'which a substantially higher proportion of one sex can comply than the other sex'. It also argued that discriminatory hiring policies in the past meant that more men were in senior positions which were immune to the retrenchment policy and hence discriminatory. It went on to conclude that 'retrenchment policies that kept alive the effects of past employment discrimination constituted, themselves, sex discrimination'.

Figure 15.4 Sexual harassment can interfere with a person's performance of their job and cause enormous stress.

Sex Discrimination Act 1984 (Cwlth)

Australia ratified the Convention on the Elimination of all Forms of Discrimination against Women (CEDAW) with the passing of the *Sex Discrimination Act 1984* (Cwlth).

The act aims to eliminate discrimination on the basis of sex, marital status or pregnancy in a number of key areas such as employment, education, the provision of services, accommodation and housing, insurance and superannuation. The act explicitly included **sexual harassment** as a form of discrimination in employment and education and makes this behaviour illegal.

The other main aim of the act is to promote community respect for the principle of the equality of men and women. It also has an educational and research role.

As such, the *Sex Discrimination Act* makes it illegal to:
- discriminate against someone on the basis of sex, marital status or pregnancy
- dismiss someone from their job on the basis of their family responsibilities
- sexually harass someone.

Sexual harassment is any unwelcome or unwanted sexual behaviour which makes a person feel offended or humiliated and where that reaction is reasonable in the circumstances. It has nothing to do with mutual attraction or friendship. It occurs when a woman is subject to unwelcome behaviour from others on the basis of her gender. The behaviour does not have to have a specifically sexual content. It can include things such as unwanted sexual advances, touching without consent, making jokes or suggestive comments that are gender oriented.

Often there is a power imbalance between the harasser and the harassed; usually the harasser occupies a higher position at the workplace. The person being harassed may think that their advancement, or indeed continued employment, depends on accepting such

sexual harassment any unwanted sexual behaviour, such as suggestive comments, inappropriate pictures hanging in the workplace, unwanted touching etc.

sexual overtures. This can be a problem in that the legislation states that the person being harassed must make it known that the overtures are unwelcome before the behaviour can legally considered 'harassment'.

The problem here is that it is the power imbalance itself that prevents the complaint from being made. This point is very clear in the case of *O'Callaghan v. Loder* [1984] EOC 92-023; [1983] 3 NSWLR 89. Loder, who was the commissioner of main roads, made sexual advances to O'Callaghan, who was a truck driver. O'Callaghan did not make it clear that she was offended by the suggestions, although she had objected to some of the comments. It was determined that Loder was not aware that what he was doing was sexual harassment and was found not to have breached the law.

If a person has a complaint under the *Sex Discrimination Act* they can take action through the Human Rights and Equal Opportunity Commission (HREOC) set up under the *Human Rights and Equal Opportunity Commission Act 1986* (Cwlth). How complaints are dealt with is examined in chapter 16.

Anti-Discrimination Act 1977 (NSW)

Women are also protected at a state level from sex discrimination under the *Anti-Discrimination Act 1977* (NSW). This broad-based act outlaws discrimination on the basis of race, gender, marital status, pregnancy, sexual harassment, racial vilification, disability, the provisions of services, accommodation and homosexuality. The Administrative Decisions Tribunal set up under the *Administrative Decisions Tribunal Act 1997* hears complaints of discrimination under its equal opportunity division.

HREOC and the Administrative Decisions Tribunal will be examined in more detail in chapter 16.

> **REVIEW 15.7**
>
> 1 Describe the difference between direct and indirect discrimination.
> 2 Explain why indirect discrimination is difficult to establish and then prove.
> 3 Outline the main aims of the *Sex Discrimination Act 1984* (Cwlth).
> 4 Define what is meant by 'sexual harassment'. What needs to occur before a complaint of sexual harassment can be initiated?
> 5 Describe the relevance of the *Anti-Discrimination Act 1977* (NSW) in respect to women.

Equal Opportunity for Women in the Workplace Act 1999 (Cwlth)

The principles of equal opportunity in the workplace

'reflect a personnel and management policy by which human resources management activities are carried out to give people the right to equitable access to jobs, career paths, training and staff development and equitable conditions of employment.'

(Source: www.eowa.gov.au)

In essence equal opportunity is about:

- treating people with dignity and respect
- management decisions being unbiased
- ensuring fair outcomes (equal access) in all areas of employment including recruitment, training and development, promotion transfer, access to information, supervision and management of staff and conditions of employment, with all selection based on merit (the best person for the job)
- recognition and respect for social and cultural backgrounds of staff and customers.

In other words, diversity is valued.

The act requires a number of organisations to establish a workplace program to 'remove the barriers to women entering and advancing in their organisation'.

Under the act all higher education institutions, private sector employers, community based organisations, non-government schools and unions with over 100 employees must develop workplace programs.

Advocates for the act believe that in a just and fair world there should be an equitable spread of both sexes in ancillary and management jobs across all industries. At present this is not case. It is argued that the whole structure of the workplace is structured to favour men, as men develop the rules. It is also hoped that equal opportunity will provide much needed role models in managerial positions so that younger women will aspire to these positions. As well as this, no women can be considered for a particular job that they are not suitably qualified for. The act is not about putting women in jobs ahead of men, as it clearly states that selection and promotion be based solely on merit. As well, it does not set quotas as does similar legislation in the United States. Quotas are used in the United States in affirmative action legislation, to prescribe a percentage of women who should occupy certain positions (e.g. in politics, as company executives etc.). It should be noted that US legislators have looked at the way affirmative action operates in Australia.

The act also establishes the Equal Opportunity for Women in the Workplace Agency to oversee the implementation of the act. The agency's role will be examined in chapter 16.

REVIEW 15.8

1 Explain the principles of 'equality of opportunity' in the workplace.
2 What are quota systems in respect to equal opportunity? Brainstorm the advantages and disadvantages of having a quota system as is currently used in the US.

MULTIPLE-CHOICE QUESTIONS

1 Which statement on the historical role of women is the most accurate?
   a women held jobs and worked part-time to earn extra money for their families
   b women only worked before they were married
   c women continued to work if they did not marry until their early forties
   d women had short working lives until they married and took up the role of homemaker

2 Which statement is not true in respect to the roles women filled during World War II?
   a women worked on farms in the land army
   b women worked in ammunition factories
   c women saw active service on the front
   d women helped maintain productivity at home

3 Which of the following statements best describes the legal position of a woman upon marrying?
   a their legal rights did not change
   b they took on the legal identity of their husband but could enter into legal relationships
   c they took on the legal identity of their husband
   d they had no legal rights at all

4 Emma, as a young English woman living in England in the late 1800s, believed she should have the right to vote. Which of the following people would have inspired her to fight for suffrage?
   a Rose Scott   b Kyra James
   c Beth McConnel   d Emmeline Pankhurst

5 In which year were women formally required to serve on juries?
   a 1948   b 1977
   c 1968   d 1955

CHAPTER SUMMARY TASKS

1 Explain why women were considered inferior to men in early British and Australian society.

2 Outline what was meant by 'unito caro'.
3 Compare women's right to own property today with that of the early nineteenth century.
4 Describe what the suffragette movement was and outline how successful it was.
5 Identify what rule restricted women from serving on juries prior to 1947.
6 Outline the level of participation of women today in education and the workforce.
7 Explain the particular barriers experienced by Indigenous women and migrant women.
8 Outline the extent to which international law recognises issues confronting women around the world.
9 Describe the different types of discrimination that women experience in Australian society.
10 Define the term 'affirmative action' and outline how it is recognised in law.

CHAPTER SUMMARY

- Women historically were treated as second-class citizens. They lost their legal identify upon marrying. They were explicitly discriminated against in the areas of marriage, property, the right to vote, the ability to sue and enter contracts, and jury service.
- Today women enjoy the same rights as men in most of these areas, but still experience economic, legal and social disadvantage.
- Women from non-English-speaking backgrounds and Indigenous women are the most discriminated-against women in society and face additional barriers to equality of opportunity.
- The Convention on the Elimination of all Forms of Discrimination against Women (CEDAW) came into force in 1981 and complements other international human rights treaties but is specifically aimed at addressing areas where women experience discrimination.
- Anti-discrimination and equal-opportunity legislation has been passed to address the issues women face, especially in the workplace.

CHAPTER 16

Mechanisms for achieving justice for women

THEME EMPHASIS:
LEGAL PROCESSES AND INSTITUTIONS/CONFLICT AND COOPERATION
An extensive body of law has developed over the past 150 years that has advanced the rights of women and better defined the status of women within society. The legislation passed by parliaments highlighted in the previous chapter are mechanisms in themselves for achieving justice for women.

This chapter will examine the institutions and processes that currently exist to protect the rights of women. It will also examine those institutions that are proactive in promoting political and economic equality of women in Australia today.

MECHANISMS FOR RESOLVING PARTICULAR PROBLEMS CONFRONTING WOMEN

Problems confronting women include: political and economic inequality; unequal access to education, training and development; difficulty in gaining promotion; unequal pay; and sexual harassment.

The role of the United Nations in protecting the rights of women

The United Nations is the mechanism where countries around the world meet and sign international declarations and treaties. The Convention on the Elimination of Discrimination against Women (CEDAW) has been important for forwarding the rights of women throughout the world. In 2004 there were 174 parties to the CEDAW.

However, with all aspects of international law there is a difference between signing an international treaty and ratification. Due to the sovereignty of all nation states, there generally has to be the political and/or economic will before a state will agree to sign a treaty. Most nation states act out of 'self-interest', and the United Nations can only pressure states to comply with international law. Once a nation state has signed a treaty, then the United Nations committee structure monitors and reports on the extent to which they are complying with its international obligations.

This is no different for CEDAW. The Committee for the Convention on the Elimination of Discrimination against Women was established under article 17 of the convention. The committee has twenty-three members who are considered experts in their chosen fields relevant to the treaty. This committee is different from other human-rights committees in that all the members have always been women selected from a wide variety of professional backgrounds. The members of the committee serve four-year terms and usually meet once a year for two weeks. The committee monitors the implementation of the treaty by examining reports submitted by states that have ratified or acceded to CEDAW.

Australia has a responsibility under the convention to report to the committee every four years or as the committee may require, on the steps it has taken to give full effects to the rights contained in it. As stated in the previous chapter, having a federal structure of government can present difficulties in ensuring all states within Australia are complying with the treaty.

The committee experiences significant difficulties as a mechanism set up to oversee the implementation of the treaty because the states that have become a party to it have made many **reservations**. It is well documented that CEDAW has had more reservations than any other treaty and hence the CEDAW committee has limited powers to promote the implementation of the treaty. These issues will be discussed in chapter 17.

reservation a formal declaration that nation states do not accept as binding on them a certain part or parts of the treaty

Figure 16.1 The Convention on the Elimination of Discrimination against Women aims to eradicate the trafficking in young girls and women around the world.

The Human Rights and Equal Opportunity Commission

The Human Rights and Equal Opportunity Commission (HREOC) is an independent federal statutory body created by the *Human Rights and Equal Opportunity Commission Act 1986* (Cwlth). It has the responsibility to administer the five federal discrimination laws, each with their own commissioner. There is a president who is aided by the human rights, race, sex, disability, Aboriginal and Torres Strait Islander, and social justice commissioners.

The sex discrimination commissioner's role is to promote greater equality between men and women. The main ways this is to be achieved is through the development of policy, initiation of research, and education of all people in respect to the behaviours and structures that contribute to sex discrimination. The commissioner also has responsibilities under the *Workplace Relations Act 1996* (Cwlth) in respect to federal awards and equal pay. Focus in the 2003–2004 reporting period also saw emphasis put on the trafficking of women to Australia to work in the sex industry or to be exploited in other work-related areas. The sex discrimination unit worked closely with customs on this issue.

When people have complaints under the *Sex Discrimination Act 1984* (Cwlth) they lodge these with the complaints handling section within the Human Rights and Equal Opportunity Commission (HREOC). The complaints handling section is responsible for investigating and conciliating all complaints under the *Human Rights and Equal Opportunity Commission Act 1986* (Cwlth), including complaints about sex discrimination.

CASE SPACE

Trafficking of women in Australia

A 20-year-old Thai university student arrived in Australia to be told that she was to work in a brothel as a sex worker. She was threatened physically and locked up so she could not escape. She had been accompanied travelling from Thailand with a woman who was paid $200 000 upon handing her over to one of the defendants, Ngoc Lan Tran. Tran placed her in a brothel in Annandale where she was told she was to have sex with clients. Upon threatening to kill herself Tran handed the victim to Sally Cui Mian Xu, another brothel owner. Xu told her she 'could not go home until she paid her tax'.

The student stated that there were up fourteen other girls in the house. She used the brothel phone when the reception was unattended and called 000. As a result she was rescued from the second brothel.

Tran and Xu have been charged under Commonwealth law of 'sexual servitude and slavery'. The defendants face up to 25 years in gaol.

Source: *Sydney Morning Herald*, 21 September 2004

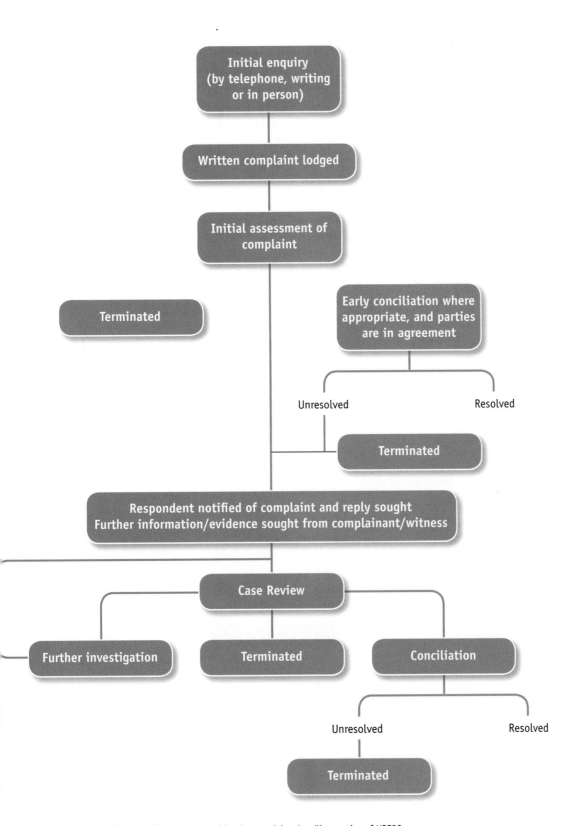

Figure 16.2 The complaint-handling process used by the complaints handling section of HREOC.

alternative dispute resolution methods of solving disputes which do not rely on the court system

The 2003–2004 HREOC annual report commented that there were 353 complaints of sex discrimination. The majority of these complaints were employment related and 28 per cent of these were of alleged pregnancy discrimination. Of all the complaints handled by HREOC, 47 per cent of these were conciliated suggesting the **alternative dispute resolution** methods adopted by the commission were able to resolve some complaints more efficiently and effectively. This might be so because they did not proceed to a more formal method of resolving the dispute via a tribunal or court. It should be remembered that for some complaints conciliation would not suffice.

Compared to the preceding years, the level of complaints had decreased by 4 per cent and the grounds and areas of complaint have been similar. There have been noticeable increases in complaints alleging pregnancy discrimination.

'… over the past three years there has been a 19 per cent increase in such complaints. The commission is of the view that this increase in complaints can, in part, be attributed to increased public awareness resulting from the Commission's ongoing policy work on pregnancy related issues.'

(Source: http:/www.hreoc.gov.au/annrep02_03/chap2.html)

TABLE 16.1

Complaints received and finalised by act 2003–2004

Act	Received	Finalised
Racial Discrimination Act	159	185
Sex Discrimination Act	353	382
Disability Discrimination Act	483	491
Human Rights and Equal Opportunity Commission Act	118	171
Total	**1113**	**1229**

TABLE 16.2

Complaints received by category of complainant by act 2003–2004

	Racial Discrimination Act	Sex Discrimination Act	Disability Discrimination Act	Human Rights and Equal Opportunity Commission Act	Total
Individual male	97	47	257	87	488
Individual female	54	305	221	22	602
Joint/multiple	4	1	4	5	14
On other's behalf	1	–	1	4	6
Organisation	3	–	–	–	3
Total	**159**	**353**	**483**	**118**	**1 113**

TABLE 16.3

Sex Discrimination Act—complaints received by ground 2003–2004

Sex Discrimination Act	Total	Percentages (%)
Sex discrimination	216	34
Marital status	28	5
Pregnancy	177	28
Sexual harassment	179	28
Parental status/family responsibility	14	2
Victimisation	19	3
Total	**633**	**100**

TABLE 16.4

Sex Discrimination Act—complaints received by area 2003–2004

Sex Discrimination Act	Total	Percentage (%)
Employment	556	88
Goods, services and facilities	41	6
Land	–	–
Accommodation	1	–
Superannuation, insurance	4	1
Education	8	1
Clubs	5	1
Administration of Commonwealth laws and programs	17	3
Application forms etc.	–	–
Trade unions, accrediting bodies	1	–
Total	**633**	**100%**

CASE SPACE

SEX DISCRIMINATION IN EMPLOYMENT

The following material has been sourced from the Australian Human Rights and Equal Opportunity Commission website. They are real-life case studies with the names of individuals and organisations changed for privacy reasons. The cases outline the events that led to a complaint being filed and the outcome.

Case 1—sexual harassment

Ms Temboli worked for a cleaning company. Mr Vassa was the nominated harassment contact officer and branch manager. Mr West was a co-worker of both Ms Temboli and Mr Vassa. Ms Temboli alleged she suffered sexual harassment and sex discrimination in employment and lodged a complaint under the *Sex Discrimination Act 1984* (Cwlth).

Ms Temboli alleged sexual harassment by Mr Vassa included: Mr Vassa making indecent gestures at her, showing her an advertisement aimed at lesbians, and saying 'I nearly grabbed a handful of a***' when he dropped a piece of paper behind her.

She alleged sexual harassment by Mr West included: Mr West stating publicly that she was having an affair with a co-worker, Mr West standing in positions where he could look down her blouse and brushing past her breast with his elbow.

Ms Temboli also alleged Mr Vassa and Mr West made comments about a piece of telephone equipment in her desk drawer, inferring it was her sex toy. The complaint was conciliated. Ms Temboli received a payment of $8000, a statement of service and an apology.

Case 2—pregnancy discrimination

Ms Frank alleged that her employer, the owner of a specialist retail store, discriminated against her on the basis of her pregnancy. Ms Frank commenced work at the store on a casual basis in September. The following February, Ms Frank informed her employer that she was pregnant and experiencing morning sickness. Ms Frank claimed that from that point onwards she was pressured in various ways to resign, but refused to do so. Ms Frank's employment was terminated in March. She lodged a complaint of pregnancy discrimination under the *Sex Discrimination Act 1984* (Cwlth). The complaint was settled by conciliation with Ms Frank receiving a payment of $2000 and an apology.

Case 3—sex discrimination

Ms Dunlop was employed in 1986, and by 1997 had been promoted to the position of group auditor. Ms Dunlop alleged that a new supervisor was appointed as her manager in 1997 and he began treating her differently to the male employees working in the same type of position. Ms Dunlop stated that she was over-scrutinised, excluded from group events and generally treated less favourably. She claimed that her salary package was less than that of male employees in equivalent positions. She also claimed that she was excluded from doing overseas audits because of her sex.

Ms Dunlop complained to management about each of these issues. She stated that the way she was treated at work then became worse. While still in her role, Ms Dunlop lodged a complaint under the *Sex Discrimination Act 1984* (Cwlth). Ms Dunlop's position was then made redundant, and she claimed she was denied a redundancy payment because she refused to sign a waiver withdrawing any action against the company. In the circumstances an immediate conciliation conference was organised in an attempt to settle the matter expeditiously. Prior to the conciliation, however, the parties settled, with a payment of over $130 000 being made to Ms Dunlop.

(Source http://www.hreoc.gov.au/
sex_discrimination/harsh_2/index.html)

REVIEW 16.1

1 Explain what the Human Rights and Equal Opportunity Commission (HREOC) is.
2 Draw a flow diagram to describe the structure of HREOC and indicate where the Sex Discrimination Commission is situated.
3 Describe the role of the Sex Discrimination Commissioner.
4 Explain how complaints under the *Sex Discrimination Act 1984* (Cwlth) are dealt with by HREOC.
5 Examine tables 16.1 to 16.4 and answer the following questions:
   a Draw a pie graph of table 16.1 to illustrate the percentage of complaints there were under each act. What percentage did sex discrimination comprise?
   b Who were the main complainants under the *Sex Discrimination Act 1984* (Cwlth) and what percentage did they comprise (Table 16.2)?
   c Examine tables 16.3 and 16.4 and write a paragraph that outlines the grounds under which the complaints were made and their area.

Equality Opportunity for Women Agency

The Equality Opportunity for Women Agency (EOWA) is a statutory body set up by the *Equal Opportunity for Women in the Workplace Act 1999* (Cwlth). It is a part of the federal Department of Employment and Workplace Relation's (DEWR) **portfolio**. EOWA's main objective is to 'create an Australia where women in the workplace can achieve their greatest potential'.

One of the challenges faced by EOWA is convince organisations that there are many benefits to having an equal opportunity workplace. Some of these are that it helps in hiring and retaining the best applicants, improves productivity and creativity, attracts more female customers and enhances the organisation's management style.

As stated in the previous chapter, organisations listed with more than 100 employees have to report annually to EOWA the steps they are taking to promote equal opportunity. Organisations that have shown 'best practice' do not have to report. EOWA's 2003–2004 annual report states that 'Seventy-three new organisations have been waived from reporting requirements as a result of their excellent workplace programs and initiatives to eliminate discrimination in the workplace'. At present there are 145 organisations across the country that have been waived of their reporting obligations.

Companies that do not comply with the legislation will face two sanctions:

- being named in the Federal Parliament in a report put on the public record (referred to as the 'naming sanction')
- being unable to tender for federal government contracts and industry assistance.

In 2003–2004 there were seventeen non-compliant organisations.

Another important role performed by EOWA is the gathering of statistical data from a number of sources to give an up-to-date overview of women in the labour force. This is compiled annually and allows EOWA to tracks trends in respect to equal opportunity in the workplace.

Through the annual EOWA Business Achievement Awards, EOWA also recognises excellence in organisations that advance women. These awards recognise those organisations around the country considered 'best practice' as examples of equal opportunity workplaces.

EOWA is an important mechanism if women are to achieve economic equality. It focuses attention on the position of women in the labour force, their representation at management levels, the level of their earnings, their participation in work-related and employer-sponsored training schemes, and their employment status (full-time, part-time or casual). All of these factors impact greatly on women's ability to enjoy economic equality. Some of these issues will be discussed in chapter 17.

portfolio a key area of government responsibility headed by a minister

REVIEW 16.2

1 Outline the role of EOWA and how it performs this role.

2 Explain what organisations have obligations under the *Equal Opportunity for Women in the Workplace Act 1999* (Cwlth). Describe these obligations.

3 What happens to those organisations that do not comply with the act?

4 Examine table 16.5 and evaluate how successful the *Equal Opportunity for Women in the Workplace Act 1999* (Cwlth) has been in getting organisations to report to EOWA. What things do the statistics not reveal about the success of the act? Explain.

5 Visit the EOWA website at http://www.eowa.gov.au/Case_Studies.asp and profile at least one category winner of an EOWA Business Achievement Award. For each organisation, outline the objectives of its program and the results they achieved.

TABLE 16.5	
EOWA reporting statistics for 2004	
Employees covered by the *Equal Opportunity for Women in the Workplace Act 1999*	2 493 906
Total number of reporting organisations in 2003–2004	2712
Number of organisations whose application to be waived from reporting for the next 1, 2 or 3 years was approved	145
Number of reporting organisations non-compliant under the act	17
Number of reporting organisations that did not have to report in 2003–2004 as they had been previously waived	177
Number of organisations that submitted compliant EOWA reports in 2002–2003	2518

(Source: http://www.eowa.gov.au)

LEGAL AND NON-LEGAL MECHANISMS: ROLE OF TRADE UNIONS, LOBBY GROUPS, WELFARE GROUPS AND GOVERNMENT AGENCIES

Legal mechanisms

The Office for Women

The Office for Women (OfW) is situated in the federal government Department of Family and Community Services. Its primary role is to provide policy advice to the 'Minister assisting the Prime Minister for women's issues' on issues that are affecting women in Australia. Being situated within the government, the OfW is well placed to influence policy making, and Cabinet and budgetary decisions, to ensure that these are made in the light of how they affect women.

The OfW also administers programs to help combat issues such as domestic violence and sexual assault and is the main avenue for consultation between the government and the women's lobby. The office also represents the Australian Government at national and international forums on women's issues and has primary responsibility within the government for Australia's obligations under the United Nations Convention on the Elimination of all Forms of Discrimination against Women.

The OfW compiles an important body of statistics that allows the position of women in Australia to be tracked historically. The extent that women have and will make gains in the areas of health, pay equity, education, occupational segregation, discrimination, leadership, sexual harassment and equal opportunity can be judged statistically. It also provides a valuable insight into the position of women in Australia today. Some of the statistics on women in chapter 15 were sourced from the OfW publication *Women in Australia 2004* which is updated every year. Some of these issues will be discussed in depth in chapter 17.

Research and publication of papers on a number of issues important to women has been a hallmark of the OfW since it began in 1974 and some of these are provided free of charge (see http://ofw.facs.gov.au/).

Office for Women NSW

The Office for Women, in the NSW Premier's Department, was established in 2004. Its mission is to 'be a credible and expert source of knowledge and strategic policy advice to government, the public and non-government sectors on emerging and complex issues relating to women in NSW'.

This is achieved through advising the government, working with the Premier's Department to have input into the policies, programs and initiatives undertaken to ensure they are relevant to women. The office also provides an avenue for dialogue, and develops partnerships between women and the government via women's organisations.

The Office for Women produces and publishes a number of valuable resources, from up-to-date statistics about women in NSW, to research papers on particular issues such as sexual assault, to fact sheets on a variety of issues concerning women. The Office for Women provides a directory of federal and state government services for women in NSW and also funds the Women's Information and Referral Service (WIRS), a confidential telephone contact point for women seeking up-to-date information concerning organisations and services for women in NSW.

Non-legal mechanisms to achieve justice for women

Legal mechanisms have been put in place to ensure that the rights and opportunities for women in society are given the attention needed to overcome the historical and cultural barriers that women still face. There are also some very effective non-legal measures that keep the issues of women on the political agenda.

Role of trade unions

In the early part of the twentieth century, unions were against women's full participation in the workplace. As women were paid less than men, unions did not want a situation where employers were able to exploit this cheap labour and force men out of jobs.

Today unions are strong advocates for the rights of women in the workplace. The Australian Council of Trade Unions (ACTU) lists the following as achievements the union movement has contributed to over the years:

- the principle of equal pay for equal work
- parental leave for women
- improvement in child care
- universal superannuation
- anti-discrimination and affirmative-action legislation.

REVIEW 16.3

1 Explain the role of the Office of Women.
2 Explain the reason behind situating the Office for Women within the federal government.
3 Visit the Office for Women NSW at http://www.women.nsw.gov.au/. Click on 'publications' and find the 'taking action' fact sheets. Select one of these and present it to the class, outlining the position of women in NSW in respect to that particular issue.

Figure 16.3 The ACTU has in recent times campaigned strongly for better rights for women in the workplace.

A fundamental challenge still facing the ACTU itself is the fact that women are still under-represented in the executive levels of the major unions in Australia compared to their level of union membership.

Some current campaigns being run by the ACTU are:

- work and family—one of the main tenets of this policy is to recognise that women have periods of time out of the workplace and that assistance in making the transition back to the workplace may be necessary
- paid maternity leave—a campaign gathering some momentum throughout the country. The ACTU believes that paid maternity leave is a 'fundamental human right, and is necessary to address the systemic discrimination and disadvantage that women suffer when they seek to combine their reproductive and productive roles'. The ACTU argues that up to 120 countries now have paid maternity leave and Australia is one of two OECD countries that does not have a system approach to it. It also believes that as the federal government is a signatory to the International Labour Organisation's Resolution 183 on paid maternity leave, it should be implemented.

Lobby groups

NON-GOVERNMENT ORGANISATIONS

Numerous non-government organisations (NGOs) throughout Australia promote issues important to women. The booklet *Australian Women Working Together* produced by the Office for Women gives the contact details of ninety-two Australian women's NGOs.

WOMEN'S ELECTORAL LOBBY (WEL)

A well-known NGO is the Women's Electoral Lobby (WEL), which was founded in 1972. WEL is dedicated to 'creating a society where women's participation and potential are unrestricted, acknowledged and respected and where women and men share equally in society's responsibilities and rewards'.

WEL is non-profit organisation that achieves its goals through lobbying governments, researching and publishing papers on issues important to women, encouraging public debate, making representation in legal cases where women's human rights are at issue, and conducting campaigns to raise awareness of these issues.

RESEARCH 16.2

1 Visit the ACTU website http://www.rightsatwork.com.au/thefacts/ and assess how the new industrial workplace laws of the Howard government may affect women. Keep in mind that women comprise the majority of part-time and casual workers.

2 Visit the webpage http://ofw.facs.gov.au/downloads/pdfs/publications_awwt_2003.pdf and research two national women's NGOs. Outline their main objectives and the methods they use to achieve their goals.

3 Visit the WEL homepage at http://www.wel.org.au/policy/Final%20revised%20policies.doc and outline some of the principles that WEL's policies are based on.

AFFIRMATIVE-ACTION AND ANTI-DISCRIMINATION LEGISLATION, EDUCATION AND TRAINING SCHEMES

Federal and state parliaments have passed numerous pieces of legislation that protect women's rights and promote equality of opportunity for women throughout Australia. Enshrining certain rights in legislation has created legal institutions and processes that promote and protect these rights.

The courts and other judicial bodies have also played a role through cases that have affirmed the current law or changed the law through the application of precedent.

Anti-discrimination and affirmative-action legislation has already been discussed in this chapter. The response by the NSW Government is evident in the *Anti-Discrimination Act 1977* (NSW), and statutory bodies such as the Office for Women in NSW that promote an affirmative action agenda.

Anti-Discrimination Act 1977 (NSW)

The *Anti-Discrimination Act 1977* (NSW) entitles all women to equality and protects all women from discrimination. This broad-based act outlaws discrimination on the basis of race, gender, marital status, pregnancy, sexual harassment, racial vilification, disability, the provisions of services, accommodation and homosexuality. It also establishes the Anti-Discrimination Board, which is part of the Attorney-General's Department, to oversee the implementation of the act. The Administrative Decisions Tribunal set up under the *Administrative Decisions Tribunal Act 1997* hears complaints of discrimination under its equal opportunity division.

Women who feel they have been discriminated against can make a complaint to the Anti-Discrimination Board, which will investigate the complaint and try to help both parties reach a solution. If the board cannot solve a complaint, women can take their case to the equal opportunity division of the Administrative Decisions Tribunal, which can make a decision like a court.

Complainants generally must make their complaint within 12 months of the alleged incident and it must be in writing.

Figure 16.4 Did she miss out on the job because she is a woman?

RESEARCH 16.3

1 Go to http://www.lawlink.nsw.gov.au/ lawlink/adb/ll_adb.nsf/pages/adb_ complaint, and click on 'complaint form'. Outline the type of information that needs to be provided to the Anti-Discrimination Board.

2 Go to the publications section of the Anti-Discrimination Board website, click on 'publications' and then 'fact sheets'. Select a fact sheet that is appropriate to women and summarise women's rights in this area.

Here are some examples of complaints that were resolved by the Anti-Discrimination Board.

Sex discrimination against a man

When a man with long hair applied for a job with a tourist company, he was told that in order to be considered for employment he would have to cut his hair. He made a complaint to the Anti-Discrimination Board because the 'no long hair' rule only applied to males and not to females. The board advised the tourist company that their policy was possibly unlawful sex discrimination. The company agreed to review and revise its grooming policy. The man was satisfied his complaint had been taken seriously and agreed to withdraw his complaint.

Sex discrimination against a woman

A woman complained to the Anti-Discrimination Board that her employer discriminated against her because of her pregnancy after she notified Workcover about safety concerns in the workplace. She was subsequently prevented from entering her work site on the grounds that it was 'too dangerous' for her. She said that when a Workcover inspector asked the employer why she was sitting outside the workshop, the manager said that it was because she was pregnant. This was despite the fact that the safety issues were of a minor nature, and other workers were allowed to continue working. She also said that she was victimised when she complained to her employer that she had nothing to do. The matter was resolved when the employer agreed to provide the employee with a written apology, a reference and an ex-gratia payment of $5000.

Sexual harassment

After being sexually harassed by her supervisor, a female security guard was dismissed. She complained to the Anti-Discrimination Board. In a conciliation conference at the board, the company agreed to pay her substantial compensation, to give her a good reference and to remove false records from her personnel file that said that her work performance was poor.

Education and training schemes

Statistics on the participation rates of girls and women in secondary and tertiary education illustrate the progress made post World War II. However, the courses studied at tertiary level tend to confirm the numbers of women in traditional areas of employment. It is also suggested that the gains made in improving educational opportunities for girls and women are not having an effect in post-school education and the workplace.

The NSW Government has taken the following initiatives over the last 10 years to try to better outcomes for girls and women in post-school education and the workplace:
- gender/equity strategies for girls and boys at school 1996–2001
- guidelines on inclusive curriculum
- promotion of gender equity by industry training advisory boards which advise the government on training priorities.

At federal level, the Australian Government Office for Women initiated a research paper in 2005 entitled 'Lifelong Learning: work related education and training for women' which specifically examined the vocational, education and training (VET) system.

Around 3000 women surveyed on their future economic security identified the following areas of high priority:

- balancing of work and family
- education and training that was affordable
- pay equity.

Part of the study examined patterns of study, especially in VET courses that young girls opt to complete. Some of these fall into the general categories of child studies, beauty and hairdressing, hospitality and business administration areas. The report suggested that these young women were not making informed choices in respect to rates of pay and the incidence of casualisation in these industries. It was argued that employment of this type 'marginalises young women and distances them from further education and on-the-job training'.

Career information that was being provided was seen to be either inaccurate or not broad enough to encourage young women to think about what career alternatives were possible, or what career offered better economic security.

In respect to women returning to the workplace there was recognition that upskilling was required for career change, and that paid maternity leave was an important feature of job security. The less time a woman is absent from the workplace, the easier the return will be. The paper addressed many other issues and could provide a good platform for the development of policy in the area of education and training for women post-school and in the workplace. For a more thorough reading of the paper, visit the website at http://www.security4women.com/.

Given the issues facing women in the workplace today, access to more meaningful and effective education and training post-school and in the workplace are needed to address issues such as pay equity and **gender segregation** in the workplace. These are discussed in chapter 17.

gender segregation
the separation of men and women into groups based on their sex

HEALTH POLICIES

'The social and biological roles of women have implications for their health and wellbeing. Women make up the majority of carers, are more likely to be in casual jobs, earn less than men and experience higher rates of violence. Women also have different expectations and preferences in the way health services are designed and delivered.'

(Source http://www.democrats.org.au/docs/2004/Womens_Health.pdf)

Men and women have some similarities in respect to their health needs, but they also have many differences. Women live longer than men, 82 years compared to 77; they bear children and suffer from specific illnesses such as breast cancer and cervical cancer.

Figure 16.5 Women have different preferences for looking after their health than men.

As a result, gender-oriented health programs have been a feature of health policies at a state and federal level for many years to the extent that Australia is a world leader in promoting women's health.

A profile of women in NSW provides some illuminating data. The main cause of death for women in NSW is cardiovascular disease, which contributes to 45.1 per cent of deaths. Cancers cause 24.2 per cent of deaths for women, of which breast cancer (29 per cent) was the most common. Lung and rectal cancers followed, with a rate of 24.9 per cent. The mortality rate for breast cancer for women aged 50–69 fell 24 per cent even though the incidence increased by 19 per cent. This suggests that early detection is having an impact.

Similarly, death rates from cervical cancer for women aged 20–60 years fell by 40 per cent in the years 1990–2000. The NSW pap test register has 1.9 million women on its books, indicating that screening is also saving lives.

Tobacco use in women is still a cause for major concern. Smoking contributes to 20 per cent of deaths for all women. Lung cancer rates among men fell 18 per cent in the last 10 years, but rose by 17 per cent for women. More girls aged 14–19 smoke than boys and the highest rate of smoking demographic is for women aged 16–24 (29 per cent). While pregnant, 97 per cent of women smokers continued into the second half of the pregnancy.

For Indigenous women, the statistics were much higher. In the 18–24 age group, 54 per cent of Indigenous women smoked, compared to 25 per cent of non-Indigenous women. As women age the picture gets worse. Of Indigenous women in the 35–44 age group, 61 per cent smoked compared to 23 per cent among non-Indigenous women.

On some indicators, women's consumption of alcohol is also increasing. The rate of hospitalisation due to alcohol was 36 per cent for women compared to 6 per cent for men. Around 40.5 per cent of women aged 16–34 have reported risk drinking.

The incidence of mental health disorders is similar for women (17.9 per cent) to men (16.9 per cent). The difference is in the types of disorders that men and women are diagnosed with. Women are more likely to be diagnosed with anxiety and or affective disorders, whereas it is more common for men to be diagnosed with disorders from substance abuse.

Obesity rates for women have risen in the years 1980–2000 from 7 to 18.9 per cent compared to men 7.2 to 17.1 per cent, with the most significant rise in obesity rates being among women aged 25–34. Women have lower physical activity participation rates than men, and it is believed that physical inactivity is a factor in contributing to disease. Women from non-English-speaking backgrounds (32 per cent) and Indigenous women (28 per cent) are less likely to be active than other Australians.

Similar patterns and issues can found around the country. As a result there have been significant federal initiatives to address some of the above health issues facing women in Australia. Some of these are:

- The National Women's Health Program established under the National Women's Health Policy in 1989. The policy is a coordinated approach to the promotion of women's health issues throughout Australia to improve health services for all women, especially those who are disadvantaged due to factors such as distance, cultural barriers and economic disadvantage.
- Breast Screen Australia, the national mammographic screening program. This free program aims to reduce deaths from breast cancer among women aged 50–69.

- The National Cervical Screening Program was established as a joint initiative of federal, state and territory governments in 1995 to prevent deaths by cancer of the cervix. It is suggested that screening every two years prevents up to 90 per cent of squamous cervical cancer, the most common form of cervical cancer. It is believed the national participation rate is approximately 70 per cent, and figures from Victoria suggest that the death rate from 1963 to 1993 went from 6.3 per 100 000 to 2.4 per 100 000.

- Prevention of female genital mutilation, which is, according to the World Health Organisation, 'all procedures involving partial or total removal of the female external genitalia or other injury to the female genital organs whether for cultural or other non-therapeutic reasons'. Genital mutilation is an unnecessary medical procedure and the law in Australia prohibits the taking of a child out of Australia for the operation to be performed. It is estimated that up 130 million women worldwide have had this procedure. Australia is a multicultural nation made up of people from many cultural backgrounds, some of whom still perceive genital mutilation to be culturally appropriate.

Figure 16.6 Some specific health issues that confront women can be totally alien to some men.

- The Australian Longitudinal Study on Women's Health, a 20-year study, the first 10 years of which were completed in 2005. Over 40 000 women are participants in three selected demographic groups aged 18–23, 45–50 and 70–75. These groups were chosen to recruit women before they passed through major turning points in their lives. The women complete a detailed survey on the state of their health every three years. The study is a world first and will provide the most comprehensive data ever collected on the health and wellbeing of Australian women. It is funded by the federal government Department of Health and Ageing. Some of the initial findings of the study after the first ten years are outlined in the box below.

LEGAL INFO

The Australian Longitudinal Study on Women's Health

The exploration of changes in individual women's lives has enabled important information to be collected which has led to many recommendations for women's health.

- Younger women are gaining weight rapidly, and the health problems associated with being overweight will start to appear much earlier than in previous generations, especially in rural areas.
- Being in a violent relationship has adverse effects on younger women's reproductive health. For example, there is greater risk of unplanned pregnancy or miscarriage.
- Younger women, particularly in cities, want to combine motherhood with paid work. The challenge is to create situations that will allow them to manage this.

- Poor mental health is associated with higher use of all drugs. While sorting out the order of causation requires more longitudinal data, recognition of the strong link should be taken into account in public health action.
- The high rate of relationship breakdown among mid-age women suggests that around a quarter will reach retirement age without partners. The effects of this on finances and lifestyle in older age have important policy implications.
- Many rural women have no access to female medical staff, or to bulk billing doctors, and this may reduce their willingness to seek help for potentially treatable conditions.
- Data collected over six years from a large sample of older women show there is no evidence to support different guidelines for alcohol consumption for older women.
- Hypertension and arthritis are the most common conditions affecting older women. While not life-threatening, stiff and painful joints cause most disability. Prevention and management of bone and joint problems should be regarded as a high priority for public health. Importantly, women should be encouraged to maintain safe and appropriate levels of physical activity.
- Widowhood is associated with poor health and high health service use in the first year or so, after which the health of widowed women becomes comparable with that of other women.
- Although there are relatively fewer providers of specialist care in rural areas, this does not translate into increased patient fees.

(Sources: http://www.newcastle.edu.au/ centre/wha/Reports/Achievements/achievements-overview.pdf

http://www.health.gov.au/internet/ministers/publishing.nsf/ Content/health-mediarel-yr2005-ta-abb110.htm)

REVIEW 16.4

1 Explain why specific health policies are required for women.
2 Outline the main issues concerning women's health. Identify some worrying recent trends in women's health and explain some possible reasons for these trends.
3 Go to to http://www.newcastle.edu. au/centre/wha/Reports/achievements_ reports.html. Select a specific area of women's health such as 'alcohol consumption and women's health' and research in greater detail an aspect of the first ten years of the Australian Longitudinal Study on Women's Health.

Figure 16.7 The way men and women sometimes stereotype and misunderstand each other has been called 'the longest war'. The fact that men hold most of the legal and economic power in society means that this misunderstanding results in discrimination against women.

MULTIPLE-CHOICE QUESTIONS

1 Which of the following statements is the most correct in describing a feature unique to the Committee for Convention on the Elimination of Discrimination against Women (CEDAW)?
   a all the members are women
   b the committee has far-reaching powers to coerce nation states into compliance with the treaty
   c the committee meets more than twice a year
   d the members serve only four year terms

2 Danielle wants to complain that she has been sexually harassed in the workplace. Which of the following statements best describes where she can take her complain to?
   a the Sex Discrimination Tribunal
   b the complaints handling section of the Human Rights and Equal Opportunity Commission (HREOC)
   c the Equal Opportunity Commission
   d the Equal Opportunity Tribunal

3 Refer to table 16.3. Which of the following options identifies the grounds for the highest number of complaints in 2004?
   a sexual harassment
   b pregnancy
   c sex discrimination
   d victimisation

4 James operates a major dot.com company with ninety-nine employees. Which body must he report to about the steps his company is taking to promote equal opportunity?
   a Equal Opportunity Commission (EOC)
   b Equality Opportunity for Women Agency (EOWA)
   c Human Rights and Equal Opportunity Commission (HREOC)
   d none of the above

5 Jacinta's company has failed to submit its annual report about the steps taken to promote equal opportunity. Which of the following best describes the sanctions the company will face?
   a a $50 000 fine
   b being named in federal parliament
   c being excluded from federal government contracts
   d being named in federal parliament and excluded from federal government contracts

CHAPTER SUMMARY TASKS

1 Outline the role of the main international mechanism that promotes the rights of women around the world.
2 Assess the extent to which it effectively carries out this role.
3 Describe what HREOC is and outline its role.
4 Explain the process followed when a woman formally complains about some form of sex discrimination to the Sex Discrimination Commission.
5 Identify what EOWA is and describe the work it performs.
6 Explain why the Australian Office for Women was established and identify at least two important roles performed by it.
7 How is the Office for Women (NSW) different from its Commonwealth counterpart?
8 Outline what is meant by the term 'non-legal' mechanisms?
9 Identify examples of non-legal mechanisms that represent the rights of women.
10 Describe why post-education and workplace training schemes are important for women.

CHAPTER SUMMARY

- The United Nations, through the Convention on the Elimination of All Forms of Discrimination against Women (CEDAW) is an important mechanism in raising awareness of the discrimination that exists against women. The convention is seen as a weak instrument due to the many reservations put in by states that are party to it.

- The Human Rights and Equal Opportunity Commission (HREOC) is a statutory body set up to administer the five federal discrimination laws, one of which is the *Sex Discrimination Act 1984* (Cwlth). The role of the commissioner is to promote greater equality between men and women through the implementation of the act, the development of policy, initiation of research and education of all people in respect to the behaviours and structures that contribute to sex discrimination.

- The Equality Opportunity for Women Agency (EOWA) is a statutory body set up by the *Equal Opportunity for Women in the Workplace Act 1999* (Cwlth). One of EOWA's main functions is to oversee the development of equality of opportunity programs within organisations required to report under the act.

- Two legal mechanisms that exist to promote the rights and equality of women are the Australian Government's Office for Women and the NSW Government's Office for Women. These bodies attempt to influence legislation and policy as it applies to women.

- The ACTU and the Women's Electoral Lobby are examples of non-legal mechanisms campaigning on issues concerning women, especially in the workplace.

- Education and training schemes post-school and in the workplace are seen as important in improving women's future economic security.

- Men and women have some similarities in respect to their health needs, but they also have many differences. The social and biological roles of women have implications for their health and wellbeing and therefore require mechanisms that address these needs. Australia is considered a leader in the development of mechanisms to address women's health issues.

CHAPTER 17

Responsiveness of the legal system to women

THEME EMPHASIS:
EFFECTIVENESS OF THE LEGAL SYSTEM; JUSTICE, LAW AND SOCIETY

'No longer should women be denied the right to vote, no longer should women
be treated as second class citizens, no longer should women not be allowed to be
a citizen at all.'

Ginny B. Waite, Member of the United States House of Representatives since 2003

THE EXTENT TO WHICH THE LAW REFLECTS THE CHANGING ROLE OF WOMEN

The law is dynamic and constantly evolving through the legislature and the courts. It must reflect the changing values of the majority of people within the society it is meant to regulate. In respect to women in Australia, the last 20 years has seen landmark legislation passed which is a reflection of the recognition of the issues facing many women in society, especially in the workplace.

Forms of response

On the face of it, women enjoy equality of opportunity with men. They have their rights protected by many laws and policies which define their status in society and protect them from discrimination. The law, however, is only a part of the solution, albeit an important one. It is not possible to legislate attitudes, and firmly held beliefs sometimes can never be changed. Hence the improvement of the rights of women in society will be generational and the importance of educative programs cannot be overstated.

Issues that have been addressed

In Australia today it would seem that women do enjoy political, economic and social equality with men. Chapter 15 examined the development of rights that women fought for throughout the last 150 years. Some of these include the right to own property, to vote, equal property rights within relationships, the right to serve on juries and the right to their own legal identity. Women have equal if not greater participation rates in higher-secondary and tertiary levels of education.

There has also been genuine progress in methods used to confront domestic violence in our society. The legal and educative measures adopted at federal and state levels since the early 1980s have recognised that domestic violence is a crime generally perpetrated by men against women. The issues and response of the law in respect to domestic violence is addressed in the unit on family law in the HSC text.

Issues still to be addressed

In spite of the many improvements that women have fought for and achieved, there are still many areas that require constant vigilance and persistence in order for change to occur. It is in this light that the legislation and mechanisms in place to ensure justice for women and the extent to which they respond to the needs of women will be evaluated. For the purposes of this chapter the responsiveness of the law will be examined in the areas of Australia's international obligations under the Convention on the Elimination of Discrimination against Women (CEDAW), discrimination, equality of opportunity (especially in the workplace), and issues emanating from these such as pay equity, gender segregation, sexual harassment and child care.

INTERNATIONAL LAW

Women around the world are exploited and abused as a result of their lack of status under the laws of their countries. The UN Convention on the Elimination of All Forms of Discrimination against Women 1981 (CEDAW) was a significant step forward in highlighting the issues confronting women around the world and getting nation states to commit themselves to ending discrimination against women.

Sovereign states can choose to ignore or comply with their international obligations and usually act out of economic or political self-interest in determining a course of action. As stated in chapter 16, CEDAW is considered a weak instrument and one of the most ignored by nation states. Those nation states that have signed the treaty have included many reservations which have allowed nations to not be accountable to certain parts of the treaty. Hence the Committee for the Convention on the Elimination of Discrimination against Women is not able to declare a nation state in violation of the treaty where it has flagged certain reservations. The committee can only continue to encourage nation states to review their current reservations.

At present the Australian government has a reservation in respect to paid maternity leave. As a result, Australia and the US are the only two OECD countries without a national paid maternity-leave scheme. Due to this reservation, over the last 21 years the Australian Government has been able to restrict paid maternity leave being used as a criticism of the steps taken to implement the articles contained in CEDAW.

Figure 17.1 Equality Now holding a press conference about women's rights at UN headquarters.

Due to these reservations there are still many areas where women throughout the world experience discrimination and have their human rights violated. It is believed that there are at least 4 million women and girls sold into sex slavery each year and that approximately a quarter of all women experience domestic violence. It is estimated that up to 130 million women are victims of genital mutilation. Literacy is still a major cause of concern, with two-thirds of all adults who are illiterate being women as a result of girls, especially in developing countries, not receiving opportunities for an adequate education compared to boys. Women are also four times more likely to be infected with HIV/AIDs than men, and up to 130 million women die from this disease each year. Education about the spread of AIDS and programs that address specific health issues relating to women is not adequate in many poorer countries.

At the same time, 179 countries have ratified the CEDAW treaty, which has been the impetus for those countries passing laws consistent with CEDAW. Millions more girls now receive a primary-school education and millions of women have been able to take out loans or now have the right to own or inherit property in their own right. The issues mentioned in the previous paragraph are now well established on the global agenda, whereas prior to CEDAW they were isolated issues in different countries, the extent of which was not effectively monitored.

At present an **optional protocol** has been approved by the UN General Assembly to provide an additional enforcement mechanism as exists with most other human-rights instruments. This would allow individuals and groups of women to be able to make a direct complaint to the CEDAW committee about alleged breaches of the treaty. The optional protocol does not add extra rights. Rather, it tries to improve the enforceability of the existing instrument.

The Australian Government has an opportunity to sign the optional protocol and send a message to the international community about its commitment to the treaty.

optional protocol
allows individuals to communicate to the committee that is overseeing the original treaty

Australia has a good record in respect to the laws and policies in place for women compared to other countries in the world. The *Sex Discrimination Act 1984* (Cwlth) is one such mechanism.

The Human Rights and Equal Opportunity Commission (HREOC) believes that there are gaps in our laws in respect to women. In the report 'Pregnancy and work: pregnant and productive' the idea that it is a right, not a privilege, to work while pregnant is discussed, and gaps in the coverage of federal anti-discrimination legislation are pointed out. Similar gaps also exist in other areas of the *Sex Discrimination Act* such as superannuation, sport, the provision of goods and services and membership of voluntary organisations.

HREOC argues that Australia signing on to the optional protocol will provide the will to correct such deficiencies, as individuals would be able to complain directly to the committee, putting added pressure on the Australian Government.

CASE SPACE

Discrimination—the basis for the torture of women

One of Amnesty International's campaigns at present is the 'Stop violence against women' campaign. The following information supplied by Amnesty International outlines the facts and issues on how discrimination can be sourced as the basis for the torture of women. Better compliance by nation states and enforcement mechanisms with CEDAW, especially article 1, would help alleviate this problem throughout the world.

The torture of women is rooted in a global culture that denies women equal rights with men, and legitimises the violent appropriation of women's bodies for individual gratification or political ends. In recent decades, women's groups and other human-rights activists and non-governmental organisations around the world have made significant advances in preventing and combating abuses, providing support and redress for survivors of abuse and winning greater equality for women. Yet women worldwide still earn less than men, own less property than men, and have less access to education, employment and health care. Pervasive discrimination continues to deny women full political and economic equality with men.

Violence against women feeds off this discrimination and reinforces it. When women are abused in custody, when they are raped by armed forces as 'spoils of war', when they are bought and sold as trafficked women, bonded labourers or in forced marriages, when they are terrorised by violence in the home, unequal power relations between men and women are both manifested and enforced. The torture of women will not be eradicated until discrimination on the grounds of gender is addressed.

Violence against women is compounded by discrimination on the grounds of race, ethnicity, sexual orientation, social status, class and age. Poor and socially marginalised women are particularly liable to torture and ill-treatment. Such multiple discrimination further restricts women's choices, increases their vulnerability to violence, and makes it even harder for them to gain redress.

Sometimes the perpetrators of these acts of violence are state officials, such as police, prison guards or soldiers. Sometimes they are members of armed groups fighting against the government. However, much of the violence faced by women is at the hands of the people with whom they share their lives, whether as members of their family, of their community, or as their employers. There is an unbroken spectrum of violence that women face at the hands of men who exert control over them.

The case of Indravani Pamela Ramjattan is one of many millions throughout the world. She was sentenced to death in May 1995 in Trinidad and Tobago for the murder of her common law husband in 1991. During her trial, the lawyers introduced evidence of the years of abuse and violence she had suffered, including beatings, death threats and rape. Despite this evidence she was convicted of murder, for which there is a mandatory death sentence. In 1999, an appeal court reduced her murder conviction to manslaughter and sentenced her to a total of 13 years imprisonment based on psychiatric evidence which showed that at the time of the murder she was suffering from 'battered women's syndrome'.

(Source: http://web.amnesty.org/library/Index/ engACT770022001?OpenDocument&of=THEMES\WOMEN#discrimination)

REVIEW 17.1

1 Assess the extent to which the law has addressed issues facing women in society today.
2 Explain with examples why there is a need for treaties such as the Convention on the Elimination of All Forms of Discrimination against Women (CEDAW).
3 What are reservations and how are they limiting the effectiveness of CEDAW?
4 Evaluate the extent to which the Australian Government has implemented the provisions of CEDAW.
5 Outline why the signing of the optional protocol for CEDAW is necessary to strengthen the enforcement of the treaty.

Figure 17.2 Pay equity for women is an issue yet to be resolved.

LEGAL INFO

International examples of pay inequality

- In the United Kingdom, women cleaners who wash floors earn 30 per cent less than wall washers (all men) and work two hours longer each week.
- In the Philippines, a car pool attendant working in a hospital earns twice as much as a female nurse, who has several years of training and high levels of responsibility for caring for patients, administration of drugs and treatment.
- In the US, local authority child care workers are responsible for supervising and looking after children under the age of five. They are paid 25 per cent less than a veterinary assistant employed to catch pests at the centre.

ISSUES TO BE ADDRESSED WITHIN AUSTRALIA

Pay equity

For many years the earnings of women have not matched those of men. Historically women have always on average earned less than men, but since the 1970s this gap has been closing. For many advocates of economic equality for women, pay equity is still an issue yet to be resolved.

Major developments in pay equity for women came about as a result of the following two test cases:

- equal pay for equal work case 1969
- equal pay for equal value case 1972

The equal pay for equal work case established that women doing the same work as men should receive the same pay. The equal pay for equal value case introduced the concept that different jobs of the same worth should get the same minimum wage. On the face of it, women's struggle to achieve equal pay had taken a quantum leap and justice had finally been achieved. What was not recognised were the explicit and implicit barriers confronting women in the workforce then and today, preventing women achieving pay equity with men.

Some of the reasons for a lack of pay equity with men are as follows:

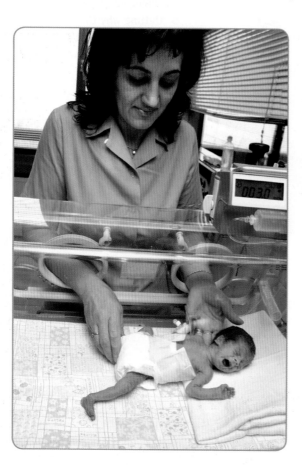

- Women are less likely to be the recipients of over-award payments than men. Women receive approximately 54 per cent of these type of payments compared to men. These payments are typically paid in occupations where there are skill shortages, usually in highly unionised, male-dominated occupations.
- Comparative worth—some occupations that predominantly employ women have been deemed to require fewer skills than occupations dominated by men, even when the educational barriers for entry are clearly higher for the predominantly female occupation. This can be seen in nursing, in which pay lags behind trades such as plumbing. In essence women's work in these occupations is under-valued.
- Less overtime—women are generally located in occupations that receive less overtime.
- Skills-based career paths—women are generally less likely to access accredited workplace training and education, even though they have the same educational qualifications and competencies as men.

Figure 17.3 In some predominantly female occupations, women's work is under-valued.

Gender segregation of the workforce

Australia has one of the most sex-segregated workforces in the developed world. This means that women do not perform the same work as men. Women generally work in different jobs and different industries. Hence some occupations have come to be considered female.

This becomes apparent when one considers the following statistics. In 1992 the Commonwealth Government report 'Half way to equal' stated that 55 per cent of women work in two occupational groups, clerks and sales people, and personnel services, whereas men are spread over a range of occupations. Evidence suggests that sex segregation is increasing. For example, women comprise 98 per cent of typists and 1 per cent of tradespersons in the fields of electrical and metal fitting and machining.

Ten years later not a lot had changed. In 2002, fifty per cent of women were still concentrated in four occupations. These were clerks (30 per cent), sales assistants (11 per cent), cleaners (4 per cent) and tellers, cashiers and ticket salespersons (4 per cent). It can be said that generally women tend to work in occupations with lower rates of pay than men.

In 2003 in NSW, 90.6 per cent of nursing professionals and 72.6 per cent of teachers were female. In contrast, 79.2 per cent of science, building and engineering professionals were men.

On getting women to enter non-traditional areas of employment, it is suggested there is what is known as a 'threshold of normality'. When women comprise at least 15 per cent of an industry workforce, this becomes sustainable in that young women have sufficient role models to encourage their participation in that industry.

Figure 17.4 Women in the armed forces perhaps have not yet reached the 'threshold of normality'...

TABLE 17.1

Employed persons by occupation, Australia, November 2003

Employed persons by occupation	Employed males (000s)	% of all employed males	Employed females (000s)	% of all employed females
Managers and administrators	**526.4**	**9.8**	**182.2**	**4.3**
Generalist managers	133.6	2.5	20.5	0.5
Specialist managers	247.1	4.6	105.6	2.5
Farmers and farm managers	145.7	2.7	56.1	1.3
Professionals	**896.8**	**16.7**	**920.2**	**21.6**
Science, building and engineering professionals	147.4	2.8	36.1	0.8
Business and information professionals	349.9	6.5	200.5	4.7
Health professionals	80.8	1.5	253.3	5.9
Educational professionals	141.0	2.6	282.2	6.6
Social, arts and miscellaneous professionals	177.6	3.3	148.1	3.5
Associate professionals	**690.6**	**12.9**	**472.4**	**11.1**
Science, engineering and related associate professionals	105.2	2.0	31.8	0.7
Business and administration associate professionals	197.9	3.7	178.8	4.2
Managing supervisors (sales and service)	291.4	5.4	186.5	4.4
Health and welfare associate professionals	25.8	0.5	48.6	1.1
Other associate professionals	70.3	1.3	26.7	0.6
Tradespersons and related workers	**1117.3**	**20.9**	**120.2**	**2.8**
Mechanical and fabrication engineering tradespersons	213.3	4.0	1.7	0.0
Automotive tradespersons	142.7	2.7	1.3	0.0
Electrical and electronics tradespersons	186.9	3.5	2.0	0.0
Construction tradespersons	302.1	5.6	5.2	0.1
Food tradespersons	60.9	1.1	28.4	0.7
Skilled agricultural and horticultural workers	73.3	1.4	11.6	0.3
Other tradespersons and related workers	138.2	2.6	69.9	1.6
Advanced clerical and service workers	**44.9**	**0.8**	**344.4**	**8.1**
Secretaries and personal assistants	3.9	0.1	181.7	4.3
Other advanced clerical and service workers	41.0	0.8	162.7	3.8
Intermediate clerical, sales and service workers	**458.2**	**8.6**	**1183.8**	**27.7**
Intermediate clerical workers	235.5	4.4	688.2	16.1
Intermediate sales and related workers	96.7	1.8	45.2	1.1
Intermediate service workers	126.0	2.4	450.4	10.6
Intermediate production and transport workers	**683.2**	**12.7**	**101.6**	**2.4**
Intermediate plant operators	176.1	3.3	8.0	0.2
Intermediate machine operators	44.2	0.8	28.5	0.7
Road and rail transport drivers	270.4	5.0	18.9	0.4
Other intermediate production and transport workers	192.5	3.6	46.1	1.1
Elementary clerical, sales and service workers	**345.9**	**6.5**	**624.9**	**14.6**
Elementary clerks	32.8	0.6	36.7	0.9
Elementary sales workers	235.7	4.4	548.8	12.9
Elementary service workers	77.4	1.4	39.4	0.9
Labourers and related workers	**595.4**	**11.1**	**319.1**	**7.5**
Cleaners	93.9	1.8	129.2	3.0
Factory labourers	141.8	2.6	81.1	1.9
Other labourers and related workers	359.7	6.7	108.7	2.5

Compiled 2004 by the Equal Opportunity for Women in the Workplace Agency

Patterns of employment

More women than men are likely to work part-time, hence women earn less and are less likely to access work benefits. In 2002, 45 per cent of females compared to 14.4 per cent of males worked part-time. This affects women's superannuation contributions and hence their retirement benefits. It also affects their capacity to save.

Women often work in industries that are generally poorly unionised and they tend not be represented in the union structure.

The enterprise bargaining system set up under the *Workplace Relations Act 1996* (Cwlth) assumed that all workers approach the bargaining table on a level playing field. However, a concentration of women in lower paid jobs requiring fewer skills has made women vulnerable in respect to pay and conditions. The new industrial laws passed through the federal parliament in 2005 strip away awards to five or six basic conditions. The rest will have to be negotiated between the worker and the employer. The deregulation of the workplace mantra in the name of flexibility and choice will further impact on pay equity for women and seriously undermine equality of opportunity in the workplace.

At the beginning of 2004, earnings nationally for full-time women employees were 84.3 per cent of men's earnings. The earnings of both full-time and part-time women employees was 65.1 per cent of men's earnings. For a lot of women, economic equality is still a long way off and is a symptom of a lack of equality of opportunity in the workplace.

TABLE 17.2

Earnings and prize money in sport

Professional sportswomen generally receive far less in prize money than men.

Sport	Men	Women
Cricket	Retainers for 25 selected Australian players range from $110 000 to $440 000 per year.	Women cricketers do not receive payment.
2002 Professional Golfers Association tour top ranking players	Tiger Woods received $6 912 625.	Annika Sorenstam received $2 863 904.
2003 Australian Open tennis	$1 127 850	$1 127 850
2002 Quicksilver Series surfing	$711 163 Mark Occhilupo	$385 000 Layne Beachley

REVIEW 17.2

1 Define pay equity and identify the extent to which women experience pay inequity on a proportional basis to men.
2 Explain with examples at least three reasons why pay inequity for women is still an issue in Australia today.
3 Define what is meant by gender segregation of the workplace.
4 Outline reasons why gender segregation contributes to pay inequity for women.
5 Explain what is needed to get women into non-traditional areas of employment.
6 Refer to table 17.1. Identify where women are over- and under-represented in certain occupational groups.

Responsiveness of the *Sex Discrimination Act*

State and federal anti-discrimination acts provide far-reaching protection to women who experience any form of discrimination in the workplace. There are few restrictions placed on women as to what they want to do. This is to some extent due to discrimination law. Women today have moved into the workforce in unprecedented numbers.

Most of the blatant forms of discrimination have disappeared due to complaints made against employers and the educative effect of the laws. Most forms of discrimination today are more subtle and covert, often involving indirect discrimination. Generally these types of discrimination involve systematic practices of disadvantage. If an employer has such a practice or policy that does disadvantage women, it is not illegal if the court believes it to be 'reasonable'.

The effectiveness of the legislation may, however, still be limited by a lack of knowledge of rights or lack of will to exercise those rights. This can be for many reasons, such as fear of dismissal, failure to recognise that there is a problem, and being unaware that such rights exist in the first place.

There are other factors that limit the effectiveness of the legislation in redressing grievances. Even if a complainant wins the case and is awarded damages, a woman may have to return to a hostile work environment. The report 'Half way to equal' recommended that women in this situation be found other employment.

On top of this, the cost—economic and emotional—may be extensive and may further constitute systems abuse and make the person feel even more of a victim.

Figure 17.5 An employment policy that disadvantages women may not be illegal if the policy is deemed 'reasonable'.

'Most people who lodge complaints end up leaving. Of those cases that go to court only 10 per cent end up staying in their job. A lot of times it is easier for the organisation to pay off the complainant than go to court.'

(*Sydney Morning Herald*, June 2004, 'The battle line for equity now focuses on the three Ps: pay, promotion and pregnancy', by Michael Pelly)

Proving that an employer or other person has discriminated against a complainant can be difficult, and most of the time not possible. At the same time, the *Sex Discrimination Act* has enabled some important cases to be won. In 1994, a woman won $160 000 after losing her career and a position as a law firm partner. This was the largest award under the act for the last 20 years, but many would argue that this is a small amount for a career. For people who win cases the damages awarded are usually under $10 000.

The provisions of the *Sex Discrimination Act* regarding sexual harassment have been effective in that the only requirement is to show that the unacceptable behaviour actually took place. Complaints of sexual harassment remain high, but this could also be attributed a greater awareness among women about their rights. A HREOC phone poll conducted in 2003 was used to gauge how prevalent sexual harassment was in society. The findings revealed that 41 per cent of Australian women aged 18–64 and 14 per cent of men had experienced sexual harassment. Of these incidences, two-thirds occurred in the workplace and less than one-third of these were reported to employers or external authorities.

HREOC also reviewed its own complaints data and found that that up to 67 per cent of those who made a complaint left their place of employment. Of these, 72 per cent stated the harassment started in the first year of employment. Although unmeasured, the economic costs to employers and the community as a result of this staff turnover is a poor use of human resources. It also reflects a residual lack of respect for female colleagues in the workplace, as women are the main complainants.

In spite of some of the criticisms outlined above, the *Sex Discrimination Act* has continued to evolve. In 1992, the act was amended to ban discrimination on the basis of the occupation or identity of ones husband or wife. The idea of 'reasonableness' as a defence for direct discrimination on the grounds of pregnancy was also banned.

In indirect discrimination cases, the onus of proof is on employers to provide a defence as to why systems and policies alleged to be indirectly discriminatory are reasonable and necessary. The definition of 'sexual harassment' was strengthened, with the complainant only having to show that they 'reasonably' felt offended, humiliated, intimidated etc.

In 1994, amendments extended the scope of protection under the act. One of these measures was to simplify the definition of 'indirect discrimination'. The number of exemptions under the act, such as those relating to superannuation and insurance, have also been recently reduced.

It should be noted that the difference between the anti-discrimination and equal-opportunity laws is that discrimination legislation is complaint based, and equal opportunity is program based.

REVIEW 17.3

Draw up a table with two columns headed 'strengths' and 'weaknesses', then list the strengths and weaknesses of the *Sex Discrimination Act 1984* (Cwlth).

Equal opportunity in the workplace

As seen in previous chapters, the *Equal Opportunity for Women in the Workplace Act 1999* (Cwlth) is the main piece of federal affirmative action legislation. The main provisions of the act and the overseeing of the act by the Equality Opportunity for Women Agency (EOWA) were discussed in chapters 15 and 16. Affirmative action legislation has been in place since 1996. The extent to which it has made a difference to the equality of opportunity of women in the workplace can be gauged by the real choices that women have.

The *Equal Opportunity for Women in the Workplace Act 1999* (Cwlth) encourages organisations to design workplace programs to 'identify issues faced by women in their workplaces and to propose, implement and evaluate actions to address those issues'. One measure of success is the proportion of women who make up company board and executive management positions. In 2004, the EOWA census revealed that women held 10.2 per cent of executive management positions and 8.6 per cent of board directorships. There were no women executive managers in 42 per cent of companies, and no women directors in 47 per cent of companies in 2004. Australia still lags behind countries such as the US and Canada. In 2004, eighty-six per cent of US Fortune 500 companies and 62.4 per cent of Canadian Financial Post 500 companies had at least one woman in an executive management position.

TABLE 17.3

International comparisons with the percentage of women board directors in Australia

Country	Latest census figures	Second census figures	First census figures
Australia	8.6% (2004)	8.4% (2003)	8.2% (2002)
United States	13.6% (2003)	8.7% (1994)	8.3% (1993)
Canada	11.2% (2003)	9.8% (2001)	6.2% (1998)
South Africa	7.1% (2004)	—	See latest

TABLE 17.4

International comparisons with the percentage of women executive managers in Australia

Country	Latest census figures	Second census figures	First census figures
Australia	8.8% (2003)	8.4% (2002)	8.4% (2002)
United States	15.7% (2002)	10.0% (1996)	8.7% (1995)
Canada	14.0% (2002)	—	12.0% (1999)
South Africa	14.7% (2004)	—	See latest

Given the statistics above it is clear that women face a **glass ceiling** effect. This refers to a situation where women can see a career path, but they are unable to progress past a certain level for a variety of reasons. Evidence suggests that it is indirect discrimination that contributes to this effect as it creates barriers to equal employment opportunities, and that it is rife both in both the private and public sector.

According to the EOWA, at the current rate of progress, employment equity for women will come in approximately 177 years. They also estimate that fewer than twenty employers have 'made significant achievements in reshaping their workplaces to make them more accommodating of a diverse workforce, including the needs of parents'.

It was also suggested that most of the employers who reported to EOWA were doing the minimum to get by under the act. They still saw equality of opportunity as an additional expense to be carried by them. The reality is that when effective EEO programs are introduced they can deliver real savings. The Hollywood Hospital in Western Australia reported that, as a result of their family-friendly policies, there was a 95 per cent saving on days lost, going from a figure of 4067 days lost in 1994 to 203 days lost in 2000.

While the rate of affirmative action progress to date has been uneven, it appears that organisations with a history of workplace segregation, where women are paid lower rewards, and where women have less access to training and promotion, need sustained affirmative action if real change is to occur.

glass ceiling
attitudinal or organisational bias preventing women and minority groups from moving into leadership positions

TABLE 17.5

The percentage of women in Australia concentrated in various leadership positions in 2004

Position	Percentage of women
ASX200 chairs	1.1%
ASX200 CEOs	2.3%
ASX200 highest titles	3.1%
ASX200 board directors	8.6%
ASX200 executive managers	10.2%
University vice-chancellors	25.0%
Federal and state politicians	28.6%
Managerial and professional positions	44.4%
Australian labour force	44.5%

At the same time, the act does enjoy sufficient community support to ensure that companies would rather comply than attract the sanction of being named in federal parliament. The naming sanction therefore ensures a high rate of compliance.

This support, however, is not matched by a good working knowledge of the issues facing women in the workplace and hence the development of programs that genuinely try to address these issues. One of the challenges faced by EOWA is to continually educate organisations and the wider community about the invisible barriers that inhibit women from being given opportunities to fill senior management and leadership roles. Given that women now make up 45 per cent of the workforce, and comprise 56 per cent of university graduates, they are well under-represented in these areas.

Figure 17.6 The number of women in senior job roles is proportionately (and significantly) lower than the number of women in the workforce.

According to the federal Employment Advocate, family-friendly practices are the key to equitable workplaces. He states:

'one of the biggest challenges we face in making the labour market more equitable remains how best to make workplaces family friendly. This includes some flexibility in allowing women and their partners to juggle work and family through more flexible hours of work, access to working conditions in part-time and casual employment etc. It is also about developing policy and practices that support and acknowledge that the stage in a family's life when raising children, especially in the early years, is short term in the context of a person's working life and allowances need to be made to allow families to better manage this.'

(Source: HREOC paid maternity leave submission, July 2002)

Paid maternity leave is also one way to minimise the separation that women experience from the workplace after childbirth. Australia's reservation to paid maternity leave under CEDAW has meant the federal government has not been under any significant external pressure to introduce a national paid maternity leave scheme. EOWA and HREOC have both advocated the benefits of paid maternity leave and allowing parents to continue their participation in the workplace after they become parents.

Quality affordable child care is another critical issue in finding the balance between work and family. Figures produced by business strategists Aegis Consulting revealed that the average cost per annum in 2004 for two children in long day care was approximately $18 000. They stated that this figure could increase up to $33 000 in Melbourne and

$46 000 in Sydney. According to Aegis, childcare 'remains the key factor in determining the workforce participation rate of women'. These costs can consume most of the income earned by returning to work, and they have risen by 32 per cent between 2003 to 2004 according to the Australian Bureau of Statistics.

Nationally, there are calls to arrest the declining birth rate, which is at 1.77 children per couple, below the replacement level of 2.1. An ageing workforce also presents challenges in maintaining a skilled workforce and our tax base. At present the two of these issues are mutually exclusive and only a radical rethink of workplace practices will provide workable solutions. The 'Fertility Decision Making Project' (2003) conducted by the Australian Institute of Family Studies found that 95 per cent of respondents wanted children. It also found that they generally desired a larger family than what they would have in reality. The reasons given for this were concerns such as job insecurity and difficulties in managing work and family responsibilities.

The federal government has taken a positive step forward in setting up an inquiry 'Balancing Work and Family'. Submissions from individuals and organisations have been taken to hear what the pressing issues and barriers to achieving this balance are. The decision around juggling work and family should not be and is not the domain of women. It is about how to achieve the best outcomes for all members of families. Giving men more flexibility to share the load is just as important for women. Essentially it is about choice.

OVERVIEW

Women have made substantal progress historically on many indicators compared to men. Having said that, they are still far from achieving equality in many areas of life. Women, like all members of society, want choice, and that means the ability to self-determine the direction and quality of their lives. Some feminists argue that conservative governments have an agenda to push women back into the home. Other sources paint a different picture. Research conducted in Australia's Household Income and Labour Dynamics in Australia (HILDA) survey, reveals that women in 2005 desire a traditional structure, with their men in full-time jobs and themselves working part-time. Susan Maushart, in her book *What Women Want Next*, points to the return of the homemaker. HILDA provides evidence that 'for most Australian women, securing high-powered jobs and long days at the office is a low priority and they are least satisfied when they work 50 hours a week'.

A second study from the University of Adelaide found that while education and career are important, Year 11 and 12 girls placed a high value on marriage, children and a balance between work and home. Sociologist Professor Susan Hakim believes that a minority of women are 'work centred' or 'home centred' and that the majority mix family and jobs without giving a priority to either.

REVIEW 17.4

1 Define the term 'affirmative action'.
2 Referring to tables 17.3 and 17.4, describe how Australia compares to other countries in respect to women executive managers and women executive directors.
3 Explain what is meant by the 'glass ceiling' effect.
4 Assess how effective the Equality Opportunity for Women Agency (EOWA) working within the *Equal Opportunity for Women in the Workplace Act 1999* (Cwlth) has been in achieving attitudinal change in the organisations that report to it.
5 Referring to table 17.5, describe in a paragraph the concentration of Australian women in leadership positions.
6 Outline why paid maternity leave and quality affordable child care are important issues for women in the workplace.
7 Visit the EOWA website at www.eowa. gov.au, click on 'publications', then 'statistics' to access Equity Statistics 2004. Select an area of concern and prepare a short fact sheet to present to the class.

At the same time, whatever length of time women spend in the workplace, the issues discussed in this chapter do limit women's choice and are discriminatory. Beth Gaze, in her article 'Twenty Years of the Sex Discrimination Act' argues:

Figure 17.7 Marching for women's rights.

'When women have equal access to economic resources, many other changes in their lives will follow. Girls and women in Australia are still in a double bind. They are told that they have equality and can pursue a career and the opportunities offered by the world equally with boys, but when they get into the workforce they find they face unequal pay, discrimination in access to good jobs and advancement in the workforce, and that they are still assigned primary responsibility for childcare by a society that devalues both motherhood and children, and is reluctant to provide adequate public support for the care and education of all its children'.

(Beth Gaze, 'Twenty Years of the Sex Discrimination Act: Assessing its achievements', in *The Alternative Law Journal*, Vol 30 No 1, Feb 2005)

If we are to prosper as a nation, we cannot continue to disenfranchise fifty per cent of the population. It is in everyone's interest to make our society more fair and just.

REVIEW 17.5

Explain what Beth Gaze in her article 'Twenty Years of the Sex Discrimination Act' sees as the dilemmas facing women achieving equality in society today.

MULTIPLE-CHOICE QUESTIONS

1 Which of the following statements best describes the extent to which the law has reflected the changing role of women?
   a women enjoy formal equality with men
   b women lack economic equality
   c women lack economic and social equality
   d all of the above

2 The Australian Government has made reservations on CEDAW. Which of the following identifies the subject of one of those reservations?
   a child care
   b quotas for equal opportunity in the workplace
   c paid maternity leave
   d all of the above

3 How may countries have signed the UN Convention on the Elimination of All Forms of Discrimination against Women (CEDAW)?
   a 190
   b 150
   c 120
   d 180

4 The optional protocol for the UN Convention on the Elimination of All Forms of Discrimination against Women (CEDAW) will allow which of the following to happen?
   a the federal government will introduce a national system of paid maternity leave
   b the Committee on the Elimination of Discrimination against Women will advise nation states on how best to implement the treaty
   c the Committee on the Elimination of Discrimination against Women will recommend trade sanctions against nation states in breach of the treaty
   d individuals will be able to complain directly to the Committee on the Elimination of Discrimination against Women

5 Which of the following best describes why women may experience pay inequity?
   a some occupations that predominantly employ women have been deemed to require fewer skills than occupations dominated by men
   b women are generally located in occupations that receive less overtime
   c more women than men are likely to work part-time, hence they earn less and are also less likely to access work benefits
   d all of the above

CHAPTER SUMMARY TASKS

1 Outline the progress women have made over the last 200 years in particular areas.
2 Explain the limitations that exist for a more effective implementation of the UN Convention on the Elimination of All Forms of Discrimination against Women (CEDAW).
3 Identify some pressing issues facing women around the world today.
4 Outline the significance of an optional protocol in respect of international human-rights treaties.
5 Outline the reasons why women still experience pay inequity in Australia today.
6 Explain the effects on a workplace that is still greatly characterised by gender segregation.
7 Discuss the effectiveness of the *Sex Discrimination Act 1984* (Cwlth).
8 Discuss the effectiveness of the *Equal Opportunity for Women in the Workplace Act 1999* (Cwlth) in removing barriers to equal opportunity in the workplace.
9 Outline why paid maternity leave is seen as an important issue for women.
10 Explain what is meant by the phrase that 'choice is the most important issue for women in Australian society today'.

CHAPTER SUMMARY

- There have been many gains for women post World War II. These include the right to own property, to vote, serve on juries and to have a legal identity. Today women still experience discrimination and lack equality of opportunity, especially in the workplace.
- The UN Convention on the Elimination of All Forms of Discrimination against Women 1981 (CEDAW) is a unique human rights treaty in that it is gender specific.
- Australia has a reservation in respect to paid maternity leave and therefore the Committee for Convention on the Elimination of Discrimination against Women is unable to apply external pressure to the Australian Government about lifting this reservation. Australia is being urged to sign the optional protocol to the treaty.
- Women still experience pay inequity compared to men. Gender segregation is still a major contributor to pay inequity in that women are confined to some occupations on lower rates of pay with minimal or no conditions.
- The *Sex Discrimination Act* 1984 (Cwlth) has been successful in reducing many overt examples of discriminatory behaviour, which is generally more subtle and systematic. Women who make complaints under the act face the prospect of returning to a hostile workplace. If they win their case the prospect of a substantial payout is unlikely given the amounts paid out in the past.

- Affirmative-action legislation has predominately failed to improve outcomes for women in executive leadership positions. It is generally accepted that family-friendly workplaces are an important step in overcoming some of the invisible barriers that exist (the glass ceiling).
- Paid maternity leave and quality affordable child care are also seen as important issues in equitable workplaces for women.

TOPIC REVIEW

EXTENDED RESPONSE

1 Define 'discrimination' and describe the main types of discrimination that women experience.
2 Outline the legal response to discrimination experienced by women.
3 Explain what action women can take when they experience discrimination. (Refer to the legal and non-legal mechanisms available).
4 Evaluate the effectiveness of the legal system in dealing with discrimination against women.

Marking criteria for extended response

Criteria	Marks
• Clearly defines discrimination and outlines the main types of discrimination that women experience and the legal and non-legal mechanisms for redress. • Makes a sound judgment based on criteria (explicit or implicit) about the effectiveness of the law in delivering justice to women who experience discrimination. • Integrates relevant legislation, documents, treaties, cases or media reports into the response. • Presents a sustained, logical and well-structured answer using relevant legal terminology.	21–25
• Defines discrimination and outlines the main types of discrimination that women experience and the legal and non-legal mechanisms for redress. • Makes a judgment based on criteria (explicit or implicit) about the effectiveness of the law in delivering justice to women who experience discrimination. • Uses relevant legislation, documents, treaties, cases or media reports in the response. • Presents a logical and well-structured answer using relevant legal terminology.	16–20
• Defines aspects of discrimination experienced by women and outlines some of the legal and non-legal mechanisms used by women for redress to discrimination. • Makes some statements based on criteria (explicit or implicit) about the effectiveness of the law in delivering justice to women who experience discrimination. • Cites some relevant legislation, documents, treaties, cases or reports in the response. • Presents a structured answer using relevant legal terminology.	11–15
• Makes references to the discrimination experienced by women and some of the legal and non-legal mechanisms available to women who experience discrimination. • Makes limited reference to the effectiveness of the law in delivering justice to women who experience discrimination. • Makes limited reference to legislation, treaties, documents, cases or media reports. • Uses some appropriate legal information with limited examples.	6–10
• Makes a general statement about discrimination relating to women. • May make limited reference to legislation, documents, treaties, cases or media reports. • Makes limited reference to legal information/terms, which may or may not be correct/appropriate.	1-5

Section D

Members of other groups not covered by human rights legislation—children and young people

CHILDREN AND YOUNG PEOPLE

The status of children and young people under the law

Historical attitudes
- lack of rights and legal recognition
- changes in policy and legislation

International developments
- Convention on the Rights of the Child
- *Gillik* case (UK)

Definition of 'child' and 'young person' in the law

Status under the law today

Family matters

Juvenile justice

Mechanisms for achieving justice for children and young people

United Nations

Committee on the Rights of the Child

Children's Court

Other mechanisms

Ombudsman, DOCS, legal aid, Administrative Decisions Tribunal

Parliament and the courts

NSW Commission for Children and Young people

Non-legal mechanisms

Unions, advocacy centres, community organisations

Responsiveness of the legal system to children and young people

International law

Problems of enforcement

Public space

Arrest/sentencing

Care and protection

CHAPTER 18

The status of children and young people under the law

THEME EMPHASIS:
CULTURE, VALUES AND ETHICS; CONTINUITY AND CHANGE

Article 12   A child capable of forming his/her views has the right to express those views, and have them taken into account in all matters affecting the child. The child has the right to be heard in administrative or judicial proceedings affecting him/her.

Article 13   The child has the right to freedom of thought, conscience and religion.

United Nations Convention on the Rights of the Child

Children and **young people** are today's future. The respect we afford them, the way in which we empower them by supporting and nurturing their social, emotional and cognitive development, is crucial to the development of a fair and just society. Children and young people are our most precious resource, and are generally undervalued and underutilised. It is hoped that through this unit of study you will gain an understanding of the nature of disadvantage that children and young people encounter, the legal and non-legal means adopted to address that disadvantage and the limitations of these means.

child generally a person aged between 0–15 years, depending on the legal context

young person in NSW, a young person is defined as being aged between 16–18

HISTORICAL ASPECTS OF THE STATUS OF CHILDREN

Historically, children had no legal rights and status until they reached adulthood, traditionally regarded as 21. It was not until the late nineteenth century, with concern over the working conditions of children, and the broader implications that child labour had on the quality of many children's lives, that significant changes began to occur.

Throughout the nineteenth century, children in poorer families were constantly threatened by the spread of disease and sickness. They lived in dirty, overcrowded housing with very poor sanitation. It is estimated that about half the funerals in London were for children under the age of ten, many of whom had died from preventable diseases. The infant mortality rate was as high as 50 per cent for children in their first year in the London area. Many children also experienced violence on a regular basis. For a lot of children, poverty and crime were significant influences in their formative years. Joining a gang, crime and prostitution were ways of surviving until adulthood.

Children convicted of offences were treated in the same way as adult offenders. The concept of an age of criminal responsibility—*doli incapax*—did not exist, and children as young as 7 or 8 were convicted of serious criminal offences.

Children were imprisoned, flogged, transported and even executed. In the year 1814, up to five children who were under the age of 14 were convicted and hung at the Old Bailey. The youngest of them was only 8 years old. By the end of the nineteenth century, there was a growing awareness that adult prisons were bad for children and young offenders were sent to reformatory schools or youth prisons.

Children were forced to work from a young age. The onset of the industrial era shifted child labour into factories where they worked long hours, usually with dangerous machinery, for very low pay. They also experienced work-related diseases due to hard physical labour or from repeatedly working with industrial chemicals, unprotected.

doli incapax a Latin term meaning 'incapable of crime', referring to the age of criminal responsibility, which in NSW is 10 years of age

Figure 18.1 The industrial era introduced young children to long work hours and dangerous machinery.

Eugene Debs was a political and social activist and a union leader in the United States early in the twentieth century. As the editor of the socialist newspaper *Appeal to Reason*, Eugene wrote:

> 'The machine became more perfect day by day: it lowered the wage of the worker and, in due course, became so perfect that it could be operated by the unskilled labor of woman, she thus became a factor in industry. The owners of these machines were in competition with each other for trade in the market; it was war: cheaper and cheaper production and labor were demanded.
>
> In the march of time it became necessary to withdraw the children from school, and these machines came to be operated by the deft touch of the fingers of the child. In the first stage, machine was in competition with man; in the next, man in competition with both; and in the next, the child in competition with the whole combination.'

The concept of public education did not exist. The education children received depended on the wealth of their family. Private tutors or governesses who taught the children at home were one option. Boys could be sent to exclusive boarding schools. There were some charity or church schools set up by unqualified teachers for poor children, but these were an exception.

Eventually, in the early 1870s, the government in England set up a subsidised system of schools, but most parents could not afford to send their children. By the 1890s, a free education system was set up with a school-leaving age of 12. Again, due to their poor economic situation, most parents needed their children to be working. It wasn't until the introduction of a minimum working age (i.e. that children attend school to a particular age) that children began to regularly attend school

By the end of the nineteenth century, many sections of society, for example governments, religious institutions and charities, began to see that children required policy and legislation to protect them from violence, abuse and poverty, and to provide them opportunities to develop socially and emotionally. From this time on, laws relating to the specific needs of children developed.

As a result of this, children began to see themselves as a distinct group of people within society and no longer as little adults who had to bear the burden of providing for their families and surviving in an adult world.

In Australia today there are many laws that acknowledge the importance of children and young people and the rationale for this is outlined below.

REVIEW 18.1

1 What challenges did children and young people experience in the nineteenth century in England? Give examples.
2 Examine the words of Eugene Debs. What explanation does he give for the use of child labour?
3 What is *doli incapax*?

HOW THE LAW DEFINES 'CHILDHOOD' AND 'YOUNG PERSON'

Traditionally, the age of adulthood was 21. In the last 20 to 30 years, this age was lowered to 18. At this age the law treats anyone over 18 as an adult. Article 1 of the Convention of the Rights of the Child (CROC) states that anyone under the age of 18 is a child unless the national law specifies an earlier age. A recent development in law has been to distinguish between a 'child' and a 'young person'. In general terms, some legislation states that childhood is said to continue until around the age of 15–16, and a young person can be anyone over 15–16. The *Children and Young Persons (Care and Protection) Act 1998* (NSW) defines a 'young person' as someone aged between 16–18.

Why does the law treat children and young people differently?

Many activities, such as drinking alcohol, buying shares, driving certain vehicles etc., are restricted or banned for children and young people under the age of 18. On the other hand, certain activities are allowed. Some services are provided free of charge or at a reduced rate. Also, if a young person commits a crime, the punishment may well take into account the offender's age.

The laws regarding young people are intended to:
* prevent them from being exploited
* protect them from the consequences of making uninformed decisions
* protect others from being disadvantaged by dealing with a person who is a minor.

STATUS OF CHILDREN AND YOUNG PEOPLE UNDER THE LAW

The status of Australian children today can be found in international instruments and domestic law which outline the rights and responsibilities of children and young people. In the 1980s, the rights of children and young people were advanced through two developments—the *Gillick* case and the adoption of the Convention on the Rights of the Child (CROC) by the United Nations General Assembly.

The *Gillik* case is an English court case that advanced the concept that children have the right and the ability to make decisions that affect their lives, and that they can do so competently given they understand the implications of such a decision. The case revolved around the claim of the mother, Mrs Gillick, that a medical practitioner should not give contraceptive advice or treatment to a teenage child without parental consent. The highest court in England dismissed the claim, arguing that if children can understand the implications of their decisions and weigh up the risks and benefits of such decisions, they are entitled to do so and this should be recognised in law.

REVIEW 18.2

1. Outline how the law defines children and young people. Use examples.
2. What was the significance of the *Gillick* case and the Convention on the Rights of the Child?
3. Take on the identity of a child in the early nineteenth century and write a two-paragraph personalised recount to explain what your life is like.

The Convention on the Rights of the Child

The main articles of the convention are:

Article 1   Defines a child as being under 18 years of age.

Article 2   A child has a right to be free from any form of discrimination.

Article 3   In all matters pertaining to children the **best interests of the child** shall be the guiding principle.

Article 6   Every child has the right to a life.

Article 7   Every child shall be given a name and nationality.

Article 9   A child shall not be separated from his/her parents and where this does occur, the best interests of the child shall be the guiding principle.

Article 12   Every child has the right to express their views and have those views heard.

Article 13   Every child has the right to freedom of expression.

Article 15   Every child has the right to freedom of association and peaceful assembly.

Article 18   Where possible, every child has the right to be raised by their parents or legal guardians.

Article 19   Children have a right to be protected from all forms of abuse.

Article 24   Children have a right to and access to proper medical and health treatments and facilities.

Article 28   Children have a right to an education.

Article 30   Indigenous children have a right to be part of, and a member of their cultural, religious and language group.

Article 32   Every child should be free from economic exploitation and there should be minimum ages set for admission to employment.

Article 35   Every child has a right to be safe from abduction, sale and trafficking of children.

Article 37   Every child has right not to be tortured or to experience cruel or degrading treatment or punishment.

Article 40   Children have a number of rights in regard to administration and procedure in the criminal justice system.

best interests of the child the standard that various judicial bodies (such as the family court) will apply when making decisions about children and young people

RESEARCH 18.1

Go to the Office of the Commissioner of Human Rights at http://www.unhchr.ch/html/menu3/b/k2crc.htm and write a one-page summary of the articles in CROC.

International law—CROC

Australia signed the Convention on the Rights of the Child (CROC) which essentially means that Australia now has an international as well as a national duty to protect the rights of children. Articles 1–40 outline the fundamental basic rights that children around the world have a right to enjoy. CROC is the most signed of all international United Nations treaties.

As a ratifying country, Australia has obligations to ensure that the policies and laws of state and federal governments do not contradict CROC at the very least and, where possible, state laws (due to federal constraints) must also uphold the principles contained within it. There are certainly many laws that uphold CROC principles and some of these will be addressed below. There are also certain laws that restrict the rights of children and young people.

Some of these laws are put in place in the best interests of the child's welfare, while some restrictions are said to curtail the rights of children and young people unnecessarily. Some of these issues are addressed later in the responsiveness of the law to children and young people.

Domestic law—civil matters

A name and a nationality

Parents have the responsibility to register the birth of their child under the *Births, Deaths and Marriages Act 1995* (NSW). The parents have 21 days after the birth to give notice of the birth, and 60 days to complete the registration process. If a child is stillborn, the registry must be notified with 48 hours. The registry will accept registration by one parent, even when the parents are married. This puts the existence of the child on the public record and gives the child a legal name, that of the father or mother in most cases. This therefore affords the child all the rights and protections under the law. The parent or parents also assume responsibilities under the law for the child's welfare.

CASE SPACE

Ms L v. the Principal Registrar of Births Deaths and Marriages (1985)

In this case, both parents had registered different surnames for their child. The registry allowed the paternal name to stand. The Equal Opportunity Tribunal found the registry practice to be unlawful in that it discriminated on the grounds of sex and marriage. The tribunal found that the registry had to register the name lodged first if two valid, but conflicting, registrations were sent.

This posed other issues for the registry because women in post-natal confinement may not be as easily disposed to quickly attend to the registration. This issue generally refers to married couples, as the requirement of a father of an **ex-nuptial child** is that he has to get agreement from the mother or a court order before he can apply to register the birth.

Under the *Australian Citizenship Act 1948* (Cwlth), any child born in Australia is automatically an Australian citizen if at least one of the parents is an Australian citizen. Children born overseas to a parent who is an Australian citizen may apply for registration as an Australian citizen by descent, if they meet certain criteria. A child who is a permanent resident and who has been legally adopted also automatically acquires Australian citizenship.

---

ex-nuptial child a child whose parents are not married at the time of conception

foundling a deserted infant whose parents' identity is unknown

adoption order a court order that establishes a new legal relationship between potential adoptive parents and a child eligible for adoption. It also severs the legal relationship that existed between the adoptive child and their natural or legally recognised parents or guardians prior to the adoption process.

If a child is a **foundling**, the person who has been granted guardianship of the child is responsible for having the child's birth registered. When an **adoption order** is made under the *Adoption Information Act 2000* (NSW), this must also be registered under the act. A child's name may be changed, and generally the child must consent to this change. The registration of the child's name can become complicated if there is disagreement between the parents as to the name to be used.

Education

Children have the right to be educated, and it is compulsory for children aged 6–15 to attend school under the *Education Reform Act 1990* (NSW). Under this act, parents must send their children to a school registered with the NSW Board of Studies, and it is the duty of the state to ensure that every child receives an education of the highest quality. The principal responsibility of the state is to ensure the above the provision of public education.

Work

Generally it is acknowledged that it is in the best interests of children that they remain in school and receive a formal primary and secondary education. According to the Office of Industrial Relations in NSW, there is no minimum legal age limit for young workers. If, however, they are under 15, they must receive authorisation from the NSW Department of Education and Training to leave school.

The NSW Commission for Children and Young People in their report 'Children at Work 2005' surveyed 10 999 children and young people in Years 7–10 living in NSW about their working experiences, and gave an interesting profile of young workers throughout the state. The report stated that approximately 56 per cent of the children and young people surveyed had completed some form of work in the last 12 months and that they were more likely to do so as they got older. Casual work was the most common form of work—49.5 per cent compared to regular work (38.2 per cent) and one-off work (12.2 per cent). The report went on to say that 61.7 per cent of children's and young people's work is flexible and insecure.

Children and young people who lived in rural areas were more likely to work (65.5 per cent) compared to children in the Sydney metropolitan area (50.4 per cent). Children and young people born in Australia are more likely to work than those born overseas (57.7 per cent compared to 48.2 per cent) and children and young people living in extended-family arrangements were less likely to work than those who did not (49.9 per cent compared to 57.2 per cent).

REVIEW 18.3

1 Which article of CROC does the *Births, Deaths and Marriages Act 1995* (NSW) comply with?
2 What are the processes that must be followed for the registering of the birth of a child?
3 What did the case *Ms L v. The Principal Registrar of Births Deaths and Marriages* (1985) establish?

TABLE 18.1

Children who work, by school grade

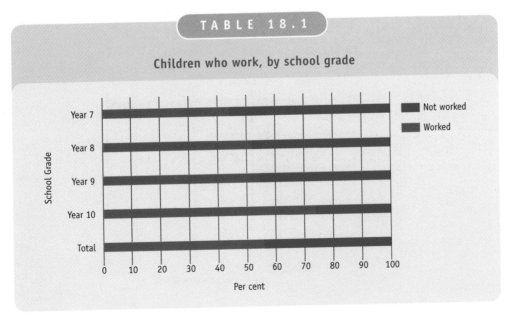

Legend: Not worked, Worked

(Per cent — axis 0 to 100; School Grade: Year 7, Year 8, Year 9, Year 10, Total)

The report went on to say that boys generally dominate work that requires more physical labour such as labouring and delivery work, while girls were more likely to dominate service and care work such as sales, clerical and service. The report also stated:

'Children and young people generally start with informal work at home, move on to do similar work for other informal employers, finally taking up a variety of jobs for formal employers (around 60 per cent) with similar pay and conditions to adults.'

The report found that rates of pay were comparable to those around the country with, about 22 per cent earning around $6 to $8.00 per hour.

Regardless of age, the worker will be covered by the relevant **award** and/or **Australian Workplace Agreement** that will cover aspects such as pay and other conditions. These should be displayed at every place of work. Some young people will be paid a 'junior rate' of pay. Regardless of this, they must be paid at least once a fortnight and receive a payslip that shows their pay, any deductions, amount paid in superannuation etc.

award an agreement between employers and employees, usually across a whole industry, in respect to pay and other working conditions, overseen by the Australian Industrial Relations Commission

Australian Workplace Agreement an individual workplace agreement between an employee and employer

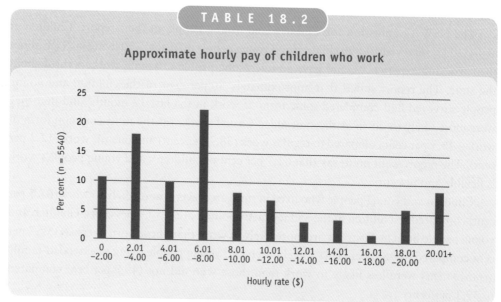

TABLE 18.2

Approximate hourly pay of children who work

TABLE 18.3

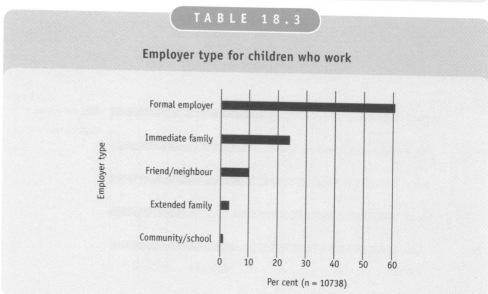

Employer type for children who work

Young people in the workplace are also covered by all the relevant workplace and safety legislation for workers in New South Wales. Issues facing young people in the workplace will be further addressed in chapter 20.

Medical treatment

Under the *Minors (Property and Contract) Act 1970* (NSW), a person aged 14 years or more can legally give consent to medical or dental treatment if the practitioner agrees to perform the treatment. Thus a doctor can prescribe contraception to a girl without her parents' knowledge or consent.

Parents have the responsibility to seek out proper medical care for their children, even if they have religious objections. If a child under 16 refuses medical treatment, parents have a right to insist that it be performed.

Religion

Section 116 of the Australian Constitution provides one of the few explicit individual rights contained in the Constitution, 'freedom of religion' or restrictions on the introduction of a 'state religion'. This means that parents have the right to decide what religion their child will be raised under. As a child grows and develops in their thinking about their religious beliefs, they naturally assume this responsibility for themselves.

Discrimination

All children and young people are treated equally under the law and protected from discrimination. Children and young people are protected from discrimination under the *Anti-Discrimination Act 1977* (NSW). This broad-based act outlaws discrimination on the basis of race, gender, marital status, pregnancy, sexual harassment, racial vilification, disability, and the provisions of services, accommodation and homosexuality. It also establishes the Anti-Discrimination Board, which oversees the implementation of the act. The Administrative Decisions Tribunal, set up under the *Administrative Decisions Tribunal Act 1997* (NSW), hears complaints of discrimination in its Equal Opportunity Division.

Contracts

People under 18 are generally not bound by a contract, lease or other transaction unless it is for their benefit. This is provided for under the *Minors (Property and Contract) Act 1970* (NSW). The courts will not enforce such contracts, even if they do exist.

Some minors may be able to enter into certain contractual arrangements if they have a parent or guardian act as a **guarantor** to ensure the contractual obligations are lived up to.

REVIEW 18.4

Refer to Tables 18.1, 18.2 and 18.3 and answer the following questions:

1 Comment on the percentage of children and young people at different grades who work.
2 Comment on the type of employers who employ children.
3 Comment on the hourly pay received by children and young people.

RESEARCH 18.2

Go to www.industrialrelations.nsw.gov.au/rights/young/ and www.lawstuff.org.au to research other aspects of work for children and young people. Summarise your findings in a few paragraphs.

---

guarantor
when a person puts their own collateral (some form of asset) up as security for another person's loan from a financial institution. If the person who took out the loan cannot repay the loan, the financial institution can seize the assets put up by the guarantor.

The exception to this is when young people enter an agreement that is for their own benefit and is a necessity such as accommodation, food, travel etc. An example could be a young person who leaves home at 16 to take an apprenticeship and has to sign a rental lease for accommodation or needs to buy a car on finance for transport. In this situation, the act states:

> 'Where a minor participates in a civil act and his or her participation is for his or her benefit at the time of his or her participation, the civil act is presumptively binding on the minor.'

Torts

There is no restriction on taking legal action because of a person's age. If a child is assaulted, battered or injured as a result of someone else's negligence, slandered, libelled, or suffers damage as a result of some other wrongful behaviour, he or she is entitled to sue the wrongdoer.

A child is also personally responsible for their wrongful acts. The general rule with parents is that they are not liable for **torts** committed by their children. It should be noted, however, that there are some instances where parents may be liable for torts committed by their children.

torts a civil wrong which can include negligence, defamation, trespass and nuisance

Leaving home

Young people do not have the right to leave home before the age of 18. However, the law would not normally force young people over the age of 16 to stay at home against their wishes. The following factors would be considered: maturity, accommodation, safe living environment, and attitude of parents. Given the number of children living on the streets for various reasons, it would seem that the law in reality can do little to stop children from leaving home if they wish.

REVIEW 18.5

Draw up a table like the one below and fill in the missing information.

Civil area of law	Legislation/cases	Status of children/ young people
Education		
Workplace		
Medical treatment		
Religion		
Discrimination		
Contracts/torts		
Leaving home		

FAMILY MATTERS

For the purposes of this unit of work not all pieces of legislation such as the *Family Law Act 1975* (Cwlth) and the *Family Law Reform Act 1995 (Cwlth)* have been referred to as these are covered in detail in the HSC course.

Inheritance and parentage

The *Status of Children Act 1996* (NSW) provides that all children, including ex-nuptial children, are treated the same as those whose parents are married in wedlock. This essentially means that ex-nuptial children have the same rights in relation to disposition of property made by a will or without a will to those born in wedlock. Any person left out of a will can contest this through the *Family Provisions Act NSW* (1982).

The *Status of Children Act 1996* (NSW) clarifies issues of parentage for children in NSW. There is a **presumption of parentage** if a child is born within a marriage. In addition if a child is born 44 weeks after the death of the husband, the child is presumed to the child of the deceased father. If a married couple separate but resume cohabitation at some stage and a child is born 44 weeks after the end of the cohabitation, and the marriage has ended, then the child is presumed to be that of the former husband.

presumption of parentage outlines a specific condition where a man and/or a woman are presumed to be the parents of a child

For couples who live together but are not married, the act goes on to state:

'A child born to a woman is presumed to be a man's child if, at any time during the period beginning not earlier than 44 weeks and ending not less than 20 weeks before the birth, the man and the woman cohabit but are not married.'

In all of the above cases the law clearly states that the birth mother is the legal mother and especially applies in case of birth technologies being used.

If a child is born through the use of fertilisation procedures the act states that the intended 'social parents' are also the legal parents. In the case of a married or de facto couple, there is presumption of knowledge of the procedure, but this can be challenged in court on the **balance of probabilities**. Men and women who donate biological material to assist in these procedures are not presumed to be the mother or father of the child as a result of that pregnancy. Under the act, the above provisions are irrefutable. It is possible to have the presumption of no paternity altered by a sperm donor and the birth mother through the *Births, Deaths and Marriages Act 1995* (NSW). This must be acknowledged in writing by the birth mother.

balance of probabilities a standard of proof in most civil matters in law that the evidence presented is more probable than not

The *Family Law Act 1975* (Cwlth) and the *Marriage Act 1961* (Cwlth) are consistent with the approach included in the *Status of Children Act 1996* (NSW). If both husband and wife have consented to the procedure, both are presumed to be the father and mother of the child. Whether the child is biologically theirs is not relevant. This presumption is also irrefutable. Presumptions of parentage are in place to ensure that all children, where possible, will have assigned to them one or two parents with the responsibility outlined under the law to care and maintain them. Parentage can be rebutted through the use of DNA samples, blood tests, voluntary recognition or other means. The standard of proof in these cases is on the balance of probabilities. It should be noted that the *Artificial Conception Act 1984* (NSW) and the *Children (Equality of Status) Act 1976* (NSW) were repealed and replaced by the *Status of Children Act 1996* (NSW).

CARE AND CONTROL

Children have the right not to be abused physically, sexually or emotionally. Child abuse in Australia is a worrying aspect of our society. Governments have passed laws to combat this, but to date the effectiveness of these initiatives has been limited.

The Department of Community Services (DOCS) is authorised to intervene between parents and children where there is a need of care and protection. A child or their parent can also request DOCS to assist where the family is having difficulties. State intervention can range from providing family support and other preventative services such as respite childcare, through to extreme action of removing children from their families or to taking police action against the perpetrators of abuse.

Why should our society protect children from abuse?

The following points outline underlying presumptions for the prevention of abuse:
- Children are important community members and they have the right to be safe from abuse.
- Children are the parents of the future. Their capacity to parent is influenced by the parenting they receive.
- Research indicates that there is a strong link between child abuse and later social problems.
- Prevention pays for itself in the long run.
- Australia's signature on the United Nations Convention on the Rights of the Child means that the Australian Government is obliged to ensure that legislation and policy is put in place to protect children.

What is abuse?

Generally, there are four types of abuse:
- sexual abuse—this can be in many forms, from suggestive comments to sexual intercourse
- physical abuse—this can involve any type of physical injury
- neglect—this can involve children not receiving adequate food, clothing, shelter, health care etc.
- emotional abuse—this can result from things that are said or implied.

Abuse generally lowers one's sense of self-worth and affects a child or young person's ability to develop socially, emotionally and cognitively. Usually a child that is abused in any of the first three ways will have suffered some form of emotional abuse as well. Regardless of the type of abuse, they all have consequences for our society. Generally, sexual abuse can be the most destructive at the time of puberty, in terms of promiscuity, and for relationships later in life.

Child sexual assault is often hidden. Children often find it hard to talk about because they think it is their fault or they think that no-one will believe them. Even if children consent, sexual and indecent assaults against children are crimes. If the offender says the child consented there is one defence only—where the child was aged 14–16 and the offender thought the child was over 16. The notification rate over the last twenty years has increased at a rate that has put DOCS resources under enormous pressure. It is believed this trend will continue at a similar or increasing rate.

LEGAL INFO

Incidence of child abuse

The following observations on the incidence of child abuse are from the Queensland Government's Department of Communities website http://www.families.qld.gov.au/projectaxis/incidence:

- One in five girls and one in ten boys may be sexually abused in childhood.
- In 90 per cent of child sexual abuse cases, the offender is known to the child.
- Anyone, male or female, could have a sexual offending problem.
- Sexual abuse of children with a disability is higher than the rate of children with no disability.
- Child sexual abuse is related to the development of psychiatric distress in adulthood and is linked to health risks over the life course.
- One in five children (10 to 17 years old) received a sexual invitation from a stranger online over the Internet.
- Those with sexual behaviour problems can include adults and young people, as well as children under 10 years. Children under 12 years are responsible for some child sexual abuse (13 per cent). Some very young children who are themselves victims of sexual abuse, act out sexually with their siblings (35 per cent) and friends (34 per cent).
- It is commonly thought the reconviction rate is high for adults who sexually abuse children. However, research shows the reconviction rate actually ranges from 13 per cent to 23 per cent, and is less for those who successfully complete a specialised treatment program.
- It is possible to identify a small group of high-risk sex offenders whose likelihood for repeat offences is greater than 50 per cent. Those who are reconvicted for child sexual abuse have often harmed a large number of children.

Children and Young Persons (Care and Protection) Act 1998 (NSW)

The guiding principles to be applied in the administration of this act are as follows:
- The safety and welfare and wellbeing of children and young people is the paramount consideration.
- Children and young people must be given an opportunity to express their views concerning their safety and welfare and these must be given due consideration.
- Culture, disability, language, religion and sexuality of the child or young person must be taken into account.
- Any course of action that must be followed should be the least intrusive for the child or young person and their family.

    Under the act, a child or young person is considered at **risk of harm** when:
- the child's or young person's basic physical or psychological needs are not being met or are at risk of not being met
- the parents or other caregivers have not arranged and are unable or unwilling to arrange for the child or young person to receive necessary medical care

risk of harm
concerns about the safety, welfare and wellbeing of a child or young person because of sexual, physical or emotional abuse and/ or neglect

- the child or young person has been, or is at risk of being, physically or sexually abused or ill-treated
- the child or young person is living in a household where there have been incidents of domestic violence and, as a consequence, the child or young person is at risk of serious physical or psychological harm
- a parent or other caregiver has behaved in such a way towards the child or young person that the child or young person has suffered or is at risk of suffering serious psychological harm.

mandatory reporting where a person working in child-related employment must by law report to care and protection agencies a child they believe to be at 'risk of harm'

Reporting of children and young people at risk

Under section 23 of the act, any person who has reasonable grounds for believing that a child or young person is at risk of harm may make a report to DOCS. **Mandatory reporting** is a responsibility of all paid workers who deliver or are responsible for the delivery of health care, welfare services, education, children's services, residential services or law enforcement wholly or partly to children. They must make a report to DOCS if they become aware that a child is at risk of harm during the course of their work.

The mechanisms in place to deal with reports of child abuse will be discussed in chapter 19.

> ### REVIEW 18.7
>
> 1 Explain why society should protect children from harm.
> 2 Describe when a child is considered at risk of harm.
> 3 Outline the different types of abuse.
> 4 What reasons could people have for not wanting to comply with mandatory reporting guidelines?

JUVENILE JUSTICE

juvenile a child or young person, generally under 18 years of age, although this may vary depending on the context

There are two recognised approaches that can be taken in dealing with issues of **juvenile** justice—the welfare model, and the justice model.

The welfare model assumes that the causes of crime can relate to the state of the economy, social and psychological factors. Under this model, there is a need to protect children and young people.

The justice model has a 'get tough on crime' stance. It generally has a 'zero tolerance' approach and emphasises punishment of offenders. To some extent the juvenile justice system takes a combination of both of these approaches when dealing with offenders.

Many pieces of legislation deal with different aspects of juvenile justice. For the purposes of this unit of study, the following legislation will be discussed:

- *Children's (Criminal Proceedings) Act 1987* (NSW)
- *Young Offenders Act 1997* (NSW)
- *Crimes Legislation Amendment (Police and Public Safety) Act 1998* (NSW)
- *Children (Protection and Parental Responsibility) Act 1997* (NSW).

Age of criminal responsibility

The *Children's (Criminal Proceedings) Act 1987* (NSW) clearly outlines the age of criminal responsibility. It states, 'It shall be conclusively presumed that no child who is under the age of 10 years can be guilty of an offence'. This is the same in all criminal jurisdictions.

Between the ages of 10–14 a child may be found guilty of a criminal offence, but the prosecution must rebut the notion of *doli incapax* and show that the child, at the time of the alleged offence, could distinguish between right and wrong. From the ages of 14–17, children and young people are held fully responsible for their actions.

The status of children appearing before a court in NSW is also outlined under the *Children's (Criminal Proceedings) Act 1987* (NSW). It requires the following principles to be taken into consideration by the court when dealing with children:

- Children have rights equal to adults and have a right to be heard and participate in the proceedings.
- Children are responsible for their actions, but require guidance and assistance.
- Where possible, the education of a child should proceed without interruption.
- Where possible, a child should be able to reside in his or her home.
- The penalty imposed on a child shall be no greater than that of an adult for the same offence.

Figure 18.2 It is presumed that no child under the age of 10 years can be guilty of an offence.

Young Offenders Act 1997 (NSW)

The Young Offenders Act became operational in NSW in 1998. Its aim is to provide diversionary measures for young offenders as alternatives to court appearances. The act only applies to summary offences and those indictable offences that can be dealt with summarily. The principles of the act are that:

- the least restrictive sanction should be applied where possible
- children should be informed of their right to seek legal advice
- criminal proceedings are not to be started if there is an appropriate alternative for dealing with matter.

Under the act, children and young offenders who have committed an offence covered in the act may proceed through a three-tiered system of diversionary processes—**warnings**, **cautions** and **youth justice conferences**.

Warnings

This is where a child may be given an official warning by an investigating official in any place and must be told of the nature, purpose and effect of the warning. A warning cannot be given for an act of violence, a repeat offence or at the discretion of the investigating officer. A record of the warning must be lodged under the act.

Cautions

A formal police caution can be given to prevent further offending. In deciding whether to give a caution or not, the investigating official will consider the seriousness of the offence, the degree of violence involved, the harm caused and number of offences by the offender.

warning this can be given to a young offender usually for a first minor offence. The offender must be told of the nature, purpose and effect of the warning.

caution can be given to a young offender depending on the seriousness of the offence, the degree of violence involved, the harm caused and number of offences by the offender

youth justice conference a measure to divert young offenders from the court system through a conference that addresses the offender's behaviour in a more holistic manner

Steps are to be taken so that the offender understands the nature and effect of the caution and the offender must sign a 'caution notice'. A specialist court officer or a court must make a record given by the officer or the court. Before an official caution is issued, the investigating officer may refer the matter to a specialist court officer to decide if the matter instead should be referred to a youth justice conference.

Youth justice conferences

The purpose of youth justice conferences is to allow the offender to take some responsibility for their actions, to promote better family understanding of the issues and to provide the offender with appropriate support services to assist them to overcome their difficulties. Youth justice conferences also enhance the rights of victims in the criminal justice process and ultimately make decisions that should reflect the offender's rights and take into account their needs. Conferences hold the offender accountable, but empower families and victims in decisions about a child's offending and, where suitable, make reparations to the victim.

Those able to participate in a conference are the child, a conference convenor, an investigating official, a member of family or extended family, the offender's legal representative, another adult chosen by the offender and a specialist youth officer. The victim can also attend, as well as any support people the victim may want present. The range of people present aims to give a picture of what is going on in the child's life and to provide enough expertise and experience to offer a more holistic approach to finding solutions for the offender's behaviour. A conference administrator ensures records of the conference are kept, as outlined under the act. The *Young Offender's Act* is generally seen to embrace the 'welfare model' of juvenile justice, in that it uses diversionary measures to find solutions to juvenile offending.

Figure 18.3 The Young Offender's Act aims to divert young offenders from the court system.

Young people and public space:
Crimes Legislation Amendment (Police and Public Safety) Act 1998 (NSW)

The *Crimes Legislation Amendment (Police and Public Safety) Act 1998* (NSW) was introduced as a result of an increase in knife-related violence in NSW. The act amended the *Summary Offences Act 1998* (NSW) by creating new knife-related offences and additional search powers and 'move on' powers for police. The act enhances police powers in regard to knife offences and street crime. It also aims to reduce the number of knives and other weapons being carried or used in a public place by:

- providing police with additional power to conduct a search on a person and to confiscate any dangerous implements found upon them
- allowing police to give reasonable directions to a person where required in public places
- enabling police to demand a person's name and residential address where they may provide information about serious offences.

The act created a new offence of having custody of a knife in a public place or school without a reasonable excuse. Police can search a person if they have a reasonable suspicion that they have a dangerous implement in a public place or school. The police also have the power to confiscate the implement.

The act also provides 'move on' powers to the police in that the police can give reasonable directions to a person in public if they believe the person's behaviour is obstructing another person or traffic, constitutes harassment or intimidation of another person, or is likely to frighten another. This part of the act is seen as an anti-gang measure to allow police to break up groups of people before situations escalate.

The police can also demand a person's name and address if they have reasonable grounds for believing that this will assist them in an investigation.

Under the act there are particular circumstances where it is deemed to be lawful for a person to be able to carry a knife. Some of these are for pursuit of one's occupation, leisure, recreation or sport. Preparation of food or drink, exhibition for knives for retail purposes, wearing official uniforms, religious purposes etc.

The *Crimes Legislation Amendment (Police and Public Safety) Act* has raised certain criticisms from some advocates in the community, who believe it affects the status of young people in their use of public space. These issues will be examined in chapter 20.

REVIEW 18.8

Refer to Table 18.4, and outline the trend of assault and robbery with and without a knife from 1996 to 1999.

RESEARCH 18.3

Go to http://www.lawlink.nsw.gov.au/lawlink/bocsar/ll_bocsar.nsf/vwFiles/bb08.pdf/$file/bb08.pdf (Knife Offences and Policing—Jacqueline Fitzgerald, June 2000, NSW Bureau of Crime Statistics and Research).

In ten lines comment on the impact the *Crimes Legislation Amendment (Police and Public Safety) Act 1998* (NSW) has had on these types of offences after it was introduced.

TABLE 18.4

Assault and robbery with and without a knife in NSW, 1996 to 1999

Offence	1996	1997	1998	1999
Assault with a knife	1180	1378	1346	1053
Assault other than with a knife	47 689	52 925	57 326	56 506
Robbery with a knife	788	1370	1704	1286
Robbery other than with a knife	6882	9637	10 100	9338

Parental responsibility: *Children (Protection and Parental Responsibility) Act 1997* (NSW)

operational areas
local government areas that can apply for police to be given additional powers under the *Parental Responsibility – Children (Protection and Parental Responsibility) Act 1997*

The *Children (Protection and Parental Responsibility) Act 1997* (NSW) enables local police to remove young people under 16 at risk in public places and return them to their parents. The act is unique in that the police are only given these powers in local government areas considered **operational areas.**

Currently in NSW there are four operational areas: Ballina, Orange, Coonamble and Moree. Local government can apply to the Attorney-General's Office to become an operational area. They must demonstrate that they have adequate crime prevention and youth support programs.

The act was designed to address rising juvenile crime problems due to a lack of parental supervision. In an operation area the police can 'safely escort' a young person under 16 from a public place if they are not being supervised by a responsible adult and if they are at risk. A young person is deemed to be at risk if:

- the person is in danger of being physically harmed or injured
- the person is in danger of abuse (including assault and sexual assault, ill-treatment, and exposure to behaviour that may cause psychological harm)
- the person is about to commit an offence.

The other main section of the act gives the Children's Court the power to make parents attend the court with their children, to make them sign an 'undertaking' for their child's behaviour. In more serious cases, the court could punish the parents where it can be shown that their neglect has caused their children's offending. Since the act has been in operation this has this has rarely occurred.

This act has also had its critics who have argued it affects the status of children and young people, as it infringes on the civil rights of young people to be able to congregate, i.e. the right of assembly. Some of these issues will also be addressed in chapter 20.

REVIEW 18.9

1 Describe how the *Young Offenders Act 1997* (NSW) can divert children and young offenders away from the traditional court system.

2 Outline two arguments for and against how the *Crimes Legislation Amendment (Police and Public Safety) Act 1998* (NSW) might protect or restrict the rights of children and young people.

3 Explain the implications of the *Children (Protection and Parental Responsibility) Act 1997* (NSW) for children, young people and adults.

MULTIPLE-CHOICE QUESTIONS

1 Which of the following is a feature of *doli incapax* in NSW?
   a children and young people are responsible for their crimes from the age of 14
   b there are certain crimes that children and young people are not responsible for
   c children and young people under the age of 10 are not responsible for their crimes
   d people with mental disabilities are not responsible for their crimes

2 Which of the following best describes the term 'young person'?
   a a person under the age of 16
   b a person between the ages of 12 and 16
   c a person aged between 16 and 18
   d a person aged between 18 and 25

3 Which of the following is not a reason for the law to treat children and young people differently?
   a to prevent them from being exploited
   b to protect them from the consequences of making uninformed decisions
   c to give them the best chance of finding appropriate employment
   d to protect others from being disadvantaged by dealing with a person who is a minor

4 Which of the following statements best describes Australia's obligations under the Convention on the Rights of the Child (CROC)?
   a laws must be passed within Australia to implement all of the provisions under CROC
   b Australia can pass whatever laws it chooses to, due to its own sovereignty
   c Australia can pass whatever laws it chooses to due to its own sovereignty, but is obliged to pass laws to implement the provisions contained in CROC
   d Australia will pass laws recommended by the United Nations

5 Jessie and Amy have just rejoiced in the birth of their first daughter. Which of the following best outlines their obligations under the *Births, Deaths and Marriages Act 1995* (NSW)?
   a they must register the birth in 60 days
   b they must register the birth in 30 days
   c they must register the birth in 21 days
   d they must register the birth 21 days after they have given notice of the birth

CHAPTER SUMMARY TASKS

1 Outline what changed in the treatment of children and young people by the end of the nineteenth century. Explain why this occurred.

2 Identify who has a right to Australian citizenship.

3 In three paragraphs, define child abuse and explain some of the issues emanating from it.

4 Explain why the mandatory reporting of children considered 'at risk' is important.

5 Outline how the presumption of paternity is affected by birth technology procedures.

6 Outline examples where the criminal justice system treats children and young people differently from adults.

7 When is it permissible for a person to carry a knife in public?

8 Explain how the *Young Offenders Act 1997* (NSW) is unique from other pieces of legislation.

9 Describe the ways the *Children (Protection and Parental Responsibility) Act 1997* (NSW) has impacted on parents and guardians of children and young people who break the law.

10 Assess the extent to which increased police 'move-on' powers in the last 10 years have been necessary.

CHAPTER SUMMARY

- Historically, children had no legal rights. Throughout the nineteenth century around the western world there developed a gradual recognition of the need to protect children and young people. As a result laws and policies relating to the specific needs of children developed.
- The Convention on the Rights of Child was an important development in promoting the rights of children and young people. It is the most signed of all international treaties.
- The law generally defines a child as being under the age of 16, and a young person as being aged 16 to 18.
- The status of children under the law is outlined mainly through various pieces of legislation in the areas of work, education, discrimination, medical treatment, contracts and leaving home.
- All states in Australia have enacted care and protection legislation over the last 30 years, This development mirrors a growing awareness that a number of children and young people in society are exploited and abused and require the protection of the state.
- Children and young people are given special consideration in respect to juvenile justice, which takes into account the age of the offender at the time of the offence. Children and young people are also given special consideration when they appear before a court.
- The police have been given additional powers to search and seize, and move on individuals or groups of children and young people when out in public.

CHAPTER 19

Mechanisms for achieving justice for children and young people

THEME EMPHASIS:
LEGAL PROCESSES AND INSTITUTIONS/CONFLICT AND COOPERATION

As seen previously, there is an extensive body of law that has been enacted to define the status of children and young people within society. The laws passed by parliaments, highlighted in the previous chapter, are mechanisms in themselves for achieving justice for children and young people.

This chapter will examine the institutions and processes that currently exist to protect the rights of children and young people. It will also examine those institutions that are proactive in promoting awareness and advancement of the rights of children and young people.

THE ROLE OF THE UNITED NATIONS IN PROTECTING THE RIGHTS OF CHILDREN AND YOUNG PEOPLE

The United Nations is the mechanism where countries around the world meet and sign international declarations and treaties. The Convention on the Rights of the Child (CROC) has been important in putting the rights of children on the global agenda.

However, with all aspects of international law there is a difference between signing an international treaty and **ratification**. Due to the sovereignty of all nation states, there generally has to be the political and or economic will before a state will agree to sign a treaty. Most nation states act out of self-interest, and the United Nations can only pressure states to comply with international law. Once a nation state has signed a treaty, the United Nations committee structure monitors and reports on the extent to which that nation is complying with its international obligations.

ratification to approve. In international law this usually means a government passing domestic laws that uphold some or all of the principles of an international treaty.

Committee on the Rights of the Child committee that oversees the implementation of the Convention on the Rights of the Child in countries which have signed that treaty

This is no different for CROC. The **Committee on the Rights of the Child** meets to examine reports from ratifying countries. The committee consists of ten members who are considered highly qualified to do this. They are elected from within ratifying countries, and, as outlined above, have no coercive power.

Australia has a responsibility under the convention to report to the committee on the steps taken to give full effect to the contained rights. As stated in chapter 18, a federal structure of government can present difficulties in ensuring all states within Australia comply with the treaty.

Figure 19.1 The United Nations' best efforts fail to impede child slavery and the use of children and young people as soldiers, despite international instruments such as the Convention on the Rights of the Child.

The committee asks countries to explain if they have developed a national strategy and plan of action within the convention, and whether the principles of CROC have been incorporated into domestic law. They also recommend that federal and state governments 'ensure that data is systematically gathered in a form that will enable an appraisal of whether laws and policies are effectively delivering the benefits provided by the Convention'.

The Australian Government has indicated that it does not intend to implement CROC through enacting it into domestic law. It has, however, been acknowledged as having a relevant mechanism under the *Human Rights and Equal Opportunity Commission Act 1986* (Cwlth) and can refer to the convention when considering complaints of discrimination. The Human Rights and Equal Opportunity Commission (HREOC) is therefore a federal mechanism that addresses instances where the rights of children have been breeched and acts accordingly.

HREOC and a large network of non-government organisations (NGOs) constantly drew attention to the plight of children in immigration detention centres prior to their subsequent release. The extent to which the Australian Government has complied with the principles outlined in CROC will be examined in chapter 20.

THE ROLE OF PARLIAMENT AND THE COURTS IN PROTECTING THE RIGHTS OF CHILDREN AND YOUNG PEOPLE

Federal and state parliaments have passed numerous pieces of legislation that protect children and young people by restricting their activities and by placing responsibilities on adults to ensure the welfare of children and young people. Certain rights have also been enshrined in legislation, which in turn has created legal institutions, and processes that promote and protect these rights.

The courts have also played a role, through cases that have affirmed the current law or changed the law through the application of precedent.

What legal institutions and processes allow children and young people to achieve justice?

The NSW Commission for Children and Young People

The NSW Commission for Children and Young People was set up under the *Commission for Children and Young People Act 1998* (NSW). This act establishes the Commission as an independent body to promote respect and understanding for the interests and needs of children and young people. It attempts to do this by increasing the participation of children and young people in decision-making that affects their lives, promoting the safety and wellbeing of children and young people, and having an input into laws and policies that affect young people.

The commission also conducts research into areas affecting children and young people (such as the NSW Child Death Review), and produces publications and resources on issues for children and young people.

The commission also implements and monitors the '**working with children check**', the mandatory employment screening by employers for job applicants working in child-related employment as outlined in the *Children and Young Persons (Care and Protection) Act 1998* (NSW). Employers can engage the commission or another approved body to carry out screening on their behalf. Screening consists of the following procedures:

- criminal record check
- apprehended violence order check
- relevant disciplinary proceedings check
- relevant probity check
- assessment of risk to children
- disclosure of results of check to employer.

The legislation also establishes the necessity of reviewing current procedures and introduces offences and penalties for employers who employ a person in child-related employment without requiring disclosure, or who knowingly employed a **prohibited person** in child-related employment.

The commission in this role, along with employers, reduces the likelihood of prohibited persons having contact with children and young people during the course of their work.

working with children check a check by the NSW Commission for Children and Young People on the appropriateness of a person in NSW to work in child-related employment

prohibited person a person prohibited from working in child-related employment

---

REVIEW 19.1

1 Outline the main role of the NSW Commission for Children and Young People.
2 Describe what is meant by the 'working with children check'.
3 Do you think it is important to have a national Commission for Children and Young People? Explain your answer.

Children's Courts

Across NSW, there are 13 children's magistrates sitting in seven specialist Children's Courts. Five of these are in metropolitan areas. There are also five children's registrars appointed under the *Children's Court Act 1987* to assist in the administration of matters before the court.

The court has a dual role, determining matters of juvenile offenders that appear before it, and also determining care and protection matters concerning children referred to it by the Department of Community Services (DOCS). Children's magistrates undergo specialist training by the Judicial Commission. They meet three times a year for conferences under section 16 of the *Children's Court Act*, where they discuss relevant issues and areas of concern and receive additional training in respect to their jurisdiction. Under the *Children's (Criminal Proceedings) Act 1987* (NSW) the main criminal jurisdiction of the Children's Court is to hear and determine matters in the following areas:

- any offence other than a serious children's indictable offence committed by a child
- committal proceedings of any indictable offence, serious ones included.

As mentioned in chapter 18, the court will follow guidelines as laid out under the *Children's (Criminal Proceedings) Act 1987* (NSW) for dealing with children and young people.

RESEARCH 19.1

Use the NSW Commission for Children and Young People home page http://www.kids.nsw.gov.au/ to outline what the commission will be doing over the next three years as a part of their strategic plan.

The NSW Commission for Children and Young People monitors appearances in the Children's Court of young offenders aged between 10 and 17. Here are some of their findings:

- The number of persons with an appearance finalised in the NSW Children's Court has fallen. From 1996–97 to 2003–04 the number decreased by 39 per cent.
- Approximately 79 per cent of persons with an appearance finalised in the NSW Children's Court were male.
- Approximately 31 per cent of persons with a proven appearance in the NSW Children's Court had a prior proven matter.

TABLE 19.1

Characteristics of persons who first appeared in the Children's Court in 1995

Juvenile characteristics	Number of juveniles	Average number of reappearances per person up to December 2003
Age at first court appearance		
10–14	1241	5.2
15–16	2371	3.4
17–18	1864	2.4
Indigenous status		
Non-Indigenous	4783	2.8
Indigenous	693	8.3
Gender		
Female	1071	2.0
Male	4405	3.8
Total	**5476**	**3.5**

TABLE 19.2

Characteristics of persons who first appeared in the Children's Court in 1995, proportion with at least one court appearance as an adult, and proportion with an adult custodial sentence

Juvenile characteristics	Number of juveniles	% with at least one adult court appearance	% with at least one adult custodial sentence within 8 years
Age at first court appearance			
10–14	1241	58.1	17.8
15–16	2371	57.2	13.1
17–18	1864	57.1	9.8
Indigenous status			
Non-Indigenous	4783	52.6	9.7
Indigenous	693	90.5	36.1
Gender			
Female	1071	38.4	4.9
Male	4405	62.0	15.0
Principal offence at first appearance			
Violent	826	59.6	14.4
Property	2780	56.6	13.7
Other	1870	57.6	11.5
Total	**5476**	**57.4**	**13.0**

REVIEW 19.2

Refer to table 19.1 and 19.2 to answer the following questions:
1 Comment on the number of appearances before the court for the members of each sub-group.
2 Describe the profile of a young offender who would be more likely to reappear before the court for subsequent offences. What types of offence would they be more likely to commit?.
3 Of all the sub-groups, which young offenders were more likely to end up with a custodial sentence?

Under the *Children and Young Persons (Care and Protection) Act 1998* (NSW) sections 71 and 72, the court may make care orders if it is satisfied on the balance of probabilities that the child or young person is in need of care or protection.

The principles that guide the court under the act are those that are least intrusive in the child or young person's life and their families, consistent with the paramount concern of protecting the child or young person from harm and promoting their development. The proceedings are conducted with as little formality and legal technicality as the case permits, and are not conducted in an adversarial manner.

restorative justice attempts to 'restore' victims, young offenders and the community in terms of dignity, injury, property loss, security etc. after a crime has been committed. A youth justice conference is used to define what restoration might mean in the context of the crime.

An order to relocate parental responsibility is the most drastic measure available and must not be made unless the court is satisfied that no other order would be sufficient to meet the needs of the child or young person.

As mentioned in the previous chapter, youth justice conferences, which are based on the concept of **restorative justice**, are an additional mechanism used to more effectively deal with young offenders, with the aim of diverting young offenders away from the court system. Children's Court magistrates can also refer a young offender to caution or a youth justice conference. This mechanism allows magistrates to have some control over the discretionary powers exercised by the police in determining who receives a caution, who goes to a youth justice conference, and so on, if they believe these powers have been exercised incorrectly.

REVIEW 19.3

1 Explain the positive messages implied by the cartoon.
2 Explain the negative messages implied by the cartoon.
3 Outline from your own knowledge and the messages contained in the cartoon why children and young people have the best chance of being rehabilitated from criminal behaviour.

Figure 19.2

The Children's Court clinic

Prior to the sentencing of children, the Department of Juvenile Justice conducts clinical assessments as a background report for all children in custody or on remand. Children and young people who are on bail or released into the community will see a private practitioner.

Under the Children's Court clinic, a trial assessment service has been put in place to better streamline the assessment service. A presiding magistrate may decide a child or young person requires assessment by the clinic. The clinic will be asked to complete an assessment where there are 'specific psychological, psycho-social or mental health issues present in the child's situation that the court needs to consider prior passing sentence'.

The Department of Community Services NSW (DOCS)

Under the *Children and Young Persons (Care and Protection) Act 1998* (NSW) the director general of the Department of Community Services (DOCS) is responsible for the care and protection of children in NSW. DOCS carries out this function on the director general's behalf.

When DOCS receives a report of a child believed to be at risk, they will first make investigations to determine whether that child or young person is at risk of harm. If DOCS is satisfied that this is the case, it can:

- arrange for support services for the family
- use alternative dispute resolution services to develop a **care plan** with the family to meet the child or young person's needs in order to reduce the need for hearings in the Children's Court.
- make a **care application** to the Children's Court for the child to be removed from their home for protection. At present there are approximately 10 000 children and young people in care. According to the Director General's 2003–04 annual report, the demand for out-of-home care continues to grow each year.

care plan an outline of how a family will meet the needs of a child or young person

care application an application made to the Children's Court to remove a child believed to be 'at risk' in their home or place of residence

'Out-of-home care is any residential care and control of a child or young person in any place other than the usual home, by any person other than a parent or relative for any period over 28 days (or 14 days if the subject of a court order). The act allows for the sharing of "parental responsibility" for a child or young person between a number of people, for example parents, the Minister, a foster carer, or an agency providing out-of-home care services...

The act also states that "children and young people in out-of-home care should participate in developing a plan for their future which includes who they should have contact with, what support services they should get, where they should live or who should have 'paternal responsibility'. Restoration plans can also be drawn up to help ensure a child is safely returned to their family wherever possible".'

(Source: www.community.nsw.gov.au)

- refer the matter to the police, who will assess whether or not there is sufficient evidence to charge anyone with an offence.

In the period 2003–04, DOCS received 185 000 reports of children at risk, which amounted to a 5 per cent increase on the previous year.

TABLE 19.3

Victims of reported offences against the person, children and young people aged 0–17, NSW (rate per 100 000)

	1995	1996	1997	1998	1999	2000	2001	2002	2003
Murder	0.6	0.5	0.3	0.6	1.3	0.8	0.7	0.5	0.8
Manslaughter	0.0	0.2	n/a	0.4	0.3	0.3	n/a	0.2	0.0
Attempted murder	0.4	0.4	0.6	0.2	0.6	0.8	1.1	0.6	1.1
Driving causing death	0.0	0.2	n/a	0.8	0.9	0.7	0.7	0.5	0.2
Kidnapping/ abduction	5.0	5.6	6.8	10.8	11.7	9.7	10.6	8.8	9.1
Blackmail/ extortion	0.0	0.0	0.6	n/a	n/a	0.3	0.5	0.2	0.4
Robbery	57.6	60.0	77.2	93.9	113.7	146.1	139.7	108.4	91.0
Assault	324.1	434.1	496.9	517.4	540.5	602.0	629.0	653.0	698.2
Sexual assault	150.5	184.7	170.4	156.2	154.5	229.7	233.1	240.5	247.6

REVIEW 19.4

1 Describe the dual role of the Children's Court in respect to children and young people.
2 Who are the main types of offenders that appear in criminal matters before the court?
3 Examine table 19.3 and identify the crimes that recorded the highest incidence from 1995 to 2003.
4 Explain the relationship between the trend in these crimes and the level of reporting made to DOCS in recent times.

Legal aid

Legal Aid NSW provides a range of services to children and young people in NSW. They represent children and young people in a variety of matters from welfare proceedings in the Children's Court to family law matters in the Family Court. They also appear for children and young people facing criminal charges in the Children's Court. There are also times when a children's representative will be appointed to advise the judge on the wishes of the child and what result will be in the best interests of the child. Legal aid will at times act in this role as a 'separate representative' of the child.

In the period of 2003–04, of all the clients that Legal Aid NSW assisted, 11.9 per cent were people under 18. They also provided legal representation to more than 2700 adults and children involved in Children's Court care matters.

The NSW Ombudsman

The main role of the NSW Ombudsman is to act as an independent review body that deals with complaints individuals may have about government agencies in the way that are administered or in the way in which they comply with specific legislation they are obliged to act within or under.

Traditionally, the office is seen as representing the people's interests, and its credibility comes from its reputation for impartiality, independence from government and confidentiality.

There have been calls for there to be a specialist 'children's Ombudsman' that can give a more targeted approach to issues facing children and young people in their dealings with government agencies. A report released from the office of the NSW Ombudsman provides important empirical evidence of areas of concern where action may need to be taken to address certain deficiencies.

The Ombudsman has certainly investigated matters in relation to children and young people. 'Reviewable Deaths Annual Report 2003–4: An Overview' is one such report that investigated the deaths of a number of children between December 2002 and December 2003. Of the 605 children and young people who died during this period, 161 (27 per cent) were reviewable. Of those 161, autopsy evidence was available for 137 of them. The deaths of 103 (75 per cent) of these 137 had been cases were there had been risk of harm reported to DOCS.

In this sense the Ombudsman's office has at times been an important advocate in highlighting serious issues and pursing procedural justice for children and young people.

Administrative Decisions Tribunal (ADT)

Under the *Anti-Discrimination Act 1977* (NSW) the Anti-Discrimination Board was established, as was the Equal Opportunity Tribunal, to hear complaints of discrimination outlined under the act. The functions of the Equal Opportunity Tribunal were transferred to the Equal Opportunity Division of the Administrative Decisions Tribunal in 1997.

Under the act, a child or young person can make a complaint if they have been discriminated against on the grounds of race, sex, marital status, transgender, homosexuality, responsibilities as a carer, age and disability alleged to have occurred in relation to employment, education, provision of goods and services, accommodation or clubs. Complaints may also be made under the ADA of vilification on the grounds of race, homosexuality, transgender or HIV/AIDS. Victimisation is also prohibited under the act.

Once a complaint is received, the President of the Anti-Discrimination Board has a duty by law to investigate these complaints. Some of these will be conciliated and others will be referred on the Equal Opportunity Division of the ADT. Children and young people cannot complain directly to the ADT. The President, as outlined above, must refer their case.

Non-legal mechanisms

The above legal mechanisms have all been put in place to ensure that the welfare of children and young people in society is paramount and is given the due attention it deserves. As children and young people cannot vote, it is difficult at times for their voices to be heard.

There are some very effective non-legal measures that keep the issues of children and young people on the political agenda.

Trade unions exist to promote the rights of workers and to agitate so that people's working conditions are not eroded. The Australian Council of Trade Unions (ACTU) provides information for children and young people who enter the workforce for the first time about pay and conditions, health and safety issues, apprenticeships etc.

The ACTU writes papers and publishes reports that highlight issues for children as well as matters that affect families such as child-care policies, women in the workplace, and family-friendly workplace policies, just to name a few.

The Worksite for Schools Website www.worksite.actu.asn.au is a valuable educative tool that provides statistics, fact sheets, case studies etc.

Figure 19.3 The ACTU provides information for children and young people entering the workforce.

In 2005, the Office of Industrial Relations also released 'Work Smart' under its 'Money Stuff' website at www.moneystuff.net.au. This publication and website contains valuable information for children and young people about their rights and responsibilities in the workplace.

In the area of advocacy, centres such as Shopfront Youth Legal Centre and the National Children's and Youth Law centre promote the rights of children and young people through advocacy and education via papers, presentations at conferences etc. These types of organisations can be very effective in highlighting how specific legislation and policy impacts on children and young people. They also can provide individual legal assistance and advice to children and young people who are in crisis.

There are also organisations that assist children and young people with emergency accommodation. The Kids Helpline on 1800 551 800 is just one of many counselling and referral organisations where children and young people in crisis can seek advice. 'Stop Child Abuse' at www.stopchildabuse.com.au/ is a service provided by the Australian Childhood Foundation to educate about child abuse and provide a directory of services in every state to assist with child abuse.

Non-legal mechanisms can be very effective in addressing issues of justice for children and young people. At times they may be the first point of call made and usually provide valuable information about a person's rights or refer them on to a point where a child or young person is able to feel empowered to see a way forward.

CONFLICT AND COOPERATION

Due to the status of children and young people under the law (as outlined in chapter 18), it is inevitable that conflict arises. Some adults still see children and young people as inferior beings until they reach 18. They are more vulnerable members of society and need greater protection. As such they can be exploited, abused and have their human rights infringed.

The legal and non-legal mechanisms mentioned above play an important role in resolving this conflict and encouraging cooperation between adults and children and young people and amongst children and young people themselves.

The extent to which this effectively resolves issues of conflict and promotes this cooperation in delivering justice for children and young people will be discussed in chapter 20.

MULTIPLE-CHOICE QUESTIONS

1 What is the main international treaty concerning children and young people?
   a Convention on the Rights of Minors
   b Convention against Discrimination of Children and Young People
   c Convention on the Rights of the Child
   d Convention to Protect Children

2 Which of the following is not a role of the NSW Commission for Children and Young People?
   a producing publications on issues affecting children and young people
   b conducting the 'working with children' check
   c supporting children and young people appearing before the courts
   d conducting research into areas affecting children and young people

3 Which of the following best describes a 'prohibited person'?
   a someone with a criminal record
   b someone banned from working in child-related employment
   c an estranged parent denied contact with their children
   d a person who has committed crimes deemed dangerous to children and young people

4 Which of the following is not a role of the Children's Court?
   a to hear care applications
   b to decide guardianship arrangements for children
   c to sentence juvenile offenders
   d to decide committal proceedings for serious criminal offences committed by children or young people

5 Which of the following represented the majority of persons with a finalised appearance before the Children's Court?
   a female—65 per cent
   b male and female—50 per cent each
   c male—79 per cent
   d none of the above

CHAPTER SUMMARY TASKS

1 Comment on the extent to which the United Nations can regulate the implementation of the Convention on the Rights of the Child throughout Australia and the rest of the world.

2 Outline the procedures that the NSW Commission for Children and Young People carry out when screening employees.

3 What are the guiding principles of the Children's Court when dealing with care orders?

4 Outline the options available to DOCS once it is satisfied that a child is at risk of harm.

5 What challenges might confront DOCS in performing their role effectively?

6 Outline the role of legal aid in assisting children and young people with legal problems.

7 What factors contribute to and inhibit the ability of the Ombudsman to effectively act as a law reform agent?

8 What avenues of redress do children and young people have if they are discriminated against?

9 Explain the ways in which the ACTU can advocate for the rights of children and young people.

10 Identify at least two other non-legal mechanisms that promote the rights of children and young people.

CHAPTER SUMMARY

- Legal and non-legal mechanisms are proactive in promoting the advancement of the rights of children and young people.
- The United Nations Committee on the Rights of the Child oversees the implementation of the Convention on the Rights of the Child. It can be effective in highlighting deficiencies in various countries' ratification of the treaty. This effectiveness can also be limited by nation states sovereignty, which allows countries to manage their own internal affairs.
- The NSW Commission for Children and Young People is an independent body that conducts research, publishes discussion papers and produces resources related to children and young people. It also conducts 'working with children' checks.
- The Children's Court has a dual role in respect to children and young people. It hears criminal matters relating to young offenders as well as care applications for children and young people considered to be at risk of harm.
- The Department of Community Services (DOCS) investigates reports of children considered at risk of harm. They can mediate with the family to arrive at a care plan in respect to the child or young person, or make a care application to the Children's Court.
- Legal Aid provides an important service by offering legal advice and representation to children and young people.
- The NSW Ombudsman acts as a general advocate for all people in their dealings with government agencies. As a result, the Ombudsman's office does some work relating to children and young people. There have been calls to have a specialist children's and young person's Ombudsman.
- Children and young people are protected against discrimination under the *Anti-Discrimination Act 1977* (NSW). It is a broad-based act, covering many areas of discrimination.
- Many non-legal mechanisms promote and advocate the rights of children and young people. These include unions, legal advocacy centres, counselling services and other community organisations. At times these organisations may be the first point of call for a child or young person in need of help or advice.

CHAPTER 20

Responsiveness of the law to children and young people

'Children today love luxury too much. They have execrable manners, flaunt authority, have no respect for their elders. They no longer rise when their parents or teachers enter the room. What kind of awful creatures will they be when they grow up?'

Socrates, 469–399 BC

Even back in Socrates' day, the extent to which the youth of the day were challenging the authority of their elders was evident. Today the adult world may still be quick to judge children and young people as they challenge the boundaries that adults impose upon them.

As they grow through adolescence and into adulthood, children and young people are more likely to take risks and, at times, their behaviour will reflect this. At the same time there are adults in society that abuse and exploit children and young people. This means that children and young people will sometimes be at risk of harm, or at risk of harming others.

It is in this light that the legislation and mechanisms in place to ensure justice for children and young people, and the extent to which they respond to the needs of children and young people, will be evaluated.

Figure 20.1 Many products sold throughout the world are still made using forced child labour.

This chapter will examine the responsiveness of the law in the areas of Australia's international obligations under the Convention on the Rights of the Child (CROC), aspects of juvenile justice, the care and protection of children, and young people and the workplace.

INTERNATIONAL LAW

Children around the world are exploited and abused as a result of their lack of status under the laws of those countries. There are approximately 250 000 000 million child labourers worldwide. In 2004 it was estimated there were as many as 300 000 children and young people involved in armed conflict, with up to 100 000 of these believed to be in Africa.

Children still suffer a lack of care and protection at rates considered too high in the developed world. In countries ravaged by war and famine, where family structures have been decimated, children lack the protection normally afforded to them within the family. In Australia, children sat in immigration detention centres, having broken no laws, while in other countries minors are still being executed for the crimes they have committed.

Australia's obligations under the Convention on the Rights of the Child

Even though CROC is the most signed international treaty, millions of children throughout the world still suffer abuses of their human rights that the world community is failing to stop. As discussed in previous chapters, the Committee on the Rights of the Child examines the reports of countries and their compliance with their obligations under the treaty. The committee can report and publish adverse findings on countries that have failed to enforce the rights of its children.

Sovereign nation states can choose to ignore or comply with such findings. Most nation states will generally act out of economic or political self-interest in their compliance with their international obligations. What CROC has done is to put the rights of children on the international agenda. The wheels of international law may turn slowly at times, but the development of CROC is universally seen as a positive step forward in the protection of all children around the world.

Australia has been a strong supporter of CROC from the very outset, and has an extensive body of federal and state law and policy in place designed to protect and promote the welfare children and young people. At the same time, there are still areas where Australia can do better. At this stage there is no legislature in Australia that has a process in place for the automatic scrutiny of draft legislation to examine if it complies with the principles outlined in CROC. There is no consistent and systematic policy developed by the state, territory or federal legislatures aimed at delivering to children and young people the rights contained in CROC.

Other examples of where Australian law does not comply with CROC include:
- There is no legislation giving children a right to a government-provided education.
- Corporal punishment is still permissible in all legislatures throughout Australia, even though it generally states that this must be 'moderate and reasonable'.
- Apart from New South Wales, adoption law throughout Australia does not establish the 'best interests' of the child as the paramount consideration.

- There are laws, especially in New South Wales, that deny children and young people use of **public space**. This is where police are able to remove children and young people, which is an infringement of their civil rights, i.e. their right to freedom of assembly.
- Children and young people are paid less for doing the same work as adults on junior rates of pay. Some states do specify a minimum age for employment.
- It is argued that the criminal age of responsibility of 10 is too low.

The holding of children in immigration detention centres hindering their social and emotional development was also a breech of CROC. It was evidence of the Australian Government's willingness to violate CROC because of its own political interests.

public space areas set aside in which members of the community can associate and assemble

CHILD EXECUTIONS

Child executions violate international law. It is acknowledged throughout the international community that putting to death child offenders negates the current thinking that children and young people have the potential for growth and change, and hence rehabilitation. It is further argued that execution denies the child or young person this chance. International law clearly denounces the death penalty for children and young people who have committed crimes under the age of 18.

Despite this some countries still use the death penalty. The number of executions is small, but as Amnesty International states, it is 'an affront to all notions of morality and decency when it comes to the protection of children—one of the most vulnerable groups in society'. Of those countries that still use the death penalty, many have publicly stated they will not use it against children and young people. This, it is said, reflects 'the conviction that the lives of child offenders—due to a young person's immaturity, impulsiveness, vulnerability and capacity for rehabilitation—should never be simply written off'.

> 'The overwhelming international consensus that the death penalty should not apply to juvenile offenders stems from the recognition that young persons, because of their immaturity, may not fully comprehend the consequences of their actions and should therefore benefit from less severe sanctions than adults. More importantly, it reflects the firm belief that young persons are more susceptible to change, and thus have a greater potential for rehabilitation than adults.'
>
> Mary Robinson, former United Nations
> High Commissioner for Human Rights

Since 1990, Amnesty International has recorded thirty-eight executions of child offenders, nineteen of them in the US. Since 2000 there have been eighteen child executions, nine of them in the US. But even in the US, such executions are not widespread: nineteen of the thirty-eight US states whose laws retain the death penalty exclude its use against child offenders, as does the federal government, and only three states—Oklahoma, Texas and Virginia—have executed child offenders since 2000.

Amnesty International believes that 'the exclusion of child offenders from the death penalty is now so widely accepted in law and practice that it has become a rule of customary international law—international rules derived from state practice and regarded as law (**opinio juris**) and therefore binding on every state, except on those that have "persistently objected" to the rule in question'.

opinio juris international rules derived from state practice and regarded as law

Child executions also breach international treaties such as:

- International Covenant of Civil and Political Rights, Article 6: 'Sentence of death shall not be imposed for crimes committed by persons below eighteen years of age'
- Convention on the Rights of the Child, Article 37: 'Neither capital punishment nor life imprisonment without the possibility of release shall be imposed for offences committed by persons below eighteen years of age'.

Figure 20.2 Napoleon Beazley was executed in 2002 in Texas for a murder committed eight years earlier when he was 17 years old. At the trial, the white prosecutor described him as an 'animal' in front of the all-white jury. Witnesses at the trial cited his potential for rehabilitation. He was a model prisoner.

CASE SPACE

Common law reform in the US

In *Roper v. Simmons* (2005), the Supreme Court found that executing child offenders violates the US Constitution, concluding that a national consensus against such executions had evolved since 1989 when it ruled that the execution of 16 and 17-year-old offenders was constitutional. The court had considered national and international trends, scientific evidence, and appeals from religious, human rights, legal and child advocacy organisations.

Amnesty International has called for an immediate end to all child executions.

TABLE 20.1

Recorded executions of child offenders since 1990

Year	Recorded executions of child offenders	Total recorded executions worldwide	Countries carrying out executions of child offenders (numbers of reported executions are shown in parentheses)
1990	2	2029	Iran (1), USA (1)
1991	0	2086	
1992	6	1708	Iran (3), Pakistan (1), Saudi Arabia (1), USA (1)
1993	5	1831	USA (4), Yemen (1)
1994	0	2331	—
1995	0	3276	—
1996	0	4272	—
1997	2	2607	Nigeria (1), Pakistan (1)
1998	3	2258	USA (3)
1999	2	1813	Iran (1), USA (1)
2000	6	1457	Congo (Democratic Republic) (1), Iran (1), USA (4)
2001	3	3048	Iran (1), Pakistan (1), USA (1)
2002	3	1526	USA (3)
2003	2	1146	China (1), USA (1)
2004	4	3797	China (1), Iran (3)
2005	6	Not available	Iran (6)

REVIEW 20.1

1 Identify five ways in which Australia does not comply with CROC.
2 Examine table 20.1. Identify the countries that still execute child offenders and highlight those countries with the most recorded executions.
3 In ten lines define and explain why child executions are an international human rights issue.

RESEARCH 20.1

Research another international human rights issue regarding children and young people. Prepare a fact sheet outlining the main issues. Two examples could include child slavery, the use of children as soldiers in conflict or forced child labour. Use the website http://web.amnesty.org/library/Index/ENGACT500152004 to get started.

CHILDREN AND YOUNG PEOPLE AND THE CRIMINAL JUSTICE SYSTEM

If children and young people come into contact with the criminal justice system, it is usually through interaction with a police officer when being arrested or questioned about some matter. This experience can influence the attitude that children and young people have to authority and to the wider community in general.

The report 'Seen and heard: Young people and the legal process', which was a joint inquiry of the Human Rights and Equal Opportunity Commission and the Australian **Law Reform Commission**, examined the relationship of children and young people and the legal process. It stated that 78 per cent of 843 children and young people surveyed said that the police rarely treated young people with a sufficient degree of respect.

It could be argued that children and young people on the whole do not have a good relationship with the police. This problem is magnified among Indigenous children and young people. This may partly be due to particular police procedures or the law-and-order policies of state governments around the country.

> 'Young people are frequently targeted for police intervention—for lacking "respect", for being "rowdy", for being part of the "rave culture", or simply for being young and out in public.'

> (Source: 'Young People and Public Space' conference workshop presented by the Youth Justice Coalition and Youth Action and Policy Association, 2002)

The 'Seen and heard' inquiry also examined how policing could become more consistent with CROC provisions and recommended that national standards via legislation or policy should exist in certain areas of concern. Some of the main areas are outlined below.

Public space

There is a need to better develop guidelines on the use of public space by children and young people. In some states the police can remove children from public places when they are considered to be at risk of offending, whether they are suspected of illegal behaviour or not. It is argued that this is a restriction of children and young people's freedom of assembly and erodes their civil rights.

The *Crimes Legislation Amendment (Police and Public Safety) Act 1998* (NSW) was introduced in response to the increased offences related to knives between 1996 and 1997. As mentioned in chapter 18, the act made it an offence to carry a knife in a public place, and gave the police the power to search people for knives and other weapons. It also gave the police the power to search people in public places if their behaviour appeared to cause fear, obstructs, harasses or intimidates.

One way to gauge the effectiveness of this legislation is the extent to which knife related offences have decreased as a result of the extra powers given to police. The NSW Ombudsman's office also conducted a review of the legislation in 1999. The Youth Action and Policy Association, in a paper entitled 'Knives Legislation to Stay', commented that the report found that the increased powers of the police led to an increase of more arbitrary stop and search procedures and that the legislation had only a modest increase in searches

Law Reform Commission
statutory body that examines the law for problems and makes recommendations

that led to a knife in the first year of operation. In contrast, it also showed that there was an enormous increase in searches where no knife was found. The report indicated that, by halfway through 1999, 81.9 per cent of people searched carried no weapon that would be a threat to public safety. The paper went on to state:

> 'As many of us had always expected, young people were the clear target of these new powers. What was surprising was the levels of harassment of young people … An incredible 68 per cent of people searched were aged 25 or under. Not only were young people targeted for these searches, they were more likely unfairly targeted. Whereas only one in seven 17 year olds who were searched were found to have knives, almost one in two 37 year olds had knives. The Youth Justice Coalition and other groups have argued that police stop and search powers should be consolidated into one piece of legislation as at present there are a minimum of six acts giving police the power to stop and search people which can cause confusion for the police and citizens alike.'

The *Children (Protection and Parental Responsibility) Act 1997* (NSW) was introduced to address the rise in juvenile crime caused by a lack of parental supervision. This act has also been criticised in the way that it impedes children and young people's use of public space. A review of policy and legislation relating youth street rights, conducted by the University of Technology Sydney's Community Law and Legal Research Centre and the Youth Justice Coalition, found that the *Children (Protection and Parental Responsibility) Act 1997* (NSW) contravened CROC. The review found that the act impedes young people's civil rights of freedom of association and assembly and that it discriminated against young people on the grounds of their visibility in public space. The review also found that the act gives the police arbitrary power of detention and does not consider the 'best interests' of the child.

The 'Seen and heard' report conducted by the Human Rights and Equal Opportunity Commission and the Australian Law Reform Commission stated that the legislation has problems. It outlined that police can scrutinise the behaviour of children and young people even if it is not criminal, and allows the police to act on stereotypes about young people.

Public space is very important to young people given that there are very few places that they can get together to meet and spend time together. Young people congregating in groups are easily branded as antisocial, even though crimes statistics show that young people are more likely to be victims rather than offenders. Move-on and stop-and-search powers serve the law-and-order agendas of governments by trying to clear the streets and supposedly making the community safer. Given this, and the diminishing ratio of public space available due to the increase in privately owned shopping malls, the civil rights of children and young people are frequently being infringed.

RESEARCH 20.2

Go to the NSW Bureau of Crime Statistics at www.lawlink.nsw.gov.au/bocsar/ Study the paper 'Knife Offences and Policing' by Jacqueline Fitzgerald and outline the effect the *Crimes Legislation Amendment (Police and Public Safety) Act 1998* (NSW) has had on assaults and robberies involving knives.

REVIEW 20.2

1 What issues have been identified with the policing of young people in areas of public space?
2 What arguments would the government and the police put forward for the necessity of laws regulating young people and public space?
3 Examine table 20.2. In what areas of crime are children and young people overrepresented as victims?

TABLE 20.2

Victimisation rate per 100 000 population for selected crimes, 2001

Age group (years)	Homicide and related offences	Assault	Sexual assault	Kidnapping	Robbery
0–14	2.3	279.2	173.3	5.9	29.5
15–24	8.5	1572.3	191.7	10.6	337.8
25–34	8.3	1409.5	73.8	4.3	141.8
35–44	6.3	900.8	38.6	2.0	88.3
45–54	4.0	510.7	17.0	0.7	69.5
55–64	4.2	265.6	6.7	0.5	55.6
65 and over	2.6	88.3	3.4	0.2	31.4
Total per 100 000 population (including victims for whom age was not specified)	5.4	782.9	86.4	3.9	111.3
Number of all recorded offences	1047	151 753	16 744	758	21 576

Arrest

In some criminal jurisdictions it is alleged that police rely heavily on arrest to gather evidence or to further the interrogation of suspects. In other words, arrest can be used as a method of investigation. This is especially so for Indigenous youth.

CROC advocates that arrest should be a 'last resort', not a first resort as it can be a very negative experience for children and young people. The 'Seen and heard' report also recommended that for children considered at risk, welfare and health services may be the more appropriate agencies to deal with the situation.

This is not to undermine the carrying out of an arrest when it is necessary for a police officer to protect the community.

Interview friend

HREOC recommends that a parent, guardian or lawyer be present during the interrogation of a child or young person as an 'interview friend'. They should be present to support the person undergoing interrogation and to witness that statements made are voluntary.

Right to legal representation

At present there is no right to have legal representation during a police interview. The 'Seen and heard' report argues that this should be a right for children and young people. It also recommends that children and young people not be detained for longer than 2 hours in all states, as is the practice at a federal level.

Sentencing of young offenders

Another area investigated by the 'Seen and heard' report was the issue of sentencing of juveniles. CROC acknowledges that children and young people, more than any other offenders, have the best chance of being rehabilitated and integrated back into society. As such, the sentence that offenders receive should take into account the circumstances under which the offence was committed.

The 'Seen and heard' report acknowledged that most jurisdictions do this. In New South Wales, the courts follow guidelines under the *Children's (Criminal Proceedings) Act 1987* (NSW) which give special consideration to juvenile offenders. The report said:

> 'Evidence to the inquiry indicated that courts do not always have sufficient regard to the totality of relevant circumstances when deciding sentences. More attention is needed to social factors such as homelessness, family circumstances, educational needs and so on in determining sentences for children. Sentences should take into account the special health and other requirements of children and young people ... these young people often have serious family or other problems.'

In respect to the sentencing options for children and young people, the report acknowledged that fines should not be used for young offenders, as they usually come from economically disadvantaged families. It commented that community service orders had benefits, as long as the conditions to fulfil them were not too difficult as to attract the legal consequences for not doing so. It also acknowledged that the statistics for youth detention indicate that it is not being used as a last resort, and that it was ineffective as a deterrent. The report stated:

> 'The relatively high youth detention rates in a number of jurisdictions may be indicative of insufficient regard for the requirement that detention should be the last resort. Available statistics and research suggest that detention and other harsh sentencing options are generally ineffective as deterrents to re-offending.'

Youth conferencing

The 'Seen and heard' report noted that conferencing schemes such as those outlined under the *Young Offenders Act 1997* (NSW) have been increasing. While youth conferencing generally deals with matters that would be dealt with summarily, it can under the act include some indictable offences such as robbery or aggravated break, enter and steal.

One of the criticisms of acts like the *Young Offenders Act* is that it is not being used for a wide enough range of offences and therefore is excluding some young offenders from the benefits that conferencing offers.

The Shopfront Youth Legal Centre in its submission in response to the NSW Law Reform Commission paper on sentencing young offenders in 2003 argued that:

'Youth justice conferencing is suitable for a wide range of offences, even very serious ones. It is not a "soft option". Indeed, it could be said that conferencing works best in the case of relatively serious offences because the young offender is obliged to consider the consequences of his or her actions, in particular the harm caused to the victim. In most cases, conferencing is a more effective mechanism than court for achieving this.'

A further criticism is made in the application of the provisions of the *Young Offenders Act*. Police discretion it is believed means that some matters that should be referred to a conference are not, even though the Children's Court can send an offender to conferencing after being referred to it. One way of ensuring that more matters get referred to conferencing would be to reduce police discretion by making some matters mandatory for referral. This, it is argued, would make the job of police easier, but it is also reasoned that there are too many variables in each case to have one rule for all.

It should be noted that approximately 50 per cent of all matters referred to conferencing come from the Children's Court, suggesting that matters have been inappropriately referred to the court by the police.

RESEARCH 20.3

Research further information on children and young people and the legal process in the 'Seen and heard' report at the HREOC home page www.hreoc.gov.au . Write a one-page report on your findings.

CARE AND PROTECTION OF CHILDREN AND YOUNG PEOPLE

The Wood Royal Commission (1997) into police corruption spent its last two years investigating issues surrounding child abuse. Evidence emerged about the lack of effective procedures and processes for reporting and following up alleged instances of child abuse within governmental agencies and the broader community. It also highlighted the magnitude of child abuse in society and the need for better legislative responses to more effectively deal with the complexity of the issues surrounding child abuse.

As the rights of children emerged (as outlined in chapter 18), so too did an awareness of the problems associated with child abuse and the long-term damage it can cause. Evidence also began to emerge that domestic violence and child abuse are linked, and are good predictors of each happening. Goddard and Carew 1993 and Tomison 1994 stated that 'a violent coercive environment, where domestic violence was identified, was almost as likely for cases of child sexual abuse as for physical abuse'. (Source: 'Child Abuse and Neglect: Part 1—Redefining the Issues', 2000, Marianne James, Australian Institute of Criminology.)

Chapter 18 illustrated some of the issues surrounding child abuse and the necessity of an effective care and protection system. The ability of governments to be able to provide this is being challenged more each year. The Australian Institute of Health and Welfare in its latest report into child abuse noted that 'the number of Australian children suspected of suffering emotional, physical, or sexual abuse or neglect has more than doubled in the last five years'.

According to DOCS, an upward trend of reports made to it continued in 2003–04. There were approximately 185 200 child protection reports made in this period which amounted to an increase of 9000 from the previous year.

The situation of child abuse portrayed by the above statistics is even more disturbing in Indigenous communities across Australia. The rate of all types of abuse in 2001–02 was

Figure 20.3 Indigenous children are overrepresented in substantiated child protection reports. In 2002–03, of those reported, 28 per cent were for physical abuse, 30 per cent sexual abuse, 8 per cent emotional abuse and 34 per cent for neglect.

estimated to be 4.3 times higher in the Indigenous population than the non-Indigenous population. Indigenous children were six times more likely to be removed from their families than other Australian children.

The Australian Institute of Health and Welfare reported that in 2003–04 222 000 children were suspected of suffering emotional, physical or sexual abuse or neglect and that this

REVIEW 20.3

1 Examine table 20.3. Compare the ratio of substatiated reports of child abuse of Indigenous children to non-Indigenous children.
2 Suggest some possible reasons for the differnce in the rates of substantiated reports.
3 Research more information on child abuse in Indigenous communities in the report by visiting http://www.aifs.gov.au/nch/issues/issues19.html. Go to the conclusion on page 53 for an overview of the report's findings.

TABLE 20.3

The number of children aged 0–16 years who were the subject of substantiated reports, rates per 1000 children by Indigenous status 2002–03

State/territory	Number of maltreated Indigenous children per 1000	Number of maltreated non-Indigenous children per 1000	Ratio of Indigenous children to non-Indigenous children
NSW	32.0	6.5	4.9 : 1
Vic	55.6	5.7	9.7 : 1
Qld	15.9	9.7	1.6 : 1
WA	9.7	1.3	7.2 : 1
SA	32.2	4.8	6.6 : 1
Tas	2.5	1.8	1.4 : 1
ACT	19.7	6.8	2.9 : 1
NT	8.7	1.6	5.5 : 1

equated to a child every two and a half minutes. Statistics such as these are putting care and protection agencies under increasing pressure to cope with such levels of reporting.

Figure 20.4 Wherever it occurs, child abuse must be identified and the causes of it addressed.

Reviewable deaths of children in New South Wales

Evidence of a lack of protection for children and young people was highlighted in the Ombudsman's reviewable deaths annual report which examined the deaths of 161 children between December 2002 to December 2003 in NSW. It found that in 137 cases 61 per cent of deaths were the result of abuse or neglect. In 103 cases the risk of harm to the children had been reported to DOCS in the three years prior. It also found that 22 per cent of the 137 cases were Aboriginal children.

The Ombudsman Bruce Barbour went on to say 'although the primary responsibility for children lay with families, there have been failures by DOCS to deal with children who were at risk of harm. There had been poor decision-making, poor intervention and cases had been closed because the risk was determined as less urgent than other cases'.

As a result, the Ombudsman recommended that, due to DOCS limited resources and therefore the need to prioritise their case load, 'they should establish a threshold of risk above which reports about children cannot be closed without some form of protective intervention'.

While he acknowledged that DOCS resources have been increased, he argued that unless additional funds were made available children would continue to remain 'unsafe and unprotected'. DOCS, through the minister, responded by saying over the following five years the number of case workers would be increased.

Research is also identifying specific factors that allow generalised statements to be made in respect to where children at risk usually come from. The Australian Institute of Health and Welfare report stated that most children at risk come from families who 'have low incomes that are financially stressed, suffer from social isolation and have less support from immediate families'.

This would suggest that to rely on the response of DOCS to solve the problems associated with child abuse in our communities is only a band aid solution. Governments increasingly have to introduce legislation and policies that attack the causes of abuse as well as continue to adequately resource intervention agencies such as DOCS.

Preventative measures that identify risk factors while enhancing protective factors would seem to be extremely important. When a child is reported to be potentially at risk to child protection agencies it already may be too late. The situation could have deteriorated to the extent that serious damage may have already been done to the child that could have been prevented.

Marianne James of the Australian Institute of Criminology in her paper 'Child Abuse and Neglect: Part 1—Redefining the Issues' (2000), identifies risk factors and prevention strategies that, if coordinated effectively between relevant services and agencies, could assist in addressing the statistics on child abuse that continue to climb each year.

RESEARCH 20.4

Go to http://www.aic.gov.au/publications/tandi/tandi146.html on page 4 and make a list of the risk factors and prevention strategies as outlined in Marianne James' paper.

REVIEW 20.4

1 What has been the trend in mandatory reporting of child abuse over the last 5 to 10 years?

2 How does this compare in Indigenous communities?

3 'The government needs to spend more time and money addressing the causes of child abuse.' Discuss this statement.

CHILDREN AND YOUNG PEOPLE IN THE WORKPLACE

Some of the types of work that young people in NSW are engaged in were outlined in chapter 18, as reported in the findings of the report 'Children at Work 2005' by the NSW Commission for Children and Young People. Sections of the report went on to examine some issues facing children and young people in the workplace.

The report found that children and young people are generally satisfied with the work they were engaged in. It stated that 40.1 per cent had suffered an injury at work and that of these 7.4 per cent had sustained a serious work-related injury. It also reported that 47.8 per cent had experienced some form of verbal harassment and 22.8 per cent had experienced some form of physical harassment. These types of harassment were more likely in formal work settings with hierarchical structures.

While the respondents in the report generally acknowledged many benefits from being in the workplace, many still felt they were treated unfairly because of their age and that they were exploited by not being paid what they felt they deserved. The commission is planning to assess the issues raised in the report and present recommendations to government about children in the workplace.

A further two issues regarding children in the workplace are rates of junior pay, which are in breach of CROC, and the use of child labour in some industries in Australia. Child labour is where children between the ages of 4 and 15 are forced to do work that affects their education and their social and psychological development. This is generally associated with poorer developing countries, but has been identified in Australia in the textile industry. Reports have been made of children working long hours at sewing machines after school and in the school holidays. As these reports are made they continue to be investigated by unions and governments.

OVERVIEW

The rights of children have come a long way. Legislation and policy has established processes and institutions that continue to agitate for better recognition of the important role that children and young people play in our society. The lack of a National Child Commissioner is cause for great concern, as is the lack of a coordinated approach by all governments in this area.

It is the children who are still unprotected, and who experience little sense of personal power. In a democratic society, the law must continue to represent their interests and fight for their rights. In some regards we have not progressed much at all since the days of Socrates.

REVIEW 20.5

1 Describe the type of problems children and young people face in the workplace.
2 What are the two main complaints that children and young people have in respect to work.
3 Assess the arguments for and against 'junior rates of pay'.

MULTIPLE-CHOICE QUESTIONS

1 Around the world, how many children and young people are estimated to be involved in armed conflict?
   a 50 000
   b 300 000
   c 100 000
   d 500 000

2 What is the most accurate reason as to why nation states at times ignore their obligations under international law?
   a it is electorally unpopular
   b they has put a reservation in for a part of the treaty
   c economic and political self-interest
   d they have a poor relationship with another nation state

3 Parents may still use corporal punishment when disciplining their children. Which statement below best describes the restrictions on its use?
   a it can only be used on children over the age of ten
   b it can be used all over the body except for the face
   c its use must be moderate
   d it use must be moderate and reasonable

4 Since 2000, eighteen children and young people have been executed in various countries around the world. Which country has carried out the most child executions?
   a Iran
   b Yemen
   c South Africa
   d United States of America

5 How many children and young people believe that the police have not treated them with a sufficient degree of respect?
   a 80 per cent
   b 50 per cent
   c 35 per cent
   d 45 per cent

CHAPTER SUMMARY TASKS

1 Identify ways in which children around the world are exploited.
2 Explain how child executions breach international law.
3 Comment on the extent to which table 20.2 supports the theory that children and young people are more likely to be victims of crimes rather than offenders.
4 Outline why it is important for communities to retain areas of public space for children and young people.
5 Describe other problems that some children and young people have in regards to the criminal justice system.
6 Explain the extent to which the sentencing of young offenders may be inconsistent with CROC.
7 Assess the effectiveness of the extent to which youth conferencing is being utilised.
8 Describe the criticisms made of DOCS in the Ombudsman's reviewable deaths annual report in 2003.
9 Compare the rates of child abuse among Indigenous children and young people to those of non-Indigenous children and young people.
10 Outline the advantages and disadvantages for children and young people working part-time.

CHAPTER SUMMARY

- Many children around the world are exploited and discriminated against as a result their powerlessness and vulnerability. Australia still has a long way to go to fully implement the provisions of the Convention on the Rights of the Child (CROC).
- Child executions are an example of nation states breaching the provisions of CROC. They also breach other human rights treaties, which are considered to be customary international law due to many countries agreeing that it is an unacceptable practice.
- Many children and young people who have contact with the police believe they are not shown a sufficient degree of respect. This problem is magnified for Indigenous children and young people.
- It is argued that the NSW Government has used various pieces of legislation to restrict and control children and young people's use of public space.
- It is also suggested that police use the power of arrest as a method of interrogation, and that more can be done by adjudicating bodies to further explore sentences that give the best chances of rehabilitation.
- The 'Seen and heard' report suggested that youth justice conferences should be expanded to hear some indictable matters. It also recommended that police discretion should be reduced for deciding what matters get referred to conferencing.

- The rates of child abuse continue to climb each year, and the rates of abuse are even higher in Indigenous communities. Over recent years the number of cases known to DOCS that resulted in a child's death have continued at an unacceptable level.
- Children and young people continue to work in high numbers and are generally satisfied at work. A number complain that they are treated unfairly because of their age and that they feel exploited being paid junior rates of pay.

TOPIC REVIEW

EXTENDED RESPONSE

1 What is juvenile justice?
2 Explain the main types of crimes that juveniles commit.
3 Explain how the legal system responds to the issue of juvenile justice. Refer to strategies for crime prevention, issues surrounding arrest and detention, diversionary schemes and court proceedings for young people.
4 Evaluate the effectiveness of the legal system in dealing with juvenile offenders.

Marking criteria for extended response

Criteria	Marks
<ul><li>Clearly defines juvenile justice and outlines the main types of crimes that children and young people commit and the issues surrounding juvenile justice.</li><li>Makes a sound judgment based on criteria (explicit or implicit) about the effectiveness of the law in delivering justice to children and young people.</li><li>Integrates relevant legislation, documents, treaties, cases or media reports into the response.</li><li>Presents a sustained, logical and well-structured answer using relevant legal terminology.</li></ul>	21–25
<ul><li>Defines juvenile justice and outlines the main types of crimes that children and young people commit and the issues surrounding juvenile justice.</li><li>Makes a judgment based on criteria (explicit or implicit) about the effectiveness of the law in delivering justice to children and young people.</li><li>Uses relevant legislation, documents, treaties, cases or media reports in the response.</li><li>Presents a logical and well-structured answer using relevant legal terminology.</li></ul>	16–20
<ul><li>Defines aspects of juvenile justice and outlines some of the crimes children and young people commit and the issues surrounding juvenile justice.</li><li>Makes some statements based on criteria (explicit or implicit) about the effectiveness of the law in delivering justice to children and young people.</li><li>Cites some relevant legislation, documents, treaties, cases or reports in the response.</li><li>Presents a structured answer using relevant legal terminology.</li></ul>	11–15
<ul><li>Makes references to juvenile justice and some of the crimes and issues surrounding it.</li><li>Makes limited reference to the effectiveness of the law in delivering justice to children and young people.</li><li>Makes limited reference to legislation, treaties, documents, cases or media reports.</li><li>Uses some appropriate legal information with limited examples.</li></ul>	6–10
<ul><li>Makes a general statement about the law relating to children and young people.</li><li>May make limited reference to legislation, documents, treaties, cases or media reports.</li><li>Makes limited reference to legal information/terms, which may or may not be correct/appropriate.</li></ul>	1-5

Glossary

adoption order a court order that establishes a new legal relationship between potential adoptive parents and a child eligible for adoption. It also severs the legal relationship that existed between the adoptive child and their natural or legally recognised parents or guardians prior to the adoption process

adultery extramarital sex that interferes with marriage relations

adversary system a legal system that relies on the skill of persons from different parties (as opposed to a neutral party, for example, a judge) in trying to come to the truth of a case

affirmative action a policy designed to address past discrimination and thus improve the economic and educational opportunities of women and minority groups

alternative dispute resolution methods of solving disputes which do not rely on the court system

anarchy the absence of order

appellate jurisdiction the ability or power of a court to hear appeals of the decisions of lower level courts and to reject, affirm, or modify those decisions

assimilation a policy based on the idea that the minority group should adopt the language and traditions of the majority group

asylum a place of protection

asylum seeker someone who has fled their own country and applies to the government of another country for protection as a refugee

ATSIC Aboriginal and Torres Strait Islander Commission, a legal branch designed to help Aboriginal and Torres Strait Islanders with the legal system, which was shut down in 2005

Australian Workplace Agreement an individual workplace agreement between an employee and employer

award an agreement between employers and employees, usually across a whole industry, in respect to pay and other working conditions, overseen by the Australian Industrial Relations Commission

balance of probabilities a standard of proof in most civil matters in law that the evidence presented is more probable than not

best interests of the child the standard that various judicial bodies (such as the family court) will apply when making decisions about children and young people

bicameral containing two chambers or houses of parliament

bill of rights a statement of basic human rights and privileges

bipartisan involving the support of two political parties

boat people people who arrive in Australia without a valid visa

border applicants people who arrive in Australia without a valid visa

bridging visa a permit to stay in Australia for a temporary period of time so that arrangements can be made to either leave or apply for permanent residency

burden of proof the responsibility of a party to prove a case in court; to show that an allegation is true

care application an application made to the Children's Court to remove a child believed to be 'at risk' in their home or place of residence

care plan an outline of how a family will meet the needs of a child or young person

caution can be given to a young offender depending on the seriousness of the offence, the degree of violence involved, the harm caused and number of offences by the offender

certiorari the issuing of a writ by a superior court requesting the record of a case heard in a lower court for the purpose of reviewing that case

child generally a person aged between 0–15 years, depending on the legal context

child care proceedings matters of child custody and access. When dealing with family law matters, the Local Court has federal jurisdiction and in these matters is essentially part of the Federal Court hierarchy.

civil law the area of the law that deals with disputes between private individuals

civil libertarians people who believe in personal freedoms such as the right to remain anonymous, the right not to be body searched at random etc; it is these issues that are becoming increasingly challenged as terrorist attacks occur around the globe

civil liberties basic individual rights, such as freedom of speech and religion, which are protected by law

colonialism the political, social, legal and cultural domination of a territory and its people by a foreign power for an extended time

committal hearing an inquiry held in the Local Court to see if there is enough evidence against the defendant to warrant a trial in a higher court (this is called establishing a prima facie case)

Committee on the Rights of the Child committee that oversees the implementation of the Convention on the Rights of the Child in countries which have signed that treaty

common law the law made by courts, historically, law common to England

conciliation a process of solving disputes verbally, or through meetings and negotiations

concurrent existing at the same time; where both state and federal parliaments can make laws on particular matters

constitution a set of rules; the fundamental law of the state

conventions procedures that people are expected to follow; a general agreement between nations

coronial inquiry an investigation into a death that has occurred in unusual circumstances, held in the Coroner's Court and overseen by a magistrate called the Coroner. The Coroner will recommend whether further action should be taken over the death.

corporations law legislation that regulates corporations and the securities and futures industry in Australia, it is administered by the Australian Securities and Investments Commission (ASIC)

customary law principles and procedures that have developed through general usage according to the customs of a people or nation, or groups of nations

customs collective habits or traditions that have been developed by a society over a long period of time

defamation an act of communication that causes someone to be shamed, ridiculed, held in contempt, and to lose their standing in the community or their place or work

delegated legislation laws made by authorities other than parliament, who are delegated the power to do this by parliament

DIMIA Department of Immigration, Multicultural and Indigenous Affairs, the federal government body that controls migration in Australia

direct discrimination when one person or group of people receives less favourable treatment than another person or group in the same position would have received, on the grounds of their race, colour, descent, or national or ethnic origin

dispersal the distribution of people over a wide area

dispossession expelling someone from the possession of land through lawful process

doctrine of precedent the process whereby decisions made in earlier court cases help decide the outcome of the present case being considered

doli incapax a Latin term meaning 'incapable of crime', referring to the age of criminal responsibility, which in NSW is 10 years of age

domestic law the law of a nation

Dreamtime also known as 'the Dreaming', the source of Indigenous Australian customary law

duty work that someone is obliged to perform for moral or legal reasons

elders older and wiser men and women who are the keepers of traditional knowledge within Indigenous communities; they are responsible for such things as initiations and the handing down of punishments when community laws are broken

equal opportunity the right to equivalent opportunities regardless of race, colour, sex, national origin, etc.

equality the equal treatment of everybody

equity judging each case on its merits to correct any injustices

ex-nuptial child a child whose parents are not married at the time of conception

ex parte refers to one side of the story; in a case this may mean the other side is absent or unrepresented

executive an arm of the federal government that is controlled by administrative law

exemption being immune from certain duties and obligations

external affairs interpreted by the High Court to mean that when the Commonwealth signs an international treaty or convention it has the authority to enact laws to give effect to this international law within Australia

Federation a national government formed through the aggregation of several states

femme sole a single woman

fiscal relating to government financial matters

foundling a deserted infant whose parents' identity is unknown

gender segregation the separation of men and women into groups based on their sex

General Assembly the main body of the United Nations, made up of all of the member nations

glass ceiling attitudinal or organisational bias preventing women and minority groups from moving into leadership positions

government policy decisions made by governments based on principles or ideals such as 'user pays', etc.

guarantor when a person puts their own collateral (some form of asset) up as security for another person's loan from a financial institution. If the person who took out the loan cannot repay the loan, the financial institution can seize the assets put up by the guarantor.

habeas corpus the idea that people should not be held indefinitely without being charged

half-caste people whose parents are of different race and/or culture

High Court the highest court in Australia, it hears appeals and decides questions of interpretation of the Australian Constitution

independent free from another person's authority; not aligned with a political party

indirect discrimination practices or policies that appear to be neutral or fair because they treat everyone in the same way, but which adversely affect a higher proportion of people from one particular group. Indirect discrimination can occur even when there is no intention to discriminate.

injunction a court order stopping an individual or organisation from performing a particular action

insider trading using information that is not available to the public for personal financial gain

judicial process allowing independent courts and judges to decide disputes

judiciary the court system

jurisdiction the power of a court; the types of matters that it is allowed to hear and decide upon

jury a group of people who listen to all of the evidence in a court case and decide on the verdict

justice the principle of upholding generally accepted rights and enforcing responsibilities, ensuring that equal outcomes are achieved for those involved

juvenile a child or young person, generally under 18 years of age, although this may vary depending on the context

kinship family relations, including all extended family relationships; an important part of Indigenous cultures and values, dictating how all people in the group behave toward each other

larceny wrongfully taking or withholding another's property with intent to permanently deprive the owner of the property

law a set of rules which are enforceable and officially recognised and binding on all members of the community

law enforcement making sure that the laws of the state are followed

Law Reform Commission statutory body that examines the law for problems and makes recommendations

legal fiction the presumption of a fact assumed by a court for convenience, consistency or to achieve justice

legislative powers having the power or capacity to make laws

libel the publication of permanent (printed etc.) material that is defamatory

mandamus a court order compelling a government official or organisation to perform a particular task

mandatory reporting where a person working in child-related employment must by law report to care and protection agencies a child they believe to be at 'risk of harm'

martial law law enforced by the military over civilian affairs that overrides civil law

mediation a process whereby a third party intervenes in a dispute between two parties with the intention of resolving the conflict. The third party does not, however, adjudicate or impose penalties.

mercantile law laws that relate to trade

merits judgment based on an analysis of the facts presented in the case

military rule the performance by the military of all the functions of government, notably the executive, legislative and judicial functions

minority group any group of people that is disadvantaged, underprivileged, excluded, discriminated against or exploited

monogamous having only one partner (refers to relationships)

mother country Britain (in 1900, 96 per cent of Australians were of British origin)

multiculturalism the recognition of cultural diversity and the right of all Australians to express and share their individual cultural heritage. It also refers to government policies and programs that are designed to support diversity.

nation state a politically independent country

native title the right of Indigenous people to their traditional lands

natural justice procedures set in place to ensure fairness in legal proceedings; in Australia it generally refers to a right to be heard, that is, present your version of the facts, and the right to freedom from bias by decision-makers, whether real or perceived

nomadic people who tend to travel and change settlements frequently

obiter dicta comments from a judge in a case not directly relevant to the case before them and therefore not legally binding

operational areas local government areas that can apply for police to be given additional powers under the *Parental Responsibility – Children (Protection and Parental Responsibility) Act 1997*

opinio juris international rules derived from state practice and regarded as law

optional protocol allows individuals to communicate to the committee that is overseeing the original treaty

original jurisdiction the ability or power of a court to hear a case in the first instance

overstayers people who come to Australia on temporary visas but who continue to stay when their visa expires

perpetrator the person who committed or is responsible for something criminally or morally wrong

police discretion the ability of police to make a decision about a situation as they see fit; for example, they do not have to follow a law in some situations

political asylum seeking refuge or shelter in a country by asking the state to protect you from another state; it usually means not being transported back to the country of origin

portfolio a key area of government responsibility headed by a minister

poverty line (also known as the Henderson poverty line) the level of personal income that defines the state of poverty

presumption of parentage outlines a specific condition where a man and/or a woman are presumed to be the parents of a child

prima facie the establishment of sufficient evidence against a defendant to warrant a trial in a higher court of law

private law also known as civil law, contract law, torts, family law and property law

prohibited person a person prohibited from working in child-related employment

prohibition a court order that forbids a lower level court from hearing or taking further action in a case or matter

public law constitutional, administrative, industrial and criminal law

public space areas set aside in which members of the community can associate and assemble

questions of law a disputed legal contention that is left for the judge to decide (e.g. whether certain evidence is admissible)

R *R* at the beginning of a case name refers to *Regina* (Latin for 'Queen'). Since Australia is a constitutional monarchy this refers to our head of state on whose behalf the prosecution case is run. If our head of state was a male the R would stand for *Rex*, which is Latin for 'King'.

racial vilification a public act based on the race, colour, national or ethnic origin of a person or group of people which is likely to offend, insult, humiliate or intimidate. Types of behaviour can include racist graffiti, speeches, posters or abuse in public.

rail gauges the distance between the inner sides of the two rails of a train line

ratification to approve. In international law this usually means a government passing domestic laws that uphold some or all of the principles of an international treaty.

ratio decidendi the legal reason why a judge came to a particular decision

real property property consisting of land and the buildings upon it

reconciliation getting two parties to correspond, or make peace

referendum the referral of a particular issue to the electorate in a vote

representative government where law-making is under the control of voters, since parliamentarians are elected by eligible voters. Abraham Lincoln famously referred to representative government as 'government of the people, by the people, for the people'.

reservation a formal declaration that nation states do not accept as binding on them a certain part or parts of the treaty

residual those matters remaining which the states can legislate on which are not referred to in the Constitution

restorative justice attempts to 'restore' victims, young offenders and the community in terms of dignity, injury, property loss, security etc. after a crime has been committed. A youth justice conference is used to define what restoration might mean in the context of the crime.

risk of harm concerns about the safety, welfare and wellbeing of a child or young person because of sexual, physical or emotional abuse and/or neglect.

sanctions official permission or approval for a course of action

Security Council a council of the United Nations responsible for preserving world peace

separation of powers the idea of preventing one person or group gaining total power by dividing power between the executive, legislature and judiciary

sexual harassment any unwanted sexual behaviour, such as suggestive comments, inappropriate pictures hanging in the workplace, unwanted touching etc.

slander the publication of non-permanent (verbal etc.) material that is defamatory

special leave where the High Court grants approval for the case to go before it on appellate jurisdiction

standard of proof the level of proof needed by each party in a court case to prove their case

statute law law made by parliament

statutory right a right that has been enshrined in statute law

suffrage the right to vote guaranteed by the law

suffragette a woman supporter of women's right to vote

tariffs a tax that must be paid on imports and exports

terra nullius land belonging to no-one—the idea and legal concept that when the first Europeans came to Australia the land was owned by no-one and thus was open to settlement. It has been judged legally invalid.

tort a civil wrong which can include negligence, defamation, trespass and nuisance

treaty an international instrument that governs relations between two or more nations

ultra vires acting beyond their power or in excess of their authority

United Nations a world organisation that is dedicated to world peace and equality for all

unito caro 'one in flesh', meaning that when a woman married, in the eyes of the law she assumed the legal identity of her husband

warning this can be given to a young offender usually for a first minor offence. The offender must be told of the nature, purpose and effect of the warning.

Western World countries such as Australia, United States of America, Great Britain and New Zealand which hold the principles of Christianity, democracy and capitalism

White Australia the official government policy of excluding non-Europeans and non-English-speaking people from coming to Australia; it was fuelled by fears of the country being overrun by Asians

working with children check a check by the NSW Commission for Children and Young People on the appropriateness of a person in NSW to work in child-related employment

young person in NSW, a young person is defined as being aged between 16–18

youth justice conference a measure to divert young offenders from the court system through a conference that addresses the offender's behaviour in a more holistic manner

Answers to multiple-choice questions

Chapter	Answers
1	1a, 2a, 3c, 4c, 5c
2	1c, 2b, 3b, 4b, 5d
3	1a, 2b, 3d, 4d, 5c
4	1b, 2c, 3d, 4b, 5c
5	1c, 2a, 3b, 4b, 5a
6	1c, 2b, 3c, 4d, 5a
7	1c, 2a, 3d, 4c, 5c
8	1c, 2a, 3c, 4c, 5d
9	1b, 2a, 3d, 4c, 5a
10	1a, 2b, 3b, 4c, 5d
11	1d, 2a, 3c, 4b, 5b
12	1b, 2d, 3c, 4c, 5d
13	1d, 2d, 3c, 4b, 5b
14	1c, 2b, 3a, 4d, 5d
15	1d, 2c, 3c, 4d, 5b
16	1a, 2b, 3c, 4c, 5d
17	1a, 2c, 3d, 4d, 5d
18	1c, 2c, 3c, 4c, 5a
19	1c, 2c, 3b, 4b, 5c
20	1b, 2c, 3d, 4d, 5a

Index

A

A v. Australia 169
Aboriginal and Torres Strait Islander peoples
  access to civil law 118
  child abuse 285, 287
  criminal offences 117
  customary law 11–14
  disadvantages 120–1
  government policies 111–13, 132–5
  health 218
  language and culture 11–14, 130–1
  legal status 114–17
  removal of children 134–5
  self-determination 126–7
  women 195–6
  see also native title
Aboriginal and Torres Strait Islander Commission Act 1989
  124
Aboriginal and Torres Strait Islander Commission (ATSIC)
  124
Aboriginal and Torres Strait Islander Heritage Protection Act 1984 65
Aboriginal and Torres Strait Islander Social Justice
  Commissioner 134
Aboriginal Land Rights Act 1976 115, 133
Aboriginal Land Rights Act 1983 65, 124
Aboriginal Legal Service (NSW/ACT) Limited (ALS) 123
Abu Ghraib prison 95
ACTU. *see* Australian Council of Trade Unions (ACTU)
Administrative Appeals Tribunal (AAT) 174, 175
Administrative Appeals Tribunals Act 1975 82
Administrative Decisions (Judicial Review) Act 1977 41, 82
Administrative Decisions Tribunal Act 1997 201
Administrative Decisions Tribunal (ADT) 58, 85, 201, 215,
  270–1
Adoption Information Act 2000 248
adoption order 248
adversarial system 22, 50–2, 118, 130
adversary system. *see* adversarial system
affirmative action 122, 235
Agha, Aziza 82
Ainsworth, Len 104
alcohol, banning of 73

alternative dispute resolution (ADR) 58–9, 208
Amnesty International 178, 277, 278
anarchy 2, 77
Anti-Discrimination Act 1977 122, 160, 201, 215, 251
Anti-Discrimination Board (ADB) 122–3, 160, 163, 216
anti-discrimination legislation 122–3, 179, 197–202
Anti-Terrorism Act 2005 102
ANZUS Treaty 95–6
appeals to High Court 40
appellate jurisdiction 37, 40
arbitration 58
arrest 282
Artificial Conception Act 1984 253
assimilation
  Indigenous peoples 111, 113
  migrants 156–7
asylum seekers 147
Atkin, Lord 91
ATSIC. *see* Aboriginal and Torres Strait Islander
  Commission (ATSIC)
Australia Acts 1986 37–8, 44
Australian Childhood Foundation 272
Australian Constitution 19, 29
  amending 35
  federal legislative powers 32–3
  freedom of religion 251
  immigration laws 139
  judicial system 36–7
  key features 31
  religious freedom 77
  separation of powers 41–2
Australian Constitutions Act 1842 44
Australian Council of Trade Unions (ACTU) 213–14, 271
Australian Courts Act 1828 44
Australian Institute of Multicultural Affairs (AIMA) 158
Australian Iron and Steel v. Banovic 199
Australian Law Reform Commission 180, 280
Australian Longitudinal Study on Women's Health 219–20
Australian multiculturalism for a new century: towards inclusiveness 159
Australian Taxation Office (ATO) 57
Australian women working together 214
Australian Women's Charter 188

Australian Workplace Agreements (AWAs) 250
authority 70–1, 72–7

B
'baggy pants' bill 74–6
Bakhtiari, Roqia 176–7
balance of power 30
balance of probabilities 253
balancing work and family. *see* Inquiry into
  Balancing Work and Family
Bankstown 152
barristers 51
Beazley, Napoleon 278
'best interests' 276
bill of rights 100, 101
birth rate, declining 237
birth registration 248
birth technologies 253
Births, Deaths and Marriages Act 1995 248, 253
boat people 148
border applicants 148
bridging visas 148
Bringing them home 135
Britain. *see* Great Britain
Builders' Labourers Federation 84
burden of proof 53, 55
Burney, Linda 125
by-laws 20

C
Cabinet 19, 20
Cabramatta 152
care and protection 254–6, 269, 284–7
care application 269
care plan 269
case law 17–18
cautions 257–8
CEDAW. *see* Convention on the Elimination of All
  Forms of Discrimination against Women (CEDAW)
certiorari 86
child care 236–7
child care proceedings 48
child labour 288
child, legal definition 246
children
    abuse 254–6, 284–7
    care and protection 254–6, 260, 269, 284–7
    criminal justice system 256–60, 282–4
    current legal status 246–52
    death penalty 277–9
    detention centres 170–1
    history 243–5
    labour and work 244–5, 249–51, 275
    parentage 253

see also Convention on the Rights of the Child
  (CROC)
*Children and Young Persons (Care and Protection)
  Act 1998* 255–6, 267, 268
Children at work 249, 288
Children (Equality of Status) Act 1976 253
*Children (Protection and Parental Responsibility)
  Act 1997* 260, 281
Children's Court Act 1987 266
Children's Court clinic 268
Children's Courts 266–8
    hearings 53
Children's (Criminal Proceedings) Act 1987 256–
  7, 266, 283
China 77
circle sentencing 105, 117
civil court proceedings 53
civil law 21, 22
civil law systems 22
civil libertarians 74
civil liberties 41
Clark, Geoff 124, 127
Coalition of Aboriginal Legal Services (COALS)
  123
codification 95
Colonial Laws Validity Act 1865 44
colonialism 42
Commission for Children and Young People 265
*Commission for Children and Young People Act
  1998* 265
commissions of inquiry 87
committal hearings 48
Committee on the Rights of the Child 264
common law 15
common law authority 71
common law duties 91
Commonwealth Franchise Act 1902 191
Commonwealth of Australia Constitution Act 1900
  19, 31, 44
Community Justice Centres (CJCs) 59–60
complaints to HREOC 208–9
conciliation within Indigenous societies 12
conscientious objectors 73
conscription 73
Constitution. *see* Australian Constitution
Constitution Act of New South Wales 1902 19
constitutional system
    division of power 32–5
    federation process 29–31
    High Court 36–40
    judicial review 41
    separation of powers 41–2
    transfer of power from Britain 42–5
Consumer, Trader & Tenancy Tribunal 58

contracts and children 251–2
Convention on the Elimination of All Forms of Discrimination against Women (CEDAW) 197, 200, 204–5, 212, 224–5
Convention on the Elimination of All Forms of Racial Discrimination 161, 178
Convention on the Prevention and Punishment of the Crime of Genocide 135
Convention on the Rights of the Child (CROC) 243, 247–8
    Australia's obligations 276–7
    child executions 278
    main articles 247
    ratification 263–4
conventions 24
coronial inquiries 48, 53
Corporations Act 1996 92
corporations law 49
Council for Multicultural Australia 159
court-made law 16
Court of Appeal 49
courts
    access by migrants 164–5
    procedures 22, 52–5
    State and Federal 47–9
Covenant on Civil and Political Rights. *see* International Covenant on Civil and Political Rights (ICCPR)
Covenant on Economic, Social and Cultural Rights. *see* International Covenant on Economic, Social and Cultural Rights (ICESCR)
Crimes Act 1900 57
Crimes Act 1914 86
Crimes Legislation Amendment (Police and Public Safety) Act 1998 258–9, 280
criminal law
    court proceedings 54–5
    vs civil law 21–2
CROC. *see* Convention on the Rights of the Child (CROC)
cultural diversity 180
cultural power 69
customary authority 71
customary law 3, 11–14, 95
customs 3, 5, 17, 24

D

death penalty 103, 277
deaths in custody 133–4
Declaration of Human Rights. *see* Universal Declaration of Human Rights (UDHR)
Declaration of the Rights of the Child. *see* Convention on the Rights of the Child (CROC)

Declaration on the Elimination of All Forms of Racial Discrimination. *see* Convention on the Elimination of all Forms of Racial Discrimination
defamation 18, 104
defence 54
delegated authority 71
delegated legislation 20–1
democracy 42
Department of Community Services (DOCS) 254, 256, 266, 268–9, 287
Department of Employment and Workplace Relations (DEWR) 211
Department of Immigration, Multicultural and Indigenous Affairs (DIMIA) 82, 140, 146, 161, 166, 174
Department of Juvenile Justice 268
deportation 166
detention 167–71
detention centres 83, 167–8, 277
dictatorship 41
DIMIA. *see* Department of Immigration, Multicultural and Indigenous Affairs (DIMIA)
direct discrimination 199
disabled parking permits 7–8
discrimination
    children 251
    migrants 160–3
    women 226–7
dispossession 113
District Court 48–9
DOCS. *see* Department of Community Services (DOCS)
doctrine of precedent 17–18
doli incapax 244, 256
domestic law 23
domestic violence 225, 284
Donaghue v. Stevenson 91
Dreamtime 12
driftnet fishing 24
duties 91–6
duty of care 91–2

E

East Timor 97, 105, 106–7
economic power 70
education
    children 245
    Indigenous school retention 121
    participation of women 191–3, 216–17
    right of children to 249
Education Reform Act 1990 249
elders 12, 111
emotional abuse 254

employment
children 249–51, 265
Indigenous peoples 121, 196
migrants 162, 194–5
sex discrimination 209–10
women 193, 227
enforcement
agencies 57
within Indigenous societies 12
equal opportunity 122, 234–7
Equal Opportunity for Women Agency (EOWA) 211
Equal Opportunity for Women in the Workplace Act 1999 201, 211, 234
equal pay. *see* pay equity
equality 4–5
equity 15
ethical duties 93
ethics 5
European Union 26
euthanasia 102
ex parte 39
executive 19
parliamentary control 80–1
Executive Council 19, 20, 23, 41
external reviews 85
extradition 166–7
Extradition Act 1988 166

F
Fair Trading Act 1987 85
fairness 4
Falun Gung 77
Family Court 37
Family Law Act 1975 188, 189, 253
Family Law Legislation Amendment (Superannuation) Act 2001 189
Family Law Reform Act 1995 253
Family Provisions Act 1982 253
family-sponsored immigration 143–4
Federal Court 37
immigration appeals 174–5
Federal Magistrates Court 37
federal parliament, legislative powers 32–3
Federation 29–31
female genital mutilation 180, 219, 225
femme sole 190
Fertility decision making project report 237
Firearms Act 1996 85
Fisheries Management Act 1994 85
Fitzgerald Report 173
Franklin Dam case 34
free speech 103
Freedom of Information Act 1982 82
Freedom of Information Act 1989 82, 85

G
Galbally Report 157
General Assembly (UN) 25
Geneva Conventions 95, 107
genocide 24, 96, 135
Gillick case 246
glass ceiling 235
Gove land rights case. *see Milirrpum v. Nabalco Pty Ltd*
government departments and law enforcement 57
Governor-General 19, 20, 35
Grassby, Al 157–8
Great Britain 15, 25, 42, 43, 101
green bans 84
Greenpeace 26, 84
Guantanamo Bay detention 107
Gutnick v. Dow Jones & Co Inc 18

H
habeas corpus 107
Half way to equal 194, 229
harassment 122
Harradine, Brian 30
health, Indigenous peoples 121
health policies 217–19
Hicks, David 107
High Court 36–40
HIV/AIDs 225
Home Building Act 1989 85
House of Representatives 19, 20, 30
'Household Income and Labour Dynamics in Australia' (HILDA) survey 237
housing, access to 163
Howard, John 83, 126
HREOC. *see* Human Rights and Equal Opportunity Commission (HREOC)
human rights
children 246–60
immigration detention abuse 169
Indigenous peoples 132–5
migrants 178–80
women 197–202
see also Universal Declaration of Human Rights (UDHR)
Human Rights and Equal Opportunity Commission Act 1986 159, 160, 206, 264
Human Rights and Equal Opportunity Commission (HREOC) 160, 206
children's rights 264
complaint handling process 207
sex discrimination complaints 201, 206, 208–9, 226
Human Rights Commission 173

humanitarian immigration   145-8

Hussein, Sadam   96

I

ICAC Act 1988   88

illegal immigrants. *see* unlawful non-citizens

immigration. *see* migration

immigration detention centres. *see* detention centres

Immigration Restriction Act 1901   30

Immigration Review Tribunal (IRT)   173

Income Tax Assessment Act 1936   57, 71

Independent Commission Against Corruption Act 1988   88

Independent Commission Against Corruption (ICAC)   88

independent judiciary   41-2

Indigenous Australians. *see* Aboriginal and Torres Strait Islander peoples

indirect discrimination   199, 235

Indonesia   51, 106, 151

injunctions   37, 87

Inquiry into Balancing Work and Family   237

inquisitorial system   22, 50-1

insider trading   92

internal reviews   85

International Court of Justice (ICJ)   26, 96

International Covenant on Civil and Political Rights (ICCPR)   169, 178, 278

International Covenant on Economic, Social and Cultural Rights (ICESCR)   105, 126, 178

International Criminal Court (ICC)   96

international customary law   24

International Decade of the World's Indigenous People   105

international governmental organisations (IGOs)   26

International Labour Organisation (ILO)   26, 98, 214

international law

limitations   106-7

protection to migrants   178

sources   23-4

women   224-7

international treaties   178

Internet   18

Iraq, invasion of   97

Irving, David   142

Israel   73

J

judges   51

judicial review   86

judiciary   19

jurisdiction

High Court   37-8

ICJ   26

jury   22, 54

Jury Act 1977   191

jury service   191

justice   4, 5

juvenile crime   260, 266-7

juvenile justice   256-7

K

Keating, Paul   116

Kids Helpline   272

kinship   12

knife-related violence   258-9, 280

'Knives legislation to stay'   280-1

L

land ownership   11-12, 14

land rights   62, 125

see also native title

Latham, Mark   87

law

definition   2

obedience to   6-8

vs rules and customs   3-5

law enforcement. *see* enforcement

legal aid   165

children   270

Indigenous peoples   123

migrants   180

purpose   57

Legal Aid Commission   57

Legal Aid Commission Act 1979 (NSW)   57

legal duties   91

legal fiction   43

legal power   70

legal professions   51-2

legislation

delegated   20-1

passing through parliament   20-21

libel   103

Local Courts   48

M

Mabo, Eddie   63, 111, 116

Mabo v. Queensland   116

Mabo v. Queensland (No.2)   63, 101, 116

magistrates   51

mandamus   37

mandatory reporting   256

mandatory sentencing laws   79

Maori land rights   62

marriage 188–9
Marriage Act 1961 253
Married Persons (Property and Torts) Act 1901
189, 190
McMahon v. Bowman 122
media 83
mediation
    alternative dispute resolution (ADR) 58
    Indigenous societies 12
medical consent 251
Members of Parliament (MPs) 83
mercantile law 15
migrant resource centres 163–4
migrants
    access to services 163–5
    discrimination 159–63
    family-sponsored 143–4
    illegal. *see* unlawful non-citizens
    refugees 145–8
    skilled 144–5
    women 194–5
migration
    applications 165, 173–7
    law 139–40
    process 141–2
Migration Act 1958 140
    1985 review 173
    2001 amendments 146, 147, 149, 175
    deportation 166
    detention 167
    unlawful non-citizens 148
Migration Internal Review Office (MIRO) 173
Migration Review Tribunal (MRT) 144, 145, 174
Milirrpum v. Nabalco Pty Ltd 115, 132
military rule 43
Milosevic, Slobodan 96
ministerial responsibility 80–1
Minogue, Kylie 69
Minors (Property and Contract) Act 1970 251
Montesquieu 41
moral duties 93
Motor Traffic Act 1909 57
Ms L v. the Principal Registrar of Births Deaths and
   Marriages 248
Muin and Lie v. Refugee Review Tribunal 175
multiculturalism 139, 156–9
Multiculturalism and the law 180
Murphyores v. The Commonwealth 39
Myall Creek massacre 114

N

nation state 23
National agenda for a multicultural Australia 159
National Child Commissioner 288

National Children's and Youth Law Centre 272
national identification card 74
National Inquiry into the Separation of Aboriginal
   and Torres Strait Islander Children from Their
   Families 134–5
National Multicultural Advisory Council (NMAC)
   159
National Parks and Wildlife Act 1974 65
nationalism 30
native title 61–5, 115, 125
Native Title Act 1993 63, 64, 116, 133
Native Title Amendment Act 1998 64, 116, 118,
   133
Native Title Tribunal 64
natural justice 41, 86
neglect 254
Neville, A.O. 113
New agenda for multicultural Australia 159
New South Wales Act 1823 44
New South Wales Constitution Act 1855 44
New Zealand 101
Non-adversarial review of migrant decisions—the
   way forward 174
non-government organisations (NGOs) 26, 84
NSW Aboriginal Land Council (NSWALC) 125
NSW Commission for Children and Young People
   266
NSW Ombudsman 87, 270

O

obiter dicta 17
observation of court proceedings 55
O'Callaghan v. Loder 201
occupations, gender segregation 230
offences 54
Office for Women (NSW) 213
Office for Women (OfW) 212
Office of Multicultural Affairs 158
offshore processing 150
offshore resettlement 147
ombudsmen, offices of 59
   see also NSW Ombudsman
one child policy 77
'Operation Hunter' 88
operational areas 260
opinio juris 277
optional protocol 225
ordinances 20
original jurisdiction 37
overstayers 148
Oxfam 84

P

Pacific Island Labourers Act 1901 30

paid maternity leave 224, 236
Palmer, Mick 85
Pankhurst, Emmeline 190
parentage 253
parliament
    passing bill through 20
    structure 19
parliamentary committees 81
Passenger Transport Act 1990 85
pay equity 227, 228
peacekeeping 25
penalties 6
people smuggling 150–1
People Smuggling, Trafficking in Persons and
    Related Transnational Crime conference 151
permanent protection visas (PPVs) 148
physical abuse 254
Pine Gap 96
police 57, 77, 280
political asylum 77
political power 70
polygamy 180
poverty 151
poverty line 193
power 69–70, 72–7
precedents 17–18
Pregnancy and work: pregnant and productive 226
pregnancy discrimination 210
prima facie 51
prisoners of war 95
Privacy Act 1988 86
*Privacy and Personal Information Protection Act
    1998* 86
private law 21
Privy Council 38
prize money in sport 231
prohibition 37, 86
property ownership 11–12, 189
*Property (Relationships) Legislation Amendment
    Act 1999* 189
prosecution 54
protection
    children. *see* care and protection
    Indigenous peoples 113
protection visas (PVs) 147
public education 245
public law 21
public space 280–1
punishment
    Indigenous societies 12
    and justice 5

R
R v. Ballard 117

R v. Brislan; ex parte Williams 39
R v. Murrell 117
R v. Williams 131
R v. Zecevic 40
racial discrimination 161
Racial Discrimination Act 1975 121, 159
Racial Hatred Act 1995 121, 159
racial 'purity' 30
racial vilification 121–2, 159, 179
rail gauges 29
ratification 23, 263
ratio decidendi 17
Rau, Cornelia 81, 85
reconciliation 127, 135
Red Cross 26
referendum process 30, 35
referendums
    Federation (1898, 1899, 1900) 31
    Indigenous peoples citizenship (1967) 35,
    115
    Republic (1999) 35, 44–5
Refugee Review Tribunal (RRT) 174
refugees 145–7, 151–2
regulations 20
religious duties 93
religious freedom 77
representative government 44
republic referendum 44–5
restorative justice 268
right to vote 190–1
rights
    to access personal information 81–2
    common law vs statutory 103
    contract 190
    domestic 101–5
    international 106–7
    legal vs moral and customary 102–3
    property 189
    voting 190
    see also human rights; land rights
Rivkin, Rene 92
*Road Transport (Safety & Traffic Management) Act
    1999* 71
Roberts, Ian 69
Roper v. Simmons 278
Royal Commission into Aboriginal Deaths in
    Custody 87, 117, 120, 124, 133–4
Royal Commission into the NSW Police Service
    87
royal commissions 87, 284
rules
    department legislation 20
    need for 3–6
    vs laws and customs 5

S

Salvation Army 164
sanctions 17
Scott, Rose 190
Security Council (UN) 25
Seen and heard: priority for children in the legal process 280, 281, 282, 283
self-defence (nation-states) 96–7
self-determination 104–5
self-help remedies 59
Senate 19, 20, 30
sentencing young offenders 283
separation of powers 19
Sex Discrimination Act 1984 188, 200, 206, 226, 232–3
sex slavery 206, 225
sexual abuse 254
sexual activity, legal vs moral rights 102
sexual harassment 200–201, 209–10, 216
shared relationship agreements (SRAs) 125
Shopfront Youth Legal Centre 272, 284
skilled migrants 144
slander 103
slavery 24
    see also sex slavery
smoking bans 72–3
social and cultural duties 93
Social justice report 2002 134
social power 69
social security
    migrants 152, 164
    women 193
Socrates 275
solicitors 51
Solon, Vivian 85
sources of law
    Australian law 15–22
    international law 23–7
sovereignty 23
spiritual nature of customary law 12
sponsorship
    employer 144
    family 143–4
squatting 103
St Vincent de Paul 164
standard of proof 53, 55
state 23
state courts 48–9
State of the nation 162
state power
    formal means to challenge 85–8
    informal means to challenge 79–84
Status of Children Act 1996 253
statute law 15, 18

Statute of Westminster 1931 44
statutory authority 71
statutory duties 92
statutory right 81
'stolen generations' 134–5
'Stop Child Abuse' 272
suffrage 190
suffragette movement 190
Summary Offences Act 1998 258
Supreme Court 49

T

Tampa incident 149
Tasmania v. Commonwealth 34
temporary protection visas (TPVs) 148
terra nullius 12, 42–3, 61–2, 112
terrorist attacks 74
torts 252
torture 24, 226–7
trade unions 83–4, 213–14
    see also Australian Council of Trade Unions (ACTU)
traditions, ritual and oral 12
Translating and Interpreting Service (TIS) 165
trauma 151
treaties 23–4, 95–6
Treaty of Waitangi 127
treaty with Indigenous peoples 126–7
trial by ordeal 16
tribunals 58

U

ultra vires 34, 41
uniform tax case 38
United Nations Children's Education Fund (UNICEF) 98
United Nations High Commission for Refugees (UNHCR) 150
United Nations Human Rights Committee (HRC) 178
United Nations (UN) 24, 25
    obligations of governments 97–8
    peacekeeping 25
    use of force 96–7
    women's rights 204–5
    see also Conventions entries; International Covenants entries; Universal Declaration of Human Rights (UDHR)
United States
    affirmative action 202
    bill of rights 101
    Iraq invasion 97
    juvenile executions 277–9
    UN Security Council 25
    see also ANZUS Treaty

unito caro 188
Universal Declaration of Human Rights (UDHR)
  24, 98, 106, 178
unlawful non-citizens 148–9, 151–3, 161

V
values 5
Vanstone, Amanda 80
Vietnam war 73
visas 147–8

W
Waite, Ginny B. 223
Walker v. New South Wales 133
warnings 257
What Women Want Next 237
Whistleblowers Australia (WBA) 83
White Australia policy 30
Whitlam, Gough 115–16
Wik case 63, 64, 118
William the Conqueror 16–17
Wireless Telegraphy Act 1919 39
women
    anti-discrimination legislation 197–202
    changing status 186–96
    current status 223–38

health 217–20
    protection of rights 204–20
Women in Australia 212
Women's Electoral Lobby (WEL) 214
Women's Information and Referral Service 213
Women's Legal Status Act 1918 192
Wood Royal Commission 284
'Work Smart' 272
workforce, aging 237
workforce, gender segregation 229–30
working with children check 265
workplace, children 270–1, 288
Workplace Relations Act 1996 206, 231
Worksite for Schools 271
World Health Organisation (WHO) 98
World Heritage (Property Conservation) Act 1983
  34
World Wildlife Fund 84

Y
Young Offenders Act 1997 257–8, 283–4
young person, legal definition 246
Youth Action and Policy Association (YAPA) 280
youth conferencing 283–4
youth justice conferences 258